Borland C++
INSIDER

THE WILEY INSIDER SERIES

If you think this book is just another computer book, stop right there. I am proud to tell you that this book is part of a stunning new series created by the Coriolis Group and published by John Wiley & Sons. What you're holding is a "tour-de-force" of Borland C++ insider tips, secrets, undocumented features, shortcuts, and technical advice that has never been available in a book format like this.

Paul Cilwa, C++ expert and author, has gathered together his best tips and techniques based on his many years of programming experience to create this new book in the INSIDER series. The book is jam-packed with innovative ideas for programming Borland C++ in ways you never thought possible. But the real kicker is that the unique format of this book will help you understand and use the tips and techniques presented as if a friendly expert were at your side, ready to answer any question you might have.

In creating the new INSIDER series, we wanted to break with tradition and develop books that go way beyond the typical "documentation approach" of most computer books. In each INSIDER book, we'll show you how to customize your software, put new features to work right away, work smarter and faster, and solve difficult problems.

What you're holding represents an innovative and highly practical guide that was developed by some of the best minds in computer book publishing. We hope you enjoy each and every INSIDER guide.

—Keith Weiskamp
INSIDER Series Editor

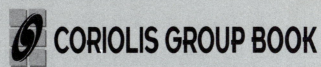

CORIOLIS GROUP BOOK

Borland C++
INSIDER

Paul Cilwa

Edited by Keith Weiskamp

John Wiley & Sons, Inc.

New York • Chichester • Brisbane • Toronto • Singapore

Library of Congress Cataloging-in-Publication Data:

Cilwa, Paul S., 1951-
    Borland C++ insider / Paul Cilwa ; edited by Keith Weiskamp.
      p. cm. -- (Wiley insider series)
    Includes index.
    ISBN 0-471-30338-0
    1. C++ (Computer program language) 2. Boralnd C++.
  I. Weiskamp, Keith. II. Title. III. Series.
  QA76.73.C153C495   1994   94-12676
  005.285--dc20   CIP

Printed in the United States of America
10 9 8 7 6 5 4 3 2 1

Contents

Chapter 13 The FileDropper Control   357

Introduction

Only a few years ago, computer programs were written by teams of programmers consisting of anywhere from ten to fifty members, with additional support personnel in the form of user-interface specialists, JCL experts, database administrators, and so on. In spite of the best efforts of this programming army, the products they produced were hard to learn and, once learned, hard to use. Now programs with ten times the power are being crafted with one-tenth the people, and users are claiming the new applications are not only *easy* to learn, but *fun* to use.

What happened?

Microsoft Windows, of course. With one stroke, the face of computing has been changed forever. The tools for computer users are now so much more powerful than before that, after sampling them, almost no one wants to go back.

The tools for Windows *programmers* have been slower to advance. Fortunately some companies have been eager to catch the thrown gauntlet. Borland Pascal version 7.0 and Borland C++ version 4.0 have been acclaimed as the premiere Windows programming environments by reviewers in one magazine after another. They take Windows programming a giant step forward, permitting the creating of applications from within the comfortable, productive, Windows environment.

Although Windows programming has traditionally been done in C, object-oriented C++ really lends itself to the Windows paradigm. A Windows application is composed of windows—many of them—and each window has certain properties and responds to messages. This parallels the behavior of C++ objects so closely that it was only a matter of time before it occurred to someone to marry the two.

In late 1990, Borland began beta testing Turbo Pascal for Windows. I was one of the beta testers. While I appreciated TPW's brilliance at the start—the idea of a Windows-hosted *compiler*, for Phillipe's sake!—it was OWL, the ObjectWindows Library, that really excited me. And Borland quickly followed up its knock-'em-dead success with Turbo C++ for Windows, which also includes OWL.

The creators of OWL did have to settle on a compromise, however; and that was, where to stop? If the native Windows API is the foundation of the house, should OWL be the first floor? The attic? The roof?

Borland settled on making OWL the *frame* of the house, and I think this was a wise decision. Starting out with OWL, you can create any kind of Windows program you can imagine: text editors, drawing programs, databases, utilities, and so on.

However, it has been my experience that the vast majority of *real* programs I have to write are all based on the same premise: a main window that consists of a dialog box with the same old menus—File, Edit, and so on. From OWL, I have created new, descendent classes that bring me as close to that generic dialog app as I can get and still be able to create "real" apps by descending from those. It is on those classes that this book concentrates.

In addition, ObjectWindows 2.0—the version accompanying Borland C++ 4.0—is a total rewrite of ObjectWindows 1.0. We have been given a whole new paradigm—the "app/document/view" paradigm on which to base our applications. The derived classes featured in this book take full advantage of this paradigm, and will help you understand how it works in the process.

Who Is This Book For

If you

- Are familiar with C++, or, at least, C
- Own a copy of Borland C++ version 4.0
- Have Windows 3.1 installed
- Want to be able to easily and quickly create Windows applications
- Would like to know as much about Windows and Borland C++ as possible without making your head hurt

then, this book is for you.

Features of This Book

This book is both an instructional manual and a reference volume. You will probably want to work with it from beginning to end. But, afterward, it will serve as a means to quickly research particular topics or refresh yourself on an unusual technique. This book is designed with this kind of easy access in mind.

Each chapter contains several major sections, such as *Menus and Commands*. Each section begins with some general information, and is then broken down further into topics. These topics describe a particular concept in more detail, showing you how to use a particular feature or solve a specific problem. Each topic begins with an informative heading, followed by a few brief sentences (printed in **bold italic type**) that tell you quickly what you can expect to learn by reading through the rest of the material in the topic.

Hot Tips

We've also included several Hot Tips throughout each chapter. Each Hot Tip provides you with information that you can use immediately to solve some of the more sticky Windows problems or to put to use some little-known techniques that we think every Borland C++ Windows programmer should know.

The INSIDER Disk

A disk is available (see back of the book for details) that contains all of the functions and programs described in these pages. Some programmers prefer to type examples in themselves, but others prefer to copy our files. With this in mind, we accommodate them all. The diskette is arranged by chapter so you can easily find the code you want. In addition, we've put some utilities on disk that you may find useful.

About the Author

Paul S. Cilwa has worked with Microsoft Windows since version 1.0, and programmed it from version 2.03. He helped beta test versions 3.0 and 3.1, as well as the first release of Turbo Pascal for Windows and Borland C++ version 4.0. As a technical writer, his in-depth research and clarity of presentation have made his articles in *PC TECHNIQUES* a favorite of that magazine's readers. His humorous fiction has appeared in the St. Augustine *Traveler* and *Changing Men* magazine. When not writing or teaching Microsoft Windows programming to corporate programmers, he can be found hiking, skiing, or white-water rafting, depending on the season.

Part Overview

1 Movin' on Up to C++ 3

In this chapter, you will learn how to get into the Borland C++ groove by looking at the powerful IDE.

2 Object-Oriented Programming 27

Get into the fast lane of C++ programming by exploring some useful OOP techniques.

3 Overloaded Operators and Streams 53

Objects are cool, and this chapter shows you how to better integrate them using overloaded operators.

4 Inheritance 73

What is inheritance? Here's your chance to find out how to really use this important OOP technique.

5 Enjoying Polymorphism 87

Next up is polymorphism, and this chapter will tell you everything you've wanted to know.

6 The Secret Life of Templates 101

In this chapter, you will learn how to extend the power of Borland C++ by using templates.

Getting the Most from C++

If you've been working with non-OOP languages like C, you'll be pleasantly surprised by the unique and powerful features found in C++. From classes to overloaded operators to polymorphism, C++ offers a wide selection of object-oriented components that can greatly help you fine-tune your coding practices.

In Part 1, we're going to examine the more useful object-oriented programming techniques available with Borland C++. We'll start with the Borland IDE in Chapter 1 and then we'll explore objects and constructors in Chapter 2, overloaded operators and streams in Chapter 3, inheritance in Chapter 4, polymorphism in Chapter 5, and finally templates in Chapter 6. After you read the chapters in Part 1, you'll be ready to move on and start creating some useful Borland C++ apps.

1

Movin' on Up to C++

I n this chapter we'll get you into the Borland C++ groove by look-ing at the powerful IDE. Then, we'll explore some useful C and C++ programming tips that you can put to work right away. There's a lot to cover, so let's get started.

Getting the Most out of the IDE

If you aren't sure what the letters *IDE* stand for, this section is for you. Computer project development has come a *long* way from its begin-nings. Long hours at the card punch have given way to dragging and dropping project components onscreen. The hours are still long—but at least the work is more fun! And using modern IDEs will help you become even more productive, and the envy of all your peers.

What Do the Letters *IDE* Stand For?

One the hardest parts in the battle to keep up with the leading edge of computer technology is the effort to keep abreast of the latest acronyms. This one is important because it represents our most important tool (next to the computer itself!).

The short answer to the question, "What does *IDE* stand for?" is, sim-ply, "Integrated Development Environment." But that doesn't tell what an integrated development *is*. And, since an IDE is our most important tool, it's worth learning a bit of history.

Years ago I worked as a fire control dispatcher for the Florida Divi-sion of Forestry. That meant I climbed a fire tower each afternoon and stared at the horizon, looking for unauthorized wisps of smoke. If I saw one (and, nearly every day I saw several), I would radio another tower and, together, we would triangulate the location of the blaze. I then radioed the nearest ranger (or, if it was a large fire, rangers) and sent him or her to put the fire out.

In spite of what you might think, it was a peaceful job. I didn't personally have to go to fires, so my greatest danger was from the wasps who lived in the upper reaches of my tower.

My first exposure to computers was the weather prediction system the state installed. It was a teletype; each afternoon, after measuring the local weather—temperature, humidity, and so on—I would dial a computer in Seattle, connect the teletype to the acoustic coupler, and key in commands that described the weather in my area. In return, the computer in Seattle would advise me how many fires to expect, how many would be set by lightning, how many by arsonists, and so on.

One of the other dispatchers, a guy named Felix, lived in terror of the computer. It seems he had come to the Division of Forestry *from* a job as a computer programmer. He explained his job to me: Day after fourteen-hour day, he plugged little wires into little holes. The pressure had gotten to him and he had fled, screaming, to the lower-paying, but infinitely more peaceful, job of dispatcher . . . but the Computer had followed him. The thought of typing the weather into that innocent little teletype was giving him nightmares.

The third dispatcher was a guy named Ralph, who chained-smoked cigars and resented any alteration in the routine he had spent years developing. He saw no point in getting a computer to tell us how many fires there would be, unless it could also tell us *when* and *where*. But his biggest problem was the letter *L*. He insisted on using it when he meant the number *1*. "I have typed lower-case *L* for *1* all my life," he'd say, "and I'm not about to stop now." He didn't, either. He sat there, literally for hours, repeating the same command and receiving the same error message: "Invalid data." He was determined to keep at it until the computer finally gave in.

It didn't, of course. And yet, in the intervening years, computer programs have become more forgiving and a lot more fun to use. Even programs used to *create* programs have become easier to use. I often wonder how poor Felix feels now that even Sears sells computers and the supermarket sells diskettes. No one programs by wiring computers anymore, and very few even use punch cards. The big, eight-inch floppies are gone and the mainframes will be, too, before long.

Just five years ago I developed hot, new systems in Clipper for dBASE-style databases. (I used dBASE to work the kinks out of the database and try out the code, then compiled it into a release app with Clipper.) I remember how amazed I was when I replaced my 8088 computer with an 80286: Compile and link time for my project went from twenty minutes to less than five!

By three years ago, I was compiling Windows apps with the Microsoft C compiler, run from the DOS command line under the control of Polymake. And then, finally, I was introduced to the Borland IDE. In one development application (two, if you count Resource Workshop separately) I could manage my project—replacing Polymake; I could compile—replace the command-line compiler; link—replacing the command-line linker; and compile and bind the resource pool—replacing the resource compiler. Everything was in one place; everything was convenient; everything contributed intelligently to the common goal of producing an executable application. Best of all, I didn't have to leave Windows to compile, then return to it to test. And the final icing on the cake: my compile and link time for my project went from five minutes to one-and-a-half—*and* produced a smaller executable!

Each generation of IDEs comes with even more abilities. The latest, Borland C++ 4.0, will even generate much of your source code for you. You answer questions on a series of dialog boxes (called "Experts" by Borland) and, the next thing you know, you have a half-dozen files containing the framework of your application. The tricky Windows stuff is done; you can concentrate on the code that makes your application *work*.

I still know a few programmers who insist on writing the Windows apps their clients demand in a DOS-based editor, compiled and linked with DOS-based tools, and tested as little as possible. But I also knew a guy who couldn't stop using lowercase *l*s when he needed to use *1*s. He wound up retiring, unable to adapt to a job that really hadn't changed very much.

IDEs are not the wave of the future; they're the wave of the *present*. Ignore them at peril of your own obsolescence.

Working with Project Components

Modern development environments are project-based. Getting the most from them requires your understanding of what, exactly, constitutes a "project."

When you first start your copy of Borland C++ 4.0 (BC4), there is no active "project." Don't be fooled by the "NONAME.CPP" window that opens; although you can *compile* a file from BC4 without having a project opened, that's *all* you can do. BC4 is project-based, and that means you have to create a new project (or open an existing one) as your first step.

Creating a new project is easy. Let's create a project called "Hello".

You start by dropping down the Project menu. To open a project, you have three choices: App Expert, New project, and Open project. The App Expert command is used for generating application skeletons; we'll look at this concept in later chapters. The Open project command accesses existing projects. That leaves New project as the command you should issue.

When you select Project, New project, the application displays the dialog box shown in Figure 1.1. Your first job is to name your project

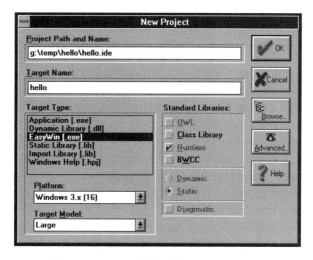

Figure 1.1 You use the New Project dialog box to create and name your project.

and select a directory for it. BC4 makes this easier than ever, because now you don't even have to pre-create the directory. Just name it—for example, "C:\HELLO\HELLO.IDE"—and BC4 will do the rest.

Keep Each Project in Its Own Directory

This may sound obvious, but I've met many programmers who rely on MAKE files (or project files) to keep track of their project components. Modern IDEs simply produce too many files to make this a feasible solution. There are files for pre-compiled headers, symbol tables, wizards and experts, not to mention the usual header, source, resource and module definition files. Do yourself a favor and segregate each project from any others.

And what about projects that share components? Easy: treat the shared components like a separate project. When you create a new project, just tell BC4 that the target type is a static library or Windows DLL. You'll find the end projects become clearer when you keep them distinct from their shared components.

Unless you change it, BC4 will give your project the same name you gave the .IDE file.

The Target Type list box allows you to choose the type of project this is. For Hello World, the easiest approach is an EasyWin project. We'll talk more about EasyWin shortly. Likewise, we'll soon cover memory models in depth. For now, any memory model you've installed will do.

Once you hit the OK button, BC4 closes that useless "noname" module and opens a Project window that looks something like the one shown in Figure 1.2.

You use the Project window as a visual MAKE file. It shows all the components of your project—even Help and resource files—and graphs their interrelationships.

When you first create the Hello project, a HELLO.CPP module does not yet exist, but its name appears in the Project window. To create one and open it for editing, simply double-click on its name in the Project window.

Here's all you need to type to create this program:

```
#include <iostream.h>

void main(void)
    {
    cout << "Hello, world!" << endl;
    }
```

To compile and link the program, drop down the Project menu again. Your three choices are Compile, Make all, and Build all. The Compile command will compile just the file in the active window, whether its part of the current project or not. The Make all command will recompile (relink, whatever) just those components that have changed since the last Make all command was issued. And the Build all command recompiles and links everything, whether BC4 thinks the component needs it or not.

To test your program, you can either double-click on HELLO.EXE in File Manager, or select Debug, Run. Either way, the window shown in Figure 1.3 appears. Note the word *Inactive* in the caption bar. HELLO.EXE runs so quickly that it is done almost as soon as it starts. Later we'll write some programs with a little more longevity!

Figure 1.2 A Project window similar to this displays when you exit the New Project dialog box.

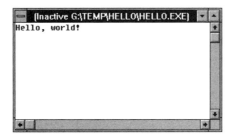

Figure 1.3 The Hello World program displays this phrase.

Using EasyWin Programs

Use the EasyWin facility to test small pieces of code or to run existing C and C++ applications in a window.

In the previous section we created a Hello World program in just a few lines of code, thanks to BC4's EasyWin facility. As I mentioned previously, to select the EasyWin facility, simply select EasyWin as your desired Target Type when you create a project.

EasyWin also makes it possible to test small, stand-alone pieces of code. As long as the Windows API or ObjectWindows isn't involved, EasyWin will be perfectly happy to accommodate a simple **main()** that exists only to exercise the questionable code. You might consider keeping a "test" project around just for that purpose.

In a EasyWin program, the "standard" I/O facilities—**stdin**, **stdout**, even **stderr**—find expression in a normal-looking Windows application window. **stdout** is used to present prompts, and input through **stdin** causes the program to pause, waiting for user input at the same window. When the program completes, the window remains open until it is closed by the user.

One word of warning: *never attempt to mix ObjectWindows and EasyWin.* A Windows application can only have one message loop active at a time, and both EasyWin and ObjectWindows try to supply one.

Understanding Declaration versus Definition

C and C++ functions and static variables are usually declared, then defined. It's helpful to know which is which.

In both C and C++, *declaration* of a variable or function occurs when the variable or function is made known to the system. *Definition* occurs when the variable or function is actually instantiated.

For example, take the function **MyFunc()**. Here's a possible declaration:

```
int MyFunc (int a, long b);
```

You can see there's no code here; it's just a function prototype, used to guarantee that callers of *MyFunc()* will get the parameter list right. The declaration can safely be **#include**d in many different modules, and even more than once in the same module. However, it can be *defined* only once:

```
int MyFunc (int a, long b)
   {
   return a * ((int) b / 4;
   }
```

If you attempt to define **MyFunc()** more than once in a source file, the compiler will issue an error. If you define it in different source files the compiler won't notice but the *linker* will issue an error.

Likewise, **extern** variables are both declared and defined—and this is done a little differently than in C. Here's the declaration of an **extern**:

```
extern int MyVar;
```

And here's the definition:

```
extern int MyVar = 17;
```

The only difference is that, in the definition, the variable is given its initial value. And, just like functions, an **extern** can be declared many, many times—but defined only once.

This means that declarations of both functions and **extern**s can (and should) be placed in header files, while the definitions of both should reside in implementation (.CPP) files. There's no harm in the file in which an **extern** is defined having previously been **#include**d a header file in which the same **extern** was declared—in fact, that's a *good* thing. It lets the compiler guarantee that there's no confusion over how the **extern** is stored.

Non-**extern** variables are unique in that they are declared and defined at the same time:

```
int MyVar;
```

In this case, the code both describes **MyVar** and allocates space for it.

Adding Modules to Your Project

A project isn't much good without the components that make it up. Here's how to add modules to the project file.

Most C++ programming involves entities called "classes." Like traditional C code modules, they are typically rendered in pairs of files. The class is declared in a header file, and defined in an implementation file. The header file, of course, has an .H extension, and the implementation file usually has a .CPP extension. (I say, "usually," because this wasn't always the case. Some early C++ compilers used .CXX extensions—the "XX" was supposed to represent plus signs lying at an angle. This has gone out of fashion, but there are still some C++ source files lying around with the old extensions.)

To add a module to your project, open the Project window (if it isn't already) and select the item to which the new module is to be a part—generally, that's the top level .EXE component. Press the Insert key; the Add to Project List dialog box appears. Simply select the file you want to add, or type in the name of a module that doesn't yet exist. Do *not* add a header file to your project; BC4 will automatically add header dependencies the first time you compile a module.

There's no rule against it, but I advise you to avoid placing more than one class description in a single pair of files. I have, several times, done so *convinced* that the second class was so closely allied with the first that they would never be used separately. So far I've *always* been wrong!

Avoiding Multiple *#includes*

#includeing the same file more than once increases compile time unnecessarily. It can also result in compile errors if the #include file contains a class declaration. Here's how to avoid multiple inclusions.

To avoid **#include**ing the same file more than once, add statements similar to the following to the beginning of each header file:

```
#ifndef __MODULE_H__
#define __MODULE_H__
```

__MODULE_H__ should be replaced by the name of your header file, of course. These should be the first two lines in the file. The last line in the file should read:

```
#endif
```

Hot Tip

Include a Newline with #endif

Be sure and place a newline character at the end of the **#endif** directive. Although this is not a problem for Borland C++ 4.0, some compilers, such as Microsoft Visual C++, erroneously report an error if a compiler directive is immediately followed by an end-of-file character. By adding the newline character to the directive, you can ease porting to another compiler platform should the need arise.

Understanding Memory Models

It's important to know what memory models are, and which ones are appropriate for various purposes. This section makes it all clear.

Most computer languages do not give the programmer a choice of memory models. For that matter, in the history of computing, most *computers* haven't given the programmer a choice of memory models. When you specify a memory model, you are stating whether pointers in your program will be "far"—that is, whether they will include segment information. You only need to specify a memory model with computer chips that use segmented memory, such as those on which the IBM-compatible PCs are based. Here are the six types of memory models:

- If your program can all be packed into a single segment—code, data, stack and heap—then it can use *small model*, where the operating system sets the segment registers and the program leaves them alone.

- *Tiny model*, a relative newcomer, is like small model except that all addresses are "fixed up" at link time. Since there's nothing else for the operating system to do, such a program loads *very* fast. Tiny model programs have a .COM extension instead of .EXE, and can only run under DOS.

- *Medium model* places all the data, along with the stack and the heap, into a single segment but allows the code to take up one segment per source module. This means that data can be accessed by **near** pointers, but function calls are made using **far** pointers. Medium model was long the model of choice for Windows programmers writing in standard C.

- *Compact model* is weird; no one I know uses it. In compact model, there may be many data segments—and, thus, data is accessed through **far** pointers—but only one code segment.

- In *Large model*, both code and data are stored in many segments; thus all pointers are **far**. Large model is all but required for DLLs, because C expects the stack and data segment registers to be pointing to the same segment; when DLL code is executing that assumption isn't true. By using Large model, where all addresses include segment information, the problem is avoided.

  Large model was once avoided for Windows applications, because you can't simultaneously run more than one copy of a large model app with multiple data segments. Modern compilers, including Borland C++ 4.0, no longer produce multiple data segments on their own, so large model is now okay for Windows apps. (However, if you use the Microsoft Foundation Classes (MFC) instead of ObjectWindows, you'll find that MFC *creates* extra data segments in large model, so you're back where you started.)

- Last in the list is *huge model*. This is similar to large model, except that the compiler supports incrementing a pointer beyond 64K. (If that happens, the selector portion of the pointer is incremented by eight, instead of one, thus directing it to the next global memory descriptor.)

Avoiding Two Common Link Errors

The most common link errors are "Duplicate definition" and "Unresolved reference." Both are easy to fix.

The linker will give you a "Duplicate definition" error if you've defined a function or **extern** variable more than once. Not only can this error occur if you have added the same component twice to your project, but It could also happen if you accidentally leave off the class specifier when you implement what you intended to be a class member function.

The opposite error, "Unresolved reference," occurs when you've *omitted* a definition. For example, you may have declared an **extern** but forgotten to define it. Or you may have included a member function in a class header but never gotten around to writing the code. If you did write it, you'll probably find that you never added the module to your project.

Things You Can't Do in C++ That You Can in C

C++ is supposed to be an *extension* of C, you'd think that anything you can do in C, you can do in C++, right? Well, for the most part you'd be right. But there are a few gotchas. In this section we'll look at the few things you *can't* do in a C++ module that are perfectly acceptable in C.

Assigning a Void Pointer to a Typed Pointer

In C it is permissible to assign a void pointer to a typed pointer; in C++ it is not.

Consider the following scrap of code:

```
void * v;
int i;
int * p = &i;
v = p; // OK
p = v; // Error in C++
```

C has traditionally been a "weakly typed" language—that is, you can assign pretty much any data type to any other. In fact, back during the C/Pascal religious wars, C programmers *bragged* that their language was weakly typed. "We can do anything we want," they said, "without having the compiler jumping all over us." However, years of experience have shown that "doing anything you want" in variable assignments leads to bugs and hard-to-maintain code; so when C++ was developed it was made "strongly typed." A *void pointer* is an intentional exception; you can assign the address of any kind of value to a void pointer—but don't expect to retrieve it without casting:

```
p = (int *) v;
```

You can cast in C++ just as you did in C. The difference is, sometimes you *have* to cast in C++, where C was a little more relaxed.

Using Old-Style Function Prototypes

As the C language evolved, its approved style of function prototyping has evolved as well. C++ throws out the old styles, and supports only the latest.

In Brian Kernigan's original vision, C was a free-wheeling, anything goes kind of language. "Prototypes?" one can almost imagine him saying. "We don't need no stinkin' prototypes!" And so the original specification for C did not require them at all. Each caller indicated the calling sequence for a function, simply by calling it.

Of course, many times programmers inadvertently listed the parameters a function was expecting, incorrectly. And so, finally, C supported prototypes of the format:

```
int MyFunc (a, b);
int a;
char b;
   {
   ...
   }
```

When the ANSI standards folks finally decided to tackle C, they changed the approved prototype style to its present form:

```
int MyFunc (int a, char b);
   {
   ...
   }
```

Of course, C compilers still support the older style, and even the original style. But C++ does not.

Omitting *return* from a Typed Function

In C++, every non-void function must return a value. The compiler flags an error if you forget.

In the original C specification, every function returned a value—that's why they're called "functions" rather than "procedures," as they are in some other languages. Of course, many times a programmer wrote a function that could return no meaningful value; in such a case he or she simply omitted the **return** statement. Still, the compiler "returned" a garbage value, and an unwary caller could assign that "value" to a variable.

The ANSI standards committee attempted to remedy this situation by inventing the **void** keyword. **void** could be used as a return type for functions, indicating the function did not return a value. However, this didn't address the common mistake of *forgetting* to include a **return** statement in a function that was *supposed* to return a value.

C++ solves this problem by *requiring* a **return** statement in any non-**void** function. Moreover, the **return** must supply a value of the same type the function is supposed to return.

return can also be used in **void** functions to signify an exit from the function to the caller; but in such a case it is used alone, without a return value.

C++ Extensions

Enough of C code that won't compile under C++! It's time to look at C++ *extensions*—things that *will* compile under C++ (but won't under C).

Most C++ extensions exist so that classes—object-oriented programming units—can be implemented. Although they could have been just stuck in, the designers of C++ chose to enhance C just enough so that classes would seem to be a logical conclusion.

Therefore, while we will *not* be looking at classes in this section, we *will* be looking at those features of C++ that make classes possible.

Understanding Overloaded Functions

Any programmer understands the notion of a "calling sequence"—the order and type of parameters to be passed to a function. In C++, the notion is taken further and formalized to support **overloaded functions.**

Consider the following two functions:

```
int MyFunc (int a, char b)
   {
   ...
   return 17;
   }
int MyFunc (char a, long b)
   {
   ...
   return 42;
   }
```

In a C program this would clearly constitute an error. How could a program have two functions with the same name? And, even if it could, how could the linker deal with it?

But that's because, in C, a function is identified by its name only. The native C calling protocol would simply send the name "MyFunc," prepended with an underscore, to the linker.

C++ doesn't work that way. Instead, C++ uses the name *and the parameter list* to generate a function name. Therefore, the first function listed in the previous code segment would have a name something like "MyFunc_with_an_Int_and_a_Char" and the second would be "MyFunc_with_a_Char_and_a_Long." Obviously there's no conflict there.

Of course, the names aren't really that wasteful of space. The various data types are encoded and delimited with characters like "@" and "!", depending on the compiler.

The process is called *name mangling*. Really, that's what it's called, unless you work for Microsoft—when that company lost its sense of humor a couple of years ago they started calling the process "name decoration." But everyone else calls it name mangling.

Everything that makes up the argument list—data types, order of types, and even modifiers like **const**—go into the mangled name. But note: the return type *does not* go into the name. So the following two prototypes *would* conflict:

```
int MyFunc (int a);
long MyFunc (int a);
```

Name mangling exists to support a concept new to C++: *overloaded functions*. You can have as many **MyFunc()** implementations as you like, as long as each has a unique function signature. Wherever you call **MyFunc()** in your program, C++ looks at the calling sequence and invokes the overloaded function whose signature matches your parameters. If it can't find a match, it tries matching to legal casts. For example, if you have this prototype

```
int MyFunc (long a, char b);
```

and you attempt to invoke it like this

```
z = MyFunc (17, 'a');
```

C++ will not be able to find a match for MyFunc_with_an_Int_and_a_Char. But it knows the value 17 can safely be cast to a long, and when it looks for MyFunc_with_a_Long_and_a_Char, a match will be found.

Avoiding Name Mangling

The only drawback to name-mangled functions is that it's the devil to try and call one of them from outside C++. In such a case, you may want to turn name mangling off.

C++ will support *one* non-mangled function of a given name. To turn off name-mangling, use the **extern** keyword in a new way:

```
extern "C"
   {
   int MyFunc (int a, char b);
   }
```

C++ is able to memorize the signature of one non-mangled function, so you can overload this function if you like—but the non-mangled one is the only version that can be called from another language.

Writing Dual-Purpose Headers

*The **extern "C"** statement is actually intended to support calling functions written and compiled in C. Any C header files you #include must be made part of an **extern "C"** statement.*

Fortunately, all the standard C library headers have already been enhanced in this way. But if you have any pre-written C functions that you want to call from both C and C++ programs, you'll want to include an **extern "C"** statement—but *only* when the functions are being processed by the C++ compiler. Fortunately, a way to accomplish this has been provided by Borland. It's the **__cplusplus** define. We are guaranteed that any C++ compiler, in C++ mode, will have this **#define** available. Therefore a dual-purpose header file can be constructed as follows:

```
#ifdef __cplusplus
extern "C" {
#endif

// Standard C function prototypes here...

#ifdef __cplusplus
}
#endif
```

This technique should be used in addition to that described in *Avoiding Multiple #includes*, earlier in this chapter.

Single-Line Comments

C++ has added a new style of denoting comments that is so refreshing it has been retrofitted into C!

Let's face it: there's no way to make standard C /* comments */ look attractive. It's also annoying that they can't be nested. How many times have you tried to "comment out" a block of code, only to discover—after a lengthy compile—that your block was brought to a premature end by an embedded comment you hadn't noticed?

C++ adds a new comment style: single-line comments, terminated by the end of the line, and beginning with a double slash:

```
int a;  // This is a comment
```

If you're saying to yourself, "This isn't new; I've been using it for a couple of years," congratulate yourself for being in the vanguard. The single-line comment syntax was invented for C++, but Microsoft and Borland programmers liked it so much they retrofitted it into their respective C compilers.

Using the New Casting Style

C++ introduces a new style of casting, although it continues to support the traditional style.

Casting, of course, occurs when a variable of a certain data type needs to look like another data type, as in:

```
unsigned a = (unsigned) -1;
```

This style is confusing to people just learning C; perhaps that's why the ANSI committee decided to reinforce it with another style, borrowed from Pascal, that makes casting look like a function call:

```
unsigned a = unsigned (-1);
```

However, the new style doesn't support multi-token data types, such as **char** *. To use the new style in such a case, you'd have to **typedef** a single-token synonym for the desired data type.

This addition to C++ doesn't seem to have been as well-thought-out as most of the others. Personally, I'm casting my lot with the old style on this one.

The Three Faces of *const*

You got to give the ANSI C++ committee credit for never using two keywords where one will do. const, *a new addition to C++, has* three *different meanings!*

With typical C brevity, **const** is short for "constant." A constant is a value that never changes, so use of the keyword **const** to indicate that is a welcome addition to C++.

In C, programmers typically use **#define**s to provide names for numbers that don't change:

```
#define MAXITEMS 32
#define MAXLENGTH 255
```

The problem is that the C preprocessor, not the compiler, performs the macro substitution; the linker never sees the names and you can't ask a debugger what the value of *MAXITEMS* is. C++ solves this problem with the concept of a "read-only variable"—a **const**:

```
const int MaxItems = 32;
const int MaxLength = 255;
```

Since a **const** variable can't be written to, it follows that it *must* be initialized. The following will provoke a compiler error:

```
const int a; // Error: no initialization
```

Now that we have **const** variables, we have a *new* problem. Suppose I make a **const struct**, and I want to pass its address to a function for efficiency reasons. The compiler doesn't know whether the function will try to change the structure, so it issues an error:

```
void MyFunc (struct MyStruct * s);
const struct MyStruct s1 = { 17, 92, 's' };
MyFunc (&s1); // Error--compiler thinks MyFunc will alter a constant
```

To solve this problem, C++ gives us the second use, the **const** argument:

```
void MyFunc (const struct MyStruct * s);
const struct MyStruct s1 = { 17, 92, 's' };
MyFunc (&s1); // OK
```

The third use of the **const** keyword is related to object-oriented classes. Classes have functions defined that work only on them, and it's possible to create a **const** object from a class. **const** is used to describe a class member function that is safe to use on a **const** object. We'll speak more of this in the next chapter.

Meanwhile, take advantage of this new feature. Any time you write a function that doesn't change the value of an argument passed to it by address or by reference (we'll talk about that shortly), remember to mark the argument as **const**. Not only will that accommodate the occasional passing of a **const** as that parameter, but the compiler will be able to optimize code more effectively, knowing the called function will not change that parameter.

Understanding *const* Pointers and Pointers to *const*

Pointers are tricky enough to grasp without having to worry about the const *keyword added to the mix. Here's some much needed help.*

Remember the old C programmer's trick: read variable definitions from right to left. For example, the definition

```
int * p;
```

reads "**p** is a pointer to an **int**."

The same trick applies when the **const** keyword tries to make things more complicated. In the example,

```
const int * p;
```

"**p** is a pointer to an **int** that's **constant**." In other words, **p** is a regular pointer whose value can be changed, but the item it *points to* cannot:

```
p = &I;
*p = 17; // Error--thing p points to can't be altered
```

A converse definition is also legal:

```
int * const p = &i;
```

In this case, **p** is a constant pointer to an **int**, so it *must* be initialized. That address cannot be changed, but **p** *can* be used to alter **i**'s value.

Finally, both the address and the target can be locked up:

```
const int * const p = &i;
```

p is now a constant pointer to a constant **int**. You probably wouldn't do this in as a function local variable, but you might declare a function parameter this way.

Declaring C++ *structs*

The syntax for declaring a **struct** *in C++ is subtly different from declaring one in C. In addition, the* **struct** *has a new significance.*

In C, a structure is simply a collection of data. In the typical declaration

```
struct X
  {
  int a, b, c;
  };
```

X is called the *tagname*. The **struct** does not, itself, allocate any space; to do that, you create an *instance* of the **struct**:

```
struct X MyX;
```

Most programmers don't want to bother repeating the keyword **struct** so often, so they declare the **struct** in a **typedef** instead.

In C++, this isn't necessary. The tagname *becomes* a data type, making the following statement legal:

```
X MyX;
```

Remember this technique when you come to the chapter on classes. In C++, a **struct** is considered to be a special kind of class; and classes are declared and defined similarly.

Unrestricted Variable Definition

In C, variables must be defined at the beginning of the block in which they will be used. C++ releases that restriction, allowing variables to be defined any time before they are actually used.

In C, the following code would provoke a compiler error:

```
void MyFunc (void)
   {
   int a;
   a = 17;
   int b;
   b = a * 3;
   }
```

However, in C++ these statements are perfectly legal.

A variable can also be defined in the code in which it is actually used:

```
for (int i= 0; i < MaxLength; i++)
   {
   ...
   }
```

Such a variable exists from the point at which it is defined, to the end of the block in which it was defined.

New Initialization Style

To support multi-argument initializations, C++ introduces a new style of initialization that can be used for any variables.

You'll see the need for multi-argument initializations when we get to classes later in this book. C++ supports the old initialization style, but on the theory that it's better to pick one initialization style and stick with it, you should plan on becoming familiar with and using the new style:

```
int a (17);
```

That's right, it makes initialization look like a function call. That's partly because, with classes, initialization *is* a function call.

Default Parameters

C++ allows us to supply default parameters to functions. This is not the same as omitting trailing parameters, as C allows. The parameter value is supplied by the compiler if you omit it in the call.

To specify a default parameter, just indicate what it should be in the function declaration:

```
int MyFunc (int a, long b = 87L, char c = 'z');
```

In this example, **MyFunc()** can be called with one, two, or three parameters. If called with two, the function will *receive* three—and the third will be the character "z." If called with one, the second will be supplied as 87.

HOT TIP

Be Careful when Overloading Functions with Default Parameters

It is possible to overload a function with default parameters, with a new function that simply *omits* those parameters. But when you try and invoke one of those functions, the compiler won't be able to tell which one you want. In such a case, the compiler will generate a message indicating your specification of an "ambiguous" function, and you'll have to figure which one to get rid of.

Understanding Argument Types and Call-By-Reference

C++ has added a new way of supplying parameters to a function. Understanding all three methods of parameter passing is essential to C++ programming.

The simplest, and original, method of passing parameters is called *call-by-value*. In this, method, a copy of the parameter is placed directly on the stack:

```
void MyFunc (int i);
```

No matter how big the parameter is—even if it's a **struct** of 4K—the whole thing is copied. That means even if the function changes the parameter internally, the caller won't see the changes.

Of course, sometimes the caller *wants* to see the changes. That's when *call-by-address* is traditionally used:

```
void MyFunc (int * i);
```

In call-by-address, instead of copying the parameter onto the stack, the *address* of the parameter is placed on the stack. The called function can then treat the parameter as the pointer that it is, and change the source variable by using the pointer de-referencing syntax:

```
*i = 17;
```

C programmers have tolerated this for years, but let's face it: that dereference syntax is just plain annoying. It's especially bothersome if you've passed the address to a **struct**, and have to change a bunch of direct-referenced data members to pointer-referenced data members.

Other languages solved this years ago, in the form of *call-by-reference*, and now C++ has it too. In call-by-reference, the parameter is passed by address—but *treated* as if it had been passed by value.

To specify a reference parameter, just use the "&" character like you would the "*" character:

```
int MyFunc (int & i);
```

Then, inside the function, treat **i** as if it were a regular variable:

```
i = 17;
```

Some C programmers find reference parameters confusing. I suppose if you spend enough years using pointers exclusively, the mind may become warped beyond all repair. Still, the cure is simple. In all your new code, use references where you would have used a pointer. Whenever you feel yourself becoming confused, remind yourself to treat the reference *exactly* as you would a non-pointer variable. And don't forget to use the **const** keyword if the reference parameter is not going to be changed.

Using *new* and *delete* to Manage Memory

C++ introduces replacements for the venerable malloc() *and* free() *functions—and, unlike* malloc() *and* free()*, they are actually part of the language!*

Quick, what's the only operator in C that is actually spelled out? Bzzt—times up! It's **sizeof**, which is an operator, not a function. But C++ adds two, *new* spellable operators: **new** and **delete**. These operators are used to allocate and release heap space, respectively.

Although **malloc()** and **free()** still exist, you shouldn't use them, because **new** and **delete** are so much better. For one thing, **malloc()** requires a byte count and returns a **void *** that you have to cast; **new** "knows" how many bytes to allocate, and returns a properly typed pointer:

```
int * i = new int;
int * j = (int *) malloc (sizeof (int));
```

delete improves over **free()**, too. For example, if you pass a NULL pointer to **free()**, you can expect a system crash. **delete** is smart enough to not try and return a NULL pointer to the heap.

new can be used to initialize the memory it obtains:

```
int * i = new int (17);
```

It can also allocate arrays:

```
int * i = new int[32]; // allocate a 32-element array
```

If you allocate an array, you must tell **delete** that it is de-allocating an array instead of a scalar variable:

```
delete [] i;
```

No, that's not a typo—yes, I know it looks weird. But they didn't check with me first, and that's how it is done.

If you compile for small, medium, or compact model, **new** and **delete** use your program's local heap as a source of memory. If you use large or huge model, they will draw from the global heap. In protected mode (as in Windows), you are limited to about 8,000 separate allocations from the global heap, due to the fact that global segment descriptors are a limited resource. However, C++ solves that, too: **new** allocates one large global segment, and sub-allocates that segment to satisfy each subsequent request. It doesn't ask for another global segment until all the space in the segment it's already asked for are used up. It will re-use space that's been deleted, too. So that's another reason to use large model.

CHAPTER

2

Object-Oriented Programming

27

I f you're new to C++, you are probably new to object-oriented programming (OOP). You'll find OOP in Smalltalk and Actor (two purely object-oriented languages) and in Borland Pascal. Time and time again, object-oriented programming has been found to produce more robust applications, make application maintenance easier, and promote reusable code—*if* you take advantage of it. But OOP isn't a matter of syntax; it's a philosophy. Writing your program as one, giant object doesn't make it an object-oriented program, any more than undressing in a phone booth makes you Superman.

Still, you've got to start somewhere. Throughout this book I hope to instill in you some of the OOP philosophy.

Objects: What You Need to Know

In this section we'll explore some useful techniques of OOP that you'll need to know, such as how to move from structures to objects, how to identify objects, and how to tell the difference between an application and a "program."

Graduating from Structures to Objects

You can hardly write a traditional C program without structs. structs *are straightforward and easy to understand, and they have equivalents in almost every other programming language. Objects, on the other hand, look intimidating. But the two are more similar than you may have guessed.*

- An **object** is very much like a **struct**. The main difference is that an object includes functions, as well as data. A **class** statement declares an object; a definition later creates the actual object, which is referred to as "instantiating an object" (and, yes, OOP progammers really talk that way).

- When declaring a **struct**, it is common practice to also **typedef** user-defined pointers to the **struct**. You can then create a pointer to a struct and allocate the space later (in C++, with the **new** operator). The same is true of objects.

- A data item in a **struct** is called a *field*. A data item in an object is called a *property*. (C++ commonly refers to properties as *member variables*; in this book I'll use both terms interchangeably.)

- The functions associated with an object are called *methods*. (C++ calls them *member functions*.) If you created a new **struct** type, you might code special functions to deal with variables of that type. That's just what an object's methods are for. By packaging them together as an inseparable object, they remain conveniently associated.

- One class can have several methods of the same name but with different signatures, just as stand-alone functions can. (Remember, these are called *overloaded* functions.) Likewise, methods for one object class can have the same names as methods for another object class. The compiler will make sure the appropriate code is invoked; this was why overloaded functions were invented.

- **struct**s can, themselves, contain **struct**s. Objects can contain other objects as properties. (Some properties might be **struct**s, as well. And a field in a **struct** could be an object.)

- If you have an existing object class that does 90 percent of what you want (or 50 percent or 10 percent), you can *derive* a new object class from it. You'll only have to add enough properties and/or methods to it to get the behavior you want. You can also override methods that are inappropriate in the descendent class. This is called *inheritance*.

- Anywhere a pointer to an object of a certain class is expected, a pointer to an object of a descendent class can be used instead. This is called *polymorphism*.

- It's best if you try not to tread a line between object-oriented programming (OOP) and conventional programming. Break each component of your project into an object, and design it as a "black box." As time goes by, you'll find yourself more able to re-use object classes and save yourself work. A program that is composed of one giant object is *not* object-oriented.

- An *abstract* class is one that cannot be used to create an actual object. It is used only as an ancestor class. When breaking a project into objects, look for classes that are similar but not identical. If you can't derive one from the other, you may be able to create a third, abstract class from which you can derive the two you need.

Identifying Objects

The first task in object-oriented programming is identifying of what objects, exactly, your application is to be composed. To develop a "feel" for objects, start by looking around you.

Objects are everywhere; they are everywhere, and you've been dealing with them since birth—possibly even earlier.

Examples of objects: cars, toasters, your own heart, your own self. If you formalize how you deal with real objects, you can learn to deal with programmatic objects the same way.

All objects can be completely described with three sets of components. First, there are the object's *properties.* What shape is it? What color is it? How much does it weigh? Of what elements is it composed? There are certain properties (such as *mass*) which apply to all objects from a quark to Whitney Houston. Others apply only to a subset of all objects, such as *number of doors.*

Second are the *events* to which an object is subject. A *doorbell* object can be *pushed.* So can a *car* object, though the result differs. So can a *homicidal maniac* object, but only so far.

Third are the *methods* an object uses to respond to events. A doorbell responds to a *push* event by *ringing.* A car responds to a *push* event by *starting* (or, in the case of the Ford Pinto, by blowing up). A homicidal maniac responds to a sufficient push by climbing a tower with an Uzi sub-machine gun and—but you get the idea.

Many *events* can occur to an object whose *method* of dealing with that event is simply to ignore it. For example, most objects respond to the *penetrated by neutrino* event just that way.

You might think that in programming, you'll actually be creating objects rather than describing them, but this isn't entirely true. You should be *formalizing* objects that already exist. For example, if you intend to write a personnel management application, don't plan on "inventing" a personnel object. One already exists, or you would never have been asked to write the app! Your job is to analyze the existing collection of employees and describe it in terms of properties, events and methods.

There's a 25¢ word for this analysis: *Encapsulation* is the process of focusing on a single object and building into it everything it needs to be self-sufficient

Understanding the Difference between an Application and a Program

Designing an object-oriented application is* not *the same as designing a "structured" program. You have to start by thinking of the application as an* object

As a DOS programmer, I always started by saying to myself, "What will my application do?" As an instructor of Windows programming, I still hear my students say the same thing. But they're asking the *wrong* question, because it's not the 70s anymore.

Today's design question is: what will my application work on? A document, a bitmap, an employee, a group of employees? This distinction is necessary because we don't write programs anymore; we write *applications*—and there *is* a difference. According to the American Heritage Dictionary, a *program* is "A listing of the order of events and other information, as for a public presentation." Usage of the word has changed, of course; a TV program was originally a listing on the TV station's "program"—its schedule. The idea was that the schedule was fixed; it had to unfold in time according to its internal sequencing. In those pre-VCR days, viewers had to accept the program schedule as it was.

Computer programs, also, are temporally fixed. They start, read their starting parameters, process, and terminate. Most of the "commands" that come with DOS such as XCOPY, CHKDSK and MEM are, in fact, programs. Once started, they must do what they were designed to do and then terminate. They are simple tools, like a screwdriver or a toaster. Or they are batch processes, like the end-of-month payroll on a mainframe.

But computer users, these days, are accustomed to working with *applications*. These "programs" may have components that do specific jobs, but the components are grouped together and are triggered at the whim of the *user*, not the computer.

SCRIPT, the IBM mainframe text formatter, was handed a file containing text plus commands; it formatted the text and printed it. That's a program.

Any modern word processor is an application. What will happen next—A character entered? A word italicized? A sentence deleted?—the word processor doesn't know. It all happens under user control; and that's the way that users like it.

Even utilities that were *always* written as programs are, more and more, being implemented as simple applications. Users no longer tolerate having to memorized arcane series of command-line options. It's a lot easier to simply check items on a dialog box and select an OK button to start the process—and *real* nice to be able to hit a Cancel button if you change your mind.

Putting OOP Programs under the Microscope

We're now ready to dig a little deeper and explore OOP programs in more detail. First, you'll need to know how to set up an application as an object—and that's where *TApplication* comes in. Then, as you create your OOP application, you'll also need to know how to construct and package the objects your program will be using.

Understanding the Application as an Object

Not only should your application be composed (almost) entirely of objects—your application itself is an object. In fact, it is the intersection of the generic TApplication class and the object that represents the problem you are trying to solve, that results in your specific application!

What could be more different, you might ask, than a word processor and the hospital collections system I plan to write?

And yet, the two do have many things in common. Assuming they are to be written as Windows applications—and what other choice is there, really?—they will manifest themselves as sizable, moveable windows; they will have menus that will operate according to the same rules; they will have dialog boxes and icons and maybe even toolbars.

Yet all these things are mere *decorations* to solving the problem of hospital collections. Yes, they'll help the hospital business office get its money more efficiently, but they have no special meaning to the concept of collections. They apply to modern *applications*, and are present for that reason.

So, no matter what application you are about to write, whether a scheduler for shop floor equipment or a MIDI random music generator, you've already identified one object of which your application is composed: the *application*. Of course, writing all the code for such a class would be a staggering chore. Fortunately, you don't have to. Borland C++ 4.0 (or specifically, ObjectWindows 2.0) gives you the **TApplication** class, almost all ready to go.

I say "almost" because an object directly instantiated from **TApplication** would not have any bearing on the app you were actually trying to write. It would have all the form, but none of the function. So, in real life, you employ *inheritance* to *derive* a new class *from* **TApplication**.

The most important addition to the derived class is a property that represents the object your application is intended to work on: the Personnel object, the Schedule object, or the randomly generated MIDI music object. This object will probably represent a document of some kind, so it will be derived from the **TDocument** class that also comes with ObjectWindows. Finally, there's another aspect of an application that is best implemented as a property of the application: the main window. Yes, users think of the main window as *being* the application, but we know better. The main window is the view that provides access to the document that the application managers. The **TWindow** class will be ancestor to the view.

Decomposing the Problem

We've established that your application will be composed of a **TWindow**-*derived object and a* **TDocument**-*derived object, which are themselves properties of a* **TApplication**-*derived object. But how can you identify the other objects that comprise the app?*

The key to decomposing the problems that modern applications are meant to solve, is to remember that *everything is an object*. To decompose the document your app works on, identify its properties as objects, then identify their properties as objects, and so on. For example, a Personnel document is a collection of employee records. Each employee record is composed of fields such as "name," "address," and "social security number," In this example, *name* and *address* are instances of *string* objects, and *SSN* might be stored as a **long**.

Eventually you get to the point where the "object" you describe is too elemental to be further reduced:

- *String* objects are already supplied by ANSI-standard C++, so you don't need to invent them or worry about how they work.

- **long** variables are a part of the C language; again, you needn't worry about their implementation.

At this point, go back to the top and examine the *view* component of the application. How best to present the document it manages to the user for manipulation? Perhaps a list box with all employees arrayed by name. And when the user selects a name, the various properties of that particular employee could be loaded into edit boxes, check boxes, etc. All those pieces become properties of the window.

You may have heard that object-oriented programming is "magic"—that objects do things "to" themselves, rather than you doing things "to" them. You may have concluded that object-oriented programming is less work than traditional programming, but this is misleading. You'll have to write at least as many lines of code as before—maybe more. But when you write the code, you'll be concentrating—focusing—on just the one object at a time. Maybe you'll be writing the other objects later; maybe someone else will. But you focus on the task at hand, which keeps each member function small and easy to test and prove. It is this microscopic approach to programming that makes object-oriented programs more robust.

Packaging Objects

An element crucial to the re-use of C++ objects is efficient packaging of those objects.

You're going to need a **TPhone** class for your employee records. You may use it in a couple of different places; home, work, and pager numbers, for example. But this is not (hopefully) the last application you'll ever write. Odds are, you'll be working with phone numbers again. And, next time, you won't have to create a **TPhone** object—you'll already have one! With each project, your decomposition should be complete at higher and higher levels as the availability of predefined classes grows. Because **TPhone** objects are totally isolated from the applications in which they are used, they will work as well in one app as another. And if you *do* notice and fix a bug in a class you wrote for an earlier app, simply recompiling the earlier app will fix the bug there, too.

But all this will work only if you help it along with a little astute packaging of your class definitions. Here's a method that's been proven to work.

First of all, give your object a meaningful name. Although I do not approve of Hungarian notation in general, it is helpful to distinguish between class names and the names of the objects instantiated from those classes. The C tradition was to put **typedef**s in UPPERCASE and variable names in lowercase. This tradition has not followed into classes. Indeed, the ANSI standard *string* class is written all lowercase, perhaps to make it fit in with built-in data types like **int** and **double**. Microsoft, in writing the Foundation Classes, begins each class name with a capital "C," for class. Borland, which originated ObjectWindows for its Pascal compiler (where classes are declared in **Type** statements), begins each class name with "T." I suppose I might begin my class names with "P," for Paul.

Whatever method you select, I advise you be consistent. Classes designed in this book will have the initial "T."

Your next job is to *abbreviate* that name so it can be used as a filename, because you should never put more than one class in a pair of files (one header and one implementation). If you have decided to prefix your class names with initials, *don't* include the initial in the filename. What's the point of having a directory filled with files, all of which begin with "P" or "R"? You've wasted a letter. Another pitfall is inadvertently duplicating a file that exists in the ObjectWindows library or the C standard library itself. But, whatever you do, *don't* follow the old COBOL technique of naming files utter nonsense that must be looked up in a manual before they can be identified. Who has time to wade through that extra layer of indirection? A little care when naming the file is all it takes to make it easy to identify and access later.

Objects, as mentioned, are rendered in a pair of files. The class declaration is found in a header file with an .H extension; the implementation is placed in a file with a .CPP extension. For example, our **TPhone** class would be rendered in PHONE.H and PHONE.CPP.

Later on we'll talk about *inline member functions.* Since these functions are not compiled until they are referenced, they have to be placed in the header file. Also, there is a type of global function called a "friend" function. Friend functions should be packaged with the class toward which they are friendly.

Declaring Objects

Finally we come to the meat of the subject: how do you declare a class? It turns out to be remarkably like declaring a struct. Here's a secret: in C++, **struct**s are actually a special kind of class! No wonder the **class** statement looks so much like the **struct** statement. Here's an example:

```
class TScaledInt
    {
    long Value;
    long Power;
    TScaledInt ();
    TScaledInt (long V, int ScalingFactor);
    };
```

This is an extremely simple example. In reality, most classes are derived from ancestor classes, and most properties are, themselves, objects. But this is a valid class declaration. (Remember, this is just the declaration. The code to implement this class is kept separately, in a .CPP file.)

In the topics in this section we'll look at each of the additional, interesting things you can do to make your **class** declaration look like you *earned* your degree in software engineering.

Don't Forget the Terminating Semicolon!

For some reason, many programmers forget it and current compilers have a hard time identifying the problem. If you get an error shortly after a class declaration and there doesn't seem to be anything wrong with the line the compiler is upset with, check the class declaration for a missing semicolon.

Using *public* versus *private*

One goal of object-oriented programming is to reduce "coupling"— the degree of interaction between unrelated components—to an absolute minimum. One way to accomplish this is judicious use of the public *and* private *keywords.*

How can you make your heart beat faster? Run around the block. How can you alter the angle at which the valves open? You can't. It's not part of the heart/body interface.

There are some aspects of an object that must be available to other objects if the object in question is to be useful. There are other aspects, crucial to the successful internal functioning of the object, which are best kept hidden. Availability of an object's properties and methods are controlled by the **public** and **private** keywords.

Their use is very simple. Here's an example:

```
class TScaledInt
   {
   private:
     long Value;
     long Power;
   public:
     TScaledInt ();
     TScaledInt (long V, int ScalingFactor);
     long GetValue (void);
   };
```

This code segment represents a fairly typical use. Properties are usually kept **private**, while most methods are **public**. There are exceptions to each, of course. But we find it helps minimize coupling to use functions to access properties, rather than directly referencing the property itself.

For example, suppose you created a **TRectangle** class that included an **Area** property. If **Area** were kept **public**, other objects needing to know the area of the rectangle could just query the property directly.

Worse, they could *change* the value without changing the dimensions of the rectangle the object represented! And suppose one day you realized that you didn't have to *store* **Area** at all—you could *calculate* it as needed. You wouldn't be able to make this enhancement to the functioning of your object, because to do so would break all the other objects that now referred to **Area** directly.

If, instead, **Area** was **private** and you provided a **public** method called, say, **GetArea()**, you'd solve both problems. No one could write to the **Area** property, and you'd be free to enhance it later once you recalled your fifth-grade geometry.

Note: *All* properties and functions are available *within* the code for that class. The **private** keyword only prevents access by code *outside the class*—that is, global code or the methods of other classes (including derived classes).

Just so you'll know, **private** is the default in a class declaration. A class with no **public** methods is pretty useless, so you'll probably always put the **public** keyword in there somewhere. The tradition is to put **public** stuff first, where it can be most easily seen by someone opening the header file, and to let the **private** parts trail. But you can use both keywords as often as you like in the same declaration, so you can arrange members however you find most convenient.

I mentioned earlier that a **struct** was a special case of a class. The primary difference (other than intent) is that, in a **struct**, the *default* access is **public**. That allows **struct**s in C++ to function similarly to those in C. It may occur to you, however, that this means a **struct** can contain methods, and this is true. However, I can think of no good reason to do this. Such a **struct** would merely be a class by another name; why confuse the issue?

Incidentally, there's another access keyword, **protected**. But we'll talk about that one a little later.

Defining and Using Objects

Now that you've declared your object class, you'll need to implement the class's methods and put the object to work. Class methods greatly resemble the C functions you've been writing all along.

Although I recommend you place one class declaration/definition in a single pair of files, there's no C++ rule that requires you do so. Suppose you did put two class declarations together. When it came time to define the member functions, how would the compiler know which class each block of code belonged to?

The answer is an operator new to C++: the *scope resolution operator.* It is two adjacent colons (::). Each function is written like any global function, but the name is fully qualified by the addition of the class name:

```
long TScaledInt::GetValue (void)
    {
    return Value * Power;
    }
```

This is just another variant of overloaded functions, which we talked about in Chapter 1. The class name is simply made part of the signature. Thus different classes can have member functions of the same name.

This is a *good* thing. If you *push* a doorbell or a baby buggy, you get different results, but the action is the same. By using consistent names for object methods, you encourage concentration on the *action*, not on the target class's implementation.

Plus, there are some really cool things you can do with this, as you'll see when we get to the section on *polymorphism.*

What's *this?*

How does class code know which object it's working on?

So you've written this great **TPhone** class, and now everybody's using it. There are **TPhone** objects from one end of your application to the other. When you call **TPhone::Dial()**, how does the **Dial()** function know *which* **TPhone** object it's supposed to use?

The answer is that (most) methods have an invisible, first parameter called **this**. **this** is a pointer to the object whose method has been invoked. Most of the time you don't have to use it. For example, in the function

```
long TScaledInt::GetValue (void)
    {
    return Value * Power;
    }
```

this is understood as the object whose **Value** is to be returned. If you wanted to, though, you could write the function

```
long TScaledInt::GetValue (void)
    {
    return this->Value * this->Power;
    }
```

with no change in the way it worked.

Remember references, discussed in Chapter 1? Sometimes a method needs to return a reference to the object. That's done with standard pointer de-referencing syntax:

```
TScaledInt & TScaledInt::SetValue (long V, int ScalingFactor)
  {
  Power = 1;
  for (register i = 0; i < ScalingFactor; i++)
    Power *= 10;
  Value = V;
  return *this;
  }
```

Instantiating Objects

So now you've declared an object class; you've fully implemented it. How can you make use of it? How can you make an object of that class?

An object is instantiated just like variables of any other type:

```
TScaledInt a;
TScaledInt b (170, 3);
TScaledInt c[50];
TScaledInt * d = new TScaledInt;
```

In this example, we declared **a** as a **TScaledInt** with no initialization, **b** initialized to 170000, **c** as an array of 50 **TScaledInts**, and **d** as a pointer to a **TScaledInt** allocated from the heap.

Putting an Object to Work

Given that you've instantiated an object, how can you reference its properties or invoke its methods?

An object's member data and functions (if public) can be accessed using the familiar struct syntax. For example:

```
TScaledInt a (170, 3);
long b;
b = a.GetValue();
```

Pointers to objects are used just like pointers to **struct**s:

```
TScaledInt * d = new TScaledInt;
d->SetValue (544, 2);
```

Six Ways Objects Are Better Than Structures

All this object business is interesting, but what's the point? What's an object got that a regular old C struct doesn't?

- **Objects are "smart" variables.** They know how to make themselves do what they have to do, so other objects don't have to.

- **Objects come into existence fully operational.** If you place a **struct** on the stack, its member data will consist of garbage until you initialize it. Objects initialize themselves when they are created. Sure, someone has to code this—but once done, you never have to worry about it again.

- **Objects automatically allocate whatever internal resources they need.** If you've created a monster **struct** of 10K or 30K, you probably won't be able to place one on the stack, even if that would have been the easy, natural thing to do. An equivalent object can store most of its contents on the heap, even though the object itself is on the stack. Again, you have to code this—but only once.

- **Objects deallocate those resources when they are destroyed.** If you've done Windows programming in C, you know there are any number of things (like brushes, pens, and device contexts) that *must* be allocated and de-allocated in pairs. Once an object has been properly coded, you never have to worry about this again; it will happen automatically.

- **There is no such thing as an "uninitialized object."** There are one or more special methods in every object called "constructors." The constructor's primary job is to initialize—*construct*—the object's properties. You don't have to remember to invoke a constructor; the compiler does it for you every time an object is instantiated. Consequently there are never uninitialized fields in an object.

- **Properly implemented objects never cause "memory leaks."** Likewise, the compiler invokes another special method, the *destructor*, when the object goes out of scope. So memory leaks, which occur when you forget to release a resource you've allocated, become a thing of the past.

Temporary Objects

And now, a few words from Andy Rooney. "Don't you just hate having to come up with names for variables you're only going to use once and then throw away?" But wait, Andy. C++ has solved that problem.

In C, you don't think it's special that you don't have to name a "7" or a "c" to pass them as parameters to a function. The designers of C++ wanted to make objects look as much as possible as part of the language, so they provided a way to create temporary, nameless objects.

Using our **TScaledInt** class as an example, you can create a temporary one simply by omitting a name:

```
TScaledInt (170, 3);
```

This is pointless, of course; the object will be destroyed as soon as it's been constructed, rather like Dan Quayle's hopes for the Presidency. But the usual use of temporary objects is as function parameters. Let's say that function **Print()** expects a **TScaledInt** parameter:

```
Print (TScaledInt (170, 3));
```

The temporary **TScaledInt** (from the previous code segment) object will exist until **Print()** has done its thing and returned.

Another purpose of a temporary object is to return a value from a function. The following usage is common:

```
int MyFunc (void)
   {
   return 53;
   }
```

So, to be consistent, C++ must allow this as well:

```
TScaledInt MyFunc (void)
   {
   return TScaledInt (53, 0);
   }
```

At this point you might be saying, "Wait a minute! If **MyFunc()** constructs a temporary **TScaledInt** on the stack, and then returns, won't that destroy the temporary object before the caller can make use of it?"

But the answer is, no. Anytime a function returns a value, that value is placed in a register (if small enough) or in a place in the stack *reserved* for it. That place was reserved by the *caller*, so it's still there when the function returns. This works for objects as well as **struct**s.

Understanding *static* Member Data

*C++ provides a type of property that can be **shared** among all instances.*

Suppose you have a **TEmployee** class, and one of the properties is an employee number. It would be nice, and very object-oriented, if the **TEmployee** constructor could come up with an employee number on its own. But doing so requires communicating with all the other **TEmployee** objects to ensure the employee number is never duplicated.

The easy way to accomplish this is to include a **static** property, **NextID**. There will be just one copy of this property; it will be stored outside all the objects (in the application's data segment, like any other **static** variable), and can be referenced by any one of them. This is how you declare such a variable:

```
class TEmployee
   {
   private:
     long ID;
   public:
     static long NextID;
     TEmployee ();
   };
```

The variable *must* be defined in the implementation file, because the compiler needs to generate just one copy of it:

```
static TEmployee::NextID = 0L;
```

Remember, **static** variables must be initialized so the compiler knows what, exactly, to put in the data segment.

The **static** property is referenced just like any other:

```
TEmployee::TEmployee ()
   : ID (NextID++)
   {
   }
```

Unlike normal properties, **static** properties can be referenced (if not **private**), without making any instances of the class, by using the class name and the scope resolution operator. For example:

```
cout << TEmployee::NextID;
```

Using *static* Member Functions

*Just as objects can have **static** properties that refer to the class as a whole, they can have **static** functions that refer to the class as a whole.*

Remember, properties are better off **private**, and that includes **static** properties. Access to **private** properties is through access functions; so access to **static** properties is, logically, through **static** access functions:

```
class TEmployee
  {
  private:
    long ID;
    static long NextID;
  public:
    TEmployee ();
    static long GetNextID (void);
  };

inline static long TEmployee::GetNextID (void)
  {
  return NextID;
  }
```

Incidentally, you cannot make a **static const** function. That's because a **static** property is not part of any one instance of a class; so changing such a property—or not—doesn't affect a **const** object per se.

Just like **static** properties, **static** methods can be invoked through an instance:

```
TEmployee Programmer;
cout << Programmer.GetNextID();
```

They can also be invoked through the class itself:

```
cout << TEmployee::GetNextID();
```

One more thing: **static** methods do not refer to specific instances of their class, so they have no **this** pointer, even when they are invoked through an instance.

The World of Constructors

When an object is instantiated, its special "constructor" method is invoked. The invocation takes place automatically, but it's up to you when designing the object class to make sure the constructor does its job.

Here's how this works: When an object is instantiated, its *construction* event occurs. This causes a member function called the constructor to be invoked. You never explicitly invoke a constructor; if there are more than one, the system chooses one that matches your initialization specification.

A constructor *always* has the same name as the class. In this class declaration

```
class TScaledInt
   {
   private:
      long Value;
      long Power;
   public:
      TScaledInt ();
      TScaledInt (long V, int ScalingFactor);
      ~TScaledInt ();
      long GetValue (void);
   };
```

there are two constructors. One expects no parameters, and the other expects two, a **long** and an **int**. In this scrap of code

```
TScaledInt a;
TScaledInt b (170, 3);
TScaledInt c ('z'); // ERROR!
```

a is constructed by the first constructor, and **b** is constructed with the second. An attempt to use initializers for which no constructor has been declared, such as with **c**, will result in a compiler error.

The constructor that requires no parameters has a special name; it is called the *default constructor*. Constructors never return a value—not even **void**—and the default constructor does not require **void** in its parameter list. It's called the default constructor because it's the one you get when you don't ask for one specifically (by including an initialization list).

For reasons that will become clear later, if you don't supply any constructors, the system will build a default constructor for you. However, it won't initialize any simple properties for you. (It will invoke the default constructors of any object properties.) If you supply even *one* constructor, though, the system will not supply one. So writing a constructor that requires parameters, but not a default constructor, will prevent any objects of that class from being instantiated without an initialization specification. Since you can't specify initialization when instantiating an *array* of objects, you would not be able to create an array of objects of such a class.

Thus, 99 percent of the time, you *will* supply a default constructor. The typical job of a constructor is to provide initialization for simple properties, and to specify initialization of object properties. In addition, resources required by the object such as heap memory or Windows pens, brushes, or device contexts are obtained.

Understanding the Member Initialization List

There's a special—weird—area in a constructor called the **member initialization list** *It looks strange and acts strange. But it's essential that you understand what it's for and how it works.*

An object with object properties *must* have those properties initialized in the constructor. Since you can't explicitly invoke a constructor, the compiler invokes the properties' default constructors automatically before the code block of your constructor is ever entered.

However, supposed you want to specify a different constructor for one or more of the properties?

C++ provides for this in the *member initialization list.* You can also initialize simple properties there.

This part of a constructor lies between the signature and the code block, and is introduced with a colon:

```
TScaledInt::TScaledInt ()
   : Value (0), Power (1)
   {
   }
```

In this example we're initializing **Value** and **Power** with the new syntax, described in Chapter 1. Note that there's nothing in the code block; after initializing the two properties, there's nothing left for the constructor to do. This is a common occurrence.

A significant weirdness of the member initialization list is that the order in which you specify initializations is *not* significant. Properties are *always* constructed/initialized in the order of their appearance in the class declaration. This can make a difference if you intend to use the result of one initialization as a parameter to another. In such a case, I recommend that you place the order-dependent initializations in the code block instead of trusting that no one will ever rearrange your class members in some compulsive-obsessive fit of order.

Why not put everything in the code block and ignore the member initialization list? Simply because you cannot implicitly invoke a constructor. That's the rule. Although the initialization specification in the member initialization list may *look* like an invocation of a constructor, it's not, because it's not code. It's just a list.

So each object property you omit from the list will be constructed anyway, using its default constructor. If it *has* no default constructor, you'll get an error message. And if you try to specify initialization in the code block, you'll get an error.

Using Destructors

When an object goes out of scope, its special "destructor" method is invoked. The invocation takes place automatically, but it's up to you when designing the object class to make sure the destructor does its job.

Here's how this works: When an object goes out of scope, its destruction event occurs. This causes a member function called the **destructor** to be invoked. You (almost) never explicitly invoke a destructor.

A destructor always has the same name as the class, with a prefixed tilde (~), as seen in the following class declaration:

```
class TScaledInt
   {
   private:
     long Value;
     long Power;
   public:
     TScaledInt ();
     TScaledInt (long V, int ScalingFactor);
     ~TScaledInt ();
     long GetValue (void);
   };
```

The destructor returns no value and takes no parameters—not even **void**. If you don't supply one, the compiler will; but such a destructor doesn't do much—certainly it wouldn't release memory or resources obtained in the object's constructor.

The rule of thumb: if you have a property that is a pointer, you almost always need an explicit destructor.

Copy Constructors

Objects are frequently passed to functions, just like* structs. *And, just like* structs, *doing so means a copy of the object is made on the stack—but this can cause problems, problems that can be solved by writing a copy constructor.

Consider the following:

```
struct SRect
   {
   int Top, Left, Right, Bottom;
   };

void MyFunc (SRect r);

   ⇩
   ⇩

SRect r1;
r1.Top = 10;
r1.Left = 10;
r1.Right = 100;
r1.Bottom = 50;
MyFunc (r1);
```

In this scrap of code, you know that the compiler will generate a byte-by-byte copy of **r1** on the stack, which **MyFunc()** will reference as **r**. You also know this is quite acceptable.

Now consider this:

```
class TString
   {
   private:
      char * Text;
      int Length;
   public:
      TString (char * aText);
      ~TString ();
   };

TString::TString (char * aText)
   : Length (strlen (aText))
   {
   Text = new char[Length+1];
   strcpy (Text, aText);
   }

TString::~TString ()
   {
   delete [] Text;
   }

void MyFunc (TString s);
   ⇩
   ⇩
```

```
TString s1 ("Fred Mertz");
MyFunc (s1);
```

If this code is executed, the call to **MyFunc()** will also cause a byte-by-byte copy of **s1** to be made on the stack. Fine, but when **MyFunc()** returns, that parameter **s** will go out of scope, causing its destructor to be invoked. The destructor frees the heap memory pointed to by **Text**. But, wait—later, **s1** will also go out of scope. When its destructor tries to delete that memory—the same memory, because the pointer values have been copied—the program will crash, because that memory was already released once.

Because the copy only goes as far as the byte level, and not to the meaning underlying the bytes, it is called a *shallow copy*.

Clearly, there are times when a shallow copy is inappropriate—basically, nearly any time the object being copied contains a pointer. Even if your object only has object properties, you don't know if any of those objects have pointer properties.

What you need is a special overloaded constructor called a *copy constructor*. This is a constructor that takes, as its only argument, a *reference* to another object of the same class:

```
class TMyClass
    {
    private:
      TMyProp Prop1;
      TMyProp Prop2;
    public:
      TMyClass (TMyClass & aMyClass);
    };
```

If you don't supply a copy constructor, the compiler will—but it's the one that does the shallow copy. The one you supply should perform a *deep copy*. If your object has any object properties, don't forget to specify *their* copy constructors in the member initialization list:

```
TMyClass::TMyClass (TMyClass & aMyClass)
    : Prop1 (aMyClass.Prop1), Prop2 (aMyClass.Prop2)
    {
    }
```

Using *const* Properties

Any object—even a non-const object—can have properties that cannot be changed once the object has been constructed. These are called const properties.

A **const** property, like a **const** variable, is one that cannot change once it's created. However, you can—and *must*—supply a value for it *when* it's created. For a **const** property, that's in the object's constructor.

Suppose you were creating a **TCrayon** class. Once a **TCrayon** is made, its color can't change. So you could give it a **const Color** property like this:

```
class TCrayon
  {
  private:
    const COLORREF Color;
  public:
    TCrayon (COLORREF aColor);
          ⇩
          ⇩
  };
```

You can only provide initialization specification in the constructor's member initialization list:

```
TCrayon::TCrayon (COLORREF aColor)
  : Color (aColor)
  {
  }
```

Since a **const** property *must* be initialized, if you forget to provide initialization of a simple **const** property in a constructor's member initialization list, the compiler will issue an error. If the property is an object, however, its default constructor will be invoked, giving it a value that you will then be unable to change.

Using *inline* and *const* Functions

As a C programmer, you're probably beginning to cringe at the thought of all these teeny functions calling each other. Imagine the overhead! Why, there must be three or four thousandths of a second spent on each one. How can you stand it? With inline functions, of course!

You'll recall from Chapter 1 that functions can be declared **inline**, in which case the code is placed at every point of invocation, saving the time it takes to call a regular function at the expense of space for the repeated machine instructions.

But some member functions exist only to provide access to **private** properties. The machine instructions for a simple assignment statement can be fewer than those involved in a function call. Such member functions are naturals for the **inline** keyword.

The code for **inline** member functions can be embedded in the class declaration, or follow it. Either way, the implementation of these functions must reside in the header file, because it isn't actually compiled until referenced by some other object.

To embed **inline** code, include the code block in place of the terminating semicolon:

```
class TScaledInt
   {
   private:
      long Value;
      long Power;
   public:
      TScaledInt ();
      TScaledInt (long V, int ScalingFactor);
      ~TScaledInt ();
      long GetValue (void) { return Value * Power }
   };
```

To provide a non-embedded **inline** function, write it normally, but preface it with the **inline** keyword and place it in the header file instead of the implementation file:

```
class TScaledInt
   {
   private:
      long Value;
      long Power;
   public:
      TScaledInt ();
      TScaledInt (long V, int ScalingFactor);
      ~TScaledInt ();
      long GetValue (void);
   };

inline long TScaledInt::GetValue (void)
   {
   return Value * Power;
   }
```

I *much* prefer the non-embedded method, for several reasons. First, debugging is much easier if there are no **inline** functions, and it's easier to pop functions into and out of the header file than it is to pop them into and out of the class declaration. Second, it's *decidedly* neater. The class declaration is hard enough to keep neat, without adding code to it.

Hot Tip

Count Your Properties before You Create an *inline* Constructor!

It is a very common practice to make constructors and destructors **inline**, because they usually don't look like they're doing much. But looks can deceive. An object with 70 object properties will be invoking 70 constructors, whether you specify them or not. Likewise, when the object is destroyed 70 destructors will be invoked. If you create many of these objects you can swell the size of your .EXE considerably.

My recommendation: use **inline** member functions only for simple access to **private** properties.

Defining *const* Functions

If you create a const int, *the compiler will not let you assign a value to it. How can the compiler know what methods are safe to call for a* const *object?*

You can create a **const** object as easily as you can any standard data type. But any method *might* change an object's value. If there were no way of telling the compiler which methods did *not* change the value, none could be called for a **const** object.

To promise that a method won't change the object, simply include the **const** keyword at the end of the function signature. You'll have to put it both on the declaration and the definition:

```
class TScaledInt
   {
   private:
     long Value;
     long Power;
   public:
     TScaledInt ();
     TScaledInt (long V, int ScalingFactor);
     ~TScaledInt ();
     long GetValue (void) const;
   };

inline long TScaledInt::GetValue (void) const
   {
   return Value * Power;
   }
```

This is only a promise. However, it's a promise the compiler will hold you to. You'll get an error message if you try to alter one of your own properties within a **const** method, or even if you dare to invoke one of your own, non-**const** methods from within it.

It's a common failing of C++ programmers that they forget to include the **const** keyword for each method that doesn't change the object. Try to remember. Not only are you providing support for **const** objects of your class, you allow the compiler to optimize some code, knowing that an object's value has not changed during the call to a **const** method.

CHAPTER 3

Overloaded Operators and Streams

53

Objects are cool, as most C programmers already know. But what would make them *really* cool would be to have them so tightly integrated into the language that they appear to be a natural part of it. That hasn't happened in Pascal, but it has in C++. Objects are so integral a part of C++ that you can even use standard C operators on them: *object + object, object / object* and so on.

In this chapter you'll learn how to overload operators for your own objects, and how to use the operators C++ has already overloaded for your benefit.

Operators—Your Ticket to Success

In this section we'll introduce you to the mysteries of C++ operators and operator overloading. As you'll see, operator overloading is a powerful technique you can use get more out of your C++ programs.

Operator Overloading

Have you ever wondered what **i * j** *actually* **means? Would it surprise you to discover that it's actually a function call? Then read on!**

The C language was originally developed on a PDP-8 minicomputer (with *far* less power than the personal computers of today). C's plethora of operators actually equate to the available machine instructions on the PDP-8.

But when C left its cradle, the language found itself on machines that didn't always *have* single machine instructions for increment, add-to-value, or multiply. The compilers for those machines had to improvise, generating two or five or ten instructions where the PDP-8 had one. Still, C programmers appreciated the rich operator set and certainly no one wanted to see it reduced—even in the case of floating-point multiply and divide operations, which, on most platforms, are such complicated operations that the code required to implement them actually resides in a subroutine.

Even the inline operations are, logically speaking, subroutines—but, in C++ parlance, they are *inline functions.*

It won't surprise you to know that the instructions emitted for the addition of one integer to another are *not* the same as the instructions emitted to add one floating-point variable to another. If data types are mixed—adding an integer to a float, for instance—the instructions are different again.

How does the compiler "know" which instructions to emit for the addition (**+**) operator? Simple. The compiler, in effect, uses the same mechanism C++ uses to identify which overloaded function to invoke—it examines the signature of the operator's parameters.

What parameters, you ask? Why, the ones involved in the operation, of course. Instead of thinking "i + j," think like the compiler. "i + j" becomes

```
operator+ (i, j);
```

where **operator+()** is the name of the overloaded function. If **i** and **j** are both integers, then C++ will invoke "operator+_with_two_ints()."

Sure, "operator+" looks like a strange name for a function. But, in C++, that's *exactly* what the function for the plus operator is called. And, there are more: **operator=()**, **operator==()**, **operator+=()** and so on.

The overloaded operators for all the standard data types have already been written and come with C++; you cannot replace them. But you *can* write operator functions for your *new* classes, thus making them appear to be integral extensions to the language.

Five Operators That Cannot Be Overloaded

Are there any operators that cannot be overloaded? Yes, but there are just a few, and, with one exception, the restriction exists because to overload these operators would "break" the C++ language.

With one exception, any operator on the "no overload" list is required by the C++ language to work in an absolutely consistent manner. Here is the list:

- The ternary operator (**?:**)
- The member selection operator (**.**)
- The scope resolution operator (**::**)
- As in C, **sizeof** is an operator, not a function; it's used internally by the **new** operator to determine how much space to allocate for an object instance
- The pointer de-referencing operator (*****)

Equalizing the Scaling Factor

The TScaledInt *class we will create in this topic will need a method for equalizing the scaling factors of two* TScaledInt *objects. Let's see how that's done.*

In the next topic, we're going to add one **TScaledInt** object to another. How can we do that?

The answer is to multiply or divide **Value** by ten, until we get the **Scale** of the one object equal to **Scale** of the other. Once the two **Scales** are equal, the **Values** can be added meaningfully.

However, it will take several pieces of code to pull this off neatly. The first segment addresses an odd lack in the C standard library: a modulo divide function for **long int**egers. (There are a couple of modulo divides for floating-point values, but I don't want to bring in the floating-point library for **TScaledInt**.) So here's the **mod()** function:

```
static long pascal mod (long Dividend, int Divisor)
  {
  long Quotient = Dividend / Divisor;
  return Dividend - (Quotient * Divisor);
  }
```

Not a big deal, of course, but we need the library for the **SetScale()** method. **SetScale()** has a more difficult job than just assigning a new value to **Scale**. In assigning that value, it also has to adjust **Value** so that the *total* value of the object is unchanged. For example, a **Value** of 45 and a **Scale** of 1 is the same as a **Value** of 450 and a **Scale** of two. Here's **SetScale()**:

```
void TScaledInt::SetScale (int NewScale)
  {
  while (Scale > NewScale)
    {
    register long v = Value / 10;
    if ((v * 10) != Value)
      return;
    Value = v;
    Scale--;
    }
  while (Scale < NewScale)
    {
    register long v = Value * 10;
    if ((v / 10) != Value)
      return;
    Value = v;
    Scale++;
    }
  }
```

The extra code is there to prevent losing validity due to overflow or underflow. It's possible, then, to call **SetScale()** and not get the **Scale** to quite the value you requested—but the object will maintain its integrity.

We're now ready for the **Equalize()** member function. **Equalize()** is intended to bring the **Scales** of two **TScaledInt** objects together. Since it is a member function, **this** will point to one of the two objects; a parameter, **other**, will be a reference to the other. Here's the code:

```
void TScaledInt::Equalize (TScaledInt & other)
   {
   if (Scale > other.Scale)
     other.SetScale (Scale);
   else if (Scale < other.Scale)
     SetScale (other.Scale);
   }
```

Since **Value** is a **long int**, not a **float**, *Scales* can only be increased, never decreased (without losing significant digits).

In addition, **Equalize()** should never be called outside the class, so I've made it a **private** member function.

When an Operator Is a Class Member

It won't surprise you to know that operator functions are often implemented as class methods. But some operators **must** *be implemented as class methods.*

Earlier in this section, I described the operator function for adding two **int**s as **operator+ (i, j)**. But some operators are class methods. When that happens, the first "parameter"—the item on the left of the operator—becomes the invisible **this** pointer.

For example, suppose you are creating a **TScaledInt** class, and you want to supply an operator function that will allow the following instructions:

```
TScaledInt s1 (37, 3), s2 (456, 1);
s1 += s2;
```

Your first thought might be to create a global operator function:

```
void operator+= (TScaledInt s1, TScaledInt s2); // This won't work!
```

But wait; the **+=** operator is supposed to make a *change to the item on the left*. Returning the modified value isn't enough; you have to actually alter **s1**.

Of course, you could always pass a *reference* to the first **TScaledInt** object. But it's far more common to make the operator function a class method:

```
class TScaledInt
   {
      ⇩
      ⇩
   public:
      TScaledInt & operator+= (const TScaledInt other);
   };
```

Now, **this** will point to the object to which **other** is being added. The function returns a reference to itself, which supports C++'s "stacking" of operators:

```
TScaledInt s1 (37, 3), s2 (456, 1), s3;
int i (92);
s3 = s1 += s2;
```

The function itself is quite simple (now that it can avail itself of the **Equalize()** method shown in the previous topic):

```
TScaledInt & TScaledInt::operator+= (TScaledInt other)
   {
   Equalize (other);
   if (Scale == other.Scale)
     Value += other.Value;
   return *this;
   }
```

Note that **other** is passed by value, not by reference. Either would be acceptable because **other** should not be altered by the function. However, **Equalize()** is *not* a **const** method, so if **other** were passed by reference, we'd have to make a copy of it to **Equalize()** anyway.

The **+=** operator just described *only* handles adding **TScaledInt** objects to **others**. If you want to add, say, an **int** to a **TScaledInt** object, you'll have to overload the **+=** operator for that, too. It is typical, then, for a class implementation to include literally *dozens* of overloaded operators, covering each operator/data type combination. But generally, one method does the real work while the others just provide conversions:

```
inline TScaledInt & TScaledInt::operator+= (int i)
   {
   return *this += TScaledInt (i);
   }
```

Because of their tendency toward minimalism, they are often written to be inline functions, as this one was.

Implementing the Equality Operator

When testing one object for equality to another, test for **logical** *equality, not* **physical** *equality . . . and know the difference!*

C has always allowed the testing for equivalence between two structures of the same type:

```
struct tagMyStruct s1, s2;
        ⇩
        ⇩
if (s1 == s2)
        ⇩
        ⇩
```

In C, the **==** operator simply performs a byte-by-byte comparison of the two structures.

In C++, the **==** operator is also automatically implemented for objects, unless you supply an explicit overload. The system-generated **operator==()** function also performs a byte-by-byte comparison, and sometimes that's enough . . . but sometimes, it's not.

For example, in the **TScaledInt** class, there are two properties: **Value** and **Scale**. Suppose that two objects of this class have the following internal values:

Object	Value	Power
s1	37	2
s2	370	1

These two objects are actually equivalent—but a byte-by-byte comparison would not show this. In order to make the **==** operator useful, we'll have to overload it ourselves.

The basic **operator==()** function compares two objects of the same type, and so is implemented as a class member of that type:

```
class TScaledInt
    {
       ⇩
       ⇩
    public:
       short operator== (const TScaledInt & other) const;
    };
```

Remember to mark the function as **const**—it isn't going to change ***this**—and also to mark **other** as **const**, because it isn't going to be changed either.

operator==() can return any value that can be interpreted as TRUE or FALSE; **short** is commonly used.

The function itself simply equalizes the two values, and then tests them for equivalence:

```
short TScaledInt::operator== (const TScaledInt & other) const
   {
   TScaledInt Temp1 (*this), Temp2 (other);
   Temp1.Equalize (Temp2);
   return (Temp1.Scale == Temp2.Scale) && (Temp1.Value == Temp2.Value);
   }
```

You'll also want to implement variants of **operator==()** to accommodate different data types. For example, without a specific operator overload for **TScaledInt**s and **int**s, the following will produce a compiler error:

```
struct tagMyStruct s;
int i;
      ⇩
      ⇩
if (s == i)
    ⇩
    ⇩
```

Fortunately, such an overload is trivial to supply:

```
short TScaledInt::operator== (int i) const
   {
   return (*this == TScaledInt (i));
   }
```

Global Operators

What happens if the item on the left of the operator isn't an object?

If **TScaledInt** is to be made a part of C++, the following construct should also be permitted:

```
struct tagMyStruct s;
int i;
      ⇩
      ⇩
if (i == s)
    ⇩
    ⇩
```

However, **i** is not an object. How then can you overload the equivalence operator for **i**?

Well, you can't—exactly. But you can write a *global* overloaded function to do the job:

```
short operator== (int i, TScaledInt & other)
  {
  return (TScaledInt (i) == other);
  }
```

Since this function is *not* a class method, there is no **this** pointer and the function prototype does not appear in the class declaration. On the other hand, it *is* an important part of the **TScaledInt** class; so its prototype should be located in the **TScaledInt** header file, and the function should be implemented in the **TScaledInt** implementation file (unless you decide to make it ans inline function, of course).

Normalizing a Scaled Integer

In the course of the next few topics we'll need to "normalize" a **TScaledInt** *object. First, let's understand what that means and see how to do it.*

As you know, **TScaledInt** stores its value in *two* properties: **Value** and **Scale**. Its true value is obtained by multiplying **Value** by 10 **Scale** times.

We've already seen the **Equalize()** method, where **Value** and **Scale** are manipulated to make **Scale** the same as that stored in another **TScaledInt**. The opposite method is also required: **Normalize()**. A **TScaledInt** object is *normalized* when the **Value** property holds as small an absolute value as possible, and **Scale** is adjusted as needed to meet this end. Normalization is accomplished by incrementing **Scale**, and dividing **Value** by 10, as long as **Value** has trailing zeros.

Here's the **Normalize()** function:

```
void TScaledInt::Normalize (void)
  {
  while (Value && (mod (Value, 10) == 0))
    {
    Value /= 10;
    Scale++;
    }
  }
```

Like **Equalize()**, **Normalize()** is a **private** function since it should not be used outside of the class.

Understanding Friend Functions

Sometimes global overloaded operator functions need access to private class data or functions to do their work. How do you tell the compiler it's okay to allow such access?

Suppose that, for efficiency reasons, you found the implementation of global **operator==()** described earlier to be too slow. (It's not, but we're just *supposing.*) Suppose further that testing showed the fastest implementation was:

```
short operator== (int i, const TScaledInt & other)
   TScaledInt Temp1 (i), Temp2 (other);
   Temp1.Equalize (Temp2);
   return (Temp1.Scale == Temp2.Scale) && (Temp1.Value == Temp2.Value);
```

You would immediately find yourself in a quandary: as a global function, **operator==()** can only access **Value** and **Scale** if they are **public** data members—but good object design dictates they be **private**. What's a poor programmer to do?

Fortunately, C++ has a solution that involves just one, new, keyword: **friend**. By stating that a global function is a "friend" of an object class, that global function obtains full access rights to any **private** data or methods the class may have.

To declare a global function a **friend**, you *do* include the function prototype in the class declaration—even though it's not a class member—with the **friend** keyword:

```
class TScaledInt
   {
      ⇩
      ⇩
   public:
      ⇩
      ⇩
      friend short operator== (int i, const TScaledInt & other);
   };
```

The function is *still* global in scope—it just has access to **TScaledInt's** **private** properties and methods, and the compiler will allow the implementation of **operator==()** shown earlier.

Only a class can declare its friends; a function can't become one on its own. And friendship isn't limited to global functions; member functions of another class can be made friends (rare), and an entire other class can be made a friend (somewhat more common).

If two classes are so intimately related that one can safely be made a **friend** of the other, they may well be implemented in the same pair of modules. But remember, even though C++ gives you this "out", you're still in the same danger with **friend** functions that you are with **public** data members: if you want to change the way a property is stored, you'll have to recompile (at the least!) any other class that references the property.

Overloading Operators

We've already introduced the topic of operator overloading and we've showed you which operators that you can't overload. Now, let's look at some techniques for overloading some of the more interesting operators inlcuing the increment/decrement operators, and the assignment operators.

Overloading the Increment/Decrement Operators

Now that you've been working with overloaded functions for a while, you may have wondered how to distinguish between the prefix and postfix increment and decrement operators. We'll explore this distinction in this topic.

Most of the operators are very clear in what operand is of which data type. The prefix increment operator is, too; if you are using it to increment a **TScaledInt** object, the signature of the overloaded operator is just what you'd expect:

```
class TScaledInt
   {
      ⇩
      ⇩
   public:
      ⇩
      ⇩
      TScaledInt & operator++ (void);
   };
```

Let's analyze the pieces; there aren't that many. First of all, the function returns a reference to a **TScaledInt** object—itself. This allows a construct such as:

```
TScaledInt s1, s2;
     ⇩
     ⇩
s1 = ++s2;
```

to be created. Since we're using a member function, we know there's
an invisible **this** pointer, but there are no other parameters because ++
is a *unary* operator—it only takes one parameter, and that's **this**.

The prefix decrement operator is declared similarly. The problem
comes with the *postfix* increment and decrement operators. They are
also unary operators, and the signatures *should* be identical. So how
can you tell them apart?

Well, at one time you couldn't. Unable to deal with this conundrum,
the original C++ specification said that, for objects, there would be no
difference between prefix and postfix increment and decrement. But
that conflicted with the desire to make objects look totally built-in to
the language, so the ANSI C++ committee took another stab at the
problem and decided to differentiate between prefix and postfix increment and decrement by adding a single, dummy parameter to post-
increment and decrement signatures:

```
class TScaledInt
    {
        ⇩
        ⇩
    public:
        ⇩
        ⇩
        TScaledInt & operator++ (int Dummy);
    };
```

The **Dummy** parameter actually exists and could be referenced, but
its value is "undefined" so you really should just pretend it isn't there.
Best bet: leave it unnamed so you won't be tempted:

```
class TScaledInt
    {
        ⇩
        ⇩
    public:
        ⇩
        ⇩
        TScaledInt & operator++ (int);
    };
```

When you implement the operators, you should be sensitive to the difference between prefix and postfix increment (and decrement). Prefix increment is the simplest to implement, of course; you simply perform the incrementation and return a reference to ***this**:

```
TScaledInt & TScaledInt::operator++ (void)
   {
   Value++;
   Normalize ();
   return *this;
   }
```

Prefix decrement is similarly simple:

```
TScaledInt & TScaledInt::operator-- (void)
   {
   SetScale (Scale - 1);
   Value--;
   Normalize ();
   return *this;
   }
```

It's with postfix that things become trickier, and all because we need to return a value to the way the object looked *before* the increment or decrement—but still perform the increment or decrement! Thus, where prefix increment and decrement return a reference to the object being manipulated, postfix increment and decrement return an object *value*— and the value returned is that of a temporary copy of the object made before the operation:

```
TScaledInt TScaledInt::operator++ (int)
   {
   TScaledInt Temp (*this);
   Value++;
   Normalize ();
   return Temp;
   }
```

```
TScaledInt TScaledInt::operator-- (int)
   {
   TScaledInt Temp (*this);
   SetScale (Scale - 1);
   Value--;
   Normalize ();
   return Temp;
   }
```

Overloading the Assignment Operator

While some operators give you a choice as to whether to implement them as global or class member functions, the assignment operator does not. Here are its requirements.

The assignment operator (=) *must* be a class member function. Furthermore, it must return a reference to itself, to support "stacking" of operations.

If you do not supply an assignment operator of your own, the system will supply one that performs a shallow (byte-by-byte) copy of the object being assigned. And, of course, the source object must be of the same object class as the target. The declaration of the system-supplied assignment operator function for **TScaledInt** class would be:

```
TScaledInt & operator== (TScaledInt source);
```

There are no automatic assignments from other data types, so if you want to support them, you'll have to supply assignment operator functions:

```
TScaledInt & TScaledInt::operator= (int i)
   {
   return *this = TScaledInt (i);
   }
```

Streams and Overloading

Before wrapping up this chapter on overloaded operators, we need to take a close look at how overloading techniques can be used with streams. In particular, we'll show you how to overload casts, how to make classes work with streams, and how to use streams with files.

Overloading Casts

In addition to overloading operators, you can also overload conversions into other data types. Continue reading to learn how to overload casts.

Wouldn't it be nice to test **TScaledInt** objects simply by posting their contents to **cout**? But **ostream**, **cout**'s class, doesn't know about **TScaledInt** objects; the class only comes with stream insertion operators for **int**s, **char**s, and so on.

We could, of course, create a **GetValue()** function. But what value type would it return? Remember, the return type of a function is *not* part of its signature, so you couldn't write **GetValue()**s for each possible data type.

However, you *can* overload casts, which solves the problem. The signature looks a little weird, though. For one thing, the function always takes a parameter of **void**. For another, it doesn't claim to return a value—not even **void**—although it *does*.

Here's **TScaledInt**'s cast to **long**:

```
TScaledInt::operator long (void) const
   {
   long Result = Value;
   register s = Scale;
   while (s < 0)
      {
      Result /= 10;
      s++;
      }
   while (s > 0)
      {
      Result *= 10;
      s--;
      }
   return Result;
   }
```

For completeness, here's the cast to **float**:

```
TScaledInt::operator float (void) const
   {
   float Result = Value;
   register s = Scale;
   while (s < 0)
      {
      Result /= 10;
      s++;
      }
   while (s > 0)
      {
      Result *= 10;
      s--;
      }
   return Result;
   }
```

Making Classes Work with Streams

We've seen how to make a class work with cout *by overriding some casts. But you don't have to "cast" an* int *or a* long, *so why should you have to cast a* TScaledInt *or a* TStarShip? *Here's how to make your classes work with streams more naturally.*

We've already seen how **istream** and **ostream** objects overloaded the << and >> operators. New classes can be made to work with streams by providing overloaded functions for those same operators.

ostream objects are intended to stream printable (ANSI) representations of other objects. The << operator, overloaded for **ostream** objects, is called the "stream insertion" operator. A sample declaration is shown here:

```
class TScaledInt
   {
   public:
     ⇩
     ⇩
     friend ostream & operator<< (ostream & os, const TScaledInt & s);
     ⇩
     ⇩
   };
```

Since the cast to **float** is already written, the definition for the stream insertion operator is simple:

```
inline ostream & operator<< (ostream & os, const TScaledInt & s)
   {
   return os << (float) s;
   }
```

Note that we must return the reference to the **ostream** object that we received. It's this reference that allows the stream insertion operators to be stacked.

You may well ask, what has this bought me? The answer is nothing in terms of machine code—but, in terms of C++ code, we have a cleaner interface of **TScaledInt**s to **ostream**s. Now, the following statements can be executed:

```
TScaledInt s1 (450, 2);
cout << s1;
```

Likewise, we can overload the **>>** operator to allow **TScaledInt** objects to work with input streams. The declaration is similar:

```
class TScaledInt
  {
  public:
     ⇩
     ⇩
     friend istream & operator>> (istream & is, TScaledInt & s);
     ⇩
     ⇩
  };
```

Notice that the **TScaledInt** parameter is *not* **const**. That's because, unlike the **ostream** stream insertion operator, the object passed *will* be changed; that's the whole idea. Here's the code:

```
istream & operator>> (istream & is, TScaledInt & s)
  {
  float f;
  is >> f;
  s = f;
  return is;
  }
```

Using Streams with Files

Once the stream insertion and extraction operators are written, stream I/O is **complete!** *Not only will your class cooperate with console streaming, it can be streamed to and from disk files as well. Here's how to use file streams.*

You know that **cout** and **cin** are pre-allocated objects of the **ostream** and **istream** classes, respectively. If you check out the class hierarchy in the online help, you'll see that **ostream** and **istream** are each derived from the **fstream** class. File streams are objects of that class.

fstream objects can be used, but more often, you'll create objects from other descendants. Input files are **ifstream** objects, and output files are **ofstream** objects. (A file used in both directions, however, is an **fstream** object.)

All you have to do to incorporate file streams in your application is to **#include** FSTREAM.H before you make use of it. Once you've overridden the **<<** and **>>** operators for any classes you want to write to or read from disk, those classes are I/O-ready.

For example, let's say you want to write a **TScaledInt** object to disk. The following scrap of code will do the trick:

```
#include <fstream.h>
      ⇩
      ⇩
TScaledInt i (4526, 2);
ofstream of ("myfile.dat");
of << i;
of.close();
```

Without further instruction you can guess that the **ofstream** constructor, when passed a C-style string, interprets that string as the name of the file that is to be opened. But that name can be supplied later as well:

```
fstream of2;
struct TMyStruct s;
      ⇩
      ⇩
of2.open ("More.dat", ios::binary);
of2.write ((LPSTR) &s, sizeof s);
of2.close ();
```

In the above example, you can also see the alternative to the stream insertion operator: the **write()** method. Use this method when sending a value to the stream that has not had the stream insertion operator overloaded for it, or for a value that wouldn't work well that way, like a structure or an array.

File input is as simple. As in file output, the filename can be specified in the constructor or later:

```
ifstream if1 ("File1.Dat");
ifstream if2;
if2.open ("File2.Dat");
struct TMyStruct s;
TScaledInt i;
if1.read ((LPSTR) &s, sizeof s);
if2 >> i;
if2.close ();
```

You can also perform other tradition file I/O tasks, such as record seeks. The following code reads the 101st **TScaledInt** in a file:

```
TScaledInt i;
ifstream if ("Myfile.Dat");
if.seekg (100 * sizeof i);
if >> i;
```

In this example, I omitted the **if.close()** call you might have expected. It isn't required; if a disk file is open when an **ifstream** or **ofstream** object is destroyed, the file will automatically be closed first.

Seeks can be used on an **ifstream** or an **ofstream** object, but more often they are used on the common ancestor to those classes, **fstream**. Objects of the **fstream** class are I/O files, used for input *and* output— but not at the same time. There is another class, **ios**, which exists primarily as a convenient gathering place for I/O-related flags. You don't normally create an **ios** object; instead you refer directly to the class's **static** data members. When opening an **fstream** object, you use **ios** flags to indicate whether you are opening for input or output:

```
fstream fs;
fs.open ("MyFile.dat", ios::out);
     ⇩
     ⇩
fs.close ();
fs.open ("MyFile.dat", ios::in);
     ⇩
     ⇩
fs.close ();
```

Let me warn you about one thing: although implementing stream insertion and extraction operators for a class totally prepares it for *stream* I/O, it is *not* usually the last word in other kinds of I/O. We'll talk more about that in the next chapter; I just wanted to prepare you in advance. Here's the key: stream I/O encourages ANSI (printable) representation, in spite of the **read()** and **write()** methods. Many applications make use of binary representation, and that's the mechanism we'll study later.

Inheritance

T he most compelling reason to write applications using objects—and the main reason to do it in C++ rather than, say, Visual Basic—is inheritance. Inheritance lets you take an object that is *almost* what you need, and derive a new class from it by specifying only the differences. In this chapter we'll take a look at what inheritance is, how to make it happen, and how to make the most of it.

So What Is Inheritance Anyway?

You might think you're already comfortable with the concept of inheritance. After all, even you are the product of traits inherited from two parents. However, object inheritance doesn't operate in quite the same way. Objects generally add traits to those they've inherited; they often modify or even delete existing traits as well.

Inheritance as it applies to individuals within a species is not a good model for object-oriented inheritance, because individuals usually mix and match traits from their parents without (usually) adding or drastically altering anything new.

However, inheritance at the evolutionary level, where new species are derived from existing species and give rise to even newer species, *is* a good example. Paws, with a little modification, become hands; legs, modified a bit, become fins or wings. As much of the ancestral design as possible is re-used; cow adrenaline is virtually identical to human or dog adrenaline, and is part of a basic system that operates similarly and serves the same function in all.

To accomplish a similar feat in an object-oriented programming environment, you first describe, in formal terms, a generalized object. This object, which will probably never be instantiated, exists just to formalize the traits that some number of other objects share. (That's why such an object class is called a *formal class*.) Using inheritance, you can then derive specific classes from the formal class as needed.

For example, suppose you wanted to build a 1986 Toyota Tercel. If you were to hand-craft each part from scratch, you could do it—but the design alone would take years and cost millions of dollars. Cars did not pop out of a vacuum; they evolved from carriages. (Even the word *car* is short for *carriage*.) To bring fresh understanding to an over-used phrase, the makers of the first cars did not have to "re-invent the wheel" to create an automobile; they literally used standard carriage wheels. Later the design for the wheel was modified and optimized for use in automobiles, but it *is* still the same, basic design.

Therefore, for our 1986 Toyota Tercel project, we don't start with cars at all. We start with *wheeled vehicles*, that being a reasonable unification of the features we'll need in the specific car we envision as an end product. A "wheeled vehicle" is intentionally vague. It can only be used as a concept; you can't build one. Therefore, in addition to being a formal object, it is also an *abstract* object.

How vague sare we being here? Well, we know the "wheeled vehicle" has some number of wheels, but we don't know how many. The number of wheels is a property of the class. We also know there must be an arrangement for carrying passengers and baggage, but we don't know what it is. We'll just have to leave room in the design for that to be specified. We'll also want to have methods for starting and stopping, but since we don't have any idea how to implement those methods, they will have to be made *pure virtual methods*—like the class, these methods will have no actual code. (In fact, the presence of one or more pure virtual methods is what *makes* a class abstract, in the physical sense!) A pure virtual method is just a placeholder. You'll see the advantage this gives you, shortly.

So now we're ready to derive an *Automobile* class from *WheeledVehicle*. We'll specify the number of wheels: four. We'll also provide a *FrontCompartment* and *RearCompartment* property to accommodate passengers, and a closed trunk, called *StorageCompartment*, (or boot, if you're reading this in England!) to transport cargo. We'll also add *Engine* and *Dashboard* properties. And we can fill in the starting and stopping methods.

Yes, it's still vague. We'll still have to pin down specifics; *Automobile* is still an abstract class. So why did we bother with the abstract *WheeledVehicle* class? Simply because *Automobile* is not the only possible wheeled vehicle. We can also derive *Carriage, Bicycle,* and *CommuterTrain* from *WheeledVehicle*. As different as each of those things is from the others, they do have traits in common; and, by putting those traits in the ancestor class they share, the traits do not have to be re-invented for each object.

But, then, why make *Automobile* an abstract class? Why not go directly from *WheeledVehicle* to *1986ToyotaTercel*? Simply because there's plenty of usable generalization left. You can, for example, derive a *Truck* class from *Automobile*. It can re-use the *Dashboard* and *FrontCompartment* properties, and simply omit the *RearCompartment*. The *StorageCompartment* is still used, but will be redefined.

Finally, between *Automobile* and *1986ToyotaTercel*, there are likely to be several intermediate classes: *CompactCar, ToyotaCar,* and

ToyotaTercel. Each provides some components to the finished product: *ToyotaCar* provides a hood ornament and ignition key design, at the least.

The whole process still takes years and millions of dollars. But at each point there are checkpoints against which you can gauge success, and intermediate products (like bicycles) that can help finance the whole project.

This is one of the key issues in object-oriented programming. Too much OOP has been sold misleadingly on the promise that "less programming will be required." This is a lie. An OOP project will need as much, possibly more, code than a project implemented in an older methodology. *But* that code will be more re-usable than standard code, more robust, and more easily maintained. And, thanks to the re-usability of the code, your *next* project may well require fewer lines of *new* code.

Inheritance in C++

Now that we've considered object-oriented inheritance in general terms, it's time to learn how to actually *do* it in C++.

Deriving a Class from a Structure

*An easy way to see how inheritance is accomplished is by example. We can use as an example something that Borland has actually done in ObjectWindows: derive a **TPoint** class from Windows' **POINT** structure.*

To understand this, you must recall that a **struct** is just a special kind of class (discussed in Chapter 2). In WINDOWS.H there is a **struct** with the following declaration:

```
typedef struct tagPOINT
  {
    int x;
    int y;
  } POINT;
```

We settle for this kind of thing in C, but let's face it: there are disadvantages involved in using plain old **struct**s. For example, you can instantiate a **struct** on the stack and forget to initialize it:

```
HDC hDC = GetPaint (...);
POINT p;
MoveTo (hDC, p); // p is uninitialized
```

It is gerenally better to make a **TPoint** class and instantiate an object from that, except that, if you make **TPoint** from scratch, you won't be able to pass it to **MoveTo()** or any other function expecting a **POINT**.

So what's the answer? Simple: don't make **TPoint** from scratch; derive it *from* **POINT**! You do it like this:

```
class TPoint : public POINT
   {
   TPoint (int _x = 0, int _y = 0);
   };
```

The ": POINT" part of the declaration is the inheritance specifier. You'll note that we did *not* have to include data members **x** and **y**; that's because we inherited those properties from **POINT**. We supplied a constructor; if **_x** and **_y** are not supplied, they will each default to zero. The constructor definition simply uses those parameters to initialize the object's properties:

```
TPoint::TPoint (int _x, int _y)
   {
   x = _x;
   y = _y;
   }
```

Thus, an object created from this class will never have garbage in its **x** and **y** properties.

Incidentally, you may be wondering why we didn't initialize **x** and **y** in the constructor's member initialization list. That's because, properly speaking, **x** and **y** are not members of **TPoint**; they are members of **POINT**, **TPoint**'s base class. Since **POINT** is a class (remember, a **struct** is a type of class), there is a default constructor already provided by the compiler for it. **x** and **y** are initialized there, although it is not a useful initialization. So, in the **TPoint** constructor, we provide useful values for those inherited properties, but we have to do it in the code section of the constructor.

Now, what have we accomplished by deriving **TPoint** from **POINT**? Several things. First of all, any **TPoint** you make, whether on the stack or the heap, will be properly initialized. Secondly, because, **TPoint** is derived from **POINT** and adds no additional properties, a **TPoint** can be passed to any function that expects either a **POINT** or a pointer to a **POINT**. And finally, we have created a framework within which we can gather, as methods, all the myriad functions that operate on **POINT**s; we can also build more. In so doing we will have created a "smart point," a point that "knows" how to perform operations on itself. We'll see the advantages to that little gem shortly.

Public? Private? Protected?

In the example just discussed we derived **TPoint** *from* **POINT** *with the* **public** *keyword. Obviously* public *cannot mean exactly what it does when applied to member data and functions. It is an* **inheritance access modifier.** *But what does that mean?*

Take the case of **TPoint** derived from **POINT** as an example. As a **struct**, **POINT**'s **x** and **y** members were **public**. You might expect that they will still be **public** when they are inherited members of **TPoint**. But suppose that isn't what you want? After all, it is considered ideal to prevent direct access to properties, as we discussed in Chapter 3. **TPoint** could be considered a greater improvement if its **x** and **y** properties were **private**.

That's what the inheritance access modifier is for. The most common inheritance access modifier is **public**. That means to keep any inherited properties just as the were in the base class. **public** members remain **public**; **private** members remain **private**.

The least common inheritance access modifier is **private**. This modifier demotes all members in the base class to **private** in the new class.

But items that were **private** in the ancestor class can't be accessed by other classes—not even derived classes. It would be nice to have another keyword sort of between **public** and **private**—one that would allow access to derived classes, but not to unrelated classes.

Such a keyword exists. It is **protected**.

When designing a new class, you can accommodate eventual derivation (even if it seems unlikely now) by making use of the **protected** keyword. Ideally, you should still make properties **private**. But methods that you would otherwise have made **private**, make **protected** instead.

The **protected** keyword can also be used as an inheritance access modifier—its value lies midway between **public** and **private**. In essence, this keyword says, "Demote any **public** members to **protected**, and leave **protected** and **private** members as they were." Using **protected** as an inheritance access modifier is rare, but not as unusual as using the **private** keyword.

(By the way, even though I say **TPoint** would be improved if **x** and **y** were made **private**, that's not what Borland chose to do in ObjectWindows.)

Table 4.1 provides a recap of the three inheritance access modifiers.

Table 4.1 Inheritance Access Modifiers

Declaration	How Often Used	Base Class' *public* members	Base Class' *protected* members	Base Class' *private* members
class CMyClass: **public** CMyBase	Usually	Visible to derived class and independent classes	Visible to derived class; hidden to other classes	Hidden from all other classes
class CMyClass: **protected** CMyBase	Rare	Visible to derived class; hidden to other classes	Visible to derived class; hidden to other classes	Hidden from all other classes
class CMyClass: **private** CMyBase	*Very* rare	Hidden from all other classes	Hidden from all other classes	Hidden from all other classes

Mother and Child Reunion

When designing a class that may be used as a base class, it is important to do the opposite of good human parenting: Never talk to your children!

A parent class can be written to *accommodate* an eventual child class. You may provide **protected** members in place of **private** ones, for example, and you may provide pure virtual methods (described briefly before and in more detail shortly). However, a parent class should never make assumptions about a child class, and it cannot communicate directly with one.

A child class, on the other hand, "knows" it has a parent. In fact, the parent's constructor is usually specified in the child's constructors' member initialization list. The child even knows what class its parent is. But the child does *not* know what class its *grandparent* is, or even if it *has* a grandparent.

These rules all promote the encapsulation of each class. The fewer assumptions any class makes about other classes, the more independent it is of those other classes.

Initialization of the parent takes place in the derived class' constructor's member initialization list. The parent is initialized *first*. If a parent constructor is not specified, the default constructor will be called by the system.

C++ wants us to be conscious of the difference between specifying a constructor and trying to *invoke* one. In C++, a constructor can *never* be invoked explicitly. However, you do tell the compiler which one *it* should invoke by supplying an argument list. I'll grant you the difference is subtle, but it's there. That's the primary reason why the member initialization list exists at all; it let's you place the argument list for the parent constructor outside the code block. Here's an example:

```
class TColorPoint : public TPoint
  {
  private:
    COLORREF Color;
  public:
    TColorPoint (int X = 0, int Y = 0, COLORREF C = RGB (0, 0, 0))
      : TPoint (X, Y), Color (C)
      {
      };
  };
```

In this example, we don't have to explicitly initialize **x** and **y**; we let the constructor for **TPoint** do it. We also initialize our new property, **Color**, in the member initialization list.

There are a few backward compatibility issues. For one thing, a **TColorPoint** object is *bigger* than a **TPoint** object because, in addition to **x** and **y**, **TColorPoint** has that **Color** property. Since it is bigger, it can't be passed in place of either a **TPoint** or a **POINT**. However, a *pointer* to a **TColorPoint** *can* be used anywhere a pointer to a **POINT** or a **TPoint** object can!

You can *always* pass a pointer to a derived class to a function expecting a pointer to an ancestor of that class. You don't even have to cast! This attribute is called *polymorphism* and, as you'll see shortly, it is an extremely powerful feature of object-oriented programming.

Deriving for Enhancement and Specialization

Why derive a new class? What benefit do you receive over simply starting from scratch? Here are the answers.

The whole idea of inheritance is that you already have something that is *almost* just what you needed. In the old days, you would have taken the old code—if you could find it all—and then made changes to it, piece by piece, until it fit into the environment of the new application and worked the way you wanted it to. Of course, this process took as long (or longer) than writing from scratch would have.

With objects, you derive a new class from the old, existing class, and change *only the things that need to be changed.* You make changes for two reasons: to enhance the behavior of the original class, or to make that behavior more appropriate to special needs.

For example, in the previous topic, we derived a **TColorPoint** class from **TPoint**. By adding the **Color** property, we enhanced the **TColorPoint** so that it could store, not only the **x** and **y** coordinates of a point, but the color of that point as well.

You can also derive for specialization by replacing inherited methods with new ones that work differently. To do this, you write new methods that have the same name and signature of the parent method they're intended to replace. For example, **TPoint** might have a method called **Display()** that draws a point on the screen. **TColorPoint** would override that method with a **Display()** of its own, that would not only draw the point, but do it in the appropriate color.

Sometimes specialization is achieved by *adding to* the ancestor method. For example, **TColorPoint**'s **Display()** method might look something like this:

```
void TColorPoint::Display (void)
  {
  SetColor (Color);
  TPoint::Display ();
  }
```

To invoke an ancestor method, use the scope resolution operator as I did here, to specify the class whose method is to be accessed. I said earlier that a derived class can know who its parent class is; this is an example of that. This same syntax will allow a class to invoke the method of a grandparent or great-grandparent as well, but it's considered poor form to do so.

Working with Constructors

*Class inheritance brings about some special considerations regarding constructors. You need to be aware of the order in which ancestral components are constructed and destructed. You also need to be aware of the fact that you do **not** inherit constructors!*

When you derive a new class from a base class, you automatically inherit all the base class's properties and methods, with one exception: a new class does *not* inherit any constructors.

Now, don't be confused: if you don't supply a constructor for the new class, the system will *generate* one—but that's not the same thing as inheriting one, even though the generated constructor will include a reference to the default parent constructor.

So usually you'll find yourself creating a slew of constructors analogous to the ones the ancestor class possessed. If the ancestor had three constructors that accepted an **int**, two **chars**, and a **long** and an **int**, respectively, you will probably need a matching set for the new class—and maybe more. Constructors generally allow arguments that are used to supply initialization values to properties; and a derived class has those same properties, (plus, perhaps, some more).

On the other hand, this is not a hard-and-fast rule. Suppose we derive this new class:

```
class TRedPoint : TColorPoint
  {
  TRedPoint (int X = 0, int Y = 0)
    : TColorPoint (X, Y, RGB (255, 0, 0))
    {
    };
  };
```

The constructor doesn't have to accept a color because, for this class, the color is understood. (It still has to be spelled out for the base class constructor, though.)

At member initialization time, each one of your constructors will include a non-explicit invocation of the base class constructor. If you don't indicate which one (by supplying an argument list for it), the system will invoke the default (no argument) constructor. It's usually best to specify the constructor you want, both as documentation and to help prevent your forgetting it.

C++ has been cleverly designed to provide the best possible order of constructor invocation. When your derived class' constructor is invoked, before it does anything else, its *parent's* constructor is invoked. If that parent was derived from yet another class, *its* parent's constructor will be invoked first thing. Thus the order of constructor is:

- Grandparents (if any)
- Parent
- Child

Likewise, the order of destruction is:

- Child
- Parent
- Grandparents (if any)

You cannot change this order—and it *is* guaranteed.

Multiple Inheritance: Two Is Better Than One

Multiple inheritance, inheriting traits from two parents (classes or human), is a concept so fraught with dangers that many object-oriented languages do not support it. In the C++ world, multiple inheritance is supported but some class libraries simply pretend it doesn't exist. ObjectWindows is not one of these. It not only acknowledges multiple inheritance, it celebrates it by basing the entire ObjectWindows hierarchy on multiple inheritance. Let's comb through some details.

Earlier I compared object-oriented inheritance to evolution, where a single species gives rise to a new species that is similar, but not identical to, its ancestor species. The new species (or class) usually adds an enhancement, or a specialization, to the abilities it inherited.

As mentioned a moment ago, C++ supports multiple inheritance, which is more like the inheritance we, personally, have experienced. Like multiply-inherited objects, we have inherited traits from *two* parents. If we're lucky (or if the new class is properly designed), we'll make use of the combined traits of both parents to fit better in our environment.

For example, suppose we had a color class:

```
class TColor
   {
   private:
     COLORREF Color;
   public:
     TColor (COLORREF C = RGB (0, 0, 0));
     void SetColor (void);
   };
```

We then could have multiply-derived **TColorPoint**:

```
class TColorPoint : public TPoint, public TColor
   {
   public:
     TColorPoint (int X = 0, int Y = 0, COLORREF C = RGB (0, 0, 0))
       : TPoint (X, Y), TColor (C)
       {
       };
     void Display (void);
   };
```

The **Display()** method would then look like this:

```
void TColorPoint::Display (void)
   {
```

```
SetColor ();
TPoint::Display ();
}
```

Notice that **SetColor()** doesn't need to be qualified with the scope resolution operator; it has not been overridden by the **TColorPoint** class and so is simply inherited. The invocation of the inherited **Display()** function does require the scope resolution operator as before.

Is this a major improvement over the previous declaration of **TColorPoint**? No, not really, although it isn't inferior either. But if you have two existing, complex classes and a new class is logically derived from both, multiple inheritance can save you a lot of work.

For example, in ObjectWindows, the processing of command messages (such as are generated by a user interface menu) is quite complex. In the ObjectWindows paradigm, windows are not the only entities that can receive and process these commands, so a class was written to encapsulate the handling of command events (such as **TEventHandler**). There are many types of windows, and so there's a **TWindow** class to encapsulate that behavior. A "view" is a window that can receive commands, so it inherits from both **TEventHandler** and **TWindow**. (This is a simplification of the actual hierarchy.)

There's no denying that multiple inheritance adds greatly to the complexity of a class hierarchy. It makes the hierarchy harder to implement and harder to document. But, used with care, it can solve problems neatly that an object-oriented language without multiple inheritance might not be able to solve at all.

To decide whether multiple inheritance is appropriate, use the "is a" test. That is, if a **TColorPoint** "is a" point *and* a color, it should be multiply-derived from **TPoint** and **TColor**. If, on the other hand, a better description is that **TColorPoint** "is a" **TPoint** *with* a **TColor**, then it should be singly-derived from **TPoint** and have a **TColor** property.

"Is a" **TView** a **TWindow** and a **TEventHandler**? Borland decided yes, and that's how they implemented it.

There is no limit to the number of parents a class can have, and the **public**, **private**, or **protected** inheritance access modifier is specified separately for each one. The derived object will contain parent properties *in the order of the inheritance list*, and they will be initialized in that order by the child's constructor.

It is possible to derive a new class from two base classes that are *already related to each other*. Doing so will give the resulting class two or more sets of inherited properties. Although this is legal, and C++ can support it, it's also hopelessly confusing to the poor human programmer who has to understand it. Therefore, to avoid conflicts between two sets of identical members, use *virtual inheritance*:

```
class x: virtual public a, virtual public b
    {
        ⇩
        ⇩
    };
```

The **virtual** keyword can be placed in any order with the **public**, **private**, or **protected** keyword.

Enjoying Polymorphism

By now, I hope you're adequately impressed with objects and the concept of inheritance. But inheritance is more than a way of saving code: it provides a way to treat similar objects in a similar manner.

One place where that ability is crucial is in the arena of *containers*. Containers are C++ objects that act as collections of other objects. What you've learned of C++ so far would not allow such a collection to hold different *kinds* of objects; unfortunately, that's just what we would most often like to do. Of course, C++ has always come to the rescue and containers are no exception.

Polymorphism is the object-oriented quality that allows us to treat related items like their ancestors, which would allow the items to be placed in containers. In this chapter you'll learn how polymorphism works, the pitfalls to avoid, and (as a side benefit) how to use C++ containers, as well!

Understanding Polymorhism

It's now time to get under the hood and explore the essentials of polymorhism. In this section, you'll learn about containers and virtual methods. Latter will show you how to put polymorphism to work and derive some classes and implement some containers.

Consider the Parking Lot

Since the objects in C++ model real-world objects, it pays to observe real-world examples to learn better how C++ objects work.

To understand how C+ containers work, let's look at a more prosaic model: a typical parking lot as shown in Figure 5.1.

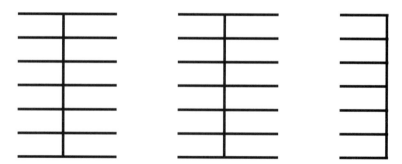

Figure 5.1 The parking lot view of polymorphism.

A parking lot, if you think about it, is designed to be a container for wheeled vehicles. In object-oriented terms, "WheeledVehicle" is just a base class from which many other classes are derived: Automobile, Motorcycle, Station Wagon. The slots in a parking lot are specifically sized and arranged for wheeled vehicles to enter, sit for a while, and then leave. Because the slots are designed for wheeled vehicles and not just cars, they can store motorcycles, station wagons and pickup trucks with equal ease. On the other hand, parking lot slots are not *totally* generic; they do not provide suitable storage for a house (too small), a CD collection (too hot), or Hilary Rodham Clinton (too healthy).

Understanding *virtual* Methods

A personnel system is an ideal example of a C++ container in use, because it must store a representation of each employee— and there are many kinds of employees.

At a typical fast food restaurant, there are several types of employees, identified by their jobs. There is a primary manager, who supervises the running of the restaurant; shift managers, who supervise their own shifts; cashiers; and cooks. If you were designing a personnel system for such a restaurant in a traditional language, you would probably develop a database table in which all records had fields for all possible details. Alternatively, you might create two tables, one for managers, the other for cooks and cashiers. Yet, even that would be inefficient, because managers are paid by salary and cooks and cashiers are paid by the hour. You would wind up having two separate paycheck routines. In fact, you might be tempted to created two personnel subsystems.

C++ containers, and polymorphic objects, solve this problem. Let's take a look. First, you could develop a **TEmployee** object that gathers the data all employees share, such as names, addresses, social security numbers, and so on. You could then derive new classes from **TEmployee** for each type of employee: **TManager**, **TCook**, and **TCashier**. You might even first derive a **TBondedEmployee** class, then derive **TManager** and **TCashier** from that.

Since objects are "smart" variables, instead of placing payroll functions in two separate modules, each **TEmployee** object "knows" how to pay itself. Therefore just one container is needed for *all* employees—even if, later, new classes have to be derived for piece workers or volunteers. That container *is*, basically, the personnel system!

This technique can work because of something called *run-time binding.* Normally, in C++ (and C) the addresses of all function calls/methods are resolved by the compiler and linker at compile-time. However, polymorphic objects sometimes need to delay that resolution until run-time, because, for instance, the container can't know in advance, which **PayMe** method should be invoked—it depends on the **TEmployee** derivative being asked to pay itself.

Some object-oriented languages, like Smalltalk, *only* provide run-time binding. However the designers of C++ couldn't bear to endorse such an inefficient technique. Instead, they provided a keyword that allows you, the programmer, to specify *which* methods should not be resolved until the application is running. That puts the responsibility on you to know which methods *need* to be resolved at run-time, and to not require this frivolity at the expense of app efficiency.

The keyword is **virtual**. This keyword enables run-time binding for the method it describes, *and all descendent methods* of the same name and signature.

Putting Polymorphism to Work

We're now ready to see what polymorphism can do for us. In this section will derive a useful class, implement a container, and explore virtual functions.

Deriving the *TMoney* Class

Putting polymorphism to use in a real C++ object, we can derive a new class from TScaledInt *The new class would be specially designed to store currency values, and could be placed in a container with* TScaledInt *objects.*

We all know the traditional problem facing programmers of financial applications: money (not lack of, programming support for!). The problem is that dollar amounts usually include pennies, which our money system represents as decimal fractions of a dollar. The obvious way to store such values is in a floating-point variable. The problem is that floating-point operations, particularly multiplication and division, do funny things with decimal fractions that cause no problems when calculating orbital trajectories, but cause the eyebrows of humorless accountants to rise.

These problems cease to exist when the dollar amounts are stored and manipulated as integers—that is, as cents instead of dollars. But doing so in a traditional environment means multiplying each dollar value by 100 on input, and remembering to divide it by 100 on output.

But wait—isn't that *exactly* what the **TScaledInt** class already does? Why not store dollar amounts in a **TScaledInt** object?

Of course, there are a couple of minor disadvantages. For one thing, each time we create a **TScaledInt** object to store a dollar amount, we'll have to specify a scaling factor of 2. It's not a big deal, but it would be nice if the object just "knew," somehow. And then there's output formatting: it would be nice if a dollar amount could be formatted, complete with dollar sign.

But, wait! We can *have* those features if we simply derive a specialized class, **TMoney**, from **TScaledInt**! We won't have to rewrite any of the basic scaled integer code; that's already there. All we have to do is code for the few differences between a generalized scaled integer and a dollar value.

The first requirement is easy: a constructor that does not require a scaling factor argument. The normal scaling factor for dollar amounts, 2, can be supplied as the default value:

```
class TMoney : public TScaledInt
    {
    public:
       TMoney (long aValue, int aScalingFactor = 2);
    ⇩
    ⇩
    }

inline TMoney::TMoney (long aValue, int aScalingFactor)
    : TScaledInt (aValue, aScalingFactor)
    {
    }
```

Formatting is a trickier problem. In **TScaledInt**, we formatted when we needed to—for example, when overloading the stream insertion and stream extraction operators. In order to make formatting work for **TMoney**, we'll have to retrofit a more modular approach to formatting in **TScaledInt**.

This modular approach requires two new methods: a C-string version of **operator()=**, and the **protected** method **Format()**. For **TScaledInt** objects, the former should remove commas and a decimal point from an input string while converting it to binary. **Format()** should add commas and the decimal point for display.

An added benefit is that by working with the decimal point manually, we won't have to bring in the floating-point library to help with conversions.

The new **TScaledInt** assignment operator looks like this:

```
TScaledInt & TScaledInt::operator= (char * Buffer)
  {
  register i,
    Length = strlen (Buffer);
  const int True = 1, False = 0;
  int DecimalPointEncountered = False;
  Value = 0;
  Scale = 0;
  for (i = 0; i < Length; i++)
    {
    if (Buffer[i] == '.')
      DecimalPointEncountered = True;
    else if (isdigit (Buffer[i]))
      {
      Value *= 10;
      Value += Buffer[i] & 0x0F;
      if (DecimalPointEncountered)
        ++Scale;
      }
    }
  return *this;
  }
```

This is actually a fun function. Did you ever wonder how **atoi()** works? Much like this, I'm sure. Starting from the beginning of the string, each character is translated directly into its binary equivalent by using just its least significant four bits. To remove commas, we simply ignore any non-digit characters—except the period, which is used to trigger adjustment of the scaling factor. Once the period is encountered, each additional digit bumps the **Scale** by one.

Given this operator, we can now easily convert strings into **TScaledInt** objects, as shown in the revised *operator>>()* method for **ostream** objects:

```
istream & operator>> (istream & is, TScaledInt & s)
  {
  char Buffer[32];
  is >> Buffer;
  s = Buffer;
  return is;
  }
```

The **Format()** method has the opposite job: using the **Value** and **Scale** properties, this function must produce a string with a decimal point and commas in the appropriate locations. This code does the job:

```
void TScaledInt::Format (char * Buffer)
   {
   register i = 0;
   register long v = Value;
   register int s = Scale;
   register char Group = 0;
   while (s < 0)
      {
      Buffer[i++] = '0';
      s++;
      if (++Group == 3)
         {
         Buffer[i++] = ',';
         Group = 0;
         }
      }
   while (v)
      {
      register long Temp = v / 10;
      char Digit = '0' + (v - (Temp * 10));
      Buffer[i++] = Digit;
      if (s)
         {
         if (--s == 0)
            Buffer[i++] = '.';
         }
      else if (++Group == 3)
         {
         Buffer[i++] = ',';
         Group = 0;
         }
      v = Temp;
      }
   if (Buffer[i-1] == ',')
      Buffer[i-1] = 0;
   else
      Buffer[i] = 0;
   Flip (Buffer, strlen (Buffer));
   if (Buffer[i-1] == '.')
      Buffer[i-1] = 0;
   }
```

The **v** and **s** variables are temporary holders for **Value** and **Scale**, respectively; the **v** and **s** will change values during the execution of this method—we wouldn't want to alter the actual property values! **i** is the ubiquitous index variable for **Buffer**, and **Group** will help us track the digits that appear between commas.

Before you start decoding, be aware that the digits will be rendered into **Buffer** in *reverse order.* This minor technicality will be repaired at the end of the method.

The first **while** loop adds the trailing zeros that should appear if the **Scale** is a negative number.

The second loop extracts each base-10 digit from **v**, and adds it to **Buffer**. Each digit allows **s** to be decremented; if and when **s** reaches zero, the decimal point can be placed into **Buffer** as well. On the other hand, if **s** is zero already (or when it turns that way), **Group** can be incremented with each digit until it reaches 3. At that time we add a comma and reset **Group** to zero.

Before reversing the string, we check for a "trailing" (actually leading) comma. If there is one, placing the terminating NULL in its placing effectively removes it. The standard library function **strrev()** reverses the string; we then look for a trailing decimal point, removing it if we find it.

The revised stream insertion operator is coded as follows:

```
ostream & operator<< (ostream & os, const TScaledInt & s)
  {
  char Buffer[32];
  s.Format (Buffer);
  return os << Buffer;
  }
```

There's one last touch to make these methods useful to a polymorphic object: both **operator==()** and **Format()** must be labeled **virtual**. This is done in the class declaration:

```
class TScaledInt
  {
  public:
    ⇩
    ⇩
    virtual TScaledInt & operator= (char * Buffer);
    ⇩
    ⇩
  protected:
    virtual void Format (char * Buffer);
    ⇩
    ⇩
  };
```

The text representation of a **TMoney** object will be just like a **TScaledInt**, with the addition of a prefixed dollar sign. As luck would have it, we won't have to override the **operator=()** method in **TMoney**; we wrote it to ignore any non-digit characters, and that will include dollar signs. (We made it **virtual** to accommodate any other derived class we might make.)

The **Format()** function just needs the addition of that leading dollar sign, so it gets written like this:

```
void TMoney::Format (char * Buffer)
  {
  Buffer[0] = '$';
  TScaledInt::Format (&Buffer[1]);
  }
```

Note that most of the work gets done by the ancestor method, which is specifically invoked.

Implementing a Simple Container

Although C++ comes with a number of containers already, you already know how to make a simple one from scratch. It's just an array of object pointers!

To test the polymorphic attributes of **TScaledInt** and **TMoney**, add the following array to your test bed:

```
TScaledInt * Container[5];
```

Then assign the addresses of various **TScaledInt** and **TMoney** objects to the array elements:

```
void main (void)
  {
  TScaledInt a;
  TScaledInt b (250, -2);
  cin >> a;
  TMoney c (2773);
  TScaledInt * Container[5];
  Container[0] = &a;
  Container[1] = &b;
  Container[2] = &c;
  Container[3] = new TScaledInt (234);
  Container[4] = new TMoney (555555555);
  register i;
```

```
for (i = 0; i < 5; i++)
   cout << i << ": "<< *Container[i] << endl;
delete Container[3];
delete Container[4];
}
```

Notice that, even though you declared **Container** to hold pointers to **TScaledInts**, the compiler doesn't complain when you assign the address of a **TMoney** object. This is always true: If you can use the address of a base class, you can use the address of a descendent class. (Of course, this applies to pointers only—the objects themselves are not interchangeable.)

How does this work? Through the magic of run-time binding! The program doesn't decide until run-time which **Format()** method to invoke, because you made **Format()** a **virtual** method. At run-time, it correctly invokes the **Format()** method of the particular object being formatted. This is how polymorphism is implemented.

How Do *virtual* Functions Work?

It's all well and good to say that the program doesn't decide until run-time which function to invoke. But how does that happen? Enquiring minds want to know!

For efficiency, C++ only does run-time binding on functions defined with the **virtual** keyword. If *any* function in the class is **virtual**, then two new, invisible properties are added. One is a **static** property, shared (as you'll recall) among all members of the class. This property is the *virtual method table* (VMT). The other, a non-**static** property, is a pointer *to* the VMT.

The entries in the VMT are pointers to virtual methods for *that class only*. Most are inherited; some will be overridden. When an object is constructed, its pointer to the VMT is set and the VMT is updated as needed. (This is why the system creates a constructor even if there are no object properties.)

Making Destructors *virtual*

As any object approaches the end of its existence, its destructor is invoked. To support polymorphism, the base class' destructor should be virtual *so that descendent classes can be destroyed by their polymorphic containers.*

Just as a container is able to format different (but related) class objects by invoking their **virtual Format()** methods, so can containers destroy related objects if their destructors are also **virtual**.

Remember, once a method is declared **virtual**, all descendent methods with the same signature are also **virtual**, *even if you omit the keyword*. (I like to use the keyword, though, as a form of documentation.)

Generally, objects that are to be given to containers are allocated on the heap via the **new** operator. The container—which is usually an object in its own right—should destroy its contents as part of its own destruct sequence. It does so by applying the **delete** operator to each of the objects it contains. Of course, it **delete**s the objects as if they were all members of the base class, which may not be true. By making sure the base class' destructor is **virtual**, you assure that the descendent classes' destructors will be invoked when appropriate.

If you neglect to do this, the omission will probably manifest itself as a memory leak.

ObjectWindows has a **TObject** class from which pretty much everything else in the OWL hierarchy is derived. This type of organization has the twin benefits of ensuring that the destructors will be **virtual**, and of allowing containers to hold any object at all (because they are designed for the **TObject** base class). You can derive new classes from **TObject** as well, if you like.

Understanding Pure Virtual Functions

Object design often involves creating a base object class that exists only to provide support to descendent classes. No instance of that base class will ever be made. As we mentioned in Chapter 4, such a class is called an **abstract class.** *Here's why you'd want to create such a class, and how to do it.*

We started this chapter off with a discussion of a hypothetical "WheeledVehicle" class. Such as class is obviously too vague to be of any use by itself—you could never build a generic wheeled vehicle; any real-life detail you add would instantly change it into something more specific: a car, a bicycle, a unicycle.

Likewise, the **TEmployee** class described earlier is also too generic to be useful, except as a base class for managers, cooks, cashiers, and other specific kinds of employees.

It's easy to see that base classes supply properties common to the descendent classes: name, address, and so on. Less obvious is the need to supply a protocol for *communicating* with objects of all descendent classes. Take the **Format()** method of **TScaledInt** as an example. The only way for a container to format **TScaledInt** objects as well as **TMoney** objects and objects of any other descendent class, is to provide a **virtual Format()** method at the base class level, and then override it in descendent classes as neccessary.

But what if the base class is abstract, and there is not enough information at that level to actually *write* the **Format()** method? That's where *pure virtual functions* (or methods) come in. These are methods in which the signature is specified—but *with no code*. Such a method provides an "anchor" for the underlying base class, but replies on the derived classes to supply the details.

A side effect is that a class with even *one* pure virtual function cannot ever be instantiated—the compiler will make sure of this. Therefore, to use a descendent class, all pure virtual functions must be overridden. Even one omission is enough to make that descendent class an abstract one, as well.

Constructors and destructors are never inherited (although they are invoked by descendent constructors and destructors, as part of the chain of inheritance). Since the base class constructor is guaranteed to be invoked first, before descendent constructors, the VMT will not yet point to overriding pure virtual functions. For this reason, you must not invoke a pure virtual function from a constructor. However, it is all right for a descendent constructor to invoke a function that *overrides* an ancestral pure virtual function.

Likewise, because the base class' destructor will be called last, by the time it is called the properties of descendent classes will already have been unraveled. Therefore, you should never invoke a pure virtual function from a destructor (although, again, it's okay to invoke an overriding method in the destructor of a base class).

In order to create a pure virtual function, you simply supply a VMT address of zero (NULL) instead of code. You do this in the class declaration:

```
class TMyBase
    {
    void MyPureVirtualMethod (void) = 0;
    };
```

There's nothing to put in the implementation file because there's no implementation of a pure virtual function—that's the point. Later, derived classes will override the pure virtual function normally:

```
TMyDerived : public TMyBase
  {
  void MyPureVirtualMethod (void);
  }

inline void MyPureVirtualMethod (void)
  {
  // Not so pure any more!
  }
```

Remember, the Function Signatures Must Match

If you write a function with the same name but a different argument list, you'll be overloading the function, not overriding it—and that's not the same thing at all! If you think you've overridden a pure virtual function, but the compiler insists that some still persist, double-check your function signatures.

Using Object Containers

Although an array of pointers to objects is technically a container, C++ class libraries supply more capable ones. These are the object-oriented equivalent to arrays, linked lists, and more. Learn to use them and you've added a powerful arsenal to your supply of programming weapons!

It is likely that the ANSI C++ committee will settle on a standard set of containers sometime soon. In the meantime, Microsoft and Borland each supply a rich set of similar, though not identical, containers. It's important to note which ones are available so you can be sure to use the right one for each job. Using the right container can save you a heck of a lot of work. Also, if none of the supplied container classes is *precisely* right for what you have in mind, don't hesitate to derive a specialized container from an existing container class.

Borland supplies thirteen general containers: Arrays, Associations, Bags, Btrees, Deques, Dictionaries, DoubleLists, HashTables, Lists, Queues, Sets, Stacks, and Vectors.

The Secret Life of Templates

I pity the poor programmer who thought that objects were the only new thing he or she would have to learn when tackling C++. Before you know it, you come crashing into a new concept called *templates.* What are they? What are they for? Why do you need them?

Briefly, templates are rather like an object's object: they carry abstraction a level further back than even C++ object classes can. In another sense, templates are a kludge to overcome a weakness of C++ that developed when the designers decided *not* to make run-time binding the default.

Still, if you can understand objects, you can *certainly* understand templates. I don't mean that they are the same thing; they're not. But they are no more complex to understand, and in the following sections, I'll hold your hand as we walk through their strange world, learning when and how to write templates of our own. Then, we'll look at Borland's major application of templates: the *container classes.*

Writing Templates

When I was in kindergarten, our teacher taught us to write our letters *before* we learned to read. The principle was, we couldn't learn to properly *use* a tool we couldn't build.

As a C++ programmer, you will *use* templates far more often than you are likely to write them. Still, we're going to start our template oddysey by learning to write our own. That way, you'll understand *why* you have to do the odd things you have to do to use them. And, besides—someday you *might* have to write one!

Why You Need Templates

Other object-oriented languages do not have templates. C doesn't, either. Why are they included in the C++ specification, and why can't you just ignore them?

Templates provide a way to write a simple piece of code that applies to an indefinite number of different data types.

For example, suppose you need a function to swap two values. Normally, you would write the following code segment:

```
void Swap (int & a, int & b)
  {
  int Temp (a);
```

```
a = b;
b = Temp;
}
```

This will work for **int**s, but what about **float**s? What about **long**s? What about object variables? Sure, you could overload **Swap()** functions for each data type you expected to use it with, but the task would grow tedious, to say the least. And, suppose you discovered a flaw in your logic. You'd have to go back and correct every variant!

This, essentially, is the dilemma that templates are meant to solve. The irony is, templates would not be neccessary if C++ had made runtime binding (the kind you get with the **virtual** keyword) the norm, and had made *all* data types objects. This is the way other object-oriented languages are designed. In the earlier example, **a** and **b** would not be **int**s; they would simply be objects, and whatever variables were passed at run-time would have their values appropriately transposed.

Even so, if you need a function like **Swap()**, but *only* for objects, you can make sure the objects are derived from a common base class and have their **operator=()** methods made **virtual**. For this situation you wouldn't need templates.

But real life is seldom so simple, and not all C++ variables are objects— many of them are scalar, like **int**s and **float**s. Templates were created for them.

Creating a Template Function

So I've decided I need to create a template function. How do I go about it?

To create a template function (or a template class, for that matter), the first thing you have to do is learn a whole new (and bizarre!) syntax. C++ has already used all the special characters on the keyboard for one thing or another; to implement templates, the C++ designers had to re-use a couple.

The second thing to realize is that a template function is *not compiled until it is used.* Think about it: if a **Swap()** function potentially exists for an infinite number of data types (including user-defined ones), then a .OBJ file containing the compiled code for them all would be also be infinitely large. To avoid this, the compiler doesn't actually generate code until needed. (This leads to more complications that we'll look at later in this chapter.) Template code, then, goes in the declaration (header) file, not an implementation file.

Let's look at a template rendition of the **Swap()** function from the previous topic:

```
template <class Type>
   void Swap (Type & a, Type & b)
      {
      Type Temp (a);
      a = b;
      b = Temp;
      }
```

First up is the keyword **template**. That's easy enough. Stranger is the entry within the angle brackets: **<class Type>**. **class** is a keyword; **Type** is just an identifier. **<class Fred>** or **<class T>** are equally valid. You are simply symbolically naming the data type that will eventually be supplied. Each occurrence of **Type** within the code will be replaced by **int** or **double** or **TStarShip** or some other data type or class name, as needed. If you need to do so, you can supply more than one substitute:

```
template <class Type1, class Type2, class Type3>
   void MyFunc (Type1 a, Type2 b, Type3 c)
      {
      ⇩
      ⇩
      }
```

The subsitutions—which are called *template parameters*—must be used in the function's signature; the way the function is called is the way the compiler can tell which version of the function to generate. You can think of a template function as being an infinite number of overloaded functions of the same name—and only those functions actually used in your program will be compiled.

Since the template parameter types will be replaced by real data types, don't forget you can add modifiers and initializations to the variables of those types:

```
template <class Type1, class Type2, class Type3>
   void MyFunc (const Type1 a, Type2 & b, Type3 * c)
      {
      ⇩
      ⇩
      }
```

Likewise, template functions can be **static**, **near**, **far**, exported and so on, just like any other function:

```
template <class Type>
   inline void Swap (Type & a, Type & b)
     {
     Type Temp (a);
     a = b;
     b = Temp;
     }
```

Later on in your program, you might have the following sequence:

```
int y, z;
     ⇩
     ⇩
Swap (y, z);
```

At this point, an overloaded **int** version of **Swap()** will come into existence. If, elsewhere, you have

```
float y, z;
     ⇩
     ⇩
Swap (y, z);
```

a **float** version will be generated at that point.

Creating a Template Class

Templates can also be used to generate distinct, but related, class declarations and definitions. Here's how and why.

Low-level languages, like C and C++, are those in which as few decisions as possible are made by the language, which defers them to the programmer. Thus, a C++ programmer, when deciding how an integer value should be stored, has several choices: **signed char**, **signed int**, **signed long**, **unsigned char**, **unsigned int**, and **unsigned long**. The price the programmer pays is having to know which data type is appropriate in which circumstance, and how to specify the one he or she wants. The benefit is that each value is stored most efficiently (assuming the programmer makes a good choice).

When we developed the **TScaledInt** class in the last few of chapters, we made the storage decision *for* the programmer: in the name of simplicity, we placed the value in a **signed long** property and said no more about it.

But what if we were loathe to presume so much? Suppose we preferred to provide a *variety* of **TScaledInt**s, from which the programmer could select—automatically, if possible—the appropriate one?

Once again, templates provide the answer.

Template classes are declared similarly to template functions. A **template** keyword sets off each block, for example a **class** statement:

```
template <class Type>
  class TScaled
    {
    public:
      TScaled ();
      TScaled (Type V, int aScale = 0);
      int GetScale (void) const;
      void SetScale (int s);
      TScaled<Type> & operator+= (TScaled<Type> other);
      TScaled<Type> & operator+= (Type i);
      short operator== (const TScaled<Type> & other) const;
      short operator== (Type i) const;
      friend short operator== (Type i, const TScaled<Type> & other);
      TScaled<Type> & operator++ (void);
      TScaled<Type> operator++ (int);
      TScaled<Type> & operator-- (void);
      TScaled<Type> operator-- (int);
      TScaled<Type> & operator= (Type i);
      TScaled<Type> & operator= (float f);
      virtual TScaled<Type> & operator= (char * Buffer);
      operator long (void) const;
      operator float (void) const;
      friend ostream & operator<< (ostream & os, const TScaled<Type>
        & s);
      friend istream & operator>> (istream & is, TScaled<Type> & s);
    protected:
      virtual void Format (char * Buffer);
    private:
      Type Value;
      int Scale;
      void Equalize (TScaled<Type> & other);
      void Normalize (void);
      static long mod (long Dividend, int Divisor);
      static float frac (double f);
    };
```

The first thing you're likely to notice is that some—but not all—of the internal references to **TScaledInt** have been changed to **TScaled<Type>**. Obviously, **<Type>** will be filled in by the compiler, but the constructor name does *not* have the **<Type>** appendage. That let's the compiler understand that this is the constructor for class **TScaled**. Hey, I *told* you the syntax for templates was weird!

A more subtle change is the addition of **mod()** and **frac()** to the list of **private** member functions. In the original version of **TScaledInt**, these were **static near** "helper" functions, not class methods. Because all template code should be placed in a header file, we can't put any "real" code there. The easiest solution is to make them **static** methods (**static** because they do not operate directly on a specific object of the class).

As I mentioned earlier, the definitions for the member functions will be placed in the header file as well, even the ones that are not **inline**. Each individual function must be part of its own template statement:

```
template <class Type>
   inline TScaled<Type>::TScaled (Type V, int aScale)
     : Value (V), Scale (aScale)
     {
     }

template <class Type>
   TScaled<Type>::TScaled ()
     : Value (0), Scale (0)
     {
     }

      ⇩
      ⇩
```

Except for the addition of the **template** statement before each function, and the replacement of the original **long** data type specifier with **Type** (where appropriate), the code is the same as we saw earlier for the **TScaledInt** class. (It's on the code disk, also.)

When we instantiated a function template earlier in the chapter, we did so by invoking the function with a specific set of parameters. The data types of the parameters told the system what version of the function to generate, making the entire thing *look* like standard function overloading.

Since a class is not a function, it can't be overloaded like a function. The designers of C++ had to find another way to specify how the compiler is to generate this class. They chose to make the programmer supply the template parameter when the class is being instantiated:

```
TScaled<char> i (9);
```

Yes, you actually specify the data type within angle brackets, as if it were actually the name of the class! And, in a way, it is; that's why we included it within the template class declaration (and definition) when specifying return value or passed parameter data types.

When declaring an instance of a template class, the data type specified within the angle brackets doesn't have to be a standard C++ data type. It can be any legal data type, including a class you've previously declared:

```
TMyTemplate<TMyClass> t;
```

This works smoothly as long as you've supplied a full set of operators when defining **TMyClass**—another reason not to skimp on class implementation.

Nesting Template Parameters

What if you want to instantiate a template class for a data type that is, itself, another instantiated template class?

Suppose you've created a template class called **TFred**. Let's say you've instantiated it for **float**s:

```
TFred<float> f;
```

Let's say further that you have another template class called **TEthel** and you'd like to instantiate it for **f**'s data type. That requires nested template parameters. You'd *like* to type

```
TEthel<TFred<float>> e;  // Will produce a warning!
```

but this will produce a warning in Borland C++ 4.0 (and will probably not compile in other C++ compilers). Instead, add a little white space to make the compiler happy:

```
TEthel<TFred<float> > e;
```

Where, Oh Where Has My Template Code Gone?

If the compiler doesn't generate code for a template class or function until a need for it is encountered, what happens if a need is encountered in more than one source file? Won't multiple copies be generated? Won't the linker complain?

The "mutliple generation" problem may be why templates were so slow to be incorporated into C++ compilers. (In fact, Borland was the first to do this for the PC world.)

Suppose that SCALED.H contains the class template presented earlier, and that this header file is **#include**d by both A.CPP and B.CPP. Suppose further that A and B *each* create an instance of **TScaled<char>**.

We've been told the compiler will generate a **char** version of **TScaled** for each module. Won't that cause the linker to cry foul (or, at least, "duplicate function")?

Actually, you have two choices, based on a compiler switch. The default switch, **-Jg**, is the one we've planned around. With the class template declaration *and* member function definitions in the header file, the compiler will indeed generate a complete set of code for each module. However, the code is marked in such a way that the linker only keeps the first set and tosses the others away. This is about as convenient as you can get, but there are a couple of drawbacks. For one, the template class code is available to be read or even changed. Another is that the compiler takes *time* to generate that code, time that is wasted on any but the first module to require the code.

So you might consider another approach. Go ahead and keep the template class code in a separate implementation file, *with instantiation statements,* but compile it once using the **-Jgd** switch. Then make the resulting object file available to the rest of your project(s), which should be compiled using the **-Jgx** switch.

Now to explain the details.To force an instantiation of a template class, just declare it complete with supplied data type. To force a **char** instantiation of **TScaled**, for example, use the following statement:

```
class TScaled<char>;
```

You can place as many of these statements in your implementation file as desired. Just remember, because you're hiding the template body from the rest of the project, the compiler will not be able to generate code for any variant you omit. Also, all the variants you *do* include will be linked into your application whether they're used or not.

HOT TIP

Generate Many Template Variants and Let the Linker Include Only the Ones You Need

The key is to get the compiler to place each variant in a separate segment, and then put the segments in a library. The linker will then add only the segments that are actually referenced to your .EXE file.

By default, code segments are named after the module in which the source code was located, but you can override this. Use the **#pragma codeseg** directive, as in this example:

```
#pragma codeseg _SCALEDCHAR
class TScaled<char>;
```

```
#pragma codeseg _SCALEDINT
class TScaled<int>;
#pragma codeseg _SCALEDLONG
class TScaled<long>;
```

Using Containers

If you had to estimate the percentage of programs you've written that did *not* use a single array or linked list, I bet the percentage would be really small. And yet, arrays and linked lists occur less often in the real world. As programmers, we use them because they're convenient; we force the problems we're trying to solve into a mold in which an array or linked list can help. No wonder we spend so much time debugging.

Borland C++ 4.0 offers something better: a whole suite of "container" classes. No matter what problem you're trying to solve, there is likely to be a pre-written container that fits exactly. All you have to know is which containers are, in fact, available, and what each can do for you. And that's what we're about to learn.

Choosing the Abstract Data Type

Do you have items that must be handled in order, but arrive at your application asynchronously? Do you have items that must be handled in reverse order? Perhaps you have a set of items that are order-independent, but that can include duplicates? Borland gives you a pre-written container class template for each of these scenarios and more—all you have to do is know when to use each one!

Borland supplies the following high-level containers, which they refer to as abstract data types (ADTs):

Array Used like a C array, but Array containers allow you to specify a *lower* bound as well as an upper one. Array containers can also grow dynamically. Items can be appended to the Array (**Add()**) or inserted in the array (**AddAt()**). You can obtain a count of used elements in the Array (**GetItemsInContainer()**), as well as the total number of elements (**ArraySize()**). The array index operator [] is implemented. Although you can iterate the items in a traditional **for** loop, consider using the **ForEach()** method instead.

Association An Association container contains just two items: a **key** and a **value**. Associations are rarely used by themselves, but they are useful components of more complex containers such as Dictionaries. Before you brush Associations off with a shrug, remember that a **value** can be an object or pointer to an object—even another container!

Bag A Bag can contain any number of items in which internal order is irrelevant. A Bag can also contain duplicate items. Since order is unimportant, there is an *Add()* method but no way to insert at a position. Likewise the array index operator [] is *not* implemented. However, you can iterate over the elements with the **ForEach()** method.

Dequeue A Dequeue is a double queue: items can be added and removed from *either* direction. Since there is no proper "head" or "tail," the directions are labeled "left" and "right." There is no add function, but there is a **PutLeft()** and **PutRight()** to match **GetLeft()** and **GetRight()** Getting an object removes it from the Dequeue container; it is also possible to **PeekLeft()** and **PeekRight()** without disturbing the object.

Dictionaries A Dictionary is a container of Association objects, intended for speedy lookups of **key**s for the purpose of returning **value**s. You can **Add()** items, but you cannot specify a position; that's inherent in the item's **key**.

Queue A Queue is a container in which items are added to the tail, but removed from the head—in other words, First In, First Out (FIFO). The **Put()** method adds items; the **Get()** method retrieves (and removes) them.

Set Sets, like Bags, contain some number of items whose relative position is unimportant. Unlike Bags though, Sets cannot contain duplicate items. They are designed to make the **Find()** method (common to all containers) particularly efficient.

Stack A Stack is a container in which items added last must be removed *before* items added earlier—in other words, First In, Last Out (FILO). The **Push()** and **Pop()** methods add and remove items, respectively.

Choosing a Fundamental Data Structure

The Borland ADTs are implemented on top of a fundamental data structure (FDS). In many cases, you can choose which FDS will underlie your choice of ADT. You can also use an FDS directly.

Borland supplies template classes for the following FDSs:

BTree Binary Search Trees are such a chore to implement that programmers usually just don't. As a container, they are almost as easy to use as arrays. The class data type must implement **operator<()** and **operator==()** so the BTree can figure out where to **Add()** each new item. You'll probably have to work with a derived class to make this low-level container useful.

DoubleList A doubly linked list is one in which it's just as easy to move backwards as forwards. Adding an item to a doubly linked list takes a little longer than the same operation on a singly linked list, the payback is *much* more flexibility. The DoubleList container expects to be filled with DoubleList elements, objects of another template class. This low-level class is the basis for the Dequeue container.

HashTable This basis for the Dictionary provides quick lookups of complex data structures by relating the structure's *hash value* to the structure itself. A hash value is any numeric value that can be derived from an item. Objects intended for use with a hashTable must therefore supply a **HashValue()** member function that makes up and returns a unique, or nearly unique, hash value for each likely real value.

List A singly linked List can provide the benefits of a doubly linked list with little overhead, as long as access is in a single direction. One problem is that additions can only be made to the *head* of the list, making the list seem to grow in reverse. If you think you want a singly linked list in which items are added to the tail, consider using a Queue container instead.

Vector The Vector is the low-level class used to implement many of the higher-level containers. It is basically a simple array, with a lower bound of zero. You should normally never need to use this container directly.

Understanding the Container Naming Convention

Borland's suite of containers not only includes eight high-level and five low-level types, but variations for storage style, programmer-supplied memory management, and more. Each option is controlled by a specific aspect of the container's name. Here's how to make sense of it all.

Remember that Borland containers, based on templates, are not actually compiled until you *use* them in an application. Borland has therefore deferred many decisions the container designers might otherwise have made to you, the programmer. You can indicate your decisions in the way you assemble the name for the class you want to use.

Here's a sample name: **TMISArrayAsVector**. What does it mean? Read on:

T This is a throwaway. All Borland classes begin with the letter *T*.

M *M* stands for *managed*, as in *memory*. You can create container classes that use a standard memory management scheme, or you can supply one of your own. The M means you'll supply your own. In general this is not worth the effort; Borland's memory management is almost always adequate.

I *I* stands for *indirect*. It means you'll be storing pointers to objects in this container, rather than copies of the objects themselves. Generally, you'll want indirect storage. Some classes require you to specify *D* for direct storage.

S *S* stands for *sorted*. Many of the containers provide automatic sorting of items as they're entered. The items stored must supply a useful **operator<()** method.

ArrayAs The name of ADT, if there is one.

Vector The name of the FDT. Some containers give you a choice of two underlying management schemes, and it is possible for you to come up with a combination of your own, using the existing ADTs and FDTs as building blocks. If you do, you should adhere to the existing naming convention.

Table 6.1 provides a list of the high-level container class templates, with a translation.

Table 6.1 High-Level Container Class Templates

Class Template	Memory Management	Storage	Sort
TMArrayAsVector	Custom	Direct	No
TArrayAsVector	Standard	Direct	No
TMIArrayAsVector	Custom	Pointer	No
TIArrayAsVector	Standard	Pointer	No
TMSArrayAsVector	Custom	Direct	Yes
TSArrayAsVector	Standard	Direct	Yes
TISArrayAsVector	Standard	Pointer	Yes
TMISArrayAsVector	Custom	Pointer	Yes
TMDDAssociation	Custom	Key: Direct	

continued

Table 6.1 High-Level Container Class Templates (Continued)

Class Template	Memory Management	Storage	Sort
Value: Direct	N/A		
TDDAssociation	Standard	Key: Direct	
Value: Direct	N/A		
TMDIAssociation	Custom	Key: Direct	
Value: Indirect	N/A		
TDIAssociation	Standard	Key: Direct	
Value: Indirect	N/A		
TMIDAssociation	Custom	Key: Indirect	
Value: Direct	N/A		
TIDAssociation	Standard	Key: Indirect	
Value: Direct	N/A		
TMIIAssociation	Custom	Key: Indirect	
Value: Indirect	N/A		
TIIAssociation	Standard	Key: Indirect	
Value: Indirect	N/A		
TMBagAsVector	Custom	Direct	N/A
TBagAsVector	Standard	Direct	N/A
TMIBagAsVector	Custom	Pointer	N/A
TIBagAsVector	Standard	Pointer	N/A
TMDequeAsVector	Custom	Direct	N/A
TDequeAsVector	Standard	Direct	N/A
TMIDequeAsVector	Custom	Pointer	N/A
TIDequeAsVector	Standard	Pointer	N/A
TMDequeAsDoubleList	Custom	Direct	N/A
TDequeAsDoubleList	Standard	Direct	N/A
TMIDequeDoubleList	Custom	Pointer	N/A
TIDequeDoubleList	Standard	Pointer	N/A
TMDictionaryAsHashTable	Custom	Direct	Yes
TDictionaryAsHashTable	Standard	Direct	Yes
TMIDictionaryAsHashTable	Custom	Pointer	Yes
TIDictionaryAsHashTable	Standard	Pointer	Yes
TMQueueAsVector	Custom	Direct	N/A

continued

Table 6.1 High-Level Container Class Templates (Continued)

Class Template	Memory Management	Storage	Sort
TQueueAsVector	Standard	Direct	N/A
TMIQueueAsVector	Custom	Pointer	N/A
TIQueueAsVector	Standard	Pointer	N/A
TMQueueAsDoubleList	Custom	Direct	N/A
TQueueAsDoubleList	Standard	Direct	N/A
TMIQueueAsDoubleList	Custom	Pointer	N/A
TIQueueAsDoubleList	Standard	Pointer	N/A
TMSetAsVector	Custom	Direct	N/A
TSetAsVector	Standard	Direct	N/A
TMISetAsVector	Custom	Pointer	N/A
TISetAsVector	Standard	Pointer	N/A
TMStackAsVector	Custom	Direct	N/A
TStackAsVector	Standard	Direct	N/A
TMIStackAsVector	Custom	Pointer	N/A
TIStackAsVector	Standard	Pointer	N/A
TMStackAsList	Custom	Direct	N/A
TStackAsList	Standard	Direct	N/A
TMIStackAsList	Custom	Pointer	N/A
TIStackAsList	Standard	Pointer	N/A

In addition to naming the container class, you'll also have to supply the name of a data type that the container is to contain—you must always supply the name of the data type when instantiating a template class. To instantiate a Dictionary class (based, as Dictionaries must be, on a HashTable) of indirectly stored Association objects (in which the key and value are both directly stored), which will themselves contain **TScaled<char>** objects, you would use the following statements:

```
class TScaled<char>;
class TArrayAsVector<TScaled<char> >;
```

Filling Containers

The container classes share a number of methods used to add items to the container. Each also has methods unique to itself. Table 6.2 provides a handy map to them all.

Table 6.2 Methods Used to Add Items to the Container

Container	Method	Purpose
Array	Add()	Adds an object to the array, in the first available position; can cause the array to grow if all available positions are already occupied
	AddAt()	Adds an object to a specified position in the array, making room, if neccessary, by shoving items between the specified position and the end of the array up one position
Bag	Add()	Adds an object to the bag; bag items are position independent of each other
Dequeue	PutLeft()	Adds an object to the left end of the Dequeue
	PutRight()	Adds an object to the right end of the Dequeue
Dictionary	Add()	Adds an Association object to the Dictionary, if one with the same key doesn't already exist
Queue	Put()	Adds an item to the tail of the Queue
Set	Add()	Adds an item to the Set, if it hasn't already been added; sets cannot contain duplicate items
Stack	Push()	Adds an item to the top of the stack

Opening Containers

There are no "black hole" containers because containers are useful only if you can get back the things you put into them. Let's look at the methods, shown in Table 6.3, that containers provide to access the items they contain.

Table 6.3 Methods That Containers Provide to Access the Items They Contain

Container	Method	Purpose
All	IsEmpty()	Returns True if there are no items in the container
	IsFull()	Returns True if all allocated slots contain items; most containers can grow if IsFull() is True and another item is added; not implemented for Dictionaries
	GetItemsInContainer()	Returns the number items actually present in the container

continued

Table 6.3 Methods That Containers Provide to Access the Items They Contain (Continued)

Container	Method	Purpose
	FirstThat()	Returns a pointer to the first item that satisfies a specified condition, or NULL if no appropriate item could be found
	LastThat()	Returns a pointer to the last item that satisfies a specified condition, or NULL if no appropriate item could be found; not implemented for Sets
Array	ArraySize()	Returns actual number of allocated slots, whether they contain items or not
	[]	Use the standard index brackets to access individual elements in the array
Bag	HasMember()	Returns True if the specified item has already been added, at least once, to the Bag
Dequeue	GetLeft()	Returns the leftmost item while removing it from the Dequeue
	GetRight()	Returns the rightmost item while removing it from the Dequeue
	PeekLeft()	Returns the leftmost item without removing it from the Dequeue
	PeekRight()	Returns the rightmost item without removing it from the Dequeue
Dictionary	Find()	Returns a pointer to the specified item
Queue	Get()	Returns the object from the tail of the Queue, removing it from the Queue
Set	HasMember()	Returns True if the specified item has already been added to the Set
Stack	Pop()	Returns the item from the top of the stack

Iterating Containers

A common use of containers is to gather together related items in order to perform some operation on all of them. This is called iteration, and the Borland containers provide two distinct ways to implement it.

You are certainly familiar with the standard C method of iterating over the elements of a simple C array:

```
float Array[32];
int i;
     ⇩
     ⇩
for (i = 0; i < 32; i++)
   Array[i] = i * 7.1;
```

This method will work with Borland Array containers, as well:

```
TArrayAsVector<float> Array (32, 1);
int i;
     ⇩
     ⇩
for (i = Array.LowerBound(); i <= Array.UpperBound(); i++)
   Array[i] = i * 7.1;
```

However, Borland has come up with a couple of new methods that work, not only with Array containers, but the other containers, as well.

The first involves a *callback function*. This is a function you write, whose address you pass to a class method. When the method is ready, *it* calls *your* function. Containers use the **ForEach()** method to invoke your callback function, once for each item they contain.

Of course, you can't use just any old function for the callback. The function you supply must have a particular calling sequence, or your application will probably crash when it is invoked. The calling sequence is different for each container/data type combination, but there is a **typedef** called **IterFunc** you can use to make sure your function fills the bill. The pattern is a void function that takes two parameters: the first is a reference to the item, and the second is a pointer you can use to pass arbitrary data through the **ForEach()** method to the callback function.

To produce an equivalent iteration to the previous example, suppose you had the following callback function:

```
void MyCallback (float & Item, void * Passthru)
   {
   int i = ((TArrayAsVector<float> *)Passthru)->Find (Item);
   Item = i * 7.1;
   }
```

The **Find()** array method returns the index of the item you pass it. Here, we are expecting the passthrough parameter to be a pointer to the array itself. The following statements create the array and iterate over its elements:

```
TArrayAsVector<float> Array (32, 1);
      ⇩
      ⇩
Array.ForEach (MyCallback, &Array);
```

Incidentally, the **FirstThat()** and **LastThat()** methods mentioned in Table 6.3 also make use of a callback function.

This method of iteration is traditional in object-oriented programming circles, and certainly COBOL programmers, already used to breaking up their code at arbitrary points, have no problem with it. But most of us prefer keeping our loop code inline, and Borland has a solution for us, as well. It *sounds* more complicated than it is, so keep calm.

Borland's trick is to supply yet another set of class templates: one for each container class template. These additional class templates create *iterators*—special objects whose job it is to return items from the container. There's an iterator template for **TArrayAsVector** containers, and another for **TSArrayAsVector** containers, and so on. Fortunately, the names of the iterator classes parallel the names of the containers.

Table 6.4 lists the iterators for the high-level container classes.

Table 6.4 Iterators for the High-Level Container Classes

Class Template	Iterator Template
TMArrayAsVector	TMArrayAsVectorIterator
TArrayAsVector	TArrayAsVectorIterator
TMIArrayAsVector	TMIArrayAsVectorIterator
TIArrayAsVector	TIArrayAsVectorIterator
TMSArrayAsVector	TMSArrayAsVectorIterator
TSArrayAsVector	TSArrayAsVectorIterator
TISArrayAsVector	TISArrayAsVectorIterator
TMISArrayAsVector	TMISArrayAsVectorIterator
TMDDAssociation	TMDDAssociationIterator
TDDAssociation	TDDAssociationIterator
TMDIAssociation	TMDIAssociationIterator
TDIAssociation	TDIAssociationIterator
TMIDAssociation	TMIDAssociationIterator

continued

Table 6.4 Iterators for the High-Level Container Classes (Continued)

Class Template	Iterator Template
TIDAssociation	TIDAssociationIterator
TMIIAssociation	TMIIAssociationIterator
TIIAssociation	TIIAssociationIterator
TMBagAsVector	TMBagAsVectorIterator
TBagAsVector	TBagAsVectorIterator
TMIBagAsVector	TMIBagAsVectorIterator
TIBagAsVector	TIBagAsVectorIterator
TMDequeAsVector	TMDequeAsVectorIterator
TDequeAsVector	TDequeAsVectorIterator
TMIDequeAsVector	TMIDequeAsVectorIterator
TIDequeAsVector	TIDequeAsVectorIterator
TMDequeAsDoubleList	TMDequeAsDoubleListIterator
TDequeAsDoubleList	TDequeAsDoubleListIterator
TMIDequeDoubleList	TMIDequeDoubleListIterator
TIDequeDoubleList	TIDequeDoubleListIterator
TMDictionaryAsHashTable	TMDictionaryAsHashTableIterator
TDictionaryAsHashTable	TDictionaryAsHashTableIterator
TMIDictionaryAsHashTable	TMIDictionaryAsHashTableIterator
TIDictionaryAsHashTable	TIDictionaryAsHashTableIterator
TMQueueAsVector	TMQueueAsVectorIterator
TQueueAsVector	TQueueAsVectorIterator
TMIQueueAsVector	TMIQueueAsVectorIterator
TIQueueAsVector	TIQueueAsVectorIterator
TMQueueAsDoubleList	TMQueueAsDoubleListIterator
TQueueAsDoubleList	TQueueAsDoubleListIterator
TMIQueueAsDoubleList	TMIQueueAsDoubleListIterator
TIQueueAsDoubleList	TIQueueAsDoubleListIterator
TMSetAsVector	TMSetAsVectorIterator
TSetAsVector	TSetAsVectorIterator
TMISetAsVector	TMISetAsVectorIterator
TISetAsVector	TISetAsVectorIterator
TMStackAsVector	TMStackAsVectorIterator

continued

Table 6.4 Iterators for the High-Level Container Classes (Continued)

Class Template	Iterator Template
TStackAsVector	TStackAsVectorIterator
TMIStackAsVector	TMIStackAsVectorIterator
TIStackAsVector	TIStackAsVectorIterator
TMStackAsList	TMStackAsListIterator
TStackAsList	TStackAsListIterator
TMIStackAsList	TMIStackAsListIterator
TIStackAsList	TIStackAsListIterator

Our example loop, implemented using iterators, looks like this:

```
TArrayAsVector<float> Array (32, 1);
TArrayAsVectorIterator<float> i (Array);
     ⇩
     ⇩
while (i)
   {
   (float) i.Current = Array.Find(i) * 7.1;
   i++;
   }
```

In this case, **i** is an iterator, not an **int**. The iterator's **Current( )** method returns the object to which the iterator currently refers; this reference is changed via the **++** operator. The **--** operator is *not* supported; you can go only move forward with an iterator. You can, however, invoke the iterator's **Restart( )** method to begin again.

You might ask, if the iterator returns an object (actually a reference to an object), why did I cast it to **float**? Wasn't it already a **float**? The answer is, iterators return **const** objects. In this example, I wanted to alter the object's value so I did something you may not have realized was possible: *I cast away* **const** *ness!* Obviously, this is a technique you should only attempt when you are *certain* it is safe to do so.

Emptying Containers

There comes a time in the life of any container when it must be emptied. For some containers, this happens often! Borland containers provide several methods to allow varying degrees of contents disposal under programmer control.

The removal of one or more objects from a container is less simple a task than it seems to be simply because some containers are indirect: they contain pointers to other objects, rather than the objects themselves. The question that then arises is this: Does the container *own* the objects it contains? This question is important because it suggests the answer to the next question: If the container removes an object from itself, should it also **delete** that object?

To formalize the answers to these questions, Borland has provided the **TShouldDelete** class. You don't have to deal explicitly with this class; it is a virtual base class for all the containers, which therefore inherit **TShouldDelete**s methods and properties. Direct containers will set these properties to say, "Yes, I own all my own objects; so when I remove them, I should destroy them as well." Indirect containers, by default, do not own their objects but destroy them anyway—but you can override that, either for the entire container, or on an item-by-item basis.

To change the default for the container, supply one of the values **NoDelete**, **DefDelete**, or **Delete** to the **public** property **DeleteType**:

```
MyContainer.DeleteType = Delete;
```

The meanings of **NoDelete** and **Delete** should be obvious. **DefDelete** means that, if the container owns its objects, they should be deleted; otherwise not. By default, direct containers own their objects; indirect containers do not. You can change this value by passing TRUE or FALSE to the **OwnsElements()** method. (This method can also be used without parameters to report the current ownership status.)

That said, we can look at the various means of removing and/or destroying items from a container. First and most permanent, of course, is the destruction of the container itself. As part of any container's destructor logic, the container deletes (and, depending on its ownership and delete states, destroys) its contained items before allowing itself to be destroyed. This occurs, as with any object, whenever a container goes out of scope.

The next most thorough clearing is done under programmer control via the **Flush()** method. **Flush()**, in fact, is the method the container invokes when it is about to be destroyed, to delete all contained elements. Called from outside the destructor, **Flush()** simply removes the contained items but leaves the container in suitable shape for re-use. How much memory is freed by the operation depends on the underlying FDT. If the FDT is a Vector, only the objects themselves will be freed; the Vector remains unchanged. If the FDT is a linked or doubly linked List, the links are freed as well.

Overriding the ownership and/or delete states, the **Destroy()** method, supported only by arrays, removes *and* destroys the specified element. There are two overloaded **Destroy()** methods; one is passed the index of the item to be destroyed; the other is passed a reference to the item itself. Remember that when passing a reference after **Destroy()** has been invoked, the reference is no longer valid.

Less drastic is **Detach()**. This method is supported by indirect Arrays, Bags, Dictionaries, and Sets. For all these except Dictionaries, you pass a reference to the item you want removed. For Dictionaries, you must pass a pointer. For Arrays, there's an overloaded version that allows you to indicate the index. In all cases, there's an optional second parameter that gives you a chance to supply a **TShouldDelete** value of **NoDelete**, **DefDelete**, or **Delete**. Interestingly, the default is **NoDelete**. I'll offer a solution to this oddity in the next topic.

Dequeues do not have either **Destroy()** or **Delete()** methods. However, as mentioned previously, the **GetRight()** and **GetLeft()** methods not only retrieve items; they remove them at the same time. They do not destroy the items; presumably you retrieved them because you want them. You'll have to delete the objects explicitly if appropriate, when you're through. Queues have a **Get()** method which operates similarly.

A Container of One's Own

Borland's container class templates are very powerful. What's more powerful? A container class you design to specification!

As I see it, there are two weaknesses in Borland's container class templates. One is minor: I don't like that default parameter in the **Detach()** methods (described in the previous topic). The other is even more minor, but extremely annoying: the awkward syntax of template instantiation.

The syntax can be smoothed, of course, by the simple use of a **typedef**:

```
typedef TFloatArray TArrayAsVector<float>;
typedef TFloatArrayIterator TArrayAsVectorIterator<Float>;
```

Sure, the terms are lengthy, but at least they are free of those oddlooking angle brackets.

But, if you are creating an indirect container, you can get the same syntax smoothing *plus* "fix" that default parameter by simply deriving a new class:

```
class TFloatArray : public TIArrayAsVector<float>
   {
   public:
     TFloatArray (int upper, int lower = 0, int delta = 0)
       : TIArrayAsVector<float> (upper, lower, delta) {}
     int Detach
       (
       int loc,
       TShouldDelete::DeleteType dt = TShouldDelete::DefDelete
       );
     int Detach
       (
       const float & i,
       TShouldDelete::DeleteType dt = TShouldDelete::DefDelete
       );
   };
```

```
inline int TFloatArray::Detach
    (
    int loc,
    TShouldDelete::DeleteType dt
    )
  {
  return TIArrayAsVector<float>::Detach (loc, dt);
  }

inline int TFloatArray::Detach
    (
    const float & i,
    TShouldDelete::DeleteType dt
    )
  {
  return TIArrayAsVector<float>::Detach (i, dt);
  }
```

Of course, you can derive a new class whether the container is indirect or not. And you can also add methods unique to your needs. After all, that's what object-oriented programming is all about!

Part Overview

PART 2

Getting into Windows

If you're familiar with the linear design of typical DOS programs, the user-pampering requirements of a Windows application may seem daunting. When you hear about the API with anywhere from 400 to 1,000 functions (depending on whether you include DDEML, OLE, the Common Dialogs, and other optional components), the arcane memory management, and the GUI interface, you probably cringe.

I'm here to tell you it's not that bad. As with any programming assignment, you just have to break up the task of learning to program for Windows into small, manageable pieces.

In Part 2, we're going to start creating useful Windows applications. We'll look at what physically makes up a Windows application and how it differs from a DOS program. For our project, we'll create a full-fledged drawing application.

CHAPTER

7

Anatomy of a Windows Application

Windows has the reputation of being difficult to program. After all, you hear that it is "message-driven" (whatever *that* means) and that it has almost a thousand functions in its API (with more in each release!). And then there are those other programmers you may know who have "managed" to learn to program for Windows but found it a thoroughly dreadful, or at least draining, experience.

The problem, though, isn't Windows: It's the programmer. If you approach Windows with the idea that it's "just another graphics library," you, too, will be jolted by its apparent complexity. If you take apart a complete recording studio under the impression that it is a turntable, that, too, might overwhelm you. But once you understand the breadth of the Windows environment, you'll be better able to program in it with the proper mind-set.

But first, to enable you to actually write for this environment, we'll look at an example program: Borland C++ for Windows.

Inside Borland C++ for Windows

Borland C++ for Windows Version 4.0 (BC4) is actually *two* compilers. The full package includes both the Windows-hosted IDE (Integrated Development Environment) and equivalent DOS command-line tools (except for an editor—DOS freaks will have to use their own editors).

This is an interesting departure for Borland, whose Borland Pascal 7.0 included *two* full-blown DOS IDEs, as well as the Windows IDE. Apparently, Borland feels that the few DOS die-hards are not worth the overhead of supporting two or three versions of the IDE.

As with Borland Pascal 7.0, BC4 compilers (both Windows-hosted and command-line) will generate applications for a number of targets:

- Real-mode DOS
- 16-bit Windows
- 32-bit Windows

It's interesting to see the differences between BC4 and the previous version, 3.1. The support for 32-bit Windows (Windows NT) is new. Interestingly, support for protected-mode DOS has been omitted. It's clear that Borland sees the market for DOS apps (and tools) diminishing in favor of Windows.

A nice addition of BC4 is the rich set of target *variations*: A distinction is made between vanilla DOS apps and those that require overlays, for example. And Windows apps—which come in standard as well as EasyWin—are supplemented by Windows DLLs (Dynamic Link Libraries) and **static** libraries.

All of these targets are supported by both the Windows-hosted and DOS compilers. Therefore, even if you feel you *must* write a DOS program, you won't have to "shell to DOS" to compile it—or test it! But, although BC4 lets you compile a Windows application from the DOS command line, I advise against it. As I said earlier, you can't learn the Windows style if you aren't immersed in it. When the Borland C++ for Windows installation program asks, tell it to install just the Windows-hosted IDE. Whether you want it to include libraries for DOS as well as for Windows is between you and your client base. What consenting adults do behind closed computer-room doors is their business.

My C++ Coding Style

The success or failure of any program does not depend on whether the braces line up with the function header or are indented from it. It helps if you can be consistent, but programs can have as many different styles as prose or poetry.

As long as you're clear and precise, there is no reason why you shouldn't develop your own programming style. That said, there is the fact that BC4 *generates* a great deal of code for you, but does so using its *own* coding style. There is, therefore, some pressure to conform.

So far I've been able to fight that pressure. I like to code C and C++ using the indentation you've seen earlier in this book. The primary difference is that Borland uses "indent-after-brace" and I prefer "indent-before-brace." Consequently, you'll be able easily to distinguish code I've written myself, and that generated by the AppExpert or ClassExpert. My feeling is that if you indent differently and, as a result, you cannot understand a program indented any other way, you've been programming too long—you've *got* to get out more.

Other than indentation, I use the following coding conventions:

- There are few, if any, comments. Instead, blocks of code that might otherwise be unclear are broken into short functions whose names tell you what they do.

- I never skimp on names, either variable or procedure. I only have to type a method once, but I may have to read it many times.

- I use Hungarian Notation only when I'm in Hungary—and that's not very often!. This coding technique came from the same country that gave us the Gabor sisters, which should give you a clue right there.Putting unpronounceable letters in front of a variable does not make its meaning clearer. Pronounceable letters are even worse; they can change the meaning of the word itself. Hungarian Notation became popular with C, which performs inadequate type checking. Its use is superfluous in C++, so leave it alone. The exceptions, of course, are Windows record structures and some OWL properties and methods that were unduly influenced by those prefix freaks at Microsoft.

- In some circles, it is popular to prefix a variable with a few letters identifying the record or object of which it is a member. This originated with COBOL, where the technique enables the programmer to use a field name without fully qualifying it. In C/C++, you must fully qualify the member name, so the prefix is redundant and, like Hungarian Notation, obscures the meaning of the variable name.

- There is one traditional prefix with which I agree. **typedef**s are a special case because generally the most descriptive name for a type definition is the same I want to give a variable of that type. Borland tradition places the letter *T* in front of the **typedef** name. Please note that the C tradition of using uppercase names for **typedef**s and the same name in lowercase for the variable has not been carried forward into C++.

Choosing Compiler Options

The Options, Project command reveals a complex, multi-tiered dialog box with many, many options. Don't be overwhelmed; they are logically organized and easy to set.

The Project Options dialog box is arranged as an outline, with major categories on the left, expandable to minor categories, each of which reveals a set of options on the right. Figure 7.1 shows a typical Project Options dialog box.

To expand any of the major categories, simply click once on the plus sign of a category. To change the value of any of the minor category options, select the category and adjust the desired option on the right.

Producing Smaller .EXE Files

Programmers are on a seemingly endless mission to cut down on the size of their .EXE files. Luckily, the Project Options dialog box provides the means to relieve minor headache.

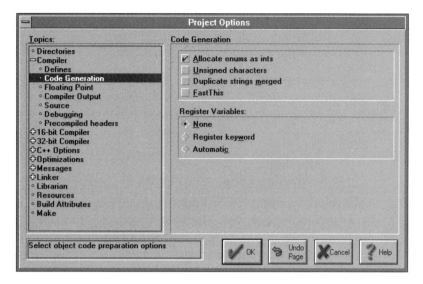

Figure 7.1 A typical Project Options dialog box.

To make your .EXE files smaller, try selecting the following options:

Compiler
    Code Generation
        Duplicate Strings Merged = Checked

This option searches your code for multiple occurences of identical strings. If it finds any, the duplicates are discarded and the additional references are made to point to the original string.

Compiler
    Code Generation
        Register Variables = Automatic

This option will speed up your .EXE as well as making it smaller. It tells the compiler to determine which, if any, variables in a function could more efficiently be stored in CPU registers than in slower RAM. Alternative: use the **register** keyword on appropriate variables (such as **for** loop indexes) and set the Register Variables option to Register Keyword. Just remember that there are a limited number of registers. Also remember that if you call another function, your register variables will have to be popped onto the stack anyway. If that function call is in a loop, it can be faster to keep the variables on the stack to begin with.

Compiler
  Code Generation
    FastThis = Checked

This option applies only to C++ objects. It causes the **this** pointer to be passed in a register instead of on the stack. This is a global setting that can (and often is) overridden on a class-by-class basis.

Compiler
  Floating Point
    No floating point = Checked

Check this option if you know your application will not perform any floating-point operations. The floating-point libraries will then be omitted from the resulting .EXE. If it turns out you were mistaken, you'll get a link error; if that happens, just uncheck this option and remake.

16-Bit Compiler
  Processor
    Instruction set = 80386

Although Windows stills runs (in "standard" mode) on 80286 CPUs, statistics show that most Windows users have 386s. The 386 instruction set includes a few instructions that do the work of several 286 instructions, so choosing this option can produce a slightly smaller (and faster) .EXE. *But*—don't use it if there's a chance your app will be run on a 286!

16-Bit Compiler
  Entry/Exit Code
    Windows Smart Callbacks, Explicit Functions Exported

Windows has to call some of your functions—your Window procedures, for example—directly. These are called *callback* functions. For callbacks to succeed, Windows needs special code to be inserted at the beginning of the functions it calls.

By default, BC4 places this code in front of *all* far functions. That means you don't have to explicitly export anything, but it's wasteful. If you can remember to include the **_export** keyword with the signature of any callback function, you can save .EXE size by choosing Windows Smart Callbacks, Explicit Functions Exported.

Incidentally, smart callbacks themselves save time and programmer effort by eliminating the need for the **MakeProcInstance()** function calls required by Microsoft compilers.

Optimizations
    Specific
        Common subexpressions = Optimize globally

This option locates duplicate subexpressions and saves the results, re-using them afterwards. This saves both time and space.

A subexpression is an expression that is part of another expression. For example, in the assignments

```
a = 17 * (b + 3);
c = (b + 3) / 4;
```

b + 3 is a subexpression. Furthermore, this subexpression is used twice.

Optimization
    Size
        All options = Checked

Among these optimizations, the most interesting is "Windows prolog/ epilog." This optimization suppresses the generation of a 2-instruction sequence otherwise inserted into exported functions. The sequence isn't needed any more; it was required by real-mode Windows (version 3.0 and earlier). However, the sequence *is* used by some debuggers. It is safe to leave it out of later release versions.

Optimization
    Speed
        Inline intrinsic functions = *not* Checked

Although getting the compiler to insert **inline** versions of **strcpy()** or **memset()** can save some execution time, the resulting .EXE is slightly larger. Rather than using a project-wide compiler switch, consider using this optimization on a case-by-case basis. For example, suppose that you had a loop in which **strcpy()** is called many, many times. For that specific instance, it might help to put **strcpy() inline**. So, preceed the loop with the compiler directive:

```
#pragma intrinsic strcpy
```

After the loop, you can return things to normal:

```
#pragma intrinsic -strcpy
```

Optimization
  Speed
    Invariant code motion = Checked

There's no harm in checking this option, even though I would *hope* it could have no effect on your code. Suppose you've written the following sequence:

```
for (i = 0; i < 10; i++)
  {
  a = 17;
  b[i] = a;
  }
```

With this optimization activated, the compiler would move the *a = 17* statement out of the loop . . . as *you* should have done.

Optimization
  Speed
    Induction variables = Checked

This optimization speeds up indexing in loops by changing index references to pointer references. However, doing so can *also* make your .EXE smaller, because indexing often requires multiplication at the machine-code level, while pointers can simply be incremented.

Linker
  General
    Include debug information = *not* Checked

"Debug information" means your application's entire symbol table, plus line number information and other stuff. Including this in a .EXE can make the file many times bigger. Of course, while you are debugging an application, you'll *want* the debugging information around.

BC4 as a Windows Application

Since a good Windows application looks and acts like other Windows applications, it stands to reason that you must be familiar with many existing Windows applications before you can write one of your own. Let's look at the application closest at hand: Borland C++ for Windows.

Most Windows apps are file oriented, and BC4 is no exception. It has a File menu, with the standard commands New, Open, Save, and so on.

However, BC4 has an aesthetic flaw (which it shares with Visual C++): Its *primary* file is the project file, yet it's not the file managed by the File menu! Instead, there's a separate Project menu for this purpose.

Some Windows apps only allow a view of one file at a time (Single Document Interface, or SDI), and others allow several views of a single document, or access to many documents at once (Mutliple Document Interface, or MDI). BC4 is an MDI application. MDI apps always have a Window menu that provides control (cascading, tiling, and so on) of the document windows (views).

When BC4 is performing a time-consuming operation, such as a compile, it internally breaks up that operation so that other applications can continue to process. To be honest, this cooperation isn't quite what I'd hoped for; smaller pieces would have allowed *meaningful* use of other apps while a compile takes place.

Context-sensitive help is well-implemented. Placing the cursor on any keyword and tapping the F1 key brings up the Windows Help Engine, displaying the topic appropriate to that keyword.

Other aspects of the environment work well together. For example, after a compile, double-clicking on an error or warning message will cause BC4 to locate the file and line that caused the message, make that window the active view, and set the cursor to the very word that's at fault.

As you design your own Windows apps, always be aware of how other applications handled similar situations. If you disapprove of a technique, then don't use it; but never be different just to be different. Users are always more comfortable with the safe and familiar; give it to them.

A Programmer's-Eye View of Windows

As a Windows user, you've seen applications share the screen and other system resources. You've seen graphics co-exist with text, and you've made use of the Clipboard and perhaps even embedded or linked objects. Here's how it all works . . . in a nutshell.

Ten Things You Should Know About a Windows Application

The fact that Windows is an entire operating environment affects every aspect of a Windows app—even the format of its executable file. Knowing the differences in the basic structure of Windows apps versus DOS programs is essential to the completion of a successful Windows project.

1. A Windows executable (.EXE) file is not like a DOS .EXE file. In fact, a Windows .EXE file *contains* a DOS .EXE file called a *stub program.* The usual stub program simply displays a one-line message: "This program requires Microsoft Windows." Only if you start the program from Windows will the Windows part of the .EXE file run.

2. In addition to machine code, a Windows .EXE file contains various resources: images of dialog boxes, pictures, icons, menus, and so on. You have to describe those things in a non-procedural step, and use a special linker that attaches them to the .EXE. (The Borland C++ built-in linker does this automatically.)

3. A traditional C program begins execution with the first line of code of the **main( )** function. Windows applications begin instead with a function called **WinMain( )**. OWL supplies a **WinMain( )** for you, which calls a function you provide called **OwlMain( )**. Neither **WinMain( )** nor **OwlMain( )** automatically creates a window!

4. A DOS program moves under its own thrust; if it wants user input, it must loop until a key is pressed. A Windows application moves only in response to messages, which may come from the keyboard, the mouse, or the system itself.

5. A DOS program is written linearly, that is, from top to bottom. Even if it has been broken into many procedures, its main program basically goes from initialize, through process, to terminate. A Windows app is entirely responsive to messages that may arrive in any order. Mostly the messages come in response to user action, such as the push of a button or selection of a menu command.

6. The core of a Windows application is the message dispatcher, also known as the message loop. (In an OWL application, the message loop is hidden in the *TApplication* class, but it's there, nevertheless.) The body of a Windows application is a message switch; it is from there that all procedures are called. (The message switch is also hidden in OWL; messages result in various event handlers being invoked.) The message switch is usually called a *window procedure.* Even in a non-object-oriented Windows app, you can think of a window procedure as a set of methods that define the window object.

7. The outer area of a Windows window is handled automatically. This is called the non-client area, and includes the caption bar, menu, minimize and maximize buttons, and the size-adjusting frame. Your program will receive messages when these pieces are manipulated, but these messages are usually ignored. Thus the user

interface part—the menu's dropping down, items being high-lighted—is all done for you by Windows.

8. Each individual visual component is called a *child window* or *control.* Generally, you can use the two terms interchangeably; if there is a difference, it is that a control is a child window that sends notification messages back to its parent. While each child window has its own window procedure, Windows comes with a set of predefined controls that will satisfy 90 percent of your user interface needs. The predefined controls for Windows 3.1 are the static text, edit box, list box, combo box, check box, radio button, pushbutton, and scroll bar.

9. A window is much like an object. Its window procedure defines the methods that respond to the various messages it receives. It can have properties, and you can derive a new window type from an old one that inherits some or all of the ancestor's methods. For this reason, OWL object classes can be made to represent various window types very cleanly.

10. Windows applications are meant to run concurrently, but there is no aspect of the Windows 3.1 environment that can enforce this. You could write a linear application in the Windows environment that initialized, processed for an hour, then terminated, but it wouldn't be a "true" Windows application because it wouldn't co-operate with the other applications in sharing the system resources. This sharing takes place in between the processing of the various messages. There are ways to share the system if processing a particular message is expected to take an unreasonable amount of time, but you'll have to implement them deliberately. The processing of most messages doesn't take that long, anyway.

Writing "Good" Windows Applications versus "Bad" Windows Applications

Of all the material to cover in a Windows programming book, probably the most important point to stress is how vital it is for you to adhere to the accepted style of a Windows application.

In the old days of programming, whether on mainframes or PCs, every application was a new adventure. When starting the design, you'd ask yourself, "What is the best way I can present control of this application's functions to the user?" Consistency in user interface was sometimes stressed within companies, but never beyond that: witness Lotus' lawsuits against competing spreadsheets for copying 1-2-3's "look and feel."

Unfortunately, *no one* benefited from this (least of all Lotus, whose attempts at twisting the Windows application style to their own image have not been applauded by reviewers). The biggest sufferers were the users, who had to learn new rules for each program they operated. Thus, computers got the reputation of being "hard to use." *Computers* aren't hard to use—you just flip a switch and type. It was never computers that were hard to use, it was computer *programs*; and it was non-standard user interfaces that were largely to blame.

Some people who develop Windows applications don't understand what Windows really means. To them, it's just a graphics library like a dozen others that are available for enhancing DOS programs. Or, worse, it's just a *buzzword* that will help sell more copies of their products! It saddens me to think of the number of times I've been told by marketing departments that following the Windows style "doesn't matter" because "people will not be running our program at the same time as any others." If that is true, *why program for Windows at all?*

The strength of Windows does not come from its user interface or its multi-billion-dollar parentage. And it *certainly* does not come from its bug-free, lightning-like execution! Compared to text-mode DOS, Windows still crawls. But *user* speed is more important than screen speed, and Windows allows a user to accomplish a given job in a fraction of the time required by a stand-alone DOS application. Windows' strength comes primarily from its acceptance as an environment in which many applications can run together, sharing functions and information so that they are much more powerful *and useful* than any application could ever be alone.

Given, then, that the Windows environment is primarily one of multi-tasking, it is important that a new Windows application follow the style of the other programs in that environment, just as it is important that a newcomer to a social gathering follow the same style of dress as the other attendees. Wearing a tuxedo to a bowling tournament or tank-top and cut-offs to a New Year's Eve gala may make a statement, but usually that statement is, "I don't fit in here—and I don't care." Fitting in may not be your preference, but, and I can't stress this enough, we are all creatures of habit, and Windows users have formed a doozy of a habit with all the Windows programs now in use!

The best way to become familiar with Windows applications—which will help you to write good Windows apps—is to *use* them. All the time. Constantly. Never, *never* go to DOS if you can help it. Your AUTOEXEC.BAT file should start Windows, and you should remove the DOS icon from Program Manager. If you have a DOS program you *must* run because you don't have a Windows replacement for it, fine; but create a PIF for it. Don't let yourself even *look* at an archaic C> prompt. Especially, this means:

- Use the File Manager for *all* your file management needs. The speed problems that plagued it in the past have been fixed in Windows 3.1; even network accesses are now agile. Use drag-and-drop for copying and moving files. Use the online help! You'll be surprised how easy it is to copy, move, rename, change attributes, manage directories, and so on, when you don't have to type filenames.

- Set up the Program Manager groups to suit *your* way of working. *Don't* accept the defaults that Windows Setup left you with. Better yet, get *Norton Desktop for Windows* (or another Windows shell) that allows you to have *nested* program groups. I *had* to do this; nested projects is the way *I* work. (I would be happy to deal with my problems one at a time if they would only line up!)

- Purge your old DOS applications from your hard disk, bundle up the original disks and manuals, and donate them to the church of a religion you don't like. Then take a deep breath and smile. Today is the first day of the rest of your programming life.

Learning Windows Terminology

References to CRTs, modems, and mouse pads would have brought blank stares from a 1950s programmer. Likewise, the Windows environment brings new terminology. Learning it now will make programming easier.

Do you know the name for the little groove under your nose? As the "user" of a human body, you don't need to. But, if you became a plastic surgeon, it would be an important term to learn.

As a Windows user, you've been running Windows apps for some time, probably without knowing the proper terminology for the things you've been manipulating. Figure 7.2 shows a typical Windows app, Write.

Most main application windows have sizable borders, as Write does. Such a border allows the application to be resized by placing the mouse cursor on the border and then dragging that border to the desired position. Likewise, the entire window can be dragged by its *caption bar* to any location on screen.

The *System-menu* button is used to drop down the System menu. It is this menu that offers keyboard commands to move, resize, minimize, maximize, or close the window. System menu buttons are also found

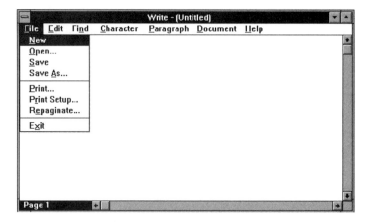

Figure 7.2 A typical Windows application.

on some dialog boxes and on the document windows of MDI apps (more on them in a moment).

For mouse users—that is, most of us—the *minimize button* is a more direct way to make the app show itself as an icon. Although most apps don't do anything while in icon form, this is not a requirement. Some apps continue background processing even while iconized.

To make the app take up the entire screen, click on the *maximize button*. When maximized, this button changes to one pointing both up and down; it is then called the *restore button*. Restoring a window returns the window to its previous size and placement.

Selecting a menu bar item either through the *speed key* or by clicking on it with the mouse, results in a subsidiary menu appearing. Even though the menu appears to drop down from the menu bar, tradition calls it a *popup menu*. Any item that produces an action, rather than a subsidiary menu, is called a *command*.

You have probably noticed that one letter on each of the items in the *menu bar* is underlined. This letter is called the *hot key* or *speed key*, depending on whose documentation you're reading. Please do *not* confuse this with the *accelerator key*, which may also exist and produces similar results through different means.

Scroll bars, when they appear, show up on the right and/or bottom of the window. The little button in the middle of a scroll bar is called the *thumb*. Every part of a scroll bar is functional. The up and down (or left and right) buttons call for a movement of one "line" (whatever that means to that application). Clicking on the broad area between the up or down buttons and the thumb results in a "page up" or "page down" action. Dragging the thumb directly can position the view to that relative part of the document.

The menu bar, scroll bars, and window border surround the *client area.* This is the part of the window you, as programmer, control. Windows provides management for all the other parts, but the client area is yours. You'll have to draw on it and receive user input through it.

That could be a daunting task, but Windows simplifies that, too. Most user input is facilitated by *dialog boxes,* windows with *controls* through which users interact with your application. Figure 7.3 shows a typical dialog box.

Dialog boxes usually do *not* have sizable borders. The style of the border in Figure 7.3 is called "dialog border."

You do not have to explicitly draw a dialog box. Instead, you place *child windows*—also called *controls*—in specific places. Each software control has a consistent response to user interaction, just like the mechanical controls on a tape deck or toaster. Windows comes with a generous set of predefined controls (called *standard* controls), and you can buy or write more controls (called *custom* controls).

Understanding Windows Multitasking

Everyone knows that Windows allows several applications to run at the same time. How does this happen without their treading on each other's toes?

The first thing you have to understand is that Windows is a cooperative multitasking environment. By comparison, DOS is *not* a multitasking environment at all. Sure, it's possible to get a DOS TSR to work while a foreground program is executing, but DOS didn't help—all the work is being done by the TSR.

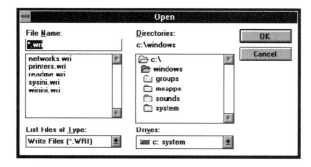

Figure 7.3 A typical dialog box.

Windows, on the other hand, provides an environment *friendly* to multitasking. Each application *expects* to share the system with others. A Windows application never writes directly to the screen, for instance, as many DOS apps do. Instead, a Windows app asks for a *device context* and draws (or writes) on that. Windows takes care of transferring the drawing from the device context to the application's client area. In fact, the purpose of the majority of functions in the Windows API is to support this sharing of system resources.

The sharing of time is the trickiest part. OS/2, another multitasking operating system, is called "pre-emptive" because the operating system itself makes sure no application hogs the machine: It *preempts* each app to allow the next app time to execute. The *time slices* are small, so OS/2 apps *seem* to run simultaneously.

Windows multitasking relies on the applications themselves to make multitasking work. Each application must be written so that it doesn't try to do too much at one shot, or other applications will not get their share of processing time. Although this puts the burden of multitasking on the programmer, it is not a heavy burden. It is true, through, that cooperative multitasking presents a somewhat jerky look to the user. One app will paint itself, for example, before the next one does. A file open operation may hold up the clock for a few seconds. Still, more CPU time is spent executing applications, rather than context-switching.

What Is a Window, Anyway?

When I start an application, sure—there's the application window. What's so special about that? Isn't it just like programming for a small screen?

It's important to realize that, when you see a main application window, you are *not* looking at a tiny monitor. You are looking at a *window*, which may stand alone, but which also may consist of dozens or even hundreds of child windows. It is the encapsulation of each of these windows, each with its own purpose and appearance, that makes Windows programming possible.

Many aspects of Windows programming will remind you of object-oriented programming. That's because the designers of Windows had studied and liked object-oriented techniques. If Microsoft had had a C++ compiler at the time, I'm sure they'd have used it. But, while C++ makes it *easy* to write an object-oriented program, it isn't the only way.

So, using object-oriented terminology, Windows apps wait for an *event* to wake them up: window creation, a user keystroke or mouse movement, or a timer tick are all events that a Windows app's main window may notice.

In fact, *all* windows are "objects"—not C++ objects, but objects just the same. They respond to events, have methods, and possess properties. Since C is *not* C++, though, the only way to access these items is by sending the window a *message*.

As I mentioned earlier, every window has a *window procedure*. This is a C function that processes all the messages a window might get. In object-oriented terms, all windows are descended from an abstract window; to implement this in C, any message a specific window doesn't handle is passed on to the abstract window's window procedure. This is done by calling **DefWindowProc( )**.

Note that Windows itself calls the window procedure; a window procedure is never called directly by the application owning the window. Thus, the window procedure is called a *callback* function and must be *exported* so that Windows can properly switch tasks, from the Windows kernel to the application.

So, writing a Windows app really means writing the window procedure for the application's main window, as well as window procedures for any other custom child windows. In designing a window procedure, you decide to what messages you'll respond and how. Your response to the **WM_PAINT** message, for example, will determine how your window will look, while its response to **WM_CHAR** will determine how it will respond to character keystrokes. There are nearly 300 messages a window can receive (not including programmer-defined ones!), but most of them can safely be passed on to **DefWindowProc( )**.

The biggest difference, then, between a Windows app and a DOS program is that the Windows app's "rest" state has it waiting passively for a message, rather than frantically checking the keyboard buffer for another keystroke. To be more precise, the application's *windows* each do this waiting—and they do it asynchronously of each other. Each window should communicate with the others entirely via messages. Robust Windows apps have few global variables, and *never* use them for inter-window communication.

While this is a difference between Windows apps and DOS apps, it is a *similarity* between Windows apps and object-oriented C++ programs!

Communicating with a Window

If a window is a completely encapsulated entity, how can you get through to it to send a message?

The answer is that every window has a handle—a 16-bit (32-bits in Windows NT) value that uniquely identifies that window. Windows re-uses handles, so they are unique only for the lifetime of the window. Still, that's good enough to send messages; you can think of the window's handle as its address (in the message sense, not the pointer sense).

So what is a message? In a practical sense, it is just a structure, composed of the destination window handle, a numeric message identifier, a couple of message-specific parameters, and a little more.

The message identifiers are listed in WINDOWS.H as **#define**s: **WM_CREATE**, **WM_PAINT**, **WM_DESTROY** and so on. The meanings of the two parameters depend on the message being sent, so you pretty much have to have access to documentation. BC4's online help contains this information. Interpreting the parameters in light of the message to which they apply is called *message cracking*.

Messages can be sent to a window either immediately, or placed into a queue. The **PostMessage( )** function places the message into the application's queue. By default, the queue only holds 16 messages. It can be made bigger, but most messages are sent immediately via the **SendMessage( )** function. **SendMessage( )** also allows the window procedure to return a value, making **SendMessage( )** the only way to query a window's properties.

Although messages can only be sent *to* a window, the queue is usually managed by the application itself. That is, the app examines the queue for messages and, if it finds any, dispatches those messages to the appropriate window. (Remember, an application only has one main window, but that main window may have hundreds of child windows.)

That would be quite a job if you had to program it yourself, but the work has all been done and is wrapped up in four or five API functions you call in a cookbook manner.

We'll see all this in the next section, where we'll use Borland C++ for Windows to actually create a simple, traditional C Windows app.

Hello World—Taking the First Steps into Windows Programming

To put things in perspective, we're going to create a few "Hello, World" applications. "Hello, World" is, of course, the traditional first program of all C students (as well as those learning pretty much any other PC-based language). By keeping to a simple and constant application function, we can pay attention to the mechanics of implementing that function.

Writing "Hello, World" in Traditional C/Windows API

The original Windows "Hello, World" application, as presented in Petzold's classic **Programming Windows**, *ran 2 pages long. Surprise: we can make it* **bigger!**

The classic "Hello, World" app in C, using the Windows API, is actually a bad example of a Windows app. Written properly, it should function as a usable skeleton.

To create the first "Hello, World" project, start BC4 and choose Project, New Project to display the New Project dialog box. Fill in the dialog box as shown in Figure 7.4 (allowing for your own directory structure, of course).

Let's consider each of these fields. First, of course, is Project Path and Name. If you like, you can use the Browse button to bring up another dialog box that will help you select a subdirectory for your project. Note that BC4 will happily *create* the subdirectory for you, if it doesn't exist. This is a feature we've all wished for, for a long time.

The next field, Target Name, fills in automatically when you type in the name of your project. You can override this name, if you prefer. But I find that having the project share a name with its subdirectory makes the project easier to find on a crowded hard disk.

The Target Type field should, of course, be set to Application (.exe). When you do so, the Standard Libraries check boxes will default to those appropriate for an ObjectWindows application, which this version of

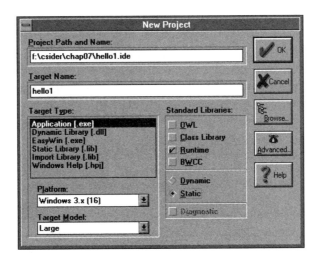

Figure 7.4 The New Project dialog box.

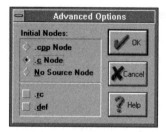

Figure 7.5 Use this dialog box to select the default file creation type.

"Hello, World" is *not.* So we have to uncheck as shown: Only the Runtime check box should be checked. And there's no reason to require the presence of a DLL to allow this application to run, so we also choose the Static option.

The platform, for me, is Windows 3.x (16). If you are running Windows NT, you can go ahead and choose Win32. And I've chosen the Large memory model, for the reasons outlined in Chapter 1.

Before clicking on the OK button, click on Advanced to display the Advanced Options dialog box, shown in Figure 7.5

Since traditional Windows apps are written in C, not C++, you'll want to choose the .c Node option, which means that new source code files will be created for C, not C++. By unchecking .rc and .def, we tell BC4 not to create default resource and module definition files for us. (A useful application would need them, but "Hello, World" does not.)

In the Advanced Options dialog box, click on OK to return to the New Project dialog box. Then, click on OK to generate the HELLO1 project. The project file itself is named HELLO1.IDE. The project file replaces the old-fashioned MAKE files we used to have to contend with. It should look like the one in Figure 7.6.

With the press of a couple of buttons, we've been given a C source file and a project. And, yet, if we use the File Manager to peek into this directory, we'll find it is empty. The files have been added to the project, but they haven't been saved to hard disk yet—so they haven't been added to the *directory*.

Figure 7.6 The HELLO1 project.

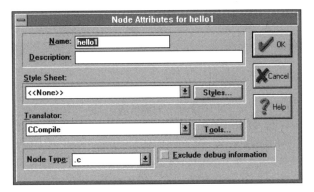

Figure 7.7 Use the Edit Node Attributes dialog box to rename your project files.

Now, it's personal preference—but I don't like to have a *source* file named after the project. I break projects up into several files, and I find it easier to find things if the names are consistent. So my next step (and yours, too, if you want to follow along) is to rename HELLO1.C to MAIN.C. To do this, click with the *right* mouse button on HELLO1.C, and select Edit Node Attributes from the floating "object menu." The resulting dialog box can be seen in Figure 7.7.

Change *hello1* to *main* and click on OK. The dialog box will close, and in the Project window, HELLO1.C will change to MAIN.C.

Double-clicking on MAIN.C is the way to open a window on this source code. The window is a standard edit window, with some enhancements—for example, most syntactic elements of C and C++ are displayed in different colors.

Make the Windows Editors Work for You!

I've heard a lot of people complain about editing source code in Windows, and, without exception, the complaints have come from people whose primary gripe is that Windows edit boxes don't act like Brief, or some other DOS-mode editor.

These people have never given much thought how to edit effectively in the Windows environment. The primary tool, after the keyboard, is the Clipboard. Once you get used to thinking ahead, copying text into the Clipboard, and then pasting it appropriately, you'll find your old DOS-mode editor is hardly missed. Use the Macro Recorder to automate keystrokes, and for really complex automation, use Word for Windows or Visual Basic to generate code and pop it into the Clipboard for you—then paste it into your BC4 app.

The first three lines in MAIN.C should read as follows:

```
#define STRICT
#include <windows.h>
#include "main.h"
```

The first line **#define**s **STRICT**. The **#define** is used by WINDOWS.H, which is **#include**d in the next line. **STRICT** causes WINDOWS.H to be less forgiving of sloppy coding than it once was. Using **STRICT** does cause a couple of annoying errors, but in general it results in syntax checking *almost* as powerful as C++'s.

The inclusion of MAIN.H accesses the header file for the project. Although there may still be an old C programmer out there who eschews function prototypes, the rest of us have discovered that using them eliminates errors caused by faulty parameter lists.

The next three lines provide for three globals needed by the project:

```
extern HINSTANCE Instance = 0;
extern HWND MainWindow = 0;
extern char AppName[] = "Hello";
```

I *hate* globals—but I'm willing to use these three without guilt, because they are set during program initialization and never again, although they are referenced throughout the code. **Instance** will contain the instance handle passed to the application in **WinMain()**. **MainWindow** will hold the handle to the application's main window. And **AppName** provides the string by which this application (and the main window class) will be called.

Next we come to the function **WinMain()**. A function by this name is required by every C language Windows application, just as the function **main()** is required by every C language DOS program. In Petzold's original, the various tasks **WinMain()** had to accomplish were all strung out inline. I prefer more structured code, both for aesthetic and practical reasons; there are performance benefits to shunting as much of the initialization code as possible into a separate code module (as we'll see shortly).

Here's my **WinMain()**:

```
#pragma argsused
int PASCAL WinMain
    (
    HINSTANCE ThisInstance,
    HINSTANCE PrevInstance,
    LPSTR CmdLine,
```

```
    int CmdShow
    )
{
MSG Message;

Instance = ThisInstance;
if (! PrevInstance)
   if (! InitApplication ())
      return 0;

MainWindow = InitInstance (CmdShow);
if (! MainWindow)
   return 0;

while (GetMessage (&Message, NULL, 0,0))
   {
   TranslateMessage (&Message);
   DispatchMessage (&Message);
   }

return Message.wParam;

}
```

The **#pragma argsused** directive tells BC4 to consider that the function parameters have all been referenced, even if they have not. This trick supresses a warning message that one or more of the parameters has not been used. Such a warning would not be useful, since we cannot shorten the function signature anyway. It must be just as it is.

The **ThisInstance** parameter is a handle to the application's own instance. In a typical application, such as might be derived from this skeleton, the instance handle would be referenced often; so we save it—in the **Instance** global.

The **PrevInstance** handle points to a *previous* copy of the application that may already be running. If this is the first copy, **PrevInstance** will be zero (FALSE) and thus can be used in a test to determine if first-copy processing should take place. That processing is done by **InitApplication()**, which returns TRUE if it succeeds.

Each running copy of the application is called an "instance" (which **ThisInstance** is a handle to). Each instance has its own initialization, accomplished by **InitInstance()**. This function returns a handle to the main window, if it was successful in creating one.

The next block of code implements the message loop. This is a simplified message loop; an MDI application, or one with floating toolboxes or status boxes, would have a slightly more complex message loop.

The loop retrieves the next message from the queue, possibly translates keydown and keyup messages into character messages, and dispatches the message to the appropriate window's window procedure. The message loop runs until a **WM_QUIT** message is retreived; at that time the **wParam** value sent with the message is made the application's return value, and the application terminates.

Obviously the application and instance initialization functions are doing something important, but what you've just seen is the essence of a windows application. The rest is, quite literally, "window" dressing!

I said that **InitInstance()** would create and return the handle to a main window. I also said earlier that all windows must have a window procedure. Here's HELLO1's window procedure:

```
LRESULT _export FAR PASCAL WndProc
    (
    HWND Window,
    UINT Msg,
    WPARAM wParam,
    LPARAM lParam
    )
{
LRESULT Result = 0;
switch (Msg)
    {
    case WM_DESTROY:
       PostQuitMessage (0);
       break;
    default:
       Result = DefWindowProc (Window, Msg, wParam, lParam);
    }
return Result;
}
```

Don't miss the **_export** keyword in the function's signature. This tells the compiler (and, eventually, the linker) that this function will be called directly by Windows.

This is, literally, as simple as a main window's procedure can get. The four parameters are the four most-often used components of any message. **Msg** is actually the message code. The window procedure is often expected to return a value—which is usually zero—so **Result** is initialized to that value.

The only message this window procedure handles explicitly is **WM_DESTROY**. This message will be received just before the main window is deleted from the system, after it's been closed. The application window *must* call **PostQuitMessage()** in response to this message, otherwise the message loop in **WinMain()** will never get the WM_QUIT message, and will therefore never fall out of the loop. The application would *look* like it had terminated, but it would still be in memory—not an attractive prospect.

For the rest of the nearly 300 windows messages, we just want to provide default processing. That's what **DefWindowProc()** is for. We pass the message components on to it, and it gives back a new value for **Result**, which we then return to *our* caller.

Now we can get back to the initialization code. This goes in a code module called INIT.C. But, wait—there's no such module in our project! How can we add it?

It's easy as crashing OS/2. Just click on HELLO1.EXE in the Project window with the *right* button and select Add Node. When the Add To Project List dialog box appears, just type INIT.C and click on OK. Then, to edit the file, double-click on the new INIT.C entry in the Project window.

The first few lines of INIT.C bring in the header files, and define a **static** structure used to register the main window class:

```
#define STRICT
#include <windows.h>
#include "main.h"

static WNDCLASS WndClass =
  {
  CS_HREDRAW | CS_VREDRAW,
  WndProc,
  0,
  GWW_EXTRA,
  0,
  NULL,
  NULL,
  COLOR_WINDOW + 1,
  NULL,
  AppName
  };
```

The **WndClass** structure will be passed to the **RegisterClass()** function in **InitApplication()**. Don't confuse **RegisterClass()** with C++ object classes. Windows was written in C, but with many object-oriented concepts. These concepts make it easy to map Windows elements to objects, but they also make the issue somewhat confusing: Windows objects (windows, brushes, memory blocks) are not identical to ObjectWindows objects, although there are many parallels. But you'll have to keep the distinction in mind.

InitApplication() has one job: performing the application initialization that an needs to be done just once, when the *first* copy (instance) of the application is started. Usually there is just one task to that job: "registering" the window class of the main window (if there were additional window classes unique to this application, they would also be registered at this time):

```
BOOL FAR PASCAL InitApplication (void)
   {
   WndClass.hInstance    = Instance;
   WndClass.hIcon        = LoadIcon (NULL, IDI_APPLICATION);
   WndClass.hCursor      = LoadCursor (NULL, IDC_ARROW);
   return (RegisterClass (&WndClass) ! = 0);
   }
```

By making **WndClass** a **static** structure, we let the compiler do most of the work—faster than requiring the fields to be set at runtime. The only fields that have to be set programmatically are **hInstance**, which isn't *known* until runtime, and the icon and cursor handles, which must be retrieved from the executable's resource pool.

RegisterClass() returns a non-zero value if it succeeds, so it's easy to use that value to return **TRUE** or **FALSE** to the caller (**WinMain()**).

Normally the instance initialization done for each copy of the app consists of creating and displaying the main window—a window of the class registered in **InitApplication()**. This initialization is performed in the **InitInstance()** function:

```
HWND FAR PASCAL InitInstance (int CmdShow)
   {
   HWND Window = CreateWindow
      (
      AppName,                       // Window class name
      "Hello, World, from Windows!", // Window caption
      WS_OVERLAPPEDWINDOW,           // Window style: top app
      CW_USEDEFAULT,                 // Initial x position
      CW_USEDEFAULT,                 // Initial y position
      CW_USEDEFAULT,                 // Initial x size (width)
      CW_USEDEFAULT,                 // Initial y size (height)
      NULL,                          // Parent window handle
      NULL,                          // Window menu handle
      Instance,                      // Application instance
      NULL                           // lParam for WM_CREATE
      );
```

```
if (Window)
  {
  ShowWindow (Window, CmdShow);
  UpdateWindow (Window);
  }
return Window;
}
```

There are three crucial steps to creating and displaying a registered window. First, **CreateWindow()** is called. This will create the window, but not show it. That's done by **ShowWindow()**; the **CmdShow** parameter tells *how* it should be shown: normal, maximized, minimized (as an icon) or even hidden, which doesn't truly "show" it at all. The third step, **UpdateWindow()**, is less crucial than the first two. If you omit it, the window will still be painted—eventually, but not until all the other applications have cleared their message queues. **UpdateWindow()** forces the window to be painted *now*.

You can see the string "Hello, World, from Windows!" as the second parameter to **CreateWindow()**. For this first experiment, that will be our app's only "output."

The last source file needed for now is MAIN.H. To add MAIN.H to the project, select MAIN.C, click the *right* mouse button, and select Add Node. Type MAIN.H and click on OK. Once the file has been added to the project, you can open an edit window on it as you did before, by double-clicking on the filename. You should enter the following:

```
extern HINSTANCE Instance;
extern HWND MainWindow;
extern char AppName[];

#define GWW_EXTRA 0

// MAIN.C
LRESULT _export FAR PASCAL WndProc
    (
    HWND Window,
    UINT Msg,
    WPARAM wParam,
    LPARAM lParam
    );

// INIT.C
BOOL FAR PASCAL InitApplication (void);
HWND FAR PASCAL InitInstance (int CmdShow);

// PAINT.C
```

I like to include comments indicating in which definition files the bodies of the functions listed reside.

Don't forget the shortcut of selecting the function signatures from the definition files, copying them into the Clipboard, and pasting them in the declaration (header) file. That gives you a function prototype with no typing (and no *typos*), other than the semi-colon that must be added to the end of each.

Now you're ready to compile and test. Another shortcut: use the Debug, Run command. This will compile and link your application, and then run it if the compile and link were successful.

If they were not, the errors will appear in an Output window. If there are any warnings, they'll appear there as well (in addition to merely informative messages). In fact, there will be two warnings. The first is "Warning INIT.C 14: Nonportable pointer conversion." If you double-click on the warning, BC4 will jump you directly to the cause of the warning

```
COLOR_WINDOW + 1,
```

which is in the definition of **WndClass**.

Unfortunately, this is a warning you'll just have to live with. The problem is that this particular field in **WndClass** is declared to be a handle to a brush, but Windows was written to allow another use. By specifying **COLOR_WINDOW + 1**, we tell Windows to use the *standard* brush in the color the user has already defined as appropriate to window backgrounds. You might think we could simply cast the value to an HBRUSH, but doing so alters the value and gives an invalid brush handle to Windows.

In fact the only way to avoid the warning is to either create a specific brush—wasteful of system resources—or to remove the **STRICT #define**. **STRICT** is too helpful, overall, to let go; so I just tolerate the warning.

The second warning is easier to ignore: "Linker Warning: No module definition file specified: using defaults." We could write a module definition file—and we will, later—but for now the defaults are adequate.

Adding Client-Area Painting

In a way, we've cheated. Sure, we placed an application onscreen with a caption that says "Hello, World" but the caption is part of the Windows presentation, not the application itself. To be fair, we really should write the "Hello" string in the application's client area. Here's how.

Shock number one for programmers writing their first Windows app: stuff you write (or draw) onscreen doesn't stay there. If an app writes in its client area, is then covered by another app, and then uncovered, the client area will not be restored automatically. Each application must, at all times, retain enough information to repaint its client area.

This requires a change in drawing logic. In a DOS app, when you want to place some text on the screen, you just do it. But, in most Windows apps, you instead add to the stockpile of drawing instructions, and then tell the app to paint itself. Thus the *repaint* logic is one and the same with the original *paint* logic.

Painting is done in response to the **WM_PAINT** message, so a minor change must be made to the window procedure:

```
LRESULT _export FAR PASCAL WndProc
    (
    HWND Window,
    UINT Msg,
    WPARAM wParam,
    LPARAM lParam
    )
    {
    LRESULT Result = 0;
    switch (Msg)
        {
        case WM_PAINT:
            OnPaint (Window);
            break;
        case WM_DESTROY:
            PostQuitMessage (0);
            break;
        default:
            Result = DefWindowProc (Window, Msg, wParam, lParam);
        }
    return Result;
    }
```

The **OnPaint()** function is kept in a new module, PAINT.C:

```
#define STRICT
#include <windows.h>
#include "main.h"

void far pascal OnPaint (HWND Window)
    {
    PAINTSTRUCT ps;
    HDC dc = BeginPaint (Window, &ps);
```

```
OnDraw (Window, dc);
EndPaint (Window, &ps);
}
```

As you can see, **OnPaint()** does not, itself, actually do any drawing. Rather, it performs required housekeeping: getting a handle to a device context from the **BeginPaint()** function, and later returning it via **EndPaint()**. By separating this task from the drawing itself, we leave open the possibility of calling **OnDraw()** in another context—drawing to the printer, for example.

OnDraw() is simplicity itself, since the contents of this app's client area never changes:

```
#pragma argsused
void far pascal OnDraw (HWND Window, HDC dc)
  {
  TextOut (dc, 0, 0, "Hello, World!", 13);
  }
```

In a real application, of course, much more work would be involved; and access to the application's data would have to be provided. Still, this is adequate for a skeleton.

The final touch adds the new function prototypes to MAIN.H:

```
// PAINT.C
void far pascal OnPaint (HWND Window);
void far pascal OnDraw (HWND Window, HDC dc);
```

That's all it takes. When you choose Debug, Run from the menu, the "Hello" application will have the text *Hello, World!* displayed in its client area.

Hello World: ObjectWindows

Writing "Hello, World" in ObjectWindows is much less work than in C... and provides a needed opportunity to see ObjectWindows at work. It's important you see this close-up, because in the future this code will be generated for you!

In a broad sense, a standard Windows app is represented by its **WinMain()** function, while its main window is represented by the window's window procedure. The same dichotomy can be seen in ObjectWindows: the application is represented by an instance of **TApplication** (or, more commonly, a descendent) while the main window is represented by an instance of **TFrameWindow** (or, again, more commonly by a descendent). All the raw work of being an application—the window registration and creation, the message loop—are hidden away in **TApplication**'s methods, while the default handling of all those messages is hidden in **TFrameWindow**.

Therefore, the simplest ObjectWindows "Hello" application you can write fits in a single module, as seen in the BC4 ObjectWindows tutorial—but we won't do it that way. As you'll remember from earlier chapters on object-oriented programming, each class declaration should go in a separate header file; each class definition in a separate code module. All we have to decide in advance is what we'll name the **TFrameWindow** and **TApplication** derivatives and their respective files. Properly set up, the Project window should look as shown in Figure 7.8.

Once you've got the nodes properly set up, you can edit MAIN.H by double-clicking on the filename:

```
#ifndef __MAIN_H__
#define __MAIN_H__
#include <owl\applicat.h>

class TMyApp : public TApplication
  {
  public:
    TMyApp();
    void InitMainWindow (void);
  };

#endif
```

OWL\APPLICAT.H has to be included for the declaration of **TApplication**. We have to include supply a constructor for **TMyApp**; that's expected. But why did we have to override **TApplication**'s **InitMainWindow()** method? Let's look at MAIN.CPP:

```
#include "main.h"
#include "frame.h"
```

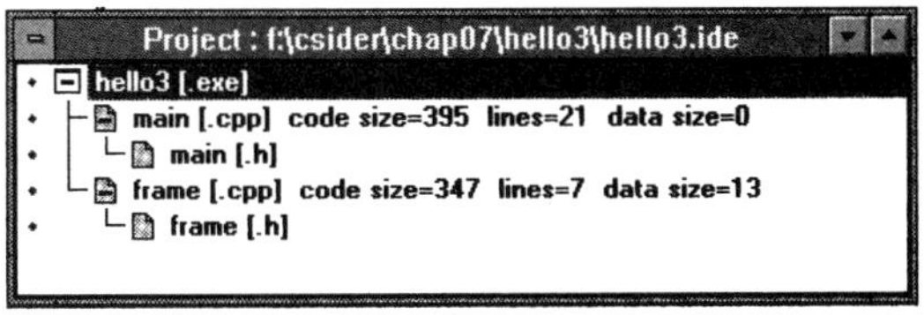

Project : f:\csider\chap07\hello3\hello3.ide
hello3 [.exe]
    main [.cpp] code size=395 lines=21 data size=0
        main [.h]
    frame [.cpp] code size=347 lines=7 data size=13
        frame [.h]

Figure 7.8 The ObjectWindows "Hello" Project.

```
TMyApp::TMyApp ()
  : TApplication()
  {
  }

void TMyApp::InitMainWindow (void)
  {
  SetMainWindow (new TMyFrame ());
  }

#pragma argsused
int OwlMain (int argc, char * argv[])
  {
  TMyApp App;
  return App.Run();
  }
```

InitMainWindow() has the job of setting the application's main window. The main window must be a derivative of **TFrameWindow**; here we use an unnamed instance of **TMyFrame** (which we haven't written yet).

Don't miss the **OwlMain()** function. This replaces **WinMain()** in an ObjectWindows application. It receives the arguments of a typical C app's **main()** rather than the arguments **WinMain()** is given. That means that multi-token command lines are pre-tokenized for you.

Anyway, **OwlMain()** creates an instance of **TMyApp**, then invokes that object's **Run()** method. **TMyApp**'s constructor (through the ancestor constructor) registers the main window class and creates and shows the main window; **Run()** then activates the message loop.

If you prefer, you can use the briefer technique from the BC4 tutorial:

```
int OwlMain (int argc, char * argv[])
  {
  return TMyApp().Run();
  }
```

This creates an unnamed instance of **TMyApp** and invokes that instance's **Run()** method, all in one line.

Since we've referred to **TMyFrame** we'd better declare it in FRAME.H:

```
#ifndef __FRAME_H__
#define __FRAME_H__

#include <owl\framewin.h>

class TMyFrame : public TFrameWindow
```

```
  {
  public:
    TMyFrame ();
  };

#endif
```

The implementation file FRAME.CPP is equally simple:

```
#include "frame.h"

TMyFrame::TMyFrame ()
  : TFrameWindow (0, "Hello, World")
  {
  }
```

TFrameWindow's constructor takes two arguments. The first is a handle to a parent's window; since there is no parent window, we supply a zero. The second parameter is the window's caption. When you compile and run, you'll get an application whose caption is "Hello, World." The performance is the same as in HELLO1, but (even with the multiple code modules) substantially less typing was required.

Of course, HELLO3 has the same deficiency as HELLO1: It doesn't actually paint anything in its client area. To add this ability, we need to intercept the WM_PAINT message as we did in HELLO2. ObjectWindows is already doing that for us, however. When a WM_PAINT message arrives, ObjectWindows does the same work we did in **OnPaint( )** in a method called **EvPaint( )** (the *Ev* stands for *event*). **EvPaint( )** then calls **Paint( )**, a **virtual** method which, by default, does nothing. Since *Paint( )* is **virtual**, we can override it easily. Here's the new HELLO4 version of FRAME.H:

```
#ifndef __FRAME_H__
#define __FRAME_H__

#include <owl\framewin.h>
#include <owl\dc.h>

class TMyFrame : public TFrameWindow
  {
  public:
    TMyFrame ();
  protected:
    void Paint (TDC & dc, BOOL Clear, TRect & Invalid);
  };

#endif
```

Since **Paint( )** takes a **TDC** parameter, we **#include** DC.H, where **TDC** is declared. We made **Paint( ) protected** because there's no need to make it **public**—and, remember, no part of an object should be made visible to outsiders that doesn't have to be.

In FRAME.CPP we supply the definition for **Paint( )**:

```
#pragma argsused
void TMyFrame::Paint (TDC & dc, BOOL Clear, TRect & Invalid)
    {
    dc.TextOut (0, 0, "Hello, World from ObjectWindows!");
    }
```

Don't confuse the **TDC** member function **TextOut( )** with the Windows API function **TextOut( )**. Obviously, the one calls the other, but the calling sequences differ.

The **Clear** parameter, if **TRUE**, indicates the background of the window should be redrawn. We don't have to worry about that in this simple program, but, if we did, the **Invalid** rectangle would tell what part had to be repainted.

We'll have more to say about the **Paint( )** method in future chapters. For now, compiling and running HELLO4 will produce the desired result: a main application window whose client area reads "Hello, World from ObjectWindows!"

Hello World: AppExpert

Finally we come to the 1990s: generated code! BC4's AppExpert will do almost all the work of creating a "Hello, World" application, leaving you to write just n lines!

To create an application using AppExpert, use the Project, AppExpert command. You'll see the familiar New Project dialog box, but after entering the name of the project and clicking on OK, the AppExpert dialog box will appear, as shown in Figure 7.9.

As you can see, most of the options that were checked by default have been unchecked—even so, we'll still have a fancier user interface than any "Hello" program deserves.

One more thing to change: under Admin Options, change Description to "Hello, World, from AppExpert!"

After clicking on the Generate button, you can choose Debug, Run to compile and run as before. After a minute or two you'll see an application complete with working menu! It won't say "Hello, World" in the caption, however; it'll say something like "Untitled - hello5." However,

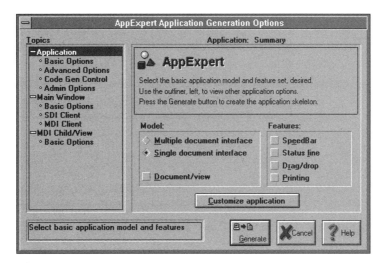

Figure 7.9 Use the AppExpert dialog box to create an app with BC4's AppExpert.

the Help, About command works—and the About box includes the line, "Hello, World, from AppExpert!"

Looking at the code, you'll find that AppExpert has basically done what we did in the previous section—but more. Lots more. What do all these extra things do? Well, frankly, you can figure them out—but why bother? Let AppExpert mind the things it's meant to mind; you can then spend your time on the fun stuff. I don't mean to sound frivolous; but it's important that you not mess with the stuff AppExpert has written. ClassExpert, whom we'll meet in a moment, relies on things being where AppExpert left them.

AppExpert has done all it's going to do for this project. However, we are obviously not done—we want to paint in the client area just as we did in the previous versions of the "Hello" app. To paint in the Hello app's client area, we'll first have to override a couple of classes. ClassExpert will help in this.

To start ClassExpert, choose View, ClassExpert to display the Class Expert window. A sample window appears in Figure 7.10

The Class Expert window is divided into three panes. At the upper left is the Classes pane. This pane contains a list of the classes ClassExpert can help you with. Some will have been generated by AppExpert; others you will have added. It's important to note, however, that *ClassExpert will not provide assistance with every class in your application.* It can only help with user-interface classes derived directly from OWL. You can't even use it to work on classes derived from classes derived from OWL! My feeling is that naming this IDE component "ClassExpert" was smacks a bit of delu-

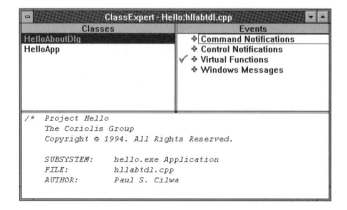

Figure 7.10 The Class Expert window.

sions of grandeur. "Class Pre-Occupied Assistant" might have been more accurate! Still, it has its uses, and we're about to exercise them.

We'll talk more about this in the next chapter, but for now just take my word that the application—Hello—must express itself through three classes: a document, a view, and a document template. Yes, that makes this program *much* more complex than the predecessor you typed in the previous section, but if OWL is going to manage the complexity, what do you care? All you have to do is add those classes (or, rather, their derivatives).

First you have to add the **TView** derivative. To do so, place the mouse cursor over the upper-left pane and press the *right* mouse button. A floating menu appears, listing the things you can do to that pane. Among the other things is an entry labeled Create new class. Select that command to display the Add New Class dialog box, which you should fill out as indicated in Figure 7.11.

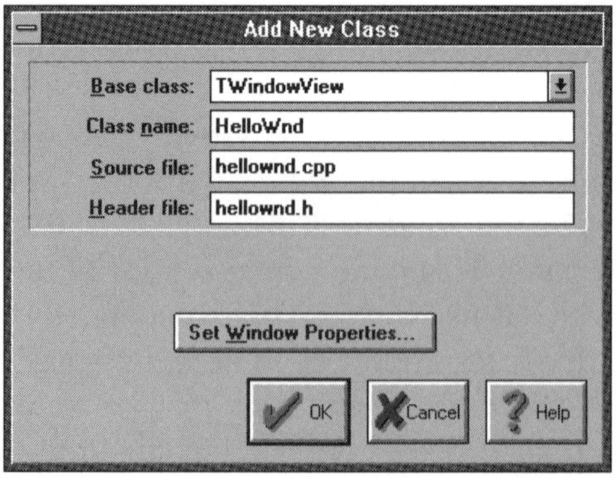

Figure 7.11 Fill out the Add New Class dialog box as it appears in this figure.

Especially important is the Base Class you choose. There are many items in the combo box, but **TWindowView** is definitely the one you want.

When you're ready, click on OK. **HelloWnd** will be added to the Classes pane and HELLOWND.CPP will be added to the Project window. It already has about 40 lines of code in it! But, as yet, it's useless because it hasn't been associated with a *document class*. To do that, return to the Classes pane and right-click again, this time choosing Create Doc Types. Choosing this command brings up the dialog box shown in Figure 7.12.

The name of the View class will, by default, be that of the **TView** derivative you just created. The only document class supported by ClassExpert is **TFileDocument**, so you don't have a choice to make there. (Borland intends to add more choices to a later version.) The Description, Filters, and Default Extension fields are also OK. Next, click on the Styles button to display the Document Styles dialog box, shown in Figure 7.13. Be sure and check the dtAutoOpen style, which opens a view window automatically when a document is created. Since documents are useless without an associated view, this style is a must.

Click on the OK button in the Document Styles dialog box, which returns you to the Add Document Type dialog box. Click on the Add button. This will cause a new entry—TFileDocument/HelloWnd—to appear in the Existing Document/View types list box at the bottom of the dialog box. But we *don't* want two entries here, not in this application.

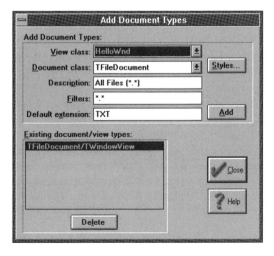

Figure 7.12 The Add Document Types dialog box allows you to associate a project file with a document class.

Figure 7.13 The Document Styles dialog box allows you to specify that a view window opens by default when a document is created.

So select the original entry (TFileDocument/TWindowView) and click on the Delete button. That will leave you with the entry you just added, the one you want to keep.

At this point—again—you could compile and run, although there would be no visual difference between now and just after you let AppExpert generate the skeleton application. We still have to add code to a **Paint( )** handler.

Now, you'd be justified in thinking that ClassExpert should help you do this. After all, to the right of the Classes pane is the Events pane, and one of the entries is Virtual Functions. **Paint( )** is a virtual function, right? And, in fact, if you had derived **HelloWnd** from **TEditView**, **Paint( )** would be on the list!

But, right now, it's not—an odd omission, but not one we can't work around. We'll just have to override the function manually; and we know how to do that (if you've forgotten, re-read the previous chapters!).

First, open the header file HELLOWND.H and modify the class declaration so that it reads:

```
//{{TWindowView = HelloWnd}}
class HelloWnd : public TWindowView {
public:
    HelloWnd (TDocument& doc, TWindow* parent = 0);
    virtual ~HelloWnd ();
    virtual void Paint(TDC&, BOOL erase, TRect&);
};    //{{HelloWnd}}
```

(How did I know the signature of **Paint( )**? Simple: I looked it up in the online help!)

Next, open HELLOWND.CPP and add the following method definition:

```
void HelloWnd::Paint(TDC& dc, BOOL erase, TRect&)
  {
  dc.TextOut (5, 5, "Hello, world!");
  }
```

Notice that I've used my preferred style of indentation. ClassExpert doesn't seem to care—probably because it's taking no responsibility for the whole procedure!

Now, recompile and run. (The Debug, Run command is the easiest way to do this.) The app starts, but at first nothing special happens. Choose the app's File, New command, though, and "Hello, world!" appears in the client area.

Why didn't it show up initially? Because the default application doesn't start with an "untitled" file.

I can hear you now, complaining that AppExpert and ClassExpert made you do *more* work, not less, in creating the Hello World app. The .EXE file is also substantially larger. But how many Hello World apps do you write? In the next chapter we'll take a look at the App/Doc/View paradigm, and see how it helps simplify the writing of real-world (as opposed to hello-world) applications.

8

Apps, Documents, and Views

For many programmers, the most puzzling aspect of ObjectWindows 2.0 (and, for that matter, Microsoft Foundation Classes 2.0) is the document/view, or doc/view, paradigm that we are now asked to follow. "Who needs it?" you might ask. But the answer is, we all do; we really do. Modern applications are just too complex to allow the division between the user interface and the data engine to fall to chance. The doc/view paradigm formalizes this division, that's all. It's really not that hard to understand; it's just different—like that new kid in your fifth-grade class who came from some other country. In this chapter, we'll explore the new paradigm and make a new friend.

Applications as Containers of Documents

Most Windows apps are file oriented. If that surprises you, you haven't been using enough Windows apps. By visualizing your application as a container of documents, you'll be well on your way to understanding the doc/view paradigm.

Here's a quick test: Name the two applications that come with Windows 3.1 that *aren't* containers of documents. Give up? The Clock app is easy to spot; I'm sure you got that one. But if you picked the Program Manager for the second, you're wrong. The Program Manager operates on files with .GRP extensions, although it doesn't use a traditional *File* menu to do so. And if you thought the Clipboard Viewer might be the second, you're wrong there, too. The Clipboard Viewer allows the user to save the current contents of the Clipboard in a .CLP file. No, the second non-file-oriented application is, of all things, the File Manager. Although it *operates* on files, it does neither stores nor saves its context in them. Like the Clock, the File Manager is a utility, not truly an application.

The thing is, we programmers don't *write* "programs" any more. We write *applications*—and there *is* a difference. According to the dictionary, a "program" is a series of chronologically related events. The word is old; centuries ago (spelled, more or less, *programme*—people used to be less fussy about such things), a program detailed the events at a fair or in a dramatic presentation. When commercial radio began broadcasting, the program let viewers (and the station management) know what shows would be broadcast at what times. However, the viewers—we would call them *users*—soon confused the *program* with the *presentation* and began referring to "radio programs." It was wrong, but the word stuck and carried into television. Such are the dynamics of language.

Meanwhile, *our* programs were still chronologically related sched-ules—of *machine instructions*. Even after the introduction of structured programming, computer programs basically started at the "top" and worked their way to the "bottom"—if not the bottom of the source file, then the bottom of the main procedure.

Event-driven, real-time programming has changed all that. Now only the handlers for specific events can be said to proceed from top to bottom; the event handlers themselves are triggered by external stimuli that is (usually) beyond the control of the programmer. Our "programs" are actually just collections of methods and event handlers, *applied* to some particular document—and, thus, called "applications."

On to our next issue. What exactly is a document? It *could* be a traditional disk file, but doesn't have to be. It is just as likely to be a database table or even a stream of bytes being transmitted over a phone line. The word *document* refers primarily to *persistence*. A document *persists* even when the application is not running, or the computer itself is not running, or even (provided you've kept backups!) if the computer is destroyed.

So, if you are writing for the Windows environment, and unless you're writing a utility like the Clock, you are going to be creating an applica-tion that is a *container* for one or more *documents*.

But a document represents only persistence, *not* user manipulation. So you need another piece that we call a *view*. The view is the user interface part; the document is the persistence engine. The view may change with fashion or the needs of the user; the document tends to be more stable. Yet either the view or the document storage can change without a change being forced on the other.

The application is simply a home for both. This brings us to a new paradigm to which we must now adhere—app/doc/view. In a tradi-tional Windows application, the application provides a place for one, and only one, document at a time. That document, in turn, is manipulated through a single view. If you start the application without specifying the file, it "loads" an "empty" one—but there is always a document there. Likewise, once the client area is painted, the view of that docu-ment is present and active.

With Word for Windows 1.0, Microsoft introduced the Multiple Docu-ment Interface (MDI). An example of this type of interface is shown in Figure 8.1. It, too, has evolved into its present, clearly stylized form. With MDI an application can, at any given moment, be host to zero or more documents. However, each document *must* be represented by at least one view. Additional views may be available. For example, in

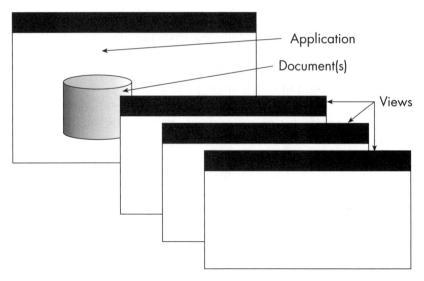

Figure 8.1 This illustration shows the relationship among applications, documents, and views.

Microsoft Excel, a worksheet may be simultaneously viewed in the form of a table of numbers *and* as a pie chart. If the numbers are changed, the chart changes as well. In a complete MDI implementation (which is rarely done) the numbers could also be changed by altering the chart.

The app/doc/view paradigm can be applied in any language; indeed, I use it in Visual Basic. But in VB, I have to do all the work. ObjectWindows 2.0 was built *assuming* app/doc/view; it's much easier to use if you accept the paradigm than if you try and fight it.

Besides, it's a *good* thing. Some years ago I wrote a Windows-hosted collections system for a small Virginia hospital. They still use the app, but would like it updated for Windows 3.1. The data engine is still valid; but user-interface fashions have changed. Updating the app *should* be a simple job and *would* be—if I had originally used the app/doc/view paradigm. Alas, neither I nor, as far as I know, anyone else had come up with the idea at the time; and my user interface and data engine are too tightly entwined for me to rip them apart. What should be a simple facelift is, instead, a rewrite.

Don't let that happen to you! Be a visionary and embrace the app/doc/view paradigm; don't let the seeming complexity bother you. Yes, the classes you'll have to master *are* complex; but once you've done so, all your applications from then on will be much, much simpler to write and maintain. I promise!

Designing a Full-Fledged Drawing Application

To provide a framework for understanding the app/doc/view paradigm, it's always easier to work with a real-life problem. Care to write a drawing program, anyone?

It's possible you look down your nose at drawing programs. After all, they're everywhere—at least, badly written ones are, although there are a few good ones. But a fully implemented drawing program, such as we are about to build, actually contains many elements in common with any prosaic business application. For example:

- Both deal with discreet units of information
- Both must paint that information on screen and be able to print it; print preview should also be supported
- Both must save that information to disk and read it back
- Both must permit all or part of that information to be copied or cut into the Clipboard, and pasted into the app from the Clipboard

In our drawing program, we'll allow the user to place shapes anywhere in the window. Consequently, we'll call the program "Shapes" as an example of clarity in program names. Each shape will maintain its integrity as a unit, and can be selected by the user after creation and moved, deleted, copied, and so on.

Once people were taught to spend days or weeks designing a program before they ever started coding it. That made sense in the days of card decks and 24-hour turnaround times for individual compiles, but it no longer does. False starts cost too little to worry about, and often provide valuable experience and insights that would otherwise have been lacking. Those weeks of preparation made sense when they preceded $10,000 worth of programming time before a result could be seen, but how much preparation is really needed before spending two minutes with a dialog box and a few check boxes? After all, if you do it wrong—you can always do it again.

Therefore, we'll start "designing" Shapes *as we write it*. However, there's only one way to make this work, and that's by use of incremental development. We'll do a little at a time, then see if we like what we've done.

To help you keep track of (and get a feel for) these minor steps, I'll present each as individual sections.

Generating the Shapes Application

You've already seen how to create a new project using App Expert; so I won't repeat the details here. However, in addition to being a code generator, App Expert can assist grappling with design issues, if you look at the various options as components of a design checklist.

The first dialog box asks for the project name; it should be "Shapes." When the App Expert Generation Options dialog box appears, we are presented with the first major decision point: will this be an MDI application or not? How can you decide?

As a non-trivial, document-based application, I would automatically use the MDI style unless I had some specific reason *not* to. SDI is appropriate for simple applications that are not document based (like the Clock) or for apps that work on documents that will never interact or need more than one simultaneous view or view format. In the case of Shapes, we can imagine the user adding shapes to different parts of a large drawing area, suggesting that multiple views might well come in handy. And we might even want to add an alternate view format in which the shapes are displayed textual; that is, displaying information on location, size and color.

So, for our purposes, we'll leave the Multiple Document Interface option button selected.

We'll *definitely* keep the Document/View check box checked, for the reasons already stated.

The list of features—Speed bar, Status line, Drag/drop and Printing—we can also leave checked. Why not? There's little harm in allowing visually oriented users to have a Speed bar if they want one. We can use the Status line to show the current mouse position. The ability to drag an appropriate file from the File Manager and drop it on the application is always a nice touch. And, of course we want to have the ability to print our shapes!

Under Basic Options, make sure the Target name is Shapes—don't forget to change the initial *S* to a capital—and you'll want to select an appropriate base directory. But what do you do about Help file support?

The problem is that you *absolutely* want a help file—but you may not want the skeleton BC4 will provide. Not that there's inherently anything wrong with it; it's just that most people don't create their own help files directly. They prefer to use one of the third-party help generation packages such as RoboHelp, Visual Help, or WinHelp+.

In the example code on disk, I'll allow BC4 to generate the help file. But for a real application, I wouldn't. (Currently, my preference is Visual Help.)

Under Advanced options, we have two sets of choices. One has to do with the way the application initially appears; the other has to do with dialog box styles.

The Startup options are Normal, Minimized and Maximized. If you are creating an application that will almost always be used in full-screen mode, choose Maximize. If, on the other hand, you are writing a monitor or demon process of some sort that will normally appear as an icon (like the Dr. Watson utility that comes with Windows), choose Minimized. Normal is usually appropriate.

The Control style group is misnamed; Dialog Box style would be more accurate, even though the style of a dialog box is achieved largely through the style of its controls. Through the years three styles have come to dominate the infinite number of ways dialog boxes could be arranged: The original Windows style is clean and simple, as shown in Figure 8.2); Borland's BWCC (Borland Workshop Custom Control) style makes use of illustrated buttons, as shown in Figure 8.3; and the 3D style is used by all Microsoft's new applications, as shown in Figure 8.4. Which you choose is entirely up to you. You can easily modify the resulting code if you change your mind, but try to resist agonizing for weeks over what is essentially a meaningless decision—no one cares which style your dialogs boxes use. If you must have a guideline, I've prepared a full-proof map for you to follow. If your political affiliation is

- Democrat, use original Windows style
- Independent, use BWCC
- Republican, use 3D

The set of Code Gen Control options simply gives you the chance to change the default file and class names for the various system components App Expert generates. To be honest, I'm not always wild about these default names. For example, *ShapesAboutDlg*—why bother prefixing everything with *Shapes*? Isn't it obvious from the context? And

Figure 8.2 The original Windows-style About box.

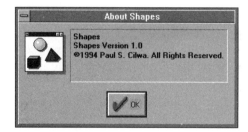

Figure 8.3 The BWCC-style About box.

Figure 8.4 The 3D-style About box.

yet, I never bother to change the names. After all, I don't really have to deal with them, and it seems to make BC4 happy.

Admin Options, on the other hand, needs some work. It would have been nice if Borland had provided us with a way to change these strings. For example, the word "Copyright" and the "©" symbol are redundant, and the name of the copyrighting party—either the author or the company—should be included on the line. The text *should* be (for me) "©1994 Paul S. Cilwa. All Rights Reserved." And why should I have to type in Author's Name every time when my name doesn't change?

Change the Default Values of the Admin Options

I've found a solution to the Admin Options Delimma. Create a new file called EXPERT.INI and place it in your Windows directory. (You can, if you prefer, put it in the \BC4\EXPERT\OWL subdirectory but it takes longer to load from there.)

Enter the following text, using your own information, so that you don't have to enter your name each time you generate a new application:

```
[Annotation]
Author=Paul S. Cilwa
Company=The Coriolis Group
Copyright=©1994 Paul S. Cilwa. All Rights Reserved.
```

The Description, of course, should be Shapes.

The next set of options comes under the heading Main Window. Be sure the window title is "Shapes."

Under MDI Child/View, we have one last set of options to modify before generating the code. The MDI client/view class should be changed to **TWindowView**. This tells App Expert to give us a vanilla derivative of **TView** in which we will build our own smarts. The default, **TEditView** would have given us a pre-built text editor, which is very nice, but not what we need for the Shapes application.

Under Description, change All Files (*.*) to Shapes files and Filters from *.* to *.shp. Here's why: If you choose the File, Open command from almost any application, you'll see a standard Windows dialog box. In the lower-left corner of the dialog box is a combo box labeled, "List files of type;" and in the combo box is a set of descriptors like "Text files" and "All files." Some applications—nearly all Microsoft apps, for instance—include the actual wildcard with the descriptor, for the user's convenience. Unfortunately, many of the descriptions are so long the wildcard rolls out the right side of the combo box, which rather defeats the purpose. And, since a wildcard in the description isn't used anyway, I prefer to simply omit it.

But you can't omit it from the list of Filters, because that's where the wildcard for filling in the File name list box comes from.

And none of this has anything to do with the Default extension, which, for this application, should be "shp."

Unfortunately, you can only supply a single filter for a given combination view/document class; I'll show you how to modify the resource file later so you can add the "All files" back that should always be included in the List Files of Type combo box.

After all that, we're finally ready to click on the Generate button. When the dust clears, BC4 will have created a new project containing eight source files. The Debug, Run command will compile and link the project and, eventually, run the resulting application, which should look like the one in Figure 8.5.

Creating a Custom View Class

When we asked App Expert to create the initial Shapes application, we specified an initial View type of TWindowView. We needn't have bothered (although we had to say something). TWindowView doesn't do anything interesting; we'll have to design a new class that does, and make that our view class.

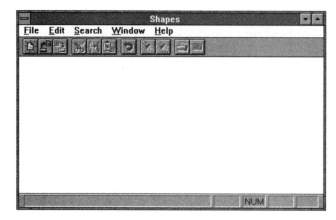

Figure 8.5 The Shapes application immediately after App Expert creates it and the IDE compiles it.

Choose the View, Class Expert command to bring up the Class Expert dialog box. As you can see in the example in Figure 8.6, the dialog box is divided into thirds. The upper left (marked "Classes") contains a list of classes that Class Expert is willing to manage for you. This will *not* be all the classes used by your application. In general, expect Class Expert to assist only with user-interface related classes. "Class Assistant" might have been a better name, but perhaps Borland hopes to make it more capable in the future.

In any case, if you click the *right* mouse button in that upper-left area, you'll get a floating menu listing the things you can do here. The first of these things is Create new class. Choose this command to derive your new **TWindowView**. In the Add New Class dialog box, set Base

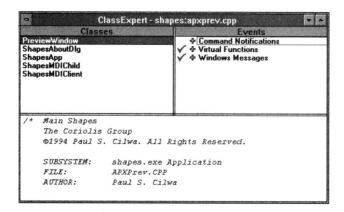

Figure 8.6 The Class Expert window.

Class to TWindowView and Class Name to TShapesView. I also suggest changing the source and header file root names to SHPSVIEW, but that's up to you. The default window properties are all fine, so when you click on OK, **TShapesView** will be added to the list of classes.

Don't like the name you chose? Too bad! *Class Expert provides no means for removing a class from its list.* In theory you could remove the implementation file from the project window by clicking on SHAPES.EXE with the right mouse button and choosing the Special, Rescan command. However, every time I've tried this approach, I've received a "rescan failed" message. Consequently, I always save the entire project to a backup subdirectory, so I can return to previous steps without having to start over from scratch.

So far we've created a **TWindowView** derivative class, but it is not yet in use. We'll have to associate it with a document type. Click the *right* mouse button in the Classes area and choosing Create doc types to display the Add Document Types dialog box. Figure 8.7 shows the dialog box *after* we finish making the necessary changes.

When the Add Document Types dialog first appears, the Existing document/view types list box will still contain the entry made by App Expert. Click on the Delete button to get rid of that. You can then drop down the View class combo box and choose TShapesView from the list. *Now* you know why we must derive the view class first: that's how it gets added to the list.

But, wait! Don't click on the Add button yet! First we must specify the styles that will be applied to the doc/view type. Click on Styles.

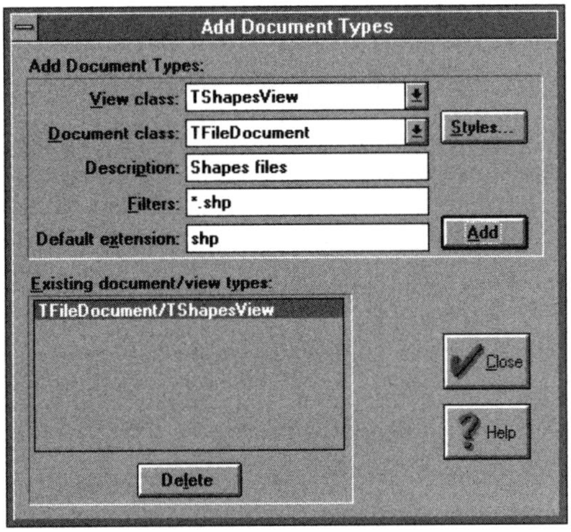

Figure 8.7 The Add Document Types dialog.

The dialog box that appears contains a list of various styles to be applied to the doc/view type—and most of them apply to the File Open common dialog box. However, one of them needs to be checked: dtAutoOpen. When you set this flag an associated view object is automatically created when a document object is created,. To do this manually is a hassle, so I don't know why they didn't make this value the default. We also need to set the dtPathMustExist and dtFileMustExist flags. These selections will let the File Open common dialog box prevent the user from "selecting" a non-existent file, without my having to write any code to do it.

Click on OK to return to the Add Document Type dialog box. *Now* you can click the Add button—and, if you forget to click Add before Close, you'll just have to start this operation over again!

Now that you're back at the Class Expert window, you'll notice that nothing has changed. To see what you've just added to your project, you'll have to open the TApplication implementation file and look for the following section:

```
//{{ShapesApp Implementation}}

//{{DOC_VIEW}}
DEFINE_DOC_TEMPLATE_CLASS(TFileDocument, TShapesView, DocType1);
//{{DOC_VIEW_END}}

//{{DOC_MANAGER}}
DocType1 __dvt1("Shapes files", "*.shp", 0, "shp", dtAutoDelete |
dtAutoOpen | dtUpdateDir | dtPathMustExist | dtFileMustExist);
//{{DOC_MANAGER_END}}
```

The **DEFINE_DOC_TEMPLATE_CLASS** macro creates a new class called **DocType1**. This unimaginatively named class is called a *document template* class. (We'll discuss document template classes later in this chapter.) A few lines later an object of this type is declared. The object's name is **__dvt1**, but don't look for it to be referenced anywhere. Simply declaring it in the static section between functions will cause its constructor to be invoked when the application is loaded. This would generally not be considered good object-oriented form, but you didn't write it, so try not to let anyone make you feel guilty. It's not your fault.

At this point you can again choose Debug, Run to compile, link, and test the result. You shouldn't notice anything different—not yet. But in the next section we'll get our **TShapesView** class to draw shapes; and in the sections following that, we'll customize the document class.

Intercepting Mouse Messages in the TShapesView Class

Nearly all applications perform their tasks in response to input from the user, in the form of keystrokes or mouse clicks. Here we'll learn how to intercept mouse click messages and respond to them.

At any given time there are dozens of messages flying about through the Windows system. Many of them are flying through *your* application. They are sent to the component they affect. For example, a paint message is sent to the window that needs repainting. A character key message is sent to the window that has the keyboard focus. There are over 260 different standard Windows messages, so you should be grateful that the **TWindow** class already has default handling built in. Each of your window classes only needs to redefine the handlers for specific messages your application needs handled differently.

You might assume that this is accomplished via a virtual function for each message; and, indeed, that's the way it would have been done— if memory usage had been no object. Unfortunately, a Windows application is likely to include many, many **TWindow**-derived classes. If each one had a virtual method table with over 260 entries (at four bytes per entry), a *lot* of space would have been devoted to the task. So Borland (and others) started looking for another approach.

Turbo C++ for Windows 3.1 used something called a *dynamic method table* (DMT). Using this approach, you could have something called a *dynamic* method, in addition to (and implemented differently than) virtual methods. Each class that implemented a dynamic method would have a DMT, but only containing pointers to its *own* dynamic methods. When a dynamic method was invoked, the CPU had to backtrack along the list of DMTs until it found the desired method. A dynamic method, then, took longer to invoke than a virtual method, but using them saved a lot of space.

Unfortunately for Borland, the ANSI C++ committee refused to include support for dynamic methods in the C++ standard. That sent Borland back to the drawing board.

The next approach was the same as Microsoft had used in their Foundation Classes library. This meant implementing the various message handlers as non-virtual functions. The only function that *has* to be virtual, after all, is the **switch** message. (That equates to the **window** procedure in the standard C Windows API.) As long as each switch invokes its parent class' switch as a default action, messages will always be intercepted by the appropriate handler.

I know this is confusing, so let's take a closer look. Say we have three window classes, **TWinA**, **TWinB**, and **TWinC**. Here are partial declarations for these classes:

```
class TWinA
  {
  protected:
    virtual LRESULT Switch (WORD Msg, WPARAM wParam, LPARAM lParam);
    LRESULT Msg1 (WORD I);
    LRESULT Msg2 (LONG 1);
    void Msg3 (void);
  };

class TWinB : public TWinA
  {
  protected:
    virtual LRESULT Switch (WORD Msg, WPARAM wParam, LPARAM lParam);
    LRESULT Msg2 (LONG 1);
  };

class TWinC : public TWinB
  {
  protected:
    virtual LRESULT Switch (WORD Msg, WPARAM wParam, LPARAM lParam);
    void Msg3 (void);
  };
```

You can see how the base class, **TWinA**, has defined handlers for three messages. **TWinB** has only defined a handler for the second message; **TWinC** only for the third—yet all three have a **Switch** method. In traditional C++ programming, there would be just one, non-virtual **Switch** method; all the message handlers would be virtual so the appropriate one would be called for each object, leading to the excessive memory usage already described. So everyone has a **switch** statement:

```
LRESULT TWinA::Switch (WORD Msg, WPARAM wParam, LPARAM lParam)
  {
  switch (Msg)
    {
    case Message1:
      return Msg1 (wParam);
    case Message2:
      return Msg2 (lParam);
    case Message3:
      Msg3 ();
```

```
          return 0;
      default:
          return 0;
      }
  }

LRESULT TWinB::Switch (WORD Msg, WPARAM wParam, LPARAM lParam)
  {
  switch (Msg)
      {
      case Message2:
          return Msg2 (lParam);
      default:
          return TWinA::Switch (Msg, wParam, lParam);
      }
  }

LRESULT TWinC::Switch (WORD Msg, WPARAM wParam, LPARAM lParam)
  {
  switch (Msg)
      {
      case Message3:
          Msg3 ();
          return 0;
      default:
          return TWinB::Switch (Msg, wParam, lParam);
      }
  }
```

As you can see, the technique is simple and straightforward—perhaps, depending on the way your mind works, simpler than making all the message handlers virtual.

So why did both Borland and Microsoft add a layer of complexity by hiding the virtual switch in macros?

Because that's what they did. The original reason, I assume, was to ease the risk of coding one of the switches wrong. In the previous example, you can see how easy it would be in **TWinC::Switch()** to accidentally call **TWinA::Switch()** in the default case, instead of **TWinB::Switch()**.

But you no longer code this stuff yourself; Class Expert (or, for Visual C++, Class Wizard) writes the code *for* you. So why add a layer of indirection to something that's quite easy to understand?

We may never know. But let's return to Class Expert and add handlers for the mouse messages we want to intercept.

Choose the View, Class Expert command, then choose TShapesView from the Classes panel. You'll see three entries in the Events panel:

Command Notifications, Virtual Functions, and Windows Messages. Each is preceded by a plus sign, indicating that this display is an outline and any of these three items may be expanded.

Click on the plus sign of Windows Messages to expand the entry. Now, Basic Messages, Other Messages, and Win32 Messages are displayed. These items, too, are preceded by plus signs.

Studying this list, you'll be interested to note that **WM_LBUTTONDOWN** and **WM_LBUTTONDBLCLK** are represented—but **WM_LBUTTONUP** is *not*. I don't know who decided which messages were "basic" and which were not, but **WM_LBUTTONUP** is in the list labeled "Other Messages." (If I had been designing this panel, I would have listed the messages by category—Mouse Messages, Clipboard Messages, and so on—but they didn't ask me.)

Anyway, if you select **WM_LBUTTONDOWN** and click the *right* mouse button on it, you'll get a short floating menu with the command Add handler. Choose that command to display the code for the new handler in the code panel below. Because of its brevity, I'll show the new function here:

```
void TShapesView::EvLButtonDown (UINT modKeys, TPoint& point)
{
    TWindowView::EvLButtonDown(modKeys, point);

    // INSERT>> Your code here.

}
```

There are two things to note here. First of all, the handler receives a reference to a **TPoint** object. This object gives the client coordinates of the mouse onscreen *at the time the button was clicked*. (Remember, these messages are processed sometime *after* they were generated.) Second, the ancestor class' **EvLButtonDown( )** method is invoked *before* you add your own processing. Some messages require ancestor processing in addition to whatever else you want to do. Class Expert knows which messages have this requirement, and writes the skeleton code accordingly.

Now, scroll upwards a little ways in the file and you'll see the following lines:

```
//
// Build a response table for all messages/commands handled
// by the application.
```

```
//
DEFINE_RESPONSE_TABLE1(TShapesView, TWindowView)
//{{TShapesViewRSP_TBL_BEGIN}}
    EV_WM_LBUTTONDOWN,
//{{TShapesViewRSP_TBL_END}}
END_RESPONSE_TABLE;
```

This is the macro I referred to. Expanded, it actually creates the virtual switch method for the **TShapesView** class. And, if this is a method, you must wonder how it is included in the class. That's in another macro—in the header file, of course:

```
class TShapesView : public TWindowView {
        ⋎

//{{TShapesViewRSP_TBL_BEGIN}}
protected:
    void EvLButtonDown (UINT modKeys, TPoint& point);
//{{TShapesViewRSP_TBL_END}}
DECLARE_RESPONSE_TABLE(TShapesView);
};      //{{TShapesView}}
```

(I apologize for the K&R-style braces, but that's the way Class Expert writes 'em.)

Now, remember, you don't have to actually write this stuff yourself—that's what Class Expert is for. I just wanted you to know how the magic works.

With that in mind, we can return to the **TShapesView::EvLButtonDown()** code. Replace the "INSERT>> Your code here." comment with a line that will actually produce a visible result; invoking the **MessageBox()** method is a good choice:

```
void TShapesView::EvLButtonDown (UINT modKeys, TPoint& point)
  {
  TWindowView::EvLButtonDown(modKeys, point);
  MessageBox ("Left button clicked");
  }
```

(By the way, you can tidy up the braces, as I did above, if you wish.) Notice that this is *not* the Windows API **MessageBox()** function; we've invoked a method inherited from **TWindow** class.

Repeating these steps, you can add handling for the right mouse button as easily:

```
void TShapesView::EvRButtonDown (UINT modKeys, TPoint& point)
  {
```

```
TWindowView::EvRButtonDown(modKeys, point);
MessageBox ("Right button clicked.");
}
```

Debug, Run will let you test your app's new abilities. Don't forget you have to create a new document (via the File, New command) before you can test; we added this behavior *only* to the **TShapesView** class—so no other windows will have their behavior modified by what we've done.

By the way, the message boxes that appear will have the caption "Error." If you don't like that, you can always add a caption of your choice—that's the second, optional, parameter of the **MessageBox( )** method. But why bother, when, in the next section, we'll be making mouse clicks do something *much* more interesting? Namely, drawing shapes.

Drawing Shapes

A shape-drawing application isn't much use until it can draw shape... but we wouldn't want the app to draw them randomly! Here we'll intercept the user's left and right mouse clicks and draw rectangles and ellipses, respectively, in response to them.

In the last section we intercepted left and right mouse clicks, displaying a message box when they occurred. Now we'll get closer to our goal by actually drawing shapes in response to those clicks.

In Chapter 7, when we built the Hello, World application, we responded to the paint message requested by the drawing of text. To do so, we needed a *device context*—commonly called a *DC*—which was supplied to the event handler.

But mouse clicks handlers are not given DCs; we'll have to make one of our own.

There's a whole hierarchy of device context classes. The base class is **TDC**, and it contains most of the functionality. The descendent classes differ mostly in where the DC comes from. For example, to create a DC for use in your client area, as we must do here, you simply create an object of **TClientDC** class. The constructor for **TClientDC** requires a handle to the window it's to draw in; but **TWindow** objects happily cast themselves to window handles so we can create the DC like this:

```
TClientDC dc (*this);
```

The base class **TDC** has two methods, **Rectangle()** and **Ellipse()**, which draw the shapes we want. Therefore, rewriting the mouse click handlers in the following manner produces the desired result:

```
void TShapesView::EvLButtonDown (UINT modKeys, TPoint& point)
  {
  TWindowView::EvLButtonDown(modKeys, point);
  TClientDC dc (*this);
  dc.Rectangle (point.x, point.y, point.x+50, point.y+50);
  }

void TShapesView::EvRButtonDown (UINT modKeys, TPoint& point)
  {
  TWindowView::EvRButtonDown(modKeys, point);
  TClientDC dc (*this);
  dc.Ellipse (point.x, point.y, point.x+50, point.y+50);
  }
```

Adding Color to a Shape

Suppose we want to fill in the shapes with some color? Rectangles and ellipses drawn using a TDC object are always filled in—but, by default, they are filled in with a white brush. We can change that; but, to do so, we have to create a new brush of the desired color, and then "select" it into the DC.

It's easy to create a new brush; there's a **TBrush** class that exists for no other reason. All you *have* to specify when creating a brush is the color you want it to be, although there are several other constructors that let you create brushes with patterns and even from bitmaps.

An easy way to specify a color is to make use of the **TColor**, a class that encapsulates color management. It includes a set of constants, such as **TColor::LtRed**, for the more commonly used colors. (We'll talk more about **TColor** in Chapter 10.) Here's the line that instantiates a red brush:

```
TBrush Brush (TColor::LtRed);
```

Now that you've got it, you have to "select" it into an existing DC. You do that with the **SelectObject()** method:

```
dc.SelectObject (Brush);
```

In the Windows API, and even in Microsoft's Foundation Classes, it is absolutely essential that you remember to restore the old brush to a

DC before the DC is destroyed. However, ObjectWindows takes care of that chore for you. Still, if you want to *use* the original brush, you can get it back by invoking the **RestoreBrush()** method:

```
dc.RestoreBrush();
```

The handler for the left mouse click now looks like this:

```
void TShapesView::EvLButtonDown (UINT modKeys, TPoint& point)
  {
  TWindowView::EvLButtonDown(modKeys, point);
  TClientDC dc (*this);
  TBrush Brush (TColor::LtRed);
  dc.SelectObject (Brush);
  dc.Rectangle (point.x, point.y, point.x+50, point.y+50);
  }
```

By the way, if you want a transparent shape—one in which the outline is drawn, but is not filled in—you can use a "hollow" brush to do the trick. Windows already has hollow brushes (as well as black, white and gray ones) created, but of course they are not **TBrush** objects. You'll need to use the API function **GetStockObject()** to return a Windows handle to one of these brushes. To use a hollow brush in ObjectWindows you'll have to use an alternate **TBrush** constructor that accepts an already-existing handle. The following line creates a hollow **TBrush** object:

```
TBrush HollowBrush ((HBRUSH) GetStockObject (HOLLOW_BRUSH));
```

Changing Pen Style and Color

As with the fill-in brush, you have a choice in color and style of the outlining pen. Here's how to create a pen to your specifications, and use it.

Creating a new pen is almost exactly like creating a brush. There's a **TPen** class, and like **TBrush** it has several constructors. The most commonly used one requires you to specify a color, and allows you to specify width and style as well.

For color you can use a **TColor** object, as you did with the brush. However, you should be aware that, while brushes can display *any* color with more or less success, pens can only display a "solid" color— and "solid" means something different for every video driver. A solid color is one in which every pixel is the same shade. If you request a brush in a color that is not available, Windows creates a dithered brush in which adjacent pixels may be different colors, but when viewed from a normal distance the pixels blur together and create the illusion of the color requested. Pens can't do this, so when you request a colored pen, Windows will give you one in the nearest solid color to the color you asked for.

The width of the pen is specified in logical units, which are usually equal to pixels, so the narrowest width is 1. However, in Windows NT, you can request a width of 0, which means a line one pixel wide no matter what size the logical units are. You can go as thick as 32K logical units, which is thicker than you're likely to want to go.

Pen styles include solid, dashed, dotted—in fact, all the ways you've ever seen a line drawn on a map. If the line is not solid, the background color—the same one used for drawing text—is used to fill the spaces between the line. Of course, as with text, you can set the mode to transparent, in which case Windows won't specifically fill in those spaces. The styles are documented in the Windows API and have easily identifyable names: **PS_SOLID**, **PS_DASH**, **PS_DASHDOT**, **PS_DASHDOTDOT**, and so on.

To create a solid blue pen of 1 unit's width, use the statement:

```
TPen Pen (TColor::LtBlue);
```

As with a brush, you must "select" the pen into the DC before it can be used:

```
dc.SelectObject (Pen);
```

Yes, this is same **SelectObject( )** we used for the brush . . . in a way. Actually, the function is overloaded, so the appropriate method is invoked based on the object being passed, **TPen** or **TBrush** (or one of several other classes). If you want to re-use the original pen, the **RestorePen( )** method will do the trick.

You always have a pen; you can't manipulate a DC in such a way that it doesn't have one. However, you can create a pen in the **PS_NULL** style; such a pen is invisible. I realize the difference between having no pen and having an invisible one is pretty subtle, but there is a difference: all pens, even invisible ones have to be created.

Rather than actually use the **PS_NULL** style, however, it would be more efficient to use the **NULL_PEN** stock object, making use of an alternate **TPen** constructor:

```
TPen NullPen ((HPEN) GetStockObject (NULL_PEN));
```

Here's the left mouse button handler, set up for red rectangles and an invisible pen:

```
void TShapesView::EvLButtonDown (UINT modKeys, TPoint& point)
  {
  TWindowView::EvLButtonDown(modKeys, point);
  TClientDC dc (*this);
  TBrush Brush (TColor::LtRed);
  dc.SelectObject (Brush);
  TPen NullPen ((HPEN) GetStockObject (NULL_PEN));
  dc.SelectObject (NullPen);
  dc.Rectangle (point.x, point.y, point.x+50, point.y+50);
  }
```

Allowing User-Specified Colors

Always drawing a red rectangle is no more interesting to the user than always drawing a black one. Giving the user some control over shape color will also give us a chance to explore the creation and management of menu commands.

Our application already has a menu. Many of the items even work: File, New and Help, About, for example. But App Expert put all that together. How can we add menu items of our own?

That answer to that requires several steps, and we'll go over all of them. In a nutshell, here are the steps you'll be following:

1. Use Resource Workshop to modify the menu, adding the desired commands.

2. Use Class Expert to add handlers for the new commands to the desired view.

3. Edit the skeleton handlers to actually implement the new commands.

Now, let's just do it.

Do *not* open Resource Workshop as an independent process, or even from BC4's Tools menu. Instead, double-click on SHAPES.RC in the Project window. That will open Resource Workshop, with the appropriate linkages between BC4, your project, and the Workshop.

When Resource Workshop comes up, you'll see a list of resources in the resource window. Scroll through the list until you come to the menu resources, then double-click on MDI_MENU to display the Menu Design window, shown in Figure 8.8.

The Menu Design window is basically divided into three areas. The left side shows (and allows editing of) the details of the currently selected

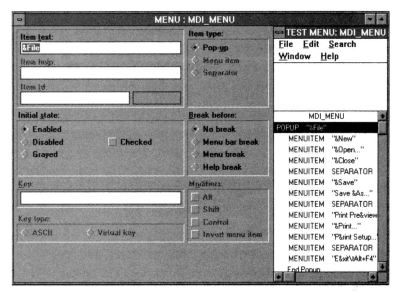

Figure 8.8 The Menu Design window.

item—the list of items being in the lower right. At the upper right is a working example of your menu as it appears so far. Clicking on one of the commands is an alternate way to select the menu description of that command for editing.

For the Shapes application, we can replace the Search menu with a Shapes menu. To do so, just click on Search and change the Item Text to "&Shapes." (The preceding ampersand makes the letter following it the menu item's hot key. To include a real ampersand, use enter two of the symbols.)

Now select "POPUP "&Shapes"" with the mouse and press the Insert key. A dummy entry will appear. Change the Item Text to "&Rectangle," and change the Item Help to "Draw a rectangle." Resource Workshop will have made up an identifier for you called CM_SHAPESRECTANGLE, which is just fine. Press the Insert key again and change the new entry to "&Ellipse." Makse sure to add appropriate help text.

Next we want a separator bar, so press Insert and then check the Separator option button in the details area. Add menu items for Red, Green and Blue—don't forget to add the ampersand for hot keys. While you're at it, add an Other . . . command (use the ellipsis to indicate that choosing his command displays a dialog box; we'll work on that later). Finally, select the Find, Find Next and Replace items left over from when this was the Search menu, hitting the Delete key to remove each one.

When you're done you can exit Resource Workshop, which will save your changes automatically. (To be true to the Windows interface it should give you a choice, but it doesn't.)

Since we've removed menu items to which the Speed bar refers, we'll have to remove the references from the Speed bar code. We'll be looking at how the Speed bar works shortly; meanwhile, humor me and remove the lines from SHPSAPP.CPP that I've commented out:

```
TControlBar* cb = new TControlBar(frame);
cb->Insert(*new TButtonGadget(CM_MDIFILENEW, CM_MDIFILENEW));
cb->Insert(*new TButtonGadget(CM_MDIFILEOPEN, CM_MDIFILEOPEN));
cb->Insert(*new TButtonGadget(CM_FILESAVE, CM_FILESAVE));
cb->Insert(*new TSeparatorGadget(6));
cb->Insert(*new TButtonGadget(CM_EDITCUT, CM_EDITCUT));
cb->Insert(*new TButtonGadget(CM_EDITCOPY, CM_EDITCOPY));
cb->Insert(*new TButtonGadget(CM_EDITPASTE, CM_EDITPASTE));
cb->Insert(*new TSeparatorGadget(6));
cb->Insert(*new TButtonGadget(CM_EDITUNDO, CM_EDITUNDO));
cb->Insert(*new TSeparatorGadget(6));
// cb->Insert(*new TButtonGadget(CM_EDITFIND, CM_EDITFIND));
// cb->Insert(*new TButtonGadget(CM_EDITFINDNEXT, CM_EDITFINDNEXT));
// cb->Insert(*new TSeparatorGadget(6));
cb->Insert(*new TButtonGadget(CM_FILEPRINT, CM_FILEPRINT));
cb->Insert(*new TButtonGadget(CM_FILEPRINTPREVIEW,
           CM_FILEPRINTPREVIEW));
```

(For neatness' sake, you can also delete the Speed bar button bitmaps from the .RC file and even from the directory. In Resource Workshop, they're the bitmaps with the IDs CM_EDITFIND and CM_EDITFINDNEXT; in the directory, they're files FIND.BMP and FINDNEXT.BMP.)

The next step is to add handlers for the new commands via Class Expert. To do that, open the Class Expert window (if it isn't already), select the TShapesView class and expand the Command Notifications entry in the Events panel. Sure enough, there in the list are CM_SHAPESRECTANGLE et al. But these are not bottom level entries; the plus sign shows that they, too, can be expanded. Beneath CM_SHAPESRECTANGLE are two handlers: Command and Command Enable.

We'll come to Command Enable in the next section. For now, just add a handler for Command. You'll be prompted for the handler's name; if you use CmShapesRectangle you'll be consistent with the names App Expert has given other command handlers. While you're at it, add handlers for the other new commands; we'll be using all of them.

Each of these commands simply sets a flag. The Red, Green, and Blue commands will set a color flag that can be used when creating the brush; the Rectangle and Ellipse commands will set a flag indicating which shape should be drawn when the left mouse button is clicked. (You can draw the opposite shape for the right mouse button.)

Where do these flags go? Why, they become properties of the **TShapesView** class, of course! But Class Expert can't help us there. We'll have to use the Project window to locate the SHPSVIEW.H file (subordinate to SHPSVIEW.CPP) and open it. We can then add the following two properties:

```
class TShapesView : public TWindowView {


protected:
  TColor Color;
  enum { SHAPE_RECTANGLE, SHAPE_ELLIPSE } Geometry;


};
```

Now that we've added properties, we *must* not forget to initialize them; so turn to the constructor next—either in a simple code window or through Class Expert; it doesn't matter. Our new constructor looks like this (with the braces tidied up):

```
TShapesView::TShapesView (TDocument& doc, TWindow* parent)
  : TWindowView(doc, parent),
    Color (TColor::LtRed),
    Geometry (SHAPE_RECTANGLE)
  {
  // INSERT>> Your constructor code here.
  }
```

With that job done, we can implement our commands. And a simple job it is, too. All each command has to do is set the appropriate property to the new value. For the **Shape** property:

```
void TShapesView::CmShapesRectangle ()
  {
  Geometry = SHAPE_RECTANGLE;
  }

void TShapesView::CmShapesEllipse ()
  {
  Geometry = SHAPE_ELLIPSE;
  }
```

For the **Color** property:

```
void TShapesView::CmShapesRed ()
   {
   Color = TColor::LtRed;
   }

void TShapesView::CmShapesGreen ()
   {
   Color = TColor::LtGreen;
   }

void TShapesView::CmShapesBlue ()
   {
   Color = TColor::LtBlue;
   }
```

Now all that's left is to modify **EvLButtonDown()** (and **EvRButtonDown()**, if you wish) to draw the desired shape in the requested color. I've removed the **NullPen**; shapes look better if they're outlined and the default pen does that nicely:

```
void TShapesView::EvLButtonDown (UINT modKeys, TPoint& point)
   {
   TWindowView::EvLButtonDown(modKeys, point);
   TClientDC dc (*this);
   TBrush Brush (Color);
   dc.SelectObject (Brush);
   if (Geometry == SHAPE_RECTANGLE)
      dc.Rectangle (point.x, point.y, point.x+50, point.y+50);
   else
      dc.Ellipse (point.x, point.y, point.x+50, point.y+50);
   }
```

Modifying the Menu at Runtime

Wouldn't it be nice if, besides using the menu to select the color of the next shape, it could also report what color had already been selected? Here's how to add check marks to menu items.

When a menu presents a set of choices, such as Rectangle or Ellipse, or Red, Green, or Blue, it is common to place a check mark by the item currently selected.

You'll remember, in Class Expert, in addition to the Command handlers were Command Enable handlers. I told you I'd have something to say about them.

While the Command handler is triggered when the user actually chooses a menu command, the Command Enable handler is triggered when the user *drops the menu down*. Specifically, it is triggered just before the drop-down menu appears; so it is the logical place to make any desired modifications to the menu item about to be displayed. Such modifications include altering the text of the item, enabling/disabling the item, and checking/unchecking the item.

Strictly speaking, a menu item doesn't need to be set and reset. It actually remembers the way it was left last—for example, if you check a menu item, it remains checked until you uncheck it. Early Windows programs were written that way. However, experience has shown that the best time to make menu modifications is just before the menu appears; hence, the Command Enable handlers.

You add these handlers the same as you added the Command handlers. I suggest the name CmShapesRectangleEnable for the Shapes, Rectangle Command Enable handler; you should be able to figure out suitable names for the others. Rather than add all the handlers at once, you may prefer to add them one at a time, using Class Expert's code window to customize them.

The code for each handler is quite simple. The methods each are passed a reference to a **TCommandEnabler** object. This object represents the specific item requesting modifications—for example, **CmShapesRectangleEnable** receives an object representing the Shapes, Rectangle menu item. You use this object to modify the item, generally through the methods **Enable()**, **SetCheck()**, and **SetText()**.

SetCheck(), for instance, takes a true-or-false parameter (it defaults to true). So, to check the Rectangle item if that is, in fact, the last of the Rectangle/Ellipse pair to be chosen, use the following one line of code:

```
tce.SetCheck (Geometry == SHAPE_RECTANGLE);
```

The other Command Enable handlers are all written similarly. Here's the set, for completeness' sake:

```
void TShapesView::CmShapesRectangleEnable (TCommandEnabler &tce)
    {
    tce.SetCheck (Geometry == SHAPE_RECTANGLE);
    }

void TShapesView::CmShapesEllipseEnable (TCommandEnabler &tce)
    {
    tce.SetCheck (Geometry == SHAPE_ELLIPSE);
    }
```

```
void TShapesView::CmShapesRedEnable (TCommandEnabler &tce)
  {
  tce.SetCheck (Color == TColor::LtRed);
  }

void TShapesView::CmShapesGreenEnable (TCommandEnabler &tce)
  {
  tce.SetCheck (Color == TColor::LtGreen);
  }

void TShapesView::CmShapesBlueEnable (TCommandEnabler &tce)
  {
  tce.SetCheck (Color == TColor::LtBlue);
  }
```

There's one other handler—for the Shapes, Other menu command—that I left out because its code is a little more complex. Although we haven't yet supplied a way to *select* a color other than red, green, or blue, there's no harm in including the test. Other should be checked any time the current color is neither red, green, *nor* blue:

```
void TShapesView::CmShapesOtherEnable (TCommandEnabler &tce)
  {
  tce.SetCheck (Color != TColor::LtRed &&
    Color != TColor::LtGreen &&
    Color != TColor::LtBlue);
  }
```

A test at this point should show the Shape menu items always correctly checked. Note: If you forgot to initialize the **Color** property, the Other menu item will probably be checked. That's because **TColor** initializes black by default.

Supporting Persistence with the TDocument Class

There's one major flaw in our program so far: windows do not repaint themselves. They can't; they don't remember what's on them! We've never built that capability into them.

It is not the job of a view to remember its contents; a view is only supposed to make the contents of a document visible in some appropriate manner. A view also conveys the wishes of the user back up to the document.

In order to add persistence to the Shapes application, we'll have to create a new **TShape** class and derivatives, derive a new class from

TDocument for our project, and get the view to tell the new document object what shapes to add to itself.

Creating the TShape Class

Considering the information that is now part of a shape—color, position, and configuration (rectangle or ellipse)—its time to encapsulate these things into a custom class.

Don't expect Class Expert to assist in creating the **TShape** class; that's not its job. Any classes needed by your application that are not directly part of the user interface have to be built entirely by you (unless you buy them or can convince someone else to write them for you!).

The **TShape** class must have as properties the object's color, geometric shape, and location. It only needs one constructor, and won't need any fancy operators. It will need to know how to paint itself, for reasons that will become clear shortly. Here's a first draft of **TShape**'s declaration:

```
typedef enum
   {
   SHAPE_RECTANGLE,
   SHAPE_ELLIPSE
   } GEOMETRY;

class TShape
   {
   public:
     TShape (SHAPE aShape,  TColor & aColor, TRect & aRect);
     void Draw (TDC & dc);
   protected:
     SHAPE Geometry;
     TColor Color;
     TRect Rect;
   };
```

As you can see, I've moved the geometry **enum** from **TShapesView** and made it a **typedef**. When the object is constructed, it will be passed a shape, color, location and (for the heck of it) size. The **Draw()** method will draw either a rectangle or ellipse.

But wait a minute. Is that the only use of the **Shape** property—to make a decision on how to draw this object? Then perhaps this is a job for polymorphism! Let's take a look at the second draft:

```
class TShape
   {
```

```
public:
   TShape (TColor & aColor, TRect & aRect);
   virtual void Draw (TDC & dc) = 0;
protected:
   TColor Color;
   TRect Rect;
};

class TShapeRectangle : public TShape
   {
   public:
   TShapeRectangle (TColor & aColor, TRect & aRect);
   void Draw (TDC & dc);
   };

class TShapeEllipse : public TShape
   {
   public:
   TShapeEllipse (TColor & aColor, TRect & aRect);
   void Draw (TDC & dc);
   };
```

With just two methods for each class (one for the base class—**Draw()**
is a pure virtual function), we can implement what we have so far even
though we suspect there may be more work ahead of us. First, though,
some housekeeping: we have to place the following lines at the top of
SHAPE.CPP:

```
#include <owl\owlpch.h>
#pragma hdrstop
#include "shape.h"
```

Without the first two lines, the pre-compiled header system will give
us grief. The third line **#include**s our own header file.

Here are the three constructors:

```
TShape::TShape (TColor & aColor, TRect & aRect)
   : Color (aColor), Rect (aRect)
   {
   }

TShapeRectangle::TShapeRectangle (TColor & aColor, TRect & aRect)
   : TShape (aColor, aRect)
   {
   }

TShapeEllipse::TShapeEllipse (TColor & aColor, TRect & aRect)
   : TShape (aColor, aRect)
```

```
{
}
```

There's nothing amazing there. Next are the two **Draw()** methods:

```
void TShapeRectangle::Draw (TDC & dc)
  {
  TBrush Brush (Color);
  dc.SelectObject (Brush);
  dc.Rectangle (Rect);
  }

void TShapeEllipse::Draw (TDC & dc)
  {
  TBrush Brush (Color);
  dc.SelectObject (Brush);
  dc.Ellipse (Rect);
  }
```

Notice how simple these functions have become (not that the drawing process was very complicated before). The decision logic—rectangle or ellipse—has been moved up to the point where the object is created, and is never again a source of concern.

On the other hand, there's common code here: the creation and selecting into the **dc** of the **Brush**. Since there's common code, maybe **TShape::Draw()** shouldn't be a pure virtual function, after all. We can modify the set of classes, making it more efficient of code space, by writing *three* **Draw()** methods:

```
void TShape::Draw (TDC & dc)
  {
  TBrush Brush (Color);
  dc.SelectObject (Brush);
  }

void TShapeRectangle::Draw (TDC & dc)
  {
  TShape::Draw (dc);
  dc.Rectangle (Rect);
  }

void TShapeEllipse::Draw (TDC & dc)
  {
  TShape::Draw (dc);
  dc.Ellipse (Rect);
  }
```

Don't forget to remove the **=0** from the declaration of **TShape::Draw( )**.

We can immediately test our **TShape** class, putting incremental development to the test by *not* adding any new abilities to the application. When we're done, the app should run just like before. Of course, first we have to let **TShapesView** know that **TShape** exists, by adding its header file to the **#include** list:

```
#include <owl\owlpch.h>
#pragma hdrstop

#include "shpsview.h"
#include "shape.h"
```

That done, we simply change the **TShapesView** left mouse button down event from an active painter to a more passive producer of an object:

```
void TShapesView::EvLButtonDown (UINT modKeys, TPoint& point)
  {
  TWindowView::EvLButtonDown(modKeys, point);
  TRect Rect (point, TSize (50, 50));
  TShape * Shape;
  if (Geometry == SHAPE_RECTANGLE)
    Shape = new TShapeRectangle (Color, Rect);
  else
    Shape = new TShapeEllipse (Color, Rect);
  TClientDC dc (*this);
  Shape->Draw (dc);
  delete Shape;
  }
```

You may have wondered why I created **Shape** in the heap, rather than on the stack. Actually, for this test, either would have worked equally well. But I placed **Shape** in the heap because that's where, eventually, it will have to be . . . as you'll see shortly.

Building a Better Document

The next step in our Shapes application is to derive a new object class from TFileDocument. Here's how it's done.

Currently Borland's Class Wizard only supports one document base class, **TFileDocument**. This class assumes disk-based storage. For Shapes, that assumption is correct. So let's see how to derive a new class from **TFileDocument**.

To begin with, forget using Class Expert. This tool will be of no help at all. We'll have to implement the new class ourselves, just as we did in the previous section with **TShape**. That means accessing the Project window, selecting the SHAPES.EXE component, clicking the right mouse button, and choosing the Add Node command. The node you should add is SHPSDOC.CPP. After you've done so, add a node to the *new* node: SHPSDOC.H.

Double-clicking on SHPSDOC.H brings up an edit window on the empty file. Add the following lines to the file:

```
#ifndef __SHPSDOC_H__
#define __SHPSDOC_H__

#include <owl\filedoc.h>

class TShapesDoc : public TFileDocument
   {
   public:
     TShapesDoc (TDocument * Parent = 0);
     virtual ~TShapesDoc ();
   };

#endif
```

This is the absolute minimum for a **TFileDocument** derivative. Likewise, we'll save the guts for later and only write the skeleton for SHPSDOC.CPP:

```
#include <owl\owlpch.h>
#pragma hdrstop
#include "shpsdoc.h"

TShapesDoc::TShapesDoc (TDocument * Parent)
   : TFileDocument (Parent)
   {
   }

TShapesDoc::~TShapesDoc ()
   {
   }
```

Of course, we'll want to fill this in later; but, for now, we just want a framework to add into the rest of the Shapes application framework.

Under Class Expert we added a view skeleton, **TShapesView**; **TShapesDoc** is our document skeleton. In ObjectWindows we need one more object to glue these two things together, called a *document template*.

It's called that partly, I think, because it actually uses the C++ template facility. Class Expert placed the class instantiation into the **TApplication** derivative definition file, SHAPSAPP, in the following snippet:

```
//{{DOC_VIEW}}
DEFINE_DOC_TEMPLATE_CLASS(TFileDocument, TShapesView, DocType1);
//{{DOC_VIEW_END}}

//{{DOC_MANAGER}}
DocType1 __dvt1("Shapes files", "*.shp", 0, "shp",
    dtAutoDelete | dtAutoOpen | dtUpdateDir | dtPathMustExist |
dtFileMustExist);
//{{DOC_MANAGER_END}}
```

I've reformatted the lines a little so they're visible on the page; Class Expert isn't so considerate. In the first block, the class **DocType1** is declared using the **DEFINE_DOC_TEMPLATE_CLASS** macro. In the second block, an instance of the new class is created with the unusual name of **__dvt1**. By simply creating this instance, **__dvt1** is attached to the doc/view facility of this application. (It is not necessary to add code to **InitMainWindow()** as the Borland documentation suggests.)

To plug your own document class into the app, just **#include** SHPSDOC.H into SHAPSAPP.CPP, and change the first block above to the one listed earlier:

```
//{{DOC_VIEW}}
DEFINE_DOC_TEMPLATE_CLASS(TShapesDoc, TShapesView, DocType1);
//{{DOC_VIEW_END}}
```

Again, compiling and running after this change should not visibly affect your application, but makes a useful sanity check before we go on.

Making TShape Container-Ready

As you may have guessed, TShapesDoc is going to function as a container of TShape objects. That means we have to make TShape container-ready; here's how.

You may recall from the earlier chapter on Borland containers that, to be used in an indirect container, an object must meet the following criteria:

- Have a default constructor
- Have implemented the == operator

We can easily upgrade **TShape** and its descendants to meet these requirements. Here's the new declaration for **TShape**:

```
class TShape
  {
  public:
    TShape () {}
    TShape (TColor & aColor, TRect & aRect);
    virtual void Draw (TDC & dc);
    int operator==(const TShape & aShape);
  protected:
    TColor Color;
    TRect Rect;
  };
```

The new default constructor simply supplies initial values to its properties; since both properties are already objects, **TShape::TShape** doesn't even have to explicitly invoke them. The **operator==()** method is added to the implementation file:

```
int TShape::operator==(const TShape & aShape)
  {
  return (Color == aShape.Color && Rect == aShape.Rect);
  }
```

Now that **TShape** is container-ready, it makes sense to **typedef** the container class right here in the implementation file:

```
#include <classlib\queues.h>
typedef TIArrayAsVector<TShape> TShapeArray;
typedef TIArrayAsVectorIterator<TShape> TShapeArrayIterator;
```

The specific kind of container we'll need is a queue. I've used an object-like naming convention for the **typedef**s, rather than the older all-caps tradition, to signify that the new entities are objects—which, of course, they are.

Adding a Container to TShapesDoc

We're ready to add the data property to TShapesDoc. This property will be a TShape container, and will hold all the TShape items TShapesView cares to send it.

Our first task in the **TShapesDoc** header file is to **#include** SHAPE.H; with that done we can add the **TShapeArray** container to **TShapesDoc**'s properties. We'll also want to supply a method for adding shape items to the container, and one for telling them to draw themselves:

```
#include "shape.h"

class TShapesDoc : public TFileDocument
  {
  public:
    TShapesDoc (TDocument * Parent = 0);
    virtual ~TShapesDoc ();
    void Add (TShape * aShape);
    void Draw (TDT & dc);
  protected:
    TShapeArray Data;
  };
```

Turning now to **TShapesDoc**'s implementation file, we'll want to specify construction details for the new property (namely, giving it the initial bounds and the number of elements by which it should grow if need be):

```
TShapesDoc::TShapesDoc (TDocument * Parent)
  : TFileDocument (Parent), Data (100, 1, 50)
  {
  }
```

The **Add()** method is trivial, since it merely passes the job onto the **Data** property:

```
void TShapesDoc::Add (TShape * aShape)
  {
  Data.Add (aShape);
  }
```

Draw() is likewise simple. It creates an iterator for the **Data** property and tells each element in the array to draw itself:

```
void TShapesDoc::Draw (TDC & dc)
  {
  TShapeArrayIterator S (Data);
  while (S)
    {
    S.Current()->Draw (dc);
    S++;
    }
  }
```

If any of this looks strange to you, re-read the chapter on container classes. And, yes, an alternate method for **Draw()** would have been a simple **for** loop. I like the iterator technique better, for no good reason.

Adding Persistence to TShapesView

Now that the container has been added to TShapesDoc, we can make use of it from TShapesView. This means adding TShape objects to the document when the left mouse button is clicked, and asking the document to draw itself when the view needs re-painting.

It is essential that a view be able to access its document. It's so universally essential, in fact, that the **TWindowView** base class has a method, **GetDocument()**, just for that purpose.

However, **GetDocument()** returns a reference to a **TDocument** object, meaning you'll always have to cast it to **TShapesDoc &** (or whatever) if it is to be useful.

We can take care of that little problem once and for all by adding a **GetDocument()** method to **TShapesView**. This all happens in the header file. First, the declaration:

```
class TShapesView : public TWindowView {


protected:


    TShapesDoc & GetDocument (void);


};
```

Note that our **GetDocument()** returns a reference to our own class, so when we call this function we will not have to do any casting. That takes place in the method implementation, which is **inline** and therefore also in the header file:

```
inline TShapesDoc & TShapesView::GetDocument (void)
   {
   return (TShapesDoc &) TWindowView::GetDocument();
   }
```

The end result? At the cost of no extra machine instructions, we have easy access to our view's document.

We had already created a **TShape** object in response to the left mouse click; we asked it to draw itself and then **delete**d it. We now modify the method to send the object to the document (which will add it to the container), instead:

```
void TShapesView::EvLButtonDown (UINT modKeys, TPoint& point)
  {
  TWindowView::EvLButtonDown(modKeys, point);
  TRect Rect (point, TSize (50, 50));
  TShape * Shape;
  if (Geometry == SHAPE_RECTANGLE)
    Shape = new TShapeRectangle (Color, Rect);
  else
    Shape = new TShapeEllipse (Color, Rect);
  TClientDC dc (*this);
  Shape->Draw (dc);
  GetDocument().Add (Shape);
  }
```

Our last task here (for now) is to add special handling for painting the screen. Your first thought, of course, will be to use Class Expert to add a handler for the **WM_PAINT** message—but don't be so fast. If we decide to work with **EvPaint()** we'll be responsible for getting our own device context, and there's already a default **EvPaint()** that does that. It calls a virtual function called, simply, **Paint()**, and *that's* the method we'll override.

So, you say, you'll look for it in Class Expert's list of virtual functions? Well, that's where it should be, but it's not there—inexplicably, it was omitted. You'll have to do this manually. First, add the declaration to **TShapesView**'s declaration:

```
class TShapesView : public TWindowView {


protected:


    virtual void Paint(TDC& dc, BOOL erase, TRect& rect);


};    //{{TShapesView}}
```

Then, add the method itself to the implementation file:

```
void TShapesView::Paint(TDC& dc, BOOL erase, TRect& rect)
  {
```

```
GetDocument().Draw (dc);
}
```

If you now compile and run, you'll see that the window repaints itself after being covered or iconized. Shapes is beginning to look like a real Windows application!

Supporting Multiple Views

As we've said, the document is the data; the view is the user interface to that data. Here's how to make the document smart enough to supply information required by the view, and how to make the view smart enough to know what to ask of the document.

The document manager does its job, important as it is, in the background. Once it's in place, we can ignore it. Not so with the document and the view; not only can we not ignore them, we have to nurture them and allow them to develop so they never lose sight of the close relationship they must always maintain.

The trick is that the view must communicate changes to the document; the document must apply those changes to itself, then inform any additional views that changes have been made. It is then up to those other views to redraw themselves if necessary.

In the Shapes application, this means that, when the **TShapesView** adds a shape to the document, it must also request the document to notify any other of its views that the shape has been added. In order to support this the view must add a new feature: *notifications*.

Notifications advise a view of some event that's occurred. In addition to the add-a-shape event, we can also imagine someday needing to advise views that shapes have been rearranged, or that they've all been cleared. So we add to the **TShapesView** header file (before the class declaration) the following event list, offset from **vnCustomBase** so they won't conflict with any internal OWL events:

```
typedef enum
    {
    vnAppend = vnCustomBase,
    vnModify,
    vnClear
    } TShapesEvents;
```

Borland uses separate **int**s in their examples:

```
const int vnAppend = vnCustomBase+0;
```

```
const int vnModify = vnCustomBase+1;
const int vnClear = vnCustomBase+2;
```

But I prefer to use a **typedef enum** so I don't have to keep track of the offset from **vnCustomBase**.

The next task is to specify the signature of the handlers for the new events. There's a macro for this, **NOTIFY_SIG**. The macro takes two parameters, the event and the data type of the handler's one parameter. In the case of **vnAppend**, we can pass the pointer to the **TShape** being appended; for **vnModify** and **vnClear** there is nothing helpful we can add so the parameter will be specified as **void**:

```
NOTIFY_SIG (vnAppend, TShape *)
NOTIFY_SIG (vnModify, void)
NOTIFY_SIG (vnClear, void)
```

Please note the macro invocations do *not* terminate in semicolons.

The next step isn't really required; but it does accommodate a handy shortcut. Here's the problem: in the **TShapesView** implementation file, we're going to have to add the event handlers to the response table. We *could* enter this:

```
DEFINE_RESPONSE_TABLE1(TShapesView, TWindowView)
//{{TShapesViewRSP_TBL_BEGIN}}


  VN_DEFINE(vnAppend, VnAppend, long),
  VN_DEFINE(vnModify, VnModify, void),
  VN_DEFINE(vnClear, VnClear, void),
//{{TShapesViewRSP_TBL_END}}
END_RESPONSE_TABLE;
```

But, let's face it, such a complex and seemingly meaningless line is asking for trouble—especially when you remember your application may have different *kinds* of views, each with its own response table. So Borland recommends we hide that complexity in another set of simpler macros:

```
#define EV_VN_APPEND VN_DEFINE(vnAppend, VnAppend, long)
#define EV_VN_MODIFY VN_DEFINE(vnModify, VnModify, void)
#define EV_VN_CLEAR VN_DEFINE(vnClear, VnClear, void)
```

You'll note that the **VN_DEFINE** for the **vnAppend** event specifies a parameter of type **long** rather than the pointer we actually intend to send. That's because the **NotifyViews()** method we have to use to trigger the events has a fixed argument list and a **long** is the largest (and most complex) thing we can pass—we'll have to cast the pointer to a **long** when the time comes. The data type we put here is actually interpreted as the *size* of the argument we'll be passing.

Then, turning to the implementation file for real, we can make the simpler modification to the response table:

```
DEFINE_RESPONSE_TABLE1(TShapesView, TWindowView)
//{{TShapesViewRSP_TBL_BEGIN}}


    EV_VN_APPEND,
    EV_VN_MODIFY,
    EV_VN_CLEAR,
//{{TShapesViewRSP_TBL_END}}
END_RESPONSE_TABLE;
```

We do have one more chore in the header file, though. (Aren't you glad the Borland IDE makes it so easy to flit from one file to the other?) We have to add the actual handler prototypes to the class declaration:

```
class TShapesView : public TWindowView {


protected:


    BOOL VnAppend (TShape * Shape);
    BOOL VnModify (void);
    BOOL VnClear (void);
    //{{TShapesViewRSP_TBL_END}}
DECLARE_RESPONSE_TABLE(TShapesView);
};      //{{TShapesView}}
```

The **VnAppend()** handler will be invoked for each view when a shape has been added. And the shape itself will be passed as part of the message, which requires us to move the painting task from the mouse button handler to **VnAppend()**. But the mouse button handler must now call another **TDocument** method, **NotifyViews()**, to trigger this event:

```
void TShapesView::EvLButtonDown (UINT modKeys, TPoint& point)
  {
  TWindowView::EvLButtonDown(modKeys, point);
  TRect Rect (point, TSize (50, 50));
  TShape * Shape;
```

```
if (Geometry -- SHAPE_RECTANGLE)
   Shape - new TShapeRectangle (Color, Rect);
else
   Shape - new TShapeEllipse (Color, Rect);
GetDocument().Add (Shape);
GetDocument().NotifyViews (vnAppend, (long) Shape);
}
```

Note that **Shape** is cast to **long**, as described earlier. If you choose to disregard my advice and compile using the medium (or small!) memory model, you'll have to enhance that cast slightly:

```
GetDocument().NotifyViews (vnAppend, (long) (TShape far *) Shape);
```

Of course, there's no harm in using the longer cast in large model.

The **VnAppend()** method now gets the simple job of telling the shape to draw itself—but, remember, this method may now be called for more than one concurrent view, thus keeping all the views of the one document in sync:

```
BOOL TShapesView::VnAppend (TShape * Shape)
   {
   TClientDC dc (*this);
   Shape->Draw (dc);
   return TRUE;
   }
```

The handler returns **TRUE** when complete, as all notification handlers must.

Although we haven't yet implemented any means of modifying or clearing the shapes document, there's no harm in implementing the handlers for those events. They're the same, anyway; in either case, the view must be invalidated, which will trigger a repaint:

```
BOOL TShapesView::VnModify (void)
   {
   Invalidate();
   return TRUE;
   }
```

```
BOOL TShapesView::VnClear (void)
   {
   Invalidate();
   return TRUE;
   }
```

A compile and run should *look* the same as at the end of the previous section . . . but you know that, behind the scenes, a lot more is going on. You are actually supporting a document, and could support multiple views if you had them, and more . . . .

And yet, you still don't have an application that's quite ready for shrink-wrap. You are lacking features like file saving, Clipboard, dialog boxes—but we'll learn how to add those in the next chapter.

Professionalizing Your Applications

Any programming book and manual in the world tells you how to get the basic jobs done. Unfortunately, what most do not tell you is how to add that bit of flash that says, "This application was written by a professional." Not only does a professional-looking and behaving application speak well of you; it also inspires confidence in the application itself. We all know that most "errors" reported by users are, in fact, caused by the user's lack of understanding the application. When an application looks and feels competent and robust, users tend to try a little harder to figure out what's wrong before they call you at 2 A.M.

Please don't mistake glitz and glitter for the kind of professional features to which I'm referring. Users can quickly see through a shallow layer of garishly colored 3-D panels when there's a lack of substance beneath.

In this chapter, we'll go through the standard menu commands one-by-one; I'll show you what each should mean and we'll implement the ones App Expert has not already implemented for us. On the way, we'll learn how to use common and custom dialog boxes; deal with the Clipboard; add real file handling to an application; and a few other surprises.

Get ready. Shrink-wrapping is not far away!

The File Menu

If you plan to write a Windows application that doesn't have a File menu, it's not really a Windows application. Oh, it may run under the Windows environment, but it won't be a true Windows app because virtually all Windows apps are document-oriented—possibly, all of them. (A utility like the Clock isn't an application.) I'll grant there may be some exceptions, somewhere, but so far no one has been able to convince me. It always turns out they've been dwelling on what their application will *do*, instead of what their application will *work on*.

Even when the document is not file-based, it is still a document. It may be in a database, on a mainframe, at the other end of a modem, or even real-time data coming from some data-gathering device. It doesn't matter. To the Windows user, it's in a file it will be managed via the File menu.

Furthermore, the user should be permitted the illusion that, when the file is "opened," it is loaded into memory where it is shared by no one, and available to be viewed or manipulated. Most important: the users must feel that they can refuse to save any changes they've made, if they like. That's one of the things that makes users feel comfortable with Windows, and we've got to encourage it, even if it means more work for us programmers.

Understanding the Three Types of Documents

Maintaining the data-in-memory illusion can be easy or tricky, depending on how much data there is to worry about. Here are a few suggestions.

It doesn't matter whether your data is kept on the local hard disk, a network disk, a database, across a modem, or in the bottom of a locked filing cabinet stuck in a disused lavatory with a sign on the door saying "Beware of the Leopard." You can still maintain what I like to call the "Windows Illusion of Safety" with one of three techniques. Which technique is right for you largely depends on *how much* data there is.

If there is a small amount, and will always be a relatively small amount, you don't have to bother with any illusions at all; simply load the whole mess into memory in response to the File, Open command. In response to File, Save, just write all the data out to disk in one shot. If you want to provide an extra level of security, save the timestamp of the file when you read it in and make sure it hasn't been updated by some other application when you are ready to overwrite it. If it has been, you can pop up a message box asking the user for instructions. The File, Save As command is also easy to implement; simply write the internal data out to a new file.

The second option is for databases only—and only those databases that support transaction consistency. In SQL, this means BEGIN TRANSACTION/COMMIT/ABORT statements are supported. You do a BEGIN TRANSACTION when the "file" is opened; you do a COMMIT in response to File, Save. As in any major database application, File, New and File, Save As are omitted from the menu. (For that matter, File, Open may not actually appear on the menu, although the operation is still there in spirit. Remember, if you omit File, Open you eliminate the possibility of testing with alternate databases.) If the user performs a *File..Exit* without saving any changes made to the database, the application can emit a ABORT.

The third option, and my favorite, is to work with *transactions*. The idea here is to access, not load, the source file (although this technique works equally well with databases). In your **TDocument** class you store a container of transactions. These transactions, which should be objects in their own right, are of three types: added, changed, and deleted. (A variation of this scheme also keeps viewed records in memory, on the theory that, once viewed, a record is likely to be requested again.) When the user requests a record, you first examine the transactions (from most recent back) for one matching the requested key. If you find it, great; otherwise, get it from the file/database.

When the user chooses the File, Save command, you apply the transactions (in order) to the file or database. File, Save As is more complex; you have to make a copy of the original file, then apply the transactions to it.

Switching to the Hourglass Cursor

As every even mildly experienced Windows user knows, the cursor switches to an hourglass whenever a lengthy operation begins, and doesn't revert to its original form until the operation is complete. Here's a handy little class to automate that task.

Switching to the hourglass cursor seems to be a trivial job at first. You simply "load" the cursor from the system resources using the Windows API call **LoadCursor()**, then call **SetCursor()** to use it. Here's the traditional code:

```
SetCursor (LoadCursor (NULL, IDC_WAIT));
```

But that's not the whole story. You have to restore the previous cursor—whatever it was—when your operation completes. Fortunately, **SetCursor()** returns a handle to that cursor, but you still have to create a variable in which to save it. And you have to call **SetCursor()** again, using the saved handle. And then there's the possibility of *nested* lengthy operations . . . .

I'm here to tell you that there's possibly no task so trivial that you can't make it even less of a pain by encapsulating it into a class, and the admittedly minor headache of the hourglass cursor is no exception.

Before we look at the code for **TWaitCursor**, let's look at how we want to *use* it. Let's say we have a function, **LengthyOperation()**, we intend to invoke. Wouldn't it be nice to do it this way:

```
void MyFunction (void)
   {
   TWaitCursor W;
   LengthyOperation();
   }
```

Here you can see that **TWaitCursor**'s constructor must do the job of loading the hourglass cursor and setting it; the destructor must restore the original cursor.

But suppose you want a little more control over *when* the cursor is changed to an hourglass? You may also want to be able to code the following:

```
void MyFunc2 (void)
  {
  TWaitCursor W (FALSE);

  W.Wait();
  LengthOperation1 ();
  W.Done();

  W.Wait();
  LengthOperation1 ();
  }
```

Constructing a **TWaitCursor** with an argument of FALSE creates the object but does not yet change the cursor. That happens when the **Wait()** method is invoked. Similarly, the **Done()** method restores the original cursor before the object is destroyed. (But if **Done()** has *not* been invoked explicitly, it will be invoked implicitly by the destructor.)

Now that you've seen **TWaitCursor** in action, let's see how it's declared. Here's WAITCUR.H:

```
#ifndef __WAITCUR_H__
#define __WAITCUR_H__

#include <owl\gdiobjec.h>

class TWaitCursor : public TCursor
  {
  public:
    TWaitCursor (BOOL StartWait = TRUE);
    ~TWaitCursor ();
    void Wait ();
    void Done ();
  private:
    HCURSOR OldCursor;
  };

#endif
```

As you can see, I've derived **TWaitCursor** from **TCursor**—we don't get a lot of benefit from doing this, but there's no harm, either. And this way, the programmer using this class can treat a wait cursor like any other **TCursor** object, in addition to its special properties.

The WAITCUR.CPP implementation file begins by including the precompiled header stuff (as any implementation file does):

```
#include <owl\owlpch.h>
#pragma hdrstop
#include "waitcur.h"
```

The constructor calls the **Wait()** method automatically if the **StartWait** parameter is TRUE—as it would be, by default:

```
TWaitCursor::TWaitCursor (BOOL StartWait)
  : TCursor (0, IDC_WAIT), OldCursor (0)
  {
  if (StartWait)
    Wait();
  }
```

Since **TWaitCursor** is derived from **TCursor**, we need to specify a base constructor. I've chosen one that will load the hourglass cursor (**IDC_WAIT**) from the Windows system resources. Notice also that **OldCursor** is initialized to zero—a signal that there is no cursor handle in there. (Zero is never a valid value for a handle.)

The destructor only has to call **Done()**:

```
TWaitCursor::~TWaitCursor ()
  {
  Done();
  }
```

The **Wait()** method simply sets the hourglass cursor, saving the return value of **SetCursor()** in **OldCursor**:

```
void TWaitCursor::Wait ()
  {
  OldCursor = SetCursor (*this);
  }
```

As a descendent of **TCursor**, **TWaitCursor** can be cast to a **HCURSOR** data type—just the data type wanted by **SetCursor()**. And, as noted before, when **TWaitCursor** was constructed, it was done specifying the hourglass cursor.

That leaves **Done()**. This method must be smart enough to not try and call **SetCursor()** too many times—that is, once waiting is done, it's done. We can accomplish this by testing the value of **OldCursor**:

```
void TWaitCursor::Done ()
  {
  if (OldCursor)
    SetCursor (OldCursor);
  OldCursor = 0;
  }
```

That's it. Even the problem of nested calls is solved, because calling **SetCursor( )** to "change" to a cursor that is, in fact, already the current cursor, is an extremely low-cost operation. Likewise, loading the handle to the hourglass cursor, as each instance of **TWaitCursor** will do, is extremely efficient. Windows makes sure access to system cursors is inexpensive anyway; and once a cursor is loaded, subsequent requests for it are filled very quickly.

Making TShapes Persistent

Before we can write full documents to disk, we'll have to enhance the TShape class so that it can be written to disk: after all, what is a Shapes document but a container of TShapes?

In an earlier chapter we covered the technique for making classes streamable. However, there is a glitch: The simple streams described earlier work only on objects whose class is known when the streaming is done, in both directions. In other words, you could always stream three **TShapeRectangle** objects followed by four **TShapeEllipse** objects, but you couldn't stream any arbitrary number of **TShape** descendents chosen by the user at runtime.

Obviously, this is a problem. What we need is some method of streaming objects out to disk (or wherever) that preserves the *type* of object along with that object's properties. Then we need a way to re-create the original objects when we bring them back from the storage medium.

Borland has provided this method, although it is poorly documented. It's encapsulated in an object class called **pstream**, located in the class library (not OWL); thus it can be used in non-ObjectWindows applications, too.

In order to stream a **TShape**, we have to stream its properties, **Color** and **Rect**—but those properties are objects of the **TColor** and **TRect** classes, respectively . . . and **TColor** *is not streamable*! That means we'll have to do some fiddling.

Basically we'll have to derive a class—call it **TXColor**—that adds no more than streamability to its base class. Fortunately this is not a lot of work (and will lead us into the project we'll create in Chapter 10).

First, we add the requisite modules XCOLOR.CPP and XCOLOR.H to the Shapes project. We **#include** CLASSLIB\OBJSTRMS.H—that's where the **pstream** macros and stuff are located—and derive the **TXColor** class from both **TColor** and **TStreamableBase**. We look up the **TColor** class in OWL\COLOR.H and copy its constructors to the Clipboard. (Remember, you can't inherit constructors.) We then paste them into the class declaration for **TXColor** and modify them so that each constructor invokes, **inline**, the corresponding base constructor. (In this way we won't add any actual runtime overhead.) Finally, we add the **DECLARE_STREAMABLE** macro and we have our XCOLOR.H header file:

```
#ifndef __XCOLOR_H__
#define __XCOLOR_H__

#include <classlib\objstrm.h>
#include <owl\color.h>

class TXColor : public TColor, public TStreamableBase
  {
  public:
    TXColor(){}
    TXColor(COLORREF value) : TColor(value) {}
    TXColor(long value) : TColor(value) {}
    TXColor(int r, int g, int b) : TColor(r,g,b) {}
    TXColor(int r, int g, int b, int f)
      : TColor (r, g, b, f) {}
    TXColor(int index) : TColor (index) {}
    TXColor(const PALETTEENTRY far & pe)
      : TColor (pe) {}
    TXColor(const RGBQUAD far& q) : TColor (q) {}
    TXColor(const RGBTRIPLE far& t) : TColor (t) {}
  DECLARE_STREAMABLE (, TXColor, 1);
  };

#endif
```

The **DECLARE_STREAMABLE** macro does more than you might expect from its unprepossessing appearance. It actually adds a *nested* class to **TXColor**. This class, **Streamer**, provides the **pstream** abilities we so desire.

The implementation file is about as simple. All we have to supply is the **IMPLEMENT_STREAMABLE** macro and the nested **Streamer** class methods **Read()** and **Write()**:

```
#include <owl\owlpch.h>
#pragma hdrstop
#include "xcolor.h"
```

```
IMPLEMENT_STREAMABLE (TXColor);

void *TXColor::Streamer::Read (ipstream & In, uint32) const
  {
  TXColor * My = GetObject();
  In >> My->Value;
  return My;
  }

void TXColor::Streamer::Write (opstream & Out) const
  {
  TXColor * My = GetObject();
  Out << My->Value;
  }
```

With the new, streamable class **TXColor** available to the project, we can now enhance **TShape**. We change the **Color** property to the new class, and add the **DECLARE_STREAMABLE** macro to **TShape**. Since **TShapeRectangle** and **TShapeEllipse** do not have any properties of their own, they get a slightly different macro, **DECLARE_STREAMABLE_BASE**. Here's SHAPE.H:

```
#ifndef __SHAPE_H__
#define __SHAPE_H__

#include <classlib\objstrm.h>
#include "xcolor.h"

class TShape : public TStreamableBase
  {
  public:
    TShape () {}
    TShape (TColor & aColor, TRect & aRect);
    virtual void Draw (TDC & dc);
    int operator==(const TShape & aShape);
  protected:
    TXColor Color;
    TRect Rect;
  DECLARE_STREAMABLE (, TShape, 1);
  };

class TShapeRectangle : public TShape
  {
  public:
    TShapeRectangle (TColor & aColor, TRect & aRect);
    void Draw (TDC & dc);
  DECLARE_STREAMABLE_FROM_BASE (, TShapeRectangle, TShape);
  };
```

```
class TShapeEllipse : public TShape
  {
  public:
    TShapeEllipse (TColor & aColor, TRect & aRect);
    void Draw (TDC & dc);
  DECLARE_STREAMABLE_FROM_BASE (, TShapeEllipse, TShape);
  };

#include <classlib\arrays.h>
typedef TIArrayAsVector<TShape> TShapeArray;
typedef TIArrayAsVectorIterator<TShape> TShapeArrayIterator;

#endif
```

Incidentally, if **TShape** had been an abstract class—for example, if its **Draw** method was pure virtual—then we'd have had to use the **DECLARE_ABSTRACT_STREAMABLE** macro, instead.

We can add the streaming stuff to the end of the implementation file. First, we implement streaming for the **TShape** base class:

```
IMPLEMENT_STREAMABLE (TShape);

void *TShape::Streamer::Read (ipstream & In, uint32) const
  {
  TShape * My = GetObject();
  In >> My->Color >> My->Rect;
  return My;
  }

void TShape::Streamer::Write (opstream & Out) const
  {
  TShape * My = GetObject();
  Out << My->Color << My->Rect;
  }
```

See how easy it is to stream the **Color** and **Rect** properties when they, too, are streamable!

Implementing streaming for **TShapeRectangle** and **TShapeEllipse** is trivial, since these derived classes have no properties of their own. It's all done with mirrors—er, macros:

```
IMPLEMENT_STREAMABLE_FROM_BASE (TShapeRectangle, TShape);
IMPLEMENT_STREAMABLE_FROM_BASE (TShapeEllipse, TShape);
```

If **TShapeRectangle** or **TShapeEllipse** *did* have additional properties, you would have to use the **DECLARE_STREAMABLE** macro and call **ReadVirtualBase()** and **WriteVirtualBase()** in the **Read()** and **Write()** methods, respectively, to stream the inherited properties before streaming the new ones.

TShape and its derived classes are now streamable. You can compile XCOLOR and SHAPE for a syntax check, but there will be no change in the running of the application—not until we've added streamability to the document class, as we do in the next section.

Writing the Document to Disk

One aspect of document persistence, the one we've already seen, is that of repainting the window after it's been moved or uncovered. The second, equally important aspect, is that of saving the document to disk between runs of the application.

When you use App Expert to generate a skeleton application for you, using the doc/view paradigm, you've already got a framework for saving your document to disk (or other storage medium). All you have to do is fill in the spaces.

In the last chapter, we created a new class, **TShapesDoc**, that was derived from **TFileDocument**. You probably have already noticed, just fooling around with the resulting application, that the File, Open and File, Save commands *appear* to work, although the file that is created is empty, and one you attempt to load isn't actually loaded. We are now going to give teeth to those commands.

Your first task is to override five methods inherited from **TFileDocument**. These methods are **IsOpen()**, **Open()**, **Commit()**, **Revert()**, and **Close()**. That means we must add them to the **TShapesDoc** class declaration in SHAPSDOC.H:

```
class TShapesDoc : public TFileDocument
  {
  public:
    TShapesDoc (TDocument * Parent = 0);
    virtual ~TShapesDoc ();
    void Add (TShape * aShape);
    void Draw (TDC & dc);
    virtual BOOL IsOpen (void);
    virtual BOOL Open (int Mode, LPCSTR Path = 0);
    virtual BOOL Commit (BOOL Force);
    virtual BOOL Revert (BOOL Clear);
    virtual BOOL Close (void);
  protected:
    TShapeArray Data;
```

```
    BOOL Opened;
};
```

We've also added a new property: **Opened**. OWL will want to know whether a file has been opened and this flag will give us the ability to answer honestly.

In SHAPSDOC.CPP, we know we're going to add some lengthy (possibly) file handling—and that means we should make use of the **TWaitCursor** class we designed earlier. To do that, we'll have to add its **#include** at the top of the file:

```
#include <owl\owlpch.h>
#pragma hdrstop
#include "shpsdoc.h"
#include "waitcur.h"
```

And, since we've added a property, we have to initialize it in the constructor:

```
TShapesDoc::TShapesDoc (TDocument * Parent)
  : TFileDocument (Parent), Data (100, 0, 50), Opened (FALSE)
  {
  }
```

We also have a small change to make to the **Add()** method. We need a way to tell the document that a change has been made, after all, so that if the user tries to close the application without saving the shapes he or she has so laboriously placed in the window, the application will display and warning and provide an opportunity to save the work. There is already a method, inherited from **TFileDocument**, that does this job; it's called **SetDirty()**. Here's the modified **Add()** method:

```
void TShapesDoc::Add (TShape * aShape)
  {
  Data.Add (aShape);
  SetDirty (TRUE);
  }
```

Now for the new methods. I mentioned that OWL would be asking whether we've opened a file or not. OWL does this by invoking the **IsOpen()** method:

```
BOOL TShapesDoc::IsOpen (void)
  {
  return Opened;
  }
```

All we have to do is return the value of the **Opened** property.

That property will be set in the **Open()** method. Here's the code:

```
BOOL TShapesDoc::Open (int, LPCSTR)
   {
   TWaitCursor Wait;
   ifpstream In (GetDocPath());
   Data.Flush();
   WORD ShapeCount;
   In >> ShapeCount;
   while (ShapeCount--)
      {
      TShape * Shape;
      In >> Shape;
      Add (Shape);
      }
   SetDirty (FALSE);
   Opened = TRUE;
   return TRUE;
   }
```

Since there's a lot of stuff here, let's look at it carefully.

First of all, you'll notice that the names of both parameters have been omitted. That's to avoid a warning from the compiler, complaining that we didn't use either one.

You can tell from the declaration in the header file that the two parameters are **Mode** and **Path**. **Mode** might indicate the file is being opened read-only; but since we're only going to read it anyway, that doesn't matter. (Some applications would save this value and refuse to enable the File, Save command if it were TRUE.) The **Path** value, one might think, would point to the name of the file to be opened . . . but this value is *always* an empty string. Apparently someone, somewhere, changed his or her mind about how **Open()** was going to be used.

So we create an instance of **TWaitCursor** (to change the cursor to an hourglass for the duration of this method), then create an instance of **ifpstream** using the **GetDocPath()** method we've inherited from **TFileDocument** to specify which file, exactly, is to be opened. You can probably figure out where **ifpstream** stands in the **pstream** hierarchy from its name: it's a **pstream** for files opened for input.

At this point we've got access to our input file, but it may not be our first—the **Data** container might already have something in it from the last time. (Not too likely in MDI mode; but you might someday re-use this class for an SDI application.) The **Flush()** method empties it out, deleting any objects it might have contained.

Next we need to know how many shape objects to read in. As you'll see when we look at the **Commit()** method, we have conveniently saved that count so all we have to do is stream it into the variable **ShapeCount**.

The loop in which we retrieve each of the previously stored objects is:

```
while (ShapeCount--)
  {
  TShape * Shape;
  In >> Shape;
  Add (Shape);
  }
```

First we create a pointer of the base **TShape** class. It's just a pointer; we don't even use the new operator on it. Instead, we stream from the **In** file directly into the pointer. That operation will actually create the object, and it won't be a **TShape** object, exactly: It will be a **TShapeRectangle** object or a **TShapeEllipse** object, whichever was stored in this position. This is polymorphism at work, here, folks. We then pass the object to the **Add()** method as usual.

After all the objects have been re-created, we can close the method by calling **SetDirty()** to mark the document as *un*changed—we just read the stuff in, after all. (**Add()** would have marked the document dirty, so we have to unmark it after all the objects have been added.) We then set **Opened** to TRUE and return TRUE.

What didn't we do? We did *not* invoke the ancestor **Open()** method. We didn't need to; it does nothing useful for us. This will not be true in the other new methods.

Commit() is the opposite of **Open()**; it's the operation in which the objects we've collected are streamed *out* to disk:

```
BOOL TShapesDoc::Commit (BOOL Force)
  {
  if (! TFileDocument::Commit (Force))
    return FALSE;
  TWaitCursor Wait;
  ofpstream Out (GetDocPath());
  WORD ShapeCount = Data.GetItemsInContainer();
  Out << ShapeCount;
  for (register WORD s = 0; s < ShapeCount; s++)
    Out << Data[s];
  SetDirty (FALSE);
  return TRUE;
  }
```

As promised, we start by invoking the inherited method—and if *it* returns FALSE, so do we, immediately. This is our only use of the **Force** parameter. It is possible to request App Expert to generate an application that has the File, Save command enabled all the time, even when the document has not been changed. If so, and the user tries to save an unchanged document, the **Force** parameter will be TRUE. I figure, if you went to the trouble of keeping File, Save enabled, you must want to allow this—so why check the flag? On the other hand, if File, Save is *disabled* for unchanged documents, **Commit()** will never be called for one of these documents . . . and you don't have to check the flag.

The rest of the method parallels the **Open()** method. Notice that we write the count of objects before streaming out the objects themselves.

Incidentally, the PSTREAM example on the Borland C++ 4.02 CDROM uses the **ForEach()** method to enumerate the objects, rather than a **for** loop. Although the example compiles and works, I couldn't get it to work here: the first two objects always failed when reading them back in. After three days of fruitless attempts, I finally switched to this technique, which worked perfectly. Someday, hopefully, Borland will get all the bugs out.

Revert() is an odd little method in that most applications do not have a File, Revert command—but, unless you request otherwise, App Expert applications do. The method is supposed to throw out changes made since the last File, Save and reload from disk:

```
BOOL TShapesDoc::Revert (BOOL Clear)
  {
  if (! TFileDocument::Revert (Clear))
    return FALSE;
  if (! Clear)
    Open (NULL);
  return TRUE;
  }
```

Clear will be FALSE unless the document was created in response to File, New. The method is easy to implement; but I question adding another command to the already-crowded File menu. Time will tell whether enough applications include it that users come to expect it there. Meanwhile, I am omitting it from *my* applications—but I still implement the method, just in case.

Finally, the **Close()** method, in addition to invoking the inherited method, has little to do but reset the **Opened** property:

```
BOOL TShapesDoc::Close (void)
  {
```

```
if (! TFileDocument::Close ())
   return FALSE;
Opened = FALSE;
return TRUE;
}
```

And that's it! Compile and run, and you'll be able to File, Save your shapes and File, Open them later.

Printing the Active View

In Microsoft's Foundation Classes, once your view window's Draw( ) method (analogous to OWL's Paint( ) method) is coded, you have print and print preview features with no further effort. It's not quite as simple in OWL but not too hard either.

After the actual file handling commands of the File menu generally come the print commands. Who knows why, in someone's mind a decade ago, it seemed reasonable to lump printing and file handling together? It doesn't matter any more. The File menu is where people expect to see it.

File, Printer Setup is already implemented for you; and, to an extent, so are File, Print and File, Print Preview. However, if you try and use either of those commands, you'll find they don't actually work.

That's because of an oddity in the way invocation of the various windows' **Paint( )** method has been distributed. When a window is actually being painted, the message gets passed to practically everyone: the MDI child window, the MDI child's client window, and the view window within the MDI child's client.

Normally the MDI child's client doesn't do any painting, and the view window's **Paint( )** method is invoked independently (because it receives its own **WM_PAINT** message from the underlying Windows system). But when the user selects File, Print or File, Print Preview the MDI child client has its **Paint( )** method invoked explicitly—from the *printing* mechanism. The view window will not get *its* **Paint( )** method invoked, unless the MDI child client does it.

The MDI child client does do this—but *only* if the view is derived from **TEditView** or **TListView**. In the demo programs supplied by Borland, the view window is always derived from **TEditView** or **TListView**, so printing appears to be effortless.

However, our Shapes program—and practically any other real-life program you write—will be derived from **TWindowView**. So you'll have to modify the MDI child client's **Paint( )** method as follows:

```
void ShapesMDIChild::Paint (TDC & dc, BOOL Erase, TRect & Rect)
  {
  ShapesApp * App = TYPESAFE_DOWNCAST(GetApplication(), ShapesApp);
  if (App)
    if (App->Printing && App->Printer && ! Rect.IsEmpty())
      {
      TWindowView * Client =
        TYPESAFE_DOWNCAST(GetClientWindow(), TWindowView);
      Client->Paint (dc, Erase, Rect);
      }
  }
```

Note that this code replaces about fifty lines of App Expert-generated code. As in the original method, we don't do anything at all unless printing is in progress. If it is, we locate the client window (which is the view) and invoke its **Paint()** method. (I could have cast the client to a **TShapesView**, but my first approach is more general and works just as well.)

Once you've made this change, you can put some shapes in a view and issue the File, Print Preview command. It will still be the user-unfriendliest print preview screen you've ever seen, but your shapes will appear on the page and you'll be able to print them by clicking on the printer button.

The Edit Menu

Windows' primary strength is not that it is simply a multitasking environment, but that it also provides a framework in which the multiple tasks can work together. The Windows Clipboard, primarily accessed through the Edit menu, is the most-used component of that framework. It lets you transfer information in various formats, and even assists the application in deciding which format should be used.

Clipboard Basics

Basic Clipboard use usually involves one format—text—and simple cutting or copying to, and pasting from, the Clipboard. Our design must be able to do that and more.

At its absolute simplest, Clipboard management is trivial. To place some text in the Clipboard, you simply:

* Open the Clipboard
* Clear its previous contents

- Place a copy of the text into the Clipboard
- Close the Clipboard

But placing text in the Clipboard, or getting it out, is only a small part of the story. Although the Clipboard is intended to hold just one *conceptual* item at a time, the fact is it can hold almost unlimited *types* of items, each a different formatting of the conceptual item. For example, if the user selects the word *Hello* in your application and chooses Edit, Copy, your app will presumably place *Hello* into the Clipboard in the CF_TEXT format. But it could also place a *picture* of the word *Hello* in CF_BITMAP format so that it could be pasted into, say, Paintbrush. It could also generate a CF_METAFILEPICT (commonly called a *picture*) of the text that could be sized and imported by Resource Workshop's Icon Editor.

Again, just placing text in the Clipboard is an extremely simple, straightforward operation. In a traditional (non object-oriented) environment, you wouldn't think twice about coding those forty or fifty lines for each application. But we would like to encapsulate the Clipboard into an object that will solve as much of the problem as possible in a re-usable class.

Some of the work has been done for us: ObjectWindows includes a **TClipboard** class. However, this class is a mere packaging of the various Windows API Clipboard functions, and not a well-thought-out object class at all. We can use it as a base for our new class: **TXClipboard**.

Having the Clipboard support multiple formats is an important consideration. Even if most of the time you intend to supply just CF_TEXT items to the Clipboard, if you ever want to include a device independent bitmap (DIB) as well, but the class can't support it, it won't have done you much good. That's why it's important to support multiple formats at the outset.

On the other hand, the implementation should not pose any extra burden when text *is* all you need to support.

Another aspect of multiple formats we'll have to contend with is that of *format negotiation*, where the Clipboard source and recipient agree in which format the item should be rendered. If your application wants to get an item from the Clipboard, and the item exists in five different formats, which one should your application take? If your application only supports one format, the answer is obvious; but suppose it supports all five. You'll want to take the format with the least loss of data. When you design your program, you'll know which that will be, but we can't guess now. The ability to specify format priority should be built into our **TXClipboard** class.

It turns out that each format can best be managed if we create a format class and a **TXClipboard** class that is a collection of format class objects. For a simple application, the only format placed in the collection might be CF_TEXT, but your app could place as many formats there as needed, in priority order. Each format object should include methods for *rendering* (placing into the Clipboard) and *garnering* (gathering from the Clipboard) data in the appropriate format.

How can we code an object that will place something into the Clipboard, when we don't know what that something will be? Simple: by making it an *abstract* class. We'll write a **TClipboardText** class, but you'll never be expected to use it directly. Instead, you'll derive a *new* class from it that will do the actual rendering to and garnering from the Windows Clipboard.

The **TXClipboard** class itself will have a container class property to hold the various formats; with enough added functionality to manage the broader aspects of the Clipboard from **TClipboard**, that will leave our **TClipboardFormat** derivatives to do the actual dirty work on demand.

The TClipboardFormat Abstract Class

As a collection of format objects, the TXClipboard class will manage the broader aspects of the Clipboard while letting the format objects render and garner the actual data. Virtual methods ensure that our application, using derived TClipboardFormat objects, will be able to place and retrieve Clipboard data as required.

Since the various Clipboard format classes and the **TXClipboard** class are inextricably linked, we can placed them in the same module, which we'll call CLIPBRD. The header file, CLIPBRD.H, starts out like this:

```
#ifndef __CLIPBRD_H__
#define __CLIPBRD_H__

#include <owl\clipboar.h>
#include <cstring.h>
#include <owl\window.h>

class TXClipboard;

class TClipboardFormat
   {
   public:
     TClipboardFormat (UINT aFormat = CF_TEXT);
     TClipboardFormat (string & aFormatName);
     virtual UINT RenderSize (void) const = 0;
```

```
   virtual void RenderToClipboard
     (TWindow & Window, LPVOID & Buffer, LONG BufferLength) const = 0;
   virtual BOOL AcceptFromClipboard
     (TWindow & Window, void far * Buffer, LONG BufferLength) const = 0;
   virtual string GetName (void) const;
   int operator==(const TClipboardFormat & aFormat) const;
   operator UINT (void) const { return Format; }
   virtual void ToClipboard (const TXClipboard & Clipboard) const;
   virtual BOOL FromClipboard (const TXClipboard & Clipboard) const;
 protected:
   UINT Format;
 };
```

```
#endif
```

There is just one property: **Format**, containing the format ID.

Several of the methods require **TXClipboard** reference parameters—however, the **TXClipboard** class has not yet been fully declared. That's okay, though; the line

```
class TXClipboard;
```

is enough to work with until we do declare it in full.

The cast operator to **UINT** will simply return the value of the **Format** property; the **Format** property in turn will contain the Clipboard format identifier: either a standard ID, or a special one for custom formats. There are quite a few standard format IDs defined in WINDOWS.H; here's a list:

CF_TEXT This format is used for standard C-style strings—that is, strings that end with a NULL character. The string may contain embedded carriage return/line feed pairs, tabs, and other formatting characters.

CF_OEMTEXT Text using the *Original Equipment Manufacturer's* font is, in other words, DOS text. The lower 128 characters match the ANSI character set used by Windows, but the upper 128 characters include the line-drawing characters familiar to DOS users. When a CF_TEXT item is added to the Clipboard, a CF_OEMTEXT entry is translated and placed as well, unless there was a CF_OEMTEXT format already there. Likewise, when a CF_OEMTEXT item is added to the Clipboard, a CF_TEXT entry is translated and placed as well, unless there was a CF_TEXT format already there.

CF_BITMAP This format is a standard Windows bitmap. Using the Windows API directly, you'd pass a bitmap handle to the Clipboard; however OWL **TBitmap** objects have a **ToClipboard()** method built into them.

CF_METAFILEPICT This format, which Windows users usually call a "picture," is a standard Windows metafile. However, the metafile handle isn't passed directly; instead, a METAFILEPICT structure (which includes a metafile handle) is passed.

CF_SYLK The *symbolic link* format is seldom used.

CF_DIF The *data interchange format* is seldom used.

CF_TIFF The *tag image file format* is another means of representing bitmaps and is used by photo, art, and desktop publishing applications.

CF_DIB A *device independent bitmap* is represented by a BITMAPINFO structure, which includes scaling information, as well as the bitmap. Don't imagine it helps much, though; scaled bitmaps are still jagged and ugly.

CF_PALETTE This format supplies a color palette. The palette specifies exactly which shade each of the 16 or 256 colors of the current video driver will take. By itself, such a palette is pretty much useless; CF_PALETTE formats usually accompany graphics formats such as CF_BITMAP.

CF_PENDATA Remember the pen extensions to the Windows operating system? Is anyone actually using them? Well, if you are, you can transfer pen information using this format.

CF_RIFF The *resource interchange file format* is seldom used as such—but see the CF_WAVE format ID entry.

CF_WAVE If you have a Sound Blaster or other Windows-compatible sound card, you are well familiar with digital sound recordings called WAVE files. WAVEs are a subset of the RIFF, though few people care. In any case, once brought into memory, WAVE information can be transfered using this format.

CF_OWNERDISPLAY This format tells the Clipboard that any Clipboard viewer shouldn't try to display the information itself. Instead, a WM_PAINTCLIPBOARD message is sent to the owner of the item. This message is conceptually similar to a WM_PAINT message, but of course the device context in the supplied PAINTSTRUCT structure won't refer to your window or even your application; the painting will take place in the Clipboard Viewer's window. This format is used when the Clipboard data is too complex for the Clipboard viewer to draw (like formatted text).

CF_PRIVATEFIRST The format IDs between this value and CF_PRIVATELAST are reserved for private formats. Studies have shown that the majority of Clipboard operations take place within the same application. An application can, of course, more efficiently work with internal data structures that no other application would understand. This range of formats permits an application to place internal structures on the Clipboard. However, there is one gotcha: the private structure handles are *not* freed when the Clipboard is emptied. Your app will have to free those handles in response to a **WM_DESTROYCLIPBOARD** message.

CF_DSPTEXT If you have placed a private format on the Clipboard, and you do *not* want to place a text format-version of the same thing, but *do* want a Clipboard viewer to be able to display text—this is the format for you. For example, suppose you have placed on the Clipboard a private format representing a map route. There is no meaningful text representation of this. You could use the CF_OWNERDISPLAY to paint the map plus the route; but an alternative would be a CF_DSPTEXT format that simply read, "Map Route." For more alternatives, see the next two formats.

CF_DSPBITMAP Like CF_DSPTEXT, this allows your app to support a Clipboard viewer by allowing your private format to be represented as a bitmap, but disallowing its being pasted into another application as a bitmap.

CF_DSPMETAFILEPICT Like CF_DSPTEXT, this format ID allows your app to support a Clipboard viewer by allowing your private format to be represented as a picture, but disallowing its being pasted into another application as a picture.

CF_GDIOBJFIRST This format ID through CF_GDIOBJLAST can be used to actually transfer GDI objects such as pens, brushes, and fonts through the Clipboard. I'm not sure why anyone would want to do this, which may explain why I've never seen it done. However, should you choose to take advantage of this feature, note two things: First, pass the *handle* of the GDI object, not a pointer to a corresponding OWL object. And second, the Clipboard will delete these GDI objects for you so make sure the **TGDI** object has been created with auto-delete turned off. (The **ShouldDelete** property is protected so you'll have to derive a new class, like **TXPen**, that sets it to FALSE for the occasion.)

We'll look at the various members of this class as we implement them in CLIPBRD.CPP.

At the top of the file (after the **#include**s) is the first of two constructors:

```
#include "clipbrd.h"
#include <string.h>


TClipboardFormat::TClipboardFormat (UINT aFormat)
```

```
: Format (aFormat)
{
}
```

This constructor is used for any of the predefined formats. You simply supply the format ID, which the constructor saves in the **Format** property.

For those occasions when none of the predefined formats will do, you can simply define your own. Call it anything you like—it can even contain embedded blanks. Just remember two things: first, the name you use will show up in Clipboard viewer's list of available formats; and second, that name will be disabled—the Clipboard viewer will not be able to display that format.

Here's the constructor for custom formats:

```
TClipboardFormat::TClipboardFormat (string & aFormatName)
    {
    Format = RegisterClipboardFormat (aFormatName.c_str());
    }
```

RegisterClipboardFormat() is a Windows API call; it returns a format ID that can be used just like one of the standard IDs.

The next two methods declared for this class, **RenderSize()** and **RenderToClipboard()** are both pure **virtual** functions. They must be implemented in descendent classes to render the specific item the user has requested. **RenderSize()** must return the number of bytes to be transferred to the Clipboard; **RenderToClipboard()** is handed a buffer of the requested size and allowed to place the data into it. Both of these methods are invoked by the **protected** method **ToClipboard()**:

```
void TClipboardFormat::ToClipboard (const TXClipboard & Clipboard)
const
    {
    LONG OriginalLength = RenderSize (Clipboard.GetWindow());
    if (OriginalLength)
        {
        HGLOBAL h = GlobalAlloc (GMEM_DDESHARE, OriginalLength);
        LPVOID Original = GlobalLock (h);
        RenderToClipboard (Clipboard.GetWindow(),
            Original, OriginalLength);
        GlobalUnlock (h);
        ((TClipboard &)Clipboard).SetClipboardData (Format, h);
        }
    }
```

ToClipboard()'s job is to simply handle the housekeeping involved in allocating a chunk of global memory to hand to the Clipboard. We use the return value of **RenderSize()** as a parameter to **GlobalAlloc()**, which provides us with the handle to the memory block. The **GMEM_DDESHARE** flag tells **GlobalAlloc()** to give us a block that can be shared among applications. Strictly speaking, this isn't required because when Clipboard takes over ownership of the block it will change the block attributes anyway. But it allows the **TClipboardFormat** items to be used in other contexts, such as DDE and OLE, should you wish.

But **RenderSize()** and **RenderToClipboard()** require a method of **TXClipboard**'s that has not yet been defined: namely, **GetWindow()**. The idea is that the **TXClipboard** object, when sending this format to the Clipboard, can supply a handle to the window with the data that needs to be sent. That's fine, but since we won't be implementing **TXClipboard** until the next section, you won't be able to compile without errors until then.

The awkward cast of the **Clipboard** parameter's **SetClipboardData()** method is due to the fact that the **TClipboard** base class was implemented without proper care given to adding the **const** keyword to the methods. As mentioned in the chapters on implementing C++ classes, any method that does not alter an object's properties should *always* be made a **const** method. However, that wasn't done in **TClipboard**.

HOT TIP

A Look at Global Handles

With the appearance of **GlobalAlloc()** we'll now go into some detail regarding Windows' memory management.

When Windows was first designed, the only PCs available had 8088 or 8086 CPUs. These ran in what we now call "real mode" and were limited to 1Mb of memory.

It was clear from the start that Windows and its applications would require much more memory than that, so the designers implemented an overlay scheme involving the segments compiled programs were already divided into. Unless otherwise marked, segments were only loaded into memory when needed, and could be discarded if the memory they occupied was needed for something else. This implied that segments might also be moved in memory, which meant traditional pointers would not provide a reliable means of accessing them. Instead, Windows relied on *handles*, 16-bit values that were actually indexes into tables where a description of the memory block was kept. There were several different tables, each used to store a different kind of object. Thus, we have window handles, handles to bitmaps and brushes, instance handles, module handles, and so on. Among this plethora of handle types are memory handles: **global** and **local**.

Global handles are created using **GlobalAlloc()**; a pointer to the allocated memory is obtained from **GlobalLock()** and released by **GlobalUnlock()**. Finally, when the memory block is no longer needed, the handle is passed to **GlobalFree()** to be released.

There is an identical set of routines with the prefix **Local** instead of **Global** for managing the local heap.

It is absolutely essential that these functions be called in pairs. Every block that is allocated must eventually be freed; every pointer that is locked must be unlocked. You are not supposed to leave a pointer locked between operations; so programmers did not usually save the pointers, just the handles. As each operation started, the handle was used to lock a pointer, the data accessed, and the handle unlocked.

GlobalAlloc() and the other global heap management functions are still used, but since Windows 3.1 cannot run in real mode, there is no longer any harm in leaving pointers locked. (Windows can move memory blocks around in protected mode without changing the segment part of the address.) With ObjectWindows the managing of handles, and the pairing of these operations, is hidden from you—but it's happening anyway. The only time you have to worry about it is when coding an object class, such as **TClipboardFormat**, that has to deal with memory management at this relatively low level.

Similarly, the pure **virtual AcceptFromClipboard()** method is handed a buffer containing the Clipboard data; **FromClipboard()** has done the housekeeping involving the global data handle:

```
BOOL TClipboardFormat::FromClipboard (const TXClipboard & Clipboard)
const
  {
  HGLOBAL h = ((TClipboard &)Clipboard).GetClipboardData (Format);
  LPVOID Buffer = GlobalLock (h);
  BOOL Result = AcceptFromClipboard (Clipboard.GetWindow(),
    Buffer, GlobalSize (h));
  GlobalUnlock (h);
  return Result;
  }
```

Normally the caller of **GlobalAlloc()** must eventually call **GlobalFree()**. However, in Clipboard use, when we give the handle to the Clipboard we also pass on ownership of the block. The Clipboard itself will free that memory block when it is no longer needed (except, as previously noted, with formats in the range of CF_PRIVATEFIRST through CF_PRIVATELAST).

FromClipboard() returns a boolean value: TRUE or FALSE. It gets this value from **AcceptFromClipboard()**. This feature will help us with format negotiation later on; if a format object tries to get data from the Clipboard that is unsuitable, it returns FALSE and the Clipboard object will try the next format.

There are times when an application would like to know a given format's name. A Clipboard viewer certainly needs this information to label the displayed data. Some applications enumerate all available formats and give the user the choice of which to paste.

The names of custom formats are easy to retrieve; you simply invoke the Windows API function **GetClipboardFormatName()**. But we are told we must *not* call this function with an identifier for one of the standard formats. Thus, in the **GetName()** method, we check for each of the standard formats before resorting to **GetClipboardFormatName()**:

```
string TClipboardFormat::GetName (void) const
  {
  switch (Format)
    {
    case CF_TEXT:
      return "Text";
    case CF_BITMAP:
      return "Bitmap";
    case CF_METAFILEPICT:
      return "Picture";
    case CF_SYLK:
      return "SYLK";
    case CF_DIF:
      return "DIF";
    case CF_TIFF:
      return "TIFF";
    case CF_OEMTEXT:
      return "OEM Text";
    case CF_DIB:
      return "DIB";
    case CF_PALETTE:
      return "Palette";
    case CF_PENDATA:
      return "Pen Data";
    case CF_RIFF:
      return "RIFF";
    case CF_WAVE:
      return "Wave";
    case CF_OWNERDISPLAY:
      return "Owner Display";
```

```
case CF_DSPTEXT:
   return "Display Text";
case CF_DSPBITMAP:
   return "Display Bitmap";
case CF_DSPMETAFILEPICT:
   return "Display Picture";
default:
   {
   char Buffer[64];
   GetClipboardFormatName (Format, Buffer, sizeof Buffer);
   return string (Buffer);
   }
};
}
```

This method returns the user-friendly name for all the standard formats except CF_PRIVATEFIRST/CF_PRIVATELAST and CF_GDIOBJFIRST/CF_GDIOBJLAST. If you actually derive one of those formats from **TClipboardFormat**, you'll need to override this method with one that returns an appropriate name.

Use the Resource Pool

Internationalize your applications by placing the text for names of formats in your application's resource pool, and change the **GetName()** method to retrieve the text from there.

You could even use the format ID itself as an offset into a string table resource to obtain the name of any format in a single function call.

Our last method for **TClipboardFormat** is the equivalence operator. This method is required in order to make a container class for these objects:

```
int TClipboardFormat::operator==(const TClipboardFormat & aFormat)
const
   {
   return (Format == aFormat.Format);
   }
```

Deriving the TXClipboard Class

Before we derive more specialized format classes, we must fully declare the TXClipboard class. This class is derived from TClipboard, but will add the features of a container of format objects.

If we want the **TXClipboard** class to include a container of formats, we should **typedef** the container class in CLIPBRD.H:

```
#include <classlib\arrays.h>
typedef TIArrayAsVector<TClipboardFormat> TClipboardFormats;
typedef TIArrayAsVectorIterator<TClipboardFormat>
TClipboardFormatsIterator;
```

With that done, we can declare (finally!) **TXClipboard**:

```
class TXClipboard : public TClipboard
  {
  public:
    TXClipboard (TWindow * Window);
    void SetData (void) const;
    void GetData (BOOL GetAll = FALSE) const;
    BOOL IsData (void) const;
    TWindow & GetWindow (void) const { return *Window; }
    TClipboardFormats Formats;
  private:
    TWindow * Window;
  };
```

The only property is **Window**, a pointer that we'll save during construction so that format objects can use it (via **GetWindow()**) for window-specific processing. (We'll have an example of that in the next section.)

Turning back to CLIPBRD.CPP, we can implement the constructor (not a big deal):

```
TXClipboard::TXClipboard (TWindow * aWindow)
  : TClipboard (*aWindow),
    Formats (10, 0, 5),
    Window (aWindow)
  {
  }
```

I've initialized the **Formats** container to ten elements, but allowed it to grow in sets of five. The memory needs of this container will never be anything but modest, so there's no need to agonize over it.

Now we get to the interesting bit—actually inducing the collection of format objects to send their guts to the Clipboard. The **SetData()** method does just that:

```
void TXClipboard::SetData (void) const
  {
  ::EmptyClipboard();
```

```
TClipboardFormatsIterator f (Formats);
while (f)
   {
   f.Current()->ToClipboard (*this);
   f++;
   }
}
```

Rather than wrestle with the fact that **TClipboard::EmptyClipboard( )** was not marked **const**, I just invoked the global Windows API function. A **TClipboardFormatsIterator** is then created, and the **ToClipboard( )** method of each format in the collection is then invoked, in order. That's important: many applications on the receiving end of the Clipboard are sensitive to the order in which formats were place there.

When most applications retrieve something from the Clipboard, they stop at the first suitable format. However, a few go for *all* the formats that are available. Our **GetData( )** method supports both scenarios:

```
void TXClipboard::GetData (BOOL GetAll) const
   {
   TClipboardFormatsIterator f (Formats);
   while (f)
      {
      TClipboardFormat * Format = f.Current();
      if (IsClipboardFormatAvailable (*Format))
         if (Format->FromClipboard (*this) && !GetAll)
            break;
      f++;
      }
   }
```

The **IsClipboardFormatAvailable( )** method takes as its first argument a **UINT**, the ID of the desired format. Since the **TClipboardFormat** class has a cast to **UINT** for just this purpose, the method is convenient to call.

As you may have noticed in the class declaration, the default value for the **GetAll** argument is FALSE. If that is not changed, the method will terminate with the first available format that matches a format in the collection . . . *if* that format's **FromClipboard( )** method returns TRUE. But if **GetAll** is TRUE, all formats in the collection for which there is data will be triggered.

Sometimes a program just wants to check to see if any suitable formats are available. The **IsData( )** method handles that job nicely:

```
BOOL TXClipboard::IsData (void) const
   {
```

```
TClipboardFormatsIterator f (Formats);
while (f)
  {
  TClipboardFormat * Format = f.Current();
  if (IsClipboardFormatAvailable (*Format))
    return TRUE;
  f++;
  }
return FALSE;
}
```

How do you add formats to the **Formats** collection? Simple—by using the collection's **Add()** method. The other standard container methods are all available, too, since **Formats** is a public data member. As a fully implemented object, **Formats** does not need to be protected (in either sense of the word!).

The TClipboardText Class

The first format class to be derived from TClipboardFormat is one designed to transfer simple text.

Unlike its base class, **TClipboardText** is *not* an abstract class—objects of this class can actually be useful; they'll pop into the Clipboard the text caption of the window that owns the **TXClipboard** object. Here's the declaration from the CLIPBRD.H file:

```
class TClipboardText : public TClipboardFormat
  {
  public:
    virtual UINT RenderSize (TWindow & Window) const;
    virtual void RenderToClipboard
      (TWindow & Window, LPVOID & Buffer, LONG BufferLength) const;
    virtual BOOL AcceptFromClipboard
      (TWindow & Window, void far * Buffer, LONG BufferLength) const;
    virtual BOOL FromClipboard (const TXClipboard & Clipboard) const;
  };
```

There isn't even a constructor! Well, there is, really. Since we haven't specified one, the system will generate a default constructor for us. The default constructor will use the default constructor of the base class, **TClipboardFormat**; and *that* constructor specifies the CF_TEXT format. So we get what we need for free.

Back to the implementation file, the first three methods we *do* have to write are trivial, since they rely on methods built into **TWindow**:

```
UINT TClipboardText::RenderSize (TWindow & Window) const
  {
  return Window.GetWindowTextLength();
  }

void TClipboardText::RenderToClipboard
    (TWindow & Window, LPVOID & Buffer, LONG BufferLength) const
  {
  Window.GetWindowText ((LPSTR) Buffer, (UINT) BufferLength);
  }

BOOL TClipboardText::AcceptFromClipboard
    (TWindow & Window, void far * Buffer, LONG) const
  {
  Window.SetWindowText ((LPSTR) Buffer);
  return TRUE;
  }
```

These methods obtain the size and text, and set the text of the **Window** argument, respectively.

The change made to the overridden **FromClipboard()** method is more subtle:

```
void TClipboardText::FromClipboard (void) const
  {
  HGLOBAL h = Clipboard->GetClipboardData (Format);
  LPSTR Buffer = (LPSTR) GlobalLock (h);
  AcceptFromClipboard (Buffer, strlen (Buffer));
  GlobalUnlock (h);
  }
```

Why did we bother? Actually, our version of **AcceptFromClipboard()** doesn't even use the **BufferLength** argument. But another text class based on this one might need to know the exact length of the string that's been fetched from the Clipboard, and one of the peculiarities of **GlobalAlloc()** is that it usually gives you a little more memory than you asked for (it allocates memory in 16-byte pieces). **GlobalSize()** therefore usually does not equal your allocation request exactly (although it will never be smaller). Therefore, you may have to take special pains to supply a correct **BufferLength** parameter to **AcceptFromClipboard()**. If, for example, you are transferring data into a structure, you should use the **sizeof** operator to determine how many bytes to copy rather than **GlobalSize()**.

This is a constant problem with CF_TEXT format, so we solve the block size problem for NULL-terminated strings by invoking **strlen()** instead of **GlobalSize()**. And now you know why **FromClipboard()**, as well as **AcceptFromClipboard()**, was made **virtual**.

Placing Bitmaps on the Clipboard

Bitmaps offer their own special challenges with regard to the Clipboard. Here's a TClipboardBitmap class you can use directly, or derive even more specialized bitmap classes from.

The OWL **TBitmap** class actually adds some helpful bitmap functionality, saving us a lot of work. All we have to do is encapsulate it into a **TClipboardFormat** derivative to get it to work with our collection-of-formats scheme.

Here's the declaration, preceded by a couple of **#include**s for **TPoint** and the GDI stuff:

```
#include <owl\point.h>
#include <owl\gdiobjec.h>
class TClipboardBitmap : public TClipboardFormat
  {
  public:
    TClipboardBitmap (TSize aBounds);
    virtual void RenderToClipboard
      (TWindow & Window, TDC & dc) const;
    virtual BOOL AcceptFromClipboard
      (TWindow & Window, TBitmap & Bitmap) const;
    virtual void ToClipboard (const TXClipboard & Clipboard) const;
    virtual BOOL FromClipboard (const TXClipboard & Clipboard) const;
  protected:
    TSize Bounds;
  private:
    virtual UINT RenderSize (void) const { return 0; }
    virtual void RenderToClipboard
      (TWindow & Window, LPVOID & Buffer, LONG BufferLength) const {}
    virtual BOOL AcceptFromClipboard
      (TWindow & Window, void far * Buffer, LONG BufSize) const {
        return FALSE; }
  };
```

Here we had an interesting challenge: the **RenderToClipboard()** and **AcceptFromClipboard()** methods suitable for bitmaps have different calling sequences than the pure virtual functions signified in the base class. Those pure virtual functions must be overridden or **TClipboardBitmap** will still be considered an abstract class by the compiler, and we won't be able to instantiate it.

If you look in the **private** section of the declaration, you'll see how that problem was solved: with inline, do-nothing versions of the required functions. That will satisfy the compiler while causing no overhead, since these methods are not called anywhere.

When creating a bitmap for the Clipboard, you have to specify the size. That's the purpose of the **Bounds** property, which is supplied in the constructor:

```
TClipboardBitmap::TClipboardBitmap (TSize aBounds)
  : TClipboardFormat (CF_BITMAP), Bounds (aBounds)
  {
  }
```

Similar to the **TClipboardText** format, the **TClipboardBitmap** class sends an image of the window that opened the Clipboard. It does this by calling that window's **Paint()** method:

```
void TClipboardBitmap::RenderToClipboard
    (TWindow & Window, TDC & dc) const
  {
  TRect Rect (TPoint (0, 0), Bounds);
  Window.Paint (dc, FALSE, Rect);
  }
```

On the other hand, there's no meaningful way we can *accept* anything from the Clipboard. Where would we put it? What we do with it? So the **AcceptFromClipboard()** method always returns FALSE:

```
BOOL TClipboardBitmap::AcceptFromClipboard
    (TWindow &, TBitmap &) const
  {
  return FALSE;
  }
```

Of course, you're always free to derive a new class from this that *does* accept bitmaps from the Clipboard.

You've got to be figuring, where is the magic? Where did the device context come from that was sent to **RenderToClipboard()**? Well, here's some of it:

```
void TClipboardBitmap::ToClipboard (const TXClipboard & Clipboard)
const
  {
  TClientDC ClientDC (Clipboard.GetWindow());
  TMemoryDC MemoryDC (ClientDC);
  TBitmap Bitmap (ClientDC, Bounds.cx, Bounds.cy);

  MemoryDC.SelectObject (Bitmap);
  MemoryDC.PatBlt (0, 0,
    Bitmap.Width(), Bitmap.Height(), WHITENESS);
  RenderToClipboard (Clipboard.GetWindow(), MemoryDC);
```

```
Bitmap.ToClipboard ((TClipboard &) Clipboard);
}
```

The code is divided into three sections. First, a device context is obtained for the window that owns the **TXClipboard** object. Then a *memory device context*, compatible with—that is, having the same characteristics as—the display screen is created. We can use this memory DC just like one that really writes to the screen, except the results stay in memory. We then create a **TBitmap** object based on the client DC; this is called a *compatible bitmap* and also will have the same characteristics as the bitmap on which the window is painted.

In the second section, we operate on the memory DC: selecting the bitmap into it and painting the bitmap white (it was originally "undefined," which is a charming shade of garbage). *Now* the memory DC is ready and we send it to **RenderToClipboard()** which, you'll recall, will pass it on the window's **Paint()** method. **Paint()** doesn't care what kind of DC it draws on.

In the final section, the bitmap sends *itself* to the Clipboard, thanks to its built-in ability to do that.

Retrieving a bitmap *from* the Clipboard turns out to be a much simpler job:

```
BOOL TClipboardBitmap::FromClipboard (const TXClipboard & Clipboard)
const
    {
    return AcceptFromClipboard (Clipboard.GetWindow(),
      TBitmap (Clipboard));
    }
```

That's because **TBitmap** comes complete with a constructor that accepts a Clipboard reference. Using that constructor does *all* the work, except for figuring out what to do with the bitmap now that you have it.

Adding Clipboard Support to Shapes

To add Clipboard support to Shapes now just requires adding a TXClipboard property to the Shapes view class, and support for the Edit, Copy and Edit, Paste commands. Try it!

Our first move for Clipboard support is to add a **TXClipboard** property to **TShapesView**. Of course, to do *that*, you have to **#include** CLIPBRD.H:

```
#include "clipbrd.h"
```

```
//{{TWindowView = TShapesView}}
class TShapesView : public TWindowView {


protected:
  TColor Color;
  enum { SHAPE_RECTANGLE, SHAPE_ELLIPSE } Geometry;
  TXClipboard Clipboard;


};    //{{TShapesView}}
```

Having added a property, we have to modify the **TShapesView** constructor:

```
TShapesView::TShapesView (TDocument& doc, TWindow* parent)
  : TWindowView(doc, parent),
    Color (TColor::LtRed),
    Geometry (SHAPE_RECTANGLE),
    Clipboard (this)
{
Clipboard.Formats.Add (new TClipboardText);
Clipboard.Formats.Add (new TClipboardBitmap (TSize (1000, 1000)));
}
```

In addition to specifying the property's constructor (and passing it the pointer to the view window), we also take this opportunity to add a couple of format objects. The view window will never have a caption (it's only the client area, remember), but there's no harm in including the text format.

Using Class Expert, you should now add support for Edit, Copy. When done the method should look like this:

```
void TShapesView::CmEditCopy ()
  {
  Clipboard.SetData();
  }
```

Yes, that's it—the rest of the job has been built into **TXClipboard** and the Clipboard format classes.

Edit, Paste is similarly implemented:

```
void TShapesView::CmEditPaste ()
  {
  Clipboard.GetData();
  Invalidate();
  }
```

To see if text can be pasted into the window, modify the **Paint()** method:

```
void TShapesView::Paint(TDC& dc, BOOL, TRect &)
  {
  char Buffer[128];
  GetWindowText (Buffer, sizeof Buffer);
  dc.TextOut (0, 0, Buffer);
  GetDocument().Draw (dc);
  }
```

Finally, support enabling Edit, Paste only if one of the desired formats is actually present in the Clipboard:

```
void TShapesView::CmEditPasteEnable (TCommandEnabler &tce)
  {
  tce.Enable (Clipboard.IsData());
  }
```

There it is: the essence of sophisticated Clipboard support that you can take as far as you like.

The Window Menu

Every MDI application should have a Window menu. The commands on this menu allow the user to manipulate the MDI child windows: cascading and tiling them, arranging the icons neatly, and so on. It also provides a list of available MDI child windows, giving the user a non-mouse method of activating any one of them.

Non-MDI applications should also have a Window menu—*if* they have modeless dialog boxes that the user can turn on or off. Visual Basic is an example of such an application; the various windows that make up the Visual Basic IDE are all actually modeless dialog boxes. In such a case, each modeless dialog box should have a name and matching entry on the Window menu. The user can open each of the windows by clicking on the entry or, if the window is already open, can close it the same way. (Entries should be checked if the window is open and unchecked if not.)

You can combine these two uses of the Window menu if you have an MDI application that also has modeless dialog boxes—but I've never seen one.

Notifying Multiple Views of Document Changes

The whole idea of the doc/view paradigm is to easily allow multiple views of the same document. To work, changes to the document by one view, must be communicated to the other views.

There are any number of reasons a view might want to communicate with another view . . . or even to send a message to itself. Notifying it of a change to the document is only one. In fact, notifying it of a change might be *many different* messages, allowing for different kinds of changes.

To support this interview communication, you have to plug into the OWL messaging system as if you belonged there. To accomplish this, add lines like the following to the document class header file (SHAPSDOC.H, in this case):

```
typedef enum
    {
    vnAppend = vnCustomBase,
    vnModify,
    vnClear
    } TShapesEvents;

NOTIFY_SIG (vnAppend, TShape *)
NOTIFY_SIG (vnModify, void)
NOTIFY_SIG (vnClear, void)

#define EV_VN_APPEND VN_DEFINE(vnAppend, VnAppend, long)
#define EV_VN_MODIFY VN_DEFINE(vnModify, VnModify, void)
#define EV_VN_CLEAR VN_DEFINE(vnClear, VnClear, void)
```

The first block of lines define the events you want to notify views of. The next block are macro invocations that map the events to response table entries. They also indicate what message cracking will be required.

The third block is optional, but makes adding the entries to the response table somewhat simpler.

With those additions, the **TShapesView** response table now looks like this:

```
DEFINE_RESPONSE_TABLE1(TShapesView, TWindowView)
//{{TShapesViewRSP TBL_BEGIN}}


    EV_VN_APPEND,
    EV_VN_MODIFY,
    EV_VN_CLEAR,
```

```
//{{TShapesViewRSP_TBL_END}}
END_RESPONSE_TABLE;
```

As an example of sending one of these notifications, consider the case where a new shape has been added to the document. The view that has added the shape can easily notify any other views that might exist by invoking the document's **NotifyViews()** method, as **EvLButtonDown()** now does (check out the last line):

```
void TShapesView::EvLButtonDown (UINT modKeys, TPoint& point)
  {
  TWindowView::EvLButtonDown(modKeys, point);
  TRect Rect (point, TSize (50, 50));
  TShape * Shape;
  if (Geometry == SHAPE_RECTANGLE)
    Shape = new TShapeRectangle (Color, Rect);
  else
    Shape = new TShapeEllipse (Color, Rect);
  GetDocument().Add (Shape);
  GetDocument().NotifyViews (vnAppend, (long) Shape);
  }
```

Responding to the notification requires a method whose calling sequence is compatible with the one defined with the **NOTIFY_SIG** macro. Here's the handler for the **vnAppend** notice:

```
BOOL TShapesView::VnAppend (TShape * Shape)
  {
  TClientDC dc (*this);
  Shape->Draw (dc);
  return TRUE;
  }
```

We've very cleverly sent the new (appended) shape to the handler; the other views can update themselves by drawing just the new shape, without having to redraw all of them.

Of course, if some modification occurred other than an append—an item was deleted, perhaps, or all of them were—then there's no recourse but for the view to redraw from scratch. The handler can make that happen by invalidating the view, thus forcing a repaint:

```
BOOL TShapesView::VnModify (void)
  {
  Invalidate();
  return TRUE;
  }
```

```
BOOL TShapesView::VnClear (void)
  {
  Invalidate();
  return TRUE;
  }
```

Now all you need is a way to open a second view of the same document as the first, and you can test! And that's just what we'll do in the next section.

Implementing a Window, New Command

Many MDI applications include a Window, New command that creates a duplicate of the active view in a new MDI child window. Unfortunately, the menu supplied by App Expert doesn't include such a command—but the logic to implement it is already there, buried in ObjectWindows. Here's how to get at it.

To add a Window, New command to your App Expert-generated application, go to the Project window and double-click on the .RC file. This will start up Resource Workshop and load your application's resources into it. Look for the main menu resource and open the menu editor.

Look for the Window menu and select it; press the Insert key to create a new item directly beneath it. This item will be initialized with the text "Item," which you should change to "&New Window." Don't worry about the comment line; amazingly, that will fill in for you automatically. The important thing is to change the identifier to CM_VIEWCREATE. Exit Resource Workshop and recompile. That's all it takes!

Part Overview

PART 3

Creating Useful Objects

As powerful as it is, ObjectWindows is just a start—a jumping-off place. To begin with, it is primarily concerned with automating the user-interface aspects of your applications. Except for the string and containers classes, when it comes to the data engine aspects of your work, you're on your own. But even with the user-interface objects, there are still a few holes. Fortunately, these holes are easy for you to fill, thanks to inheritance and the extensibility of C++ objects.

In the next few chapters we'll create a few of these object classes together and show how they can be used. These projects will help you to develop the skills necessary to create your own ObjectWindows extensions, filling needs as you find them, and building an additional arsenal of tools that you can re-use in future projects.

Building a Colorful Object

F rom the earliest days of Windows, C programmers have had access to a **typedef** called **COLORREF**. A **COLORREF** is actually just a 32-bit value that holds a color, defined by its red, green, and blue components. Each of these components is allocated eight bits, so that there are eight bits left over. Windows also supplies a macro, **RGB()**, that combines individual component values by the simple expedient of left-shifting the red and green portions. Additional macros, **GetRValue()**, **GetGValue()**, and **GetBValue()**, return the individual components.

The folks at Borland expanded **COLORREF** into a true objectcalled **TColor**. However, maybe they didn't have time to really think about what they were doing. For whatever reason, **TColor** is an extremely simple encapsulation of **COLORREF**. That's why we had to derive a **TXColor** class in the previous chapter; the **TColor** class didn't even have streaming ability built in! **TColor** stores its value, as does **COLORREF**, in a 32 bit property. But, as a simple 32-bit value, it does not lend itself to meaningful operations such as addition or multiplication; and other C++ features such as streaming are not built into it. In this chapter we'll complete the **TXColor** class by throwing out its **TColor** inheritance, starting from scratch (although we'll still derive **TXColor** from **TStreamableBase** and clear up some possibleconfusion regarding stream I/O along the way).

Designing the TXColor Class

To design a class, the first step is often to decide how the class will be used. To see how the **TXColor** class will be used, we should first look at how the **COLORREF** type it is intended to replace is used.

All color values in Windows are represented as **COLORREF**s. These values are used in creating pens and brushes, and in setting text and text background colors.

COLORREFs are generally derived in either of two ways. For the standard, user-definable system colors, we use the **GetSysColor()** function. This function is passed one of several pre-defined indexes, such as **COLOR_WINDOW** or **COLOR_BTNFACE**. (There is also a **SetSysColors()** function, although you should use this function only as a replacement for the Control Panel's Color utility—people's eyes work differently, and no application should presume to reset system colors on its own!)

For programmer-defined colors, the **RGB()** macro is most often used. From a C programmer's point of view, this macro makes relatively simple the otherwise tedious job of converting three color components—red, green, and blue—into a 32-bit number. For example, the statement that loads the color purple into a **COLORREF**

```
COLORREF MyColor = RGB (255, 0, 255);
```

expands to:

```
COLORREF MyColor = ((255 << 16) + (0 << 8) + 255);
```

Either way it works because all colors (at least, the ones humans can perceive) can be represented as varying degrees of red, green, and blue.* Equal amounts of all three produce gray shades; the maximum value (255) of all three appears white, while the minimum value (0) of all three appears black. Red and green components of 255, with a blue component of 0, produce yellow. Blue and green produce cyan; red and blue produce magenta.

Although this system allows for about 16 million different shades, don't be surprised if you can't tell the difference between RGB(255,0,0) and RGB(254,0,0). Even with a 16-million-color video driver, the human eye would find the difference too subtle to consciously detect. Such color differences only matter when there are a great many of them, adjacent to each other, producing a field of gradually varying shades.

But most of us do not use 16-million-color video drivers; we settle for 256-color or even the 16-color driver that Windows installs for standard VGA cards. In such cases, only the grossest changes to color components matter—*if* we are talking about solid colors, as are used with text and lines.

Brushes are a different matter. If you ask Windows for a brush in a color that cannot be portrayed directly with the installed video driver, Windows will create a "dithered" color. This word, which comes from the printing industry (and not, as you may have suspected, from the world of politics), means to switch back and forth from each of two values, neither of which is quite what you want, but which together give an approximation of the desired value. To see dithering at work, get a magnifying glass and look closely at a color magazine photo (or, easier, at a comic book page). You'll see that "in-between" colors such as flesh tones, purples and oranges are actually composed of varying-sized dots of different primary colors. When viewed from a normal

---

* This is using the *additive* color system, the way glowing devices like television and computer monitors work. The *subtractive* system applies to magazine printing, mixing paints, and combining crayons, and uses magenta, yellow and cyan as its base colors.

distance, the eye blends these dots together, producing the illusion of the desired color.

One of the neat things about Windows is that this dithering takes place only when needed, and without any effort on the programmer's part at all. It even applies automatically to monochrome monitors, where various requested "solid" colors are rendered as dithered shades of gray.

The fact that programmers find the **RGB()** macro to be useful reveals that the red-green-blue concept is not a hard one to grasp—or to use. In designing our **TXColor** class, we should accommodate this. It would be nice, for example, to be able to add to just the red component of a color, or to the green or blue. And, of course, we want addition operations to look like normal, built-in addition. In pseudocode, we'd like to write something like

```
MyColor += Red(16);
```

and add to just the red component without disturbing the blue or green components. We'd also want to assure that adding to a value won't cause an overflow. Say that the red component of a color is already 200; since these components are limited to 8 bits, the maximum value is 255. If I add 100 to the red component of that color, what I *want* is for the color to get redder. Such an addition should stop at 255, rather than rolling around to the much dimmer 45.

It turns out, then, that we need to create classes for each of the color components: **TRed**, **TGreen**, and **TBlue**.

Obviously these classes share much in common; so you might ask why create three classes instead of just one **TColorComponent** class. The answer lies in the example given earlier. We can overload the assignment operator separately for each of these classes, so that

```
MyColor += TRed (100);
```

is implemented to affect just **MyColor**'s red component, while

```
MyColor += TGreen (50);
```

affects just the green component. We would not be able to duplicate this effect with just a **TColorComponent** class.

Still, there's no denying that **TRed**, **TGreen**, and **TBlue** have a great deal in common—everything, in fact, but their conceptual place in the universe! They're stored the same (8-bit values), and they'll all be subject to the same normalization requirements (no arithmetic operation should allow their absolute value to rise above 255, or below 0). It's clear, then, that the best way to implement the individual color component classes is to derive them from a common base class.

And, one more thing: one of the reasons to bother with the **TXColor** class at all is to make serialization easier. That means that the **TColorComponent** and **TXColor** classes must, themselves, be derived from the ObjectWindows **TStreamableBase** class, so they can inherit the basic serialization mechanism.

Planning for TXColor's Distribution

How will **TXColor** *be distributed? It depends on how you plan to use it. Here are some guidelines for making the choice between distributing source code, a static library, or a DLL.*

You have three choices when packaging an object such as **TColor**. You can write the source code and distribute it that way, adding both the header and implementation files to all future projects that can make use of this object's functionality. This technique is appropriate if the following conditions apply:

- The object is only going to be used by a small team
- The object is "in progress" and subject to frequent changes or improvements
- You don't mind the increased compile times associated with the frequent recompiling of code

I find that developing useful objects along with the rest of a real-life project can be done this way. However, once the object has been developed and appears stable, I am ready for the second option, to place it in a "project" of its own. You can use this new project to produce a static library if it meets the following conditions:

- The object is relatively small
- You don't anticipate frequent updates or bug fixes
- You are using the object primarily in-house

Static libraries have the added benefit that *all* your in-house projects can be grouped together into one. Since the objects in the library are already compiled, the time spent compiling new projects that use these libraries are correspondingly shortened.

Your third choice is to place the object in a DLL. Please don't do this just because "DLL" sounds sexy! There are any number of maintenance problems associated with DLLs. But there are times when DLLs can add practical benefit to the distribution of your projects. Place your new object in a DLL only if it meets the following conditions:

- The object is large, or can be combined in the DLL with other objects, all of which will be used by the project, thus keeping the new .EXE's size down

- The object is likely to be used by more than one application—especially more than one application at a time, thus providing a savings in runtime memory (DLLs are loaded only once)

- The object is *very* stable, and is unlikely to be updated frequently—and any updates that *do* occur will either not change the object interface, or will only add to it

Building the COLOR Module Files

As with all programmer-defined objects, **TXColor** *was implemented in a pair of files all its own. However, since* **TColorComponent**, **TRed**, **TGreen**, *and* **TBlue** *exist only to implement* **TXColor**, *they can be added to the files.*

Remember that ClassExpert can only assist in developing classes that relate directly to Windows user-interface components such as windows and controls. Therefore we can't use it to assist in managing **TXColor**; we'll have to build the project and add the files manually. Since an earlier version of **TXColor** has already been implemented and tested, we can continue with the modules we already created. Later, we can create a standalone project that produces a static library.

To do so means using the Project, New project command. You'll fill in the resulting dialog box something like that shown in Figure 10.1. Of course, you'll want to place the project on a drive and in a directory that makes sense to you.

Figure 10.1 The New Target dialog box set up for the TXColor project.

These settings will give you a blank, or almost blank, Project window, with XCOLOR.LIB as the target and only entry. By clicking on XCOLOR.LIB with the *right* mouse button, you'll bring up the object menu. Select Add node and add XCOLOR.CPP to the project. Then click on XCOLOR.CPP with the right mouse button, select Add node again, and add XCOLOR.H.

Or you can use this alternate method: Bring up File Manager and size the Borland IDE and File Manager so they share the screen. Then, simply *drag* XCOLOR.CPP from File Manager to the XCOLOR.LIB node in the Project Window. That's all it takes to add an existing file to a node! Likewise, drag XCOLOR.H to the XCOLOR.CPP node.

Either way, when you're done, the Project window should look like that shown in Figure 10.2.

Declaring the TColorComponent Class

TColorComponent's main job is to provide arithmetic and stream I/O services for its three derived classes, **TRed**, **TGreen**, and **TBlue**. And, incidentally, it also provides storage for the color component's actual value.

To create the declaration for the **TColorComponent** class, we need to tally up the following:

- Required class derivations
- Required constructors
- Required operators
- Other required methods
- Properties

Since we want to make the **TColorComponent** class streamable, it must be derived from **TStreamableBase**. We'll want to construct it from byte values, mostly, but we'll also want a copy constructor. We'd *like* to put all arithmetic operators at this level; but in C++ assignment

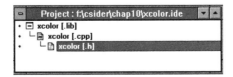

Figure 10.2 The XColor Project window.

operators are not inherited, so we can only implement the basic four—addition, subtraction, multiplication, and division—at this level. We'll have two each for addition and subtraction: one function for adding or subtracting a **BYTE** value; and another for operations involving another **TColorComponent**. It doesn't make sense to divide or multiply a color by a color, so we only need one each of those operators, set to work with a small binary value. This will allow our programmers to double or triple, or halve or third, a color's intensity.

Since the color is stored as a **BYTE**, and isn't otherwise useful in itself, the only casting operator we need is one that casts to a BYTE.

Finally, we'll need the **DECLARE_STREAMABLE** macro to make this a streamable class. The following declaration, added to the COLOR.H file, meets all these requirements:

```
class TColorComponent : public TStreamableBase
  {
  public:
    TColorComponent (BYTE aValue) : Value (aValue) {}
    TColorComponent (TColorComponent & aComponent) : Value
(aComponent.Value) {}
    TColorComponent operator+ (BYTE aValue) const;
    TColorComponent operator+ (TColorComponent aComponent) const;
    TColorComponent operator- (BYTE aValue) const;
    TColorComponent operator- (TColorComponent aComponent) const;
    TColorComponent operator* (BYTE aValue) const;
    TColorComponent operator/ (BYTE aValue) const;
    operator BYTE const() { return Value; }
  protected:
    BYTE Value;
  DECLARE_STREAMABLE (, TColorComponent, 1);
  };
```

You'll notice I made both constructors embedded **inline**. As mentioned earlier, I normally prefer external **inline** functions for neatness, but we'll be adding several other classes to this header and I didn't want it to get cluttered.

The **DECLARE_STREAMABLE** macro deserves a comment: it looks like it's missing a parameter, doesn't it? **DECLARE_STREAMABLE**'s first parameter is supposed to expand—automatically—into either the keyword **_export** or **_import**, depending on its use in a DLL. Unfortunately, Borland hasn't supplied us with that macro. Rather than confuse the issue by **#define**'ing it here, I've just left it blank—as Borland does in their example code—to indicate that this class will be neither exported from nor imported into a DLL. (Note that the *IMPEXPMACRO* used in the Borland documentation doesn't actually exist anywhere.)

That leaves **DECLARE_STREAMABLE**'s other two parameters to **DECLARE_STREAMABLE**. The purpose of the second parameter you can guess; it's the name of the class itself. The macro uses it to generate some method definitions. The last parameter is a version number; you can use any integer you like. This value should be used to accommodate future expansion of your class—not your application. Suppose you add a new property to the class. If you then specify your new stream version as 2, and try to read the first version of your object from a file, you can detect that it *is* the older version, read in the original properties, and then create default values for the new ones. Although this technique allows you to update your classes while retaining the ability to read old versions, note that there is no mechanism for *writing* old versions.

Normalizing TColorComponent Values

One of our design constraints is that the Value *property of* TColorComponent *never exceed 255, and never diminish below 0. Of course, if we simply make* Value *an* unsigned char *data type—what Windows has* typedefed *as a* BYTE—*we can meet that constraint. But we also want to prevent rollaround: 255 + 1 should equal 255, not 0.*

Modifying these operations is called *normalization*. The easiest way to implement normalization in **TColorComponent** is in a helper function, **Normalize( )**, that accepts a (possibly) invalid value as an **int**, then returns an acceptable **BYTE**. Even though we're going to put more class definitions in the header file, let's jump over to the implementation file to see how the **Normalize( )** function is implemented:

```
#include "xcolor.h"

static BYTE near Normalize (int Test)
  {
  if (Test > 255)
    return 255;
  else if (Test < 0)
    return 0;
  else
    return (BYTE) Test;
  }
```

The first line, of course, is the original **#include** of the COLOR.H declaration file. The function itself accepts, as a parameter, an **int**. This is large enough to contain the maximum result from an operation involving two **BYTE**s.

Implementing the Arithmetic Operators

Although **TColorComponent** cannot implement the arithmetic assignment operators (because assignments cannot be inherited), it *can* implement the basic arithmetic operations (which the descendent classes can then use to implement the arithmetic assignments).

The four operators—implemented as six overloaded functions—all follow the same premise: create a temporary **TColorComponent** object, initialized as a duplicate of ***this**; arithmetically combine the temporary's **Value** and the operand's value as **int**s; set the temporary's result to the value returned by **Normalize( )**. Here's the code:

```
TColorComponent TColorComponent::operator+ (BYTE aValue) const
    {
    TColorComponent Temp (*this);
    Temp.Value = Normalize ((int) Temp.Value + (int) aValue);
    return Temp;
    }


TColorComponent TColorComponent::operator+ (TColorComponent
aComponent) const
    {
    TColorComponent Temp (*this);
    Temp.Value = Normalize ((int) Temp.Value + (int) aComponent.Value);
    return Temp;
    }


TColorComponent TColorComponent::operator- (BYTE aValue) const
    {
    TColorComponent Temp (*this);
    Temp.Value = Normalize ((int) Temp.Value - (int) aValue);
    return Temp;
    }


TColorComponent TColorComponent::operator- (TColorComponent
aComponent) const
    {
    TColorComponent Temp (*this);
    Temp.Value = Normalize ((int) Temp.Value - (int) aComponent.Value);
    return Temp;
    }
```

```
TColorComponent TColorComponent::operator* (BYTE aValue) const
  {
  TColorComponent Temp (*this);
  Temp.Value = Normalize ((int) Temp.Value * (int) aValue);
  return Temp;
  }

TColorComponent TColorComponent::operator/ (BYTE aValue) const
  {
  TColorComponent Temp (*this);
  Temp.Value = Normalize ((int) Temp.Value / (int) aValue);
  return Temp;
  }
```

Making TColorComponent Streamable

We've already seen the macro and inheritance that must be applied to a class's declaration in order to make it streamable. Here's what to add to the implementation to complete the effect.

In order to make a class implementation streamable, you must do three things: first, invoke the **IMPLEMENT_STREAMABLE( )** macro; second, add a **Read( )** method; third, add a **Write( )** method. However, two of these three steps are a tad more complicated than they sound, so let's look at each step singly.

First, there's the **IMPLEMENT_STREAMABLE( )** macro. It's simple to code, but you should be aware that's it is adding *several* methods to your class implementation, including stream insertion (<<) and extraction (>>) operators. As you'll recall from the previous chapter, the macro takes, as its single parameter, the name of the class for which streamability is being implemented:

```
IMPLEMENT_STREAMABLE (TColorComponent);
```

Next is the **Read( )** method. The complication here is that it is not exactly a method of your class. Remember the **DECLARE_STREAMABLE( )** macro in your header file? Among other things, it actually declared a *nested* class called **Streamer** in your class. **Streamer** is the class whose **Read( )** method you must supply. Since **DECLARE_STREAMABLE( )** added the class and its methods, you didn't have to prototype **Read( )** in the header file; but you do have to provide the implementation. Let's look at it:

```
void * TColorComponent::Streamer::Read (ipstream & in, uint32) const
  {
```

```
TColorComponent * Me = GetObject();
in >> Me->Value;
return Me;
}
```

First of all, note the complex class affiliation:

```
TColorComponent::Streamer::Read
```

That's the way you fully qualify methods of a nested class. Next, notice that the second parameter has no name and isn't used. I assume it's there for future enhancement; I couldn't find any documentation on it at all.

Then there's the use of the **GetObject( )** function and the **My** pointer. If you're wondering why we didn't just use the **this** pointer, remember that **Read( )** is a method of **TColorComponent::Streamer**, not **TColorComponent**—**this** would refer to the streamer subobject. The **GetObject( )** function returns a typesafe pointer to **TColorComponent**'s **this**, which the code assigns to **Me** for re-use.

The actual job of the **Read( )** method is to insert any property values into the output stream, as represented by **in**. For the built-in data types, as well as object properties that are also streamable, inserting the property values can be done with the stream extraction operator (>>). **TColorComponent** only has one property, **Value**, so that's the only one we have to stream. Finally, we return **Me** to the caller, whoever that might be.

If you're sharp-eyed, you might have noted the **const** keyword on the function prototype. Surely, you may have thought, that's a mistake. The **Read( )** function is *intended* to change the object; that's the whole point, right? Well, that's true—if the object you're talking about is **TColorComponent**. But remember: **Read( )** is a method of **TColorComponent::Streamer**, not **TColorComponent**. And, while it certainly does change **TColorComponent**, it does not change **TColorComponent::Streamer** at all, so it can (and should) be a **const** method.

The **Write( )** method is similar: it, too, is a member function of the **Streamer** subclass; it, too, uses the **GetObject( )** method to retrieve the **TColorComponent** object; it, too, performs a streaming operation on the object's properties—but this time, the properties are inserted *into* the stream:

```
void TColorComponent::Streamer::Write (opstream & out) const
    {
    out << GetObject()->Value;
    }
```

Since the return value of **GetObject( )** was used just once, I didn't bother storing it in a pointer; using it directly seemed more efficient.

Defining TRed, TGreen, and TBlue

Now that **TColorComponent** has been defined and implemented, we can create the three derived classes that will actually be used as properties of **TXColor**.

TRed, **TGreen**, and **TBlue** are declared identically, except for the input parameter types of the copy constructors and assignment operators, which, of course, must be references to the **TRed**, **TGreen**, and **TBlue** class objects, respectively. Another difference is the return references of the assignment operators:

```
class TRed : public TColorComponent
   {
   public:
     TRed (TRed & R) : TColorComponent (R.Value) {}
     TRed (BYTE aValue = 0) : TColorComponent (aValue) {}
     TRed & operator= (BYTE aValue);
     TRed & operator= (TRed & R);
     TRed & operator+= (BYTE aValue);
     TRed & operator+= (TRed & R);
     TRed & operator-= (BYTE aValue);
     TRed & operator-= (TRed & R);
     TRed & operator*= (BYTE aValue);
     TRed & operator/= (BYTE aValue);
   DECLARE_STREAMABLE ( , TRed, 1);
   };

class TGreen : public TColorComponent
   {
   public:
     TGreen (TGreen & G) : TColorComponent (G.Value) {}
     TGreen (BYTE aValue = 0) : TColorComponent (aValue) {}
     TGreen & operator= (BYTE aValue);
     TGreen & operator= (TGreen & G);
     TGreen & operator+= (BYTE aValue);
     TGreen & operator+= (TGreen & G);
     TGreen & operator-= (BYTE aValue);
     TGreen & operator-= (TGreen & G);
     TGreen & operator*= (BYTE aValue);
     TGreen & operator/= (BYTE aValue);
   DECLARE_STREAMABLE ( , TGreen, 1);
   };
```

```
class TBlue : public TColorComponent
  {
  public:
    TBlue (TBlue & B) : TColorComponent (B.Value) {}
    TBlue (BYTE aValue = 0) : TColorComponent (aValue) {}
    TBlue & operator= (BYTE aValue);
    TBlue & operator= (TBlue & B);
    TBlue & operator+= (BYTE aValue);
    TBlue & operator+= (TBlue & B);
    TBlue & operator-= (BYTE aValue);
    TBlue & operator-= (TBlue & B);
    TBlue & operator*= (BYTE aValue);
    TBlue & operator/= (BYTE aValue);
  DECLARE_STREAMABLE ( , TBlue, 1);
  };
```

Notice that none of these classes is derived directly from **TStreamableBase**; they don't have to be, because their direct ancestor **TColorComponent** is. Nevertheless, they do each need the **DECLARE_STREAMABLE** macro, which is used as it was in **TColorComponent**.

Implementing TRed's Assignment Operators

A derived object cannot inherit its assignment operators, because an assignment operator returns a reference to itself—a typed reference that would conflict with the derived object's class because polymorphism can travel back towards the base class only, not forward to the derived classes. Therefore TRed (and TGreen and TBlue) must implement its own assignment operators, even though they are functionally identical to those in TColor.

Here is the implementation of **TRed**'s assignment operators:

```
TRed & TRed::operator= (BYTE aValue)
  {
  Value = aValue;
  return *this;
  }


TRed & TRed::operator= (TRed & R)
  {
  return *this = R.Value;
  }


TRed & TRed::operator+= (BYTE aValue)
  {
```

```
   Value = Normalize ((int) Value + (int) aValue);
   return *this;
   }

TRed & TRed::operator+= (TRed & R)
   {
   return *this += R.Value;
   }

TRed & TRed::operator-= (BYTE aValue)
   {
   Value = Normalize ((int) Value - (int) aValue);
   return *this;
   }

TRed & TRed::operator-= (TRed & R)
   {
   return *this -= R.Value;
   }

TRed & TRed::operator*= (BYTE aValue)
   {
   Value = Normalize ((int) Value * (int) aValue);
   return *this;
   }

TRed & TRed::operator/= (BYTE aValue)
   {
   Value = Normalize ((int) Value / (int) aValue);
   return *this;
   }
```

You've been warned that the code for **TGreen** and **TBlue** will be functionally identical. Isn't that what class templates are for?

Well, yes. However, class templates allow functionally equivalent code to be generated for different data types. The problem here is that **TRed**, **TGreen**, and **TBlue** *aren't* really different data types—they are just *conceptually* different.

If you really want to implement these classes using templates, it can be done. First create three classes **TRedBase**, **TGreenBase**, and **TBlueBase** with no properties and no methods except for constructors. Then create the template class **TColorComponent<class T>**. This class should be derived from **TStreamableBase** as before, but it can contain *all* the functionality. Finally, implement **TRed** as a **typedef** for **TColorComponent<TRedBase>**; implement the other two colors in a similar fashion.

Sound complicated? That's nothing compared to the effort you'll make when you try and debug if something goes wrong. That's why I chose to do it the way I did.

Making TRed Streamable

Implementing streamability for a derived class is a little different from doing it to a base class.

TRed is derived from **TColorComponent**, so we have to use a variant of the **IMPLEMENT_STREAMABLE()** macro. For classes derived from a single base class (as opposed to multiple inheritance), use the **IMPLEMENT_STREAMABLE1()** macro. The 1 means there's just one base class; for multiple inheritance there are versions that replace the 1 with 2, 3, 4, or even 5. If you've derived a class from more than five base classes, you'll have to write your own macro . . . as soon as you get out of therapy!

Here's the macro as entered for **TRed**:

```
IMPLEMENT_STREAMABLE1 (TRed, TColorComponent);
```

As you can see, the first parameter, as with the original version of **IMPLEMENT_STREAMABLE()**, names the class that is being made streamable. The additional parameters—the number tells how many—specify the base classes.

The next problem we encounter is that, although **TRed** has no properties of its own, its base class does. If **TRed** did have properties, it would insert or extract them just as **TColorComponent** did. But, in addition, the properties of its base class must be streamed.

In other class libraries, this would be accomplished simply by invoking the base class's **Read()** and **Write()** functions, or whatever that library called them. That's the way it was done in the previous version of ObjectWindows, but apparently Borland found that method too simple. So, instead, we must call **ReadBaseObject()** and **WriteBaseObject()**, complete with arcane macros that hide what's actually happening from us mere mortals:

```
void * TRed::Streamer::Read (ipstream & in, uint32) const
   {
   ReadBaseObject (STATIC_CAST(TColorComponent *, GetObject()), in);
   return GetObject();
   }
```

```
void TRed::Streamer::Write (opstream & out) const
   {
   WriteBaseObject (STATIC_CAST(TColorComponent *, GetObject()), out);
   }
```

If you derive a class that has properties of its own, be certain you read and write them in the same order—and that **ReadBaseObject()** and **WriteBaseObject()** are included in the same sequence. Tradition says they should be invoked first, but the important thing is that the order for reading and writing be *exactly* the same.

Implementing TGreen and TBlue

Now that we've seen how **TRed** *is implemented, we can implement* **TGreen** *and* **TBlue** *in just the same way.*

Here's the code for completeness' sake:

```
TGreen & TGreen::operator= (BYTE aValue)
   {
   Value = aValue;
   return *this;
   }

TGreen & TGreen::operator= (TGreen & G)
   {
   return *this = G.Value;
   }

TGreen & TGreen::operator+= (BYTE aValue)
   {
   Value = Normalize ((int) Value + (int) aValue);
   return *this;
   }

TGreen & TGreen::operator+= (TGreen & G)
   {
   return *this += G.Value;
   }

TGreen & TGreen::operator-= (BYTE aValue)
   {
   Value = Normalize ((int) Value - (int) aValue);
   return *this;
   }
```

```
TGreen & TGreen::operator-= (TGreen & G)
   {
   return *this -= G.Value;
   }

TGreen & TGreen::operator*= (BYTE aValue)
   {
   Value = Normalize ((int) Value * (int) aValue);
   return *this;
   }

TGreen & TGreen::operator/= (BYTE aValue)
   {
   Value = Normalize ((int) Value / (int) aValue);
   return *this;
   }

IMPLEMENT_STREAMABLE1 (TGreen, TColorComponent);

void * TGreen::Streamer::Read (ipstream & in, uint32) const
   {
   ReadBaseObject (STATIC_CAST(TColorComponent *, GetObject()), in);
   return GetObject();
   }

void TGreen::Streamer::Write (opstream & out) const
   {
   WriteBaseObject (STATIC_CAST(TColorComponent *, GetObject()), out);
   }

TBlue & TBlue::operator= (BYTE aValue)
   {
   Value = aValue;
   return *this;
   }

TBlue & TBlue::operator= (TBlue & B)
   {
   return *this = B.Value;
   }

TBlue & TBlue::operator+= (BYTE aValue)
   {
   Value = Normalize ((int) Value + (int) aValue);
   return *this;
   }

TBlue & TBlue::operator+= (TBlue & B)
   {
```

```
    return *this += B.Value;
    }

TBlue & TBlue::operator-= (BYTE aValue)
    {
    Value = Normalize ((int) Value - (int) aValue);
    return *this;
    }

TBlue & TBlue::operator-= (TBlue & B)
    {
    return *this -= B.Value;
    }

TBlue & TBlue::operator*= (BYTE aValue)
    {
    Value = Normalize ((int) Value * (int) aValue);
    return *this;
    }

TBlue & TBlue::operator/= (BYTE aValue)
    {
    Value = Normalize ((int) Value / (int) aValue);
    return *this;
    }

IMPLEMENT_STREAMABLE1 (TBlue, TColorComponent);

void * TBlue::Streamer::Read (ipstream & in, uint32) const
    {
    ReadBaseObject (STATIC_CAST(TColorComponent *, GetObject()), in);
    return GetObject();
    }

void TBlue::Streamer::Write (opstream & out) const
    {
    WriteBaseObject (STATIC_CAST(TColorComponent *, GetObject()), out);
    }
```

Declaring the TXColor Class

All that has gone before has prepared us for this moment. We created
the **TColorComponent** class so we could derive the **TRed**, **TGreen**,
and **TBlue** classes from it; we did that so we would have object properties for **TXColor**. Now we're ready to declare **TXColor** itself.

Here's the declaration:

```
class TXColor : public TStreamableBase
  {
  public:
    TXColor ();
    TXColor (TXColor & aColor);
    TXColor (TRed R, TGreen G, TBlue B);
    TXColor (COLORREF aValue);
    TXColor (int anIndex);
    TXColor(const PALETTEENTRY far & pe);
    TXColor(const RGBQUAD far& q);
    TXColor(const RGBTRIPLE far& t);
    operator COLORREF ()const;
    operator TColor () const;
    TXColor & operator= (COLORREF aValue);
    TXColor & operator= (int anIndex);
    TXColor & operator= (TRed R);
    TXColor & operator= (TGreen G);
    TXColor & operator= (TBlue B);
    TXColor & operator+= (TXColor aColor);
    TXColor & operator+= (COLORREF aColor);
    TXColor & operator+= (TRed R);
    TXColor & operator+= (TGreen G);
    TXColor & operator+= (TBlue B);
    TXColor operator+ (TXColor aColor) const;
    TXColor operator+ (COLORREF aColor) const;
    TXColor operator+ (TRed R) const;
    TXColor operator+ (TGreen G) const;
    TXColor operator+ (TBlue B) const;
    TXColor & operator-= (TXColor aColor);
    TXColor & operator-= (COLORREF aColor);
    TXColor & operator-= (TRed R);
    TXColor & operator-= (TGreen G);
    TXColor & operator-= (TBlue B);
    TXColor operator- (TXColor aColor) const;
    TXColor operator- (COLORREF aColor) const;
    TXColor operator- (TRed R) const;
    TXColor operator- (TGreen G) const;
    TXColor operator- (TBlue B) const;
    TXColor & operator*= (BYTE aValue);
    TXColor operator* (BYTE aValue) const;
    TXColor & operator/= (BYTE aValue);
    TXColor operator/ (BYTE aValue) const;
    TXColor & operator>>= (int Shift);
    TXColor & operator<<= (int Shift);
    TXColor operator>> (int Shift) const;
    TXColor operator<< (int Shift) const;
    void SetSysColor (int anIndex);
```

```
    void SelectUserColor (TWindow * Window);
    TRed RValue;
    TGreen GValue;
    TBlue BValue;
    static const COLORREF Red;
    static const COLORREF Green;
    static const COLORREF Blue;
    static const COLORREF White;
    static const COLORREF Black;
  DECLARE_STREAMABLE ( , TXColor, 1);
  };
```

TXColor is derived from **TStreamableBase**; we want to be able to read and write these things to disk (or anyplace else a stream is going).

As is customary, the class declaration begins with the constructors. In addition to the default and copy constructors, I've supplied constructors for **COLORREF** values, separate **TRed**, **TGreen**, and **TBlue** values, and even a constructor that accepts a Windows user-defined color index. Note that the **TRed**, **TGreen**, and **TBlue** constructor will also accept three constant values, each of which is between 0 and 255, which automatically converts them to **TRed**, **TGreen**, and **TBlue** objects in the process.

Next we have a single cast, which allows a **TXColor** object to be used anywhere a **COLORREF** is expected—for example, in creating a brush or pen. Since the cast is unambiguous, you won't even have to specify it.

The arithmetic operators are declared next. In addition to the four basic operations and their assigned analogs, I've added a couple of shift operators. You'll see what they're used for in an upcoming section; meanwhile, try and guess what you'd use them for. Overloading operators is only useful if the result is intuitive; otherwise, you'd be better off creating a clearly named method.

Next we have the three properties themselves: **RValue**, **GValue**, and **BValue**. They are stored separately because we intend to manipulate them separately; that's why we went to the effort of developing **TColorComponent** and its derived classes in the first place.

Why aren't the properties private? Basically because they themselves are typesafe objects with private properties. Since the programmers who use this class can't damage the objects themselves, we can allow them the benefit of accessibility.

You'll notice I've added some static constants for the sake of convenience. Being static, these constants belong to the class, not each object, and so only take up space once. And, being constants, they cannot change value. You may remember similar constants as members of **TColor**. However, where **TColor** used names like **LtRed** and **LtGreen**, I've just called mine **Red** and **Green**. The **TColor** constants are still available, so you can use whichever set you prefer.

Finally we have the (now) familiar **DECLARE_STREAMABLE()** macro.

Implementing TXColor's Constructors

TXColor provides constructors for **COLORREFs, TColorComponents,** *and even Windows' user-defined colors. Here's how they're implemented.*

TXColor's first three constructors don't require much explanation:

```
TXColor::TXColor ()
   : RValue (0), GValue (0), BValue (0)
   {
   }

TXColor::TXColor (TXColor & aColor)
   {
   RValue = aColor.RValue;
   GValue = aColor.GValue;
   BValue = aColor.BValue;
   }

TXColor::TXColor (TRed R, TGreen G, TBlue B)
   : RValue (R), GValue (G), BValue (B)
   {
   }
```

The next constructor takes its value from a **COLORREF**:

```
TXColor::TXColor (COLORREF Value)
   {
   *this = Value;
   }
```

We still don't know how the constructor works, exactly; you can deduce, we intend to implement the assignment operator to work with **COLORREFs**. That's the way it is with object-oriented programming; you never get blinded by the forest because you are forced to concentrate on the trees. But you'll never have to spend much time debugging this constructor; if it doesn't work, the problem must be in the assignment operator!

In a more subtle fashion, the next operator also relies on the assignment operator:

```
TXColor::TXColor (int anIndex)
    {
    *this = anIndex;
    }
```

This is the operator that accepts a Windows user-defined color index. Again, we'll have to wait for the assignment operators to see how this trick is actually accomplished. We'll be looking at the assignment operators shortly.

The last three constructors are here to provide compatibility with the full set of **TColor** constructors. Rather than try and figure out how **TColor** made them work, we can make use of **TColor** itself—and its own ability to cast to a **COLORREF**—to implement our own:

```
TXColor::TXColor(const PALETTEENTRY far & pe)
    {
    *this = TColor (pe);
    }

TXColor::TXColor(const RGBQUAD far & q)
    {
    *this = TColor (q);
    }

TXColor::TXColor(const RGBTRIPLE far & t)
    {
    *this = TColor (t);
    }
```

Implementing the COLORREF *and TColor* Casts

TXColor *has only two casts, and those are's to the* **COLORREF** *and TColor type it's intended to supplant.*

It's always fun to use familiar Windows/C programming constructs in C++, knowing they are doing more work than they ever could in C. Take the **RGB()** macro, for instance. It accepts three **BYTE** values, shifts them, and returns a **COLORREF**. However, in C, these are all just **typedef**s. **BYTE**s are just **signed char**s, and **COLORREF**s are just **long**s. But look at the implementation of the **COLORREF** cast operator:

```
TXColor::operator COLORREF () const
```

```
    {
    return RGB (RValue, GValue, BValue);
    }
```

It looks simple. But because **RGB()** expects three **BYTE**s, **RValue**, **GValue**, and **BValue**—which are actually objects—it automatically perform a cast to **BYTE**. And, as a macro, *RGB()* is occasionally prone to compiler confusion. But in a nice, isolated environment like a compiled function, you know it will work perfectly every time. It even saves code space, because those shift operations require more machine code than the function call!

While a cast to **COLORREF** will handle all those Windows API calls you might like to make, ObjectWindows methods mostly require **TColor** objects. Since **TXColor** is no longer a descendent of **TColor**, polymorphism can't help us here. So we have to supply a cast to **TColor** as well:

```
TXColor::operator TColor () const
    {
    return TColor ((COLORREF) *this);
    }
```

Implementing the TXColor Assignment Operators

It is normal in C++ to try and save code. When creating a bunch of assignment operators, the usual method is to put the "engine" in one operator, then let the others perform some simple conversion which then invokes the engine. Here's an example.

The first assignment operator we'll look at for **TXColor** expects a **COLORREF** on the right side of the equal sign:

```
TXColor & TXColor::operator= (COLORREF Value)
    {
    RValue = GetRValue (Value);
    GValue = GetGValue (Value);
    BValue = GetBValue (Value);
    return *this;
    }
```

GetRValue(), **GetGValue()**, and **GetBValue()** are Windows API macros—*not* functions. Each returns a **BYTE**, so that the **TColorComponent** assignments are happy to accept those values to set **RValue**, **GValue**, and **BValue**, respectively. (As in all assignment operators, we must return a reference to the object being assigned.)

The next assignment receives an **int**, which it interprets as a Windows user-defined color index:

```
TXColor & TXColor::operator= (int anIndex)
    {
    return *this = GetSysColor (anIndex);
    }
```

The index must be handed to the Windows function **GetSysColor()**, which returns a **COLORREF**. Therefore, after calling **GetSysColor()**, this operator actually invokes the previous to perform the assignments. This technique saves three lines of code!

The next three assignments accept **TRed**, **TGreen**, or **TBlue** objects, respectively:

```
TXColor & TXColor::operator= (TRed R)
    {
    RValue = R;
    return *this;
    }

TXColor & TXColor::operator= (TGreen G)
    {
    GValue = G;
    return *this;
    }

TXColor & TXColor::operator= (TBlue B)
    {
    BValue = B;
    return *this;
    }
```

With these operators, you can actually create a separate **TBlue** object of your own, give it whatever value you please, and assign it to a **TXColor** object without disturbing that object's red or green components! *This* is why we went to the effort of creating all those **TColorComponent** derivatives.

Implementing the TXColor Arithmetic Operators

Although in **TColorComponent** we coded the base arithmetic operators first and derived the assigned arithmetic operators from them, that's the opposite of the usual pattern.

Generally assigned operators are seen as more general versions and are coded first. Here are the assigned addition operators:

```
TXColor & TXColor::operator+= (TXColor aColor)
   {
   RValue += aColor.RValue;
   GValue += aColor.GValue;
   BValue += aColor.BValue;
   return *this;
   }

TXColor & TXColor::operator+= (COLORREF aColor)
   {
   TColor C (aColor);
   return *this += C;
   }

TXColor & TXColor::operator+= (TRed R)
   {
   RValue += R;
   return *this;
   }

TXColor & TXColor::operator+= (TGreen G)
   {
   GValue += G;
   return *this;
   }

TXColor & TXColor::operator+= (TBlue B)
   {
   BValue += B;
   return *this;
   }
```

As you can see, these operators follow the assignment operators in the data types they allow on the right side of the operator.

The matching + operators can then get away with creating a temporary object, then performing the arithmetic assignment on the object:

```
TXColor TXColor::operator+ (TXColor aColor) const
   {
   return TXColor (*this) += aColor;
   }

TXColor TXColor::operator+ (COLORREF aColor) const
```

```
    {
    return TXColor (*this) += aColor;
    }

TXColor TXColor::operator+ (TRed R) const
    {
    return TXColor (*this) += R;
    }

TXColor TXColor::operator+ (TGreen G) const
    {
    return TXColor (*this) += G;
    }

TXColor TXColor::operator+ (TBlue B) const
    {
    return TXColor (*this) += B;
    }
```

We follow the same pattern with the subtraction, multiplication and division operators:

```
TXColor & TXColor::operator-= (TXColor aColor)
    {
    RValue -= aColor.RValue;
    GValue -= aColor.GValue;
    BValue -= aColor.BValue;
    return *this;
    }

TXColor & TXColor::operator-= (COLORREF aColor)
    {
    TXColor C (aColor);
    return *this -= C;
    }

TXColor & TXColor::operator-= (TRed R)
    {
    RValue -= R;
    return *this;
    }

TXColor & TXColor::operator-= (TGreen G)
    {
    GValue -= G;
    return *this;
    }

TXColor & TXColor::operator-= (TBlue B)
```

```
     {
     BValue -= B;
     return *this;
     }

TXColor TXColor::operator- (TXColor aColor) const
     {
     return TXColor (*this) -= aColor;
     }

TXColor TXColor::operator- (COLORREF aColor) const
     {
     return TXColor (*this) -= aColor;
     }

TXColor TXColor::operator- (TRed R) const
     {
     return TXColor (*this) -= R;
     }

TXColor TXColor::operator- (TGreen G) const
     {
     return TXColor (*this) -= G;
     }

TXColor TXColor::operator- (TBlue B) const
     {
     return TXColor (*this) -= B;
     }

TXColor & TXColor::operator*= (BYTE aValue)
     {
     RValue *= aValue;
     GValue *= aValue;
     BValue *= aValue;
     return *this;
     }

TXColor TXColor::operator* (BYTE aValue) const
     {
     return TXColor (*this) * aValue;
     }

TXColor & TXColor::operator/= (BYTE aValue)
     {
     RValue /= aValue;
     GValue /= aValue;
     BValue /= aValue;
     return *this;
     }
```

```
TXColor TXColor::operator/ (BYTE aValue) const
   {
   return TXColor (*this) / aValue;
   }
```

Implementing the TXColor Shift Operators

If you guessed the shift operators would have something to do with stream I/O, you're wrong. Here's why, and what they really do.

Certainly you can be forgiven for associating shift operators with stream I/O, but actually it's the *stream* objects that do that particular bit of overloading. A value object such as a bit string, character string, or color shifts by rotating its components. In the case of a **TXColor** object, those components are the relative values of red, green, and blue. Here's the implementation:

```
TXColor & TXColor::operator>>= (int Shift)
   {
   Shift %= 3;
   while (Shift > 0)
      {
      TColorComponent Temp (BValue);
      BValue = GValue;
      GValue = RValue;
      RValue = Temp;
      --Shift;
      }
   return *this;
   }

TXColor & TXColor::operator<<= (int Shift)
   {
   Shift %= 3;
   while (Shift > 0)
      {
      TColorComponent Temp (RValue);
      RValue = GValue;
      GValue = BValue;
      BValue = Temp;
      --Shift;
      }
   return *this;
   }

TXColor TXColor::operator>> (int Shift) const
```

```
  {
  return TXColor (*this) >>= Shift;
  }

TXColor TXColor::operator<< (int Shift) const
  {
  return TXColor (*this) <<= Shift;
  }
```

Note that we've made this shifting more efficient by shifting, not *shift* number of times, but that value modulo 3. That means the value will only be 0, 1, or 2 and yet will produce the same result as if the red, green, and blue values had been rotated the original number of times.

If you are absolutely certain that no programmer will ever send a number greater than 2, or if you would rather save the code space than the time, you can safely delete those lines.

Changing the User-Defined System Colors

The **GetSysColors()** function changes the system colors, making it possible to implement a color-selection utility to replace the one found in the Control Panel. However, this function is awkward to use, especially when changing a single color. This method will simplify the task.

The problem is that **SetSysColors()** was really designed to change, not one color, but many of them—perhaps most of them—at a time. Therefore it requires, not simple values, but *arrays* of values: one for the color indexes, another for the matching colors.

We can implement **SetSysColor()** fairly easily, though, allowing changes of a single system color at a time:

```
void TXColor::SetSysColor (int anIndex)
  {
  COLORREF Color (*this);
  SetSysColors (1, &anIndex, &Color);
  }
```

The temporary **Color** variable is required since **SetSysColors()** is probably the only function that requires a pointer to a **COLORREF**, not a direct one.

Making TXColor Streamable

Making **TXColor** *streamable is much like making* **TColorComponent** *streamable, since each is a class derived directly from* **TStreamableBase.**

Here's the code that implements streaming for **TXColor**:
```
IMPLEMENT_STREAMABLE (TXColor);

void * TXColor::Streamer::Read (ipstream & in, uint32) const
  {
  TXColor * Me = GetObject();
  in >> Me->RValue >> Me->GValue >> Me->BValue;
  return Me;
  }

void TXColor::Streamer::Write (opstream & out) const
  {
  TXColor * Me = GetObject();
  out << Me->RValue << Me->GValue << Me->BValue;
  }
```

Note the "stacking" of properties being streamed. Also, note again the use of the **Me** pointer, which is not found in the Borland documentation. Using **Me** instead of making repeated calls to **GetObject( )** makes your code more compact *and* more efficient.

Providing Standard Color Constants

*We complete **TXColor** with a set of constants designed to make specifying standard colors, such as red and green, simpler.*

In **TXColor**'s header we indicated our intention to supply a set of static constants for standard colors. As you know, such an indication doesn't actually do the job; we have to initialize the constants in the implementation file:

```
const COLORREF TXColor::Red = RGB (255, 0, 0);
const COLORREF TXColor::Green = RGB (0, 255, 0);
const COLORREF TXColor::Blue = RGB (0, 0, 255);
const COLORREF TXColor::White = RGB (255, 255, 255);
const COLORREF TXColor::Black = RGB (0, 0, 0);
```

Obviously this set could be longer. I have a friend who tells me that printers (the people, not the devices) have a vocabulary of several dozen words that describe specific colors. Apparently there's a difference between teal and cerulean that I've been unable to distinguish. But **TXColor** is your object class. Please feel free to add as many color definitions as you like!

Since these constants are **COLORREF**s, they can be used directly by any function expecting one. they can al, or to initialize a **TXColor** object. They are static constants, so they can be referenced either from the class or from any **TXColor** object:

```
TXColor MyColor (TColor::Red);
...
MyBrush = CreateBrush (MyColor.Green); // Even though MyColor itself
is red!
```

And if any of you, Gentle Readers, know the correct RGB equivalent of mulberry or chartreuse, please don't bother to tell me. I have enough trouble telling cyan from blue!

Working with Common Dialogs

As a finaly touch to the TXColor class, let's add access to the Choose Color Common Dialog box.

When Windows first came out, all the little applications that came with it—Windows Write, Windows Paint, Notepad—used identical File Open dialog boxes to help the user select a file. Obviously, those of us who were writing Windows apps were intended to supply similar dialog boxes, but Microsoft provided no help to do so. We were on our own.

And the File Open (and File Save As) dialogs are particularly complex—much more tricky to code *and* use than most dialogs are.

Borland was the first company to offer assistance, in Borland Pascal for Windows. With the package came code for "standard" file open and save dialogs. Of course, they were "Borland standard," with graphic buttons sporting a chiselled steel look.

Between that and the claim that Microsoft was withholding parts of the Windows API to give themselves a competitive edge in the applications marketplace, Microsoft was shamed into bundling the most commonly used dialogs into a DLL and publishing its API. That DLL is called COMMDLG.DLL, and it was made available sometime between the releases of Windows 3.0 and 3.1.

In the Common Dialog API, you fill out a **struct** and pass it to a function. The dialog appears; the user pushes a button, and you query the **struct** to determine which button was pressed and, if it was the OK button, what the new, user-selectable value is.

ObjectWindows, of course, further encapsulates the operation. Unfortunately, Borland did not encapsulate it as cleanly as Microsoft's Foundation Classes did. In the ObjectWindows version, you *still* have to allocate and fill in a **struct**.

A further complication is that the standard color dialog allows the user to specify sixteen "custom" colors. In order for these colors to be retained from use to use of the dialog, we have to save them somewhere—and that somewhere winds up being static memory.

So, here's the code for **SelectUserColor( )**:

```
void TXColor::SelectUserColor (TWindow * Window)
  {
  static TChooseColorDialog::TData Data;
  static TColor CustomColors[16] =
    {
    TXColor::White, TXColor::White,
    TXColor::White, TXColor::White,
    TXColor::White, TXColor::White,
    TXColor::White, TXColor::White,
    TXColor::White, TXColor::White,
    TXColor::White, TXColor::White,
    TXColor::White, TXColor::White,
    TXColor::White, TXColor::White
      };
  if (! Data.Flags)
    {
    Data.Flags = CC_RGBINIT;
    Data.Color = *this;
    Data.CustColors = CustomColors;
    }
  if (TChooseColorDialog(Window, Data).Execute() == IDOK)
    *this = Data.Color;
  }
```

In the first line we allocate a **struct** in the data segment—so you know it will be initialized to all zeroes. Although we could have placed it on the stack and initialized it, this way there's only one and it will retain user-selected values from use to use. Likewise we place an array of 16 *CustomColors* in the data segment, all initialized to the color white. They will also retain any user modifications during the run of the application.

Data.Flags will be zero only the first time this method is invoked; if it is, we add a couple of values, specifically the address of the custom color array and the initial color are set.

Then, the dialog box is executed. That's the easy part; all we have to do is create an instance of one on the stack and invoke its **Execute( )** method. When the invocation returns, the dialog has come and gone and all we have to do is check whether the user hit the OK button on the dialog. If he or she did, we can accept the value in the **struct**'s **Color** member.

Incidentally, all the common dialogs are used similarly. The File Open and Save As dialogs are already incorporated into your application, thanks to App Expert; so are the Print and Printer Setup dialogs. We just demonstrated the Choose Color dialog, which leaves Choose Font, Find, and Replace. You won't have any trouble using them, though; they all operate similarly to the Choose Color dialog (although Find and Replace do require you to supply callback functions).

To use the new capability of **TXColor** in our Shapes application, simply add a *Shape..Other* menu command after *Red*, *Green*, and *Blue*. In the header for the **TView** module, change the *Color* property from a **TColor** object to a **TXColor** object. In the implementation file, for the handler, use the following:

```
void TShapesView::CmShapesOther ()
  {
  Color.SelectUserColor (this);
  }
```

Compile and run; when you choose the *Shapes..Other* menu, you see the standard color dialog appear just as big as life (as shown in Figure 10.3).

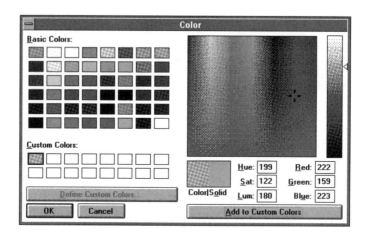

Figure 10.3 The Choose Color common dialog as it appears in the Shapes application.

Creating an .INI Managing Object

Files with the extension .INI are used by most Windows applications to store configuration information. This information might be essential (such as the name of the subdirectory in which certain files are stored) or optional (such as where the user prefers the application to appear onscreen).

Applications written for the early versions of Windows all stored their configuration information in a file called WIN.INI. But the number of applications owned by a typical user and the amount of information that had to be retained made it impractical to have just one .INI file. Nowadays, almost all applications have their own .INI files, accessed via Windows API functions like **GetPrivateProfileString()** and **WritePrivateProfileString()**. By combining the various parameters in one or another arcane ways, these two routines can be used to perform most required .INI file-management functions.

In this chapter, we'll build a **TIniData** class that will encapsulate the various methods and properties required to make maintaining and accessing your applications' .INI files a breeze.

Creating the TIniData Class

You can use the **TIniData** object class to manage your .INI files, including enumerating, adding, changing, and deleting sections and keys, and even encrypting selected values so they cannot be easily read by the casual user. Before you can start coding, however, you should know just what a .INI file is used for and how it's formatted.

Understanding the .INI File Format

Nearly all .INI files share a common structure because they are usually managed by the same API functions.

Thanks to the Windows API function **GetPrivateProfileString()** and its siblings, nearly every .INI file uses a common format. In this format, keyed values are grouped into sections. When there were just two .INI files (SYSTEM and WIN), the section was assumed to be the name of an application, and much of the documentation still refers to the section header that way. Now, with most applications owning their own, most .INI files contain only one or a few sections.

The name of the section is always set off by brackets, and may include embedded blanks. The following list contains valid section names, the way they might appear in an .INI file:

```
[Microsoft Word]

[Clock]

[Menus]
```

Section names are not case sensitive, so entering "CLOCK" or even "cloCK" would access the "Clock" section equally well.

Beneath each section name there is usually a group of keyed values (although an empty section is permissible). A typical section from a WIN.INI file is shown here:

```
[Desktop]
Pattern=(None)
GridGranularity=0
wallpaper=camper.bmp
IconSpacing=75
TileWallPaper=1
```

In this case, there are five keyed values, the first of which is "Pattern," located in the "Desktop" group. Like section names, keys are not case sensitive.

The value of a key begins at the first character past the equal sign, so

```
wallpaper=camper.bmp
```

is *not* the same as

```
wallpaper = camper.bmp
```

Incidentally, there is a Windows API variant of **GetPrivateProfileString( )** called **GetPrivateProfileInt( )** that combines the former with a built-in conversion to a binary numeric. There is no corresponding function for *writing* **int**s, however. You have to write the string equivalent with **WritePrivateProfileString( )**.

Unless you hard-code a fully qualified pathname as the filename parameter, Windows will *always* look for an .INI file in the Windows directory—not in the WINDOWS\SYSTEM directory, the application's "current" directory, nor any of the directories listed in your PATH environment variable. There is one alternative to hard-coding a fully qualified pathname: you could instead construct a fully qualified pathname at run-time; but I recommend you let your .INI file reside in the Windows directory with all the others.

Design Considerations

Clearly any **TIniData** *class we write will include, as properties, section and key names. Consider using the trick we learned in the previous chapter to make assignments to these properties simpler—by creating special* **TSection** *and* **TKey** *classes for them.*

In the last chapter, we created **TRed**, **TGreen**, and **TBlue** classes, which were functionally identical. The only reason we bothered was so that they would be *different* classes, and we saw the advantages we can reap by overloading operators to behave differently for those different classes.

In most C++ demonstrations, you would be told to make **Section** and **Key** string properties, and to provide **SetSection()**, **GetSection()**, **SetKeyName()**, and **GetKeyName()** functions; but I prefer creating **TSection** and **TKey** classes, and then overloading the assignment operators to get the same effect—but, I think, more elegantly.

The **TIniData** class we intend to create is rather elaborate. We'll include multiple-value parsing, enumeration of sections and keys within a section, and even value encryption. Trying to do all these things at once could prove to be a bit overwhelming. Therefore, let us "whelm" ourselves just right, by applying *incremental development* to this project. We'll build the class in four stages, making sure each stage works properly before going on to the next.

The TIniData Class: Stage 1

For our first trick, we're going to create not one, but *three* related classes. **TSection** and **TKey** are just derivatives of **string**, but by making each one a discreet class we can achieve the neat effect of overloading **TIniData**'s assignment operator differently for each one. This arrangement allows the assignment of a **TSection** object to a **TIniData** object set the section name, and the assignment of a **TKey** object set the key name. That leaves assignments of **string** objects available to set the current value of the preset section and key! What could be more elegant?

Creating the TIniData Files

The second step in implementing any class, after designing it, is to create the pair of files in which it will be realized. If the class is being created as a stand-alone project, it will also be necessary to create the project.

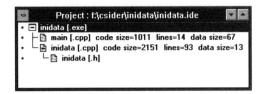

Figure 11.1 The TIniData project window.

The **TIniData** class will be one that we can use in project after project, so it makes sense to think of this as a project in its own right. That means our target will be an .LIB file. (Since **TIniData** will be implemented in a single .CPP file—with related .H file, of course—it could be distributed as a .OBJ file. But placing it in a .LIB file will make it "seem" more like a library.)

However, for now we're going to want to test our work. Since **TIniData** does not refer to any part of ObjectWindows proper, we can test it from an EasyWin application. That means the target—which we can change to a .LIB file later—will for now be an EasyWin .EXE. That also means we'll need an "extra" source module, MAIN.CPP, to contain the test code in a **main()** function.

But that's all setup. The files we're *really* interested in are INIDATA.CPP and INIDATA.H. Match your project window against the one shown in Figure 11.1 to verify that you've set up your project correctly.

The initial contents of INIDATA.H should come so automatically to you by now, you should be able to type them in your sleep:

```
#ifndef __INIDATA_H__
#define __INIDATA_H__

#include <cstring.h>

#endif
```

Okay, I did add one **#include**, a reference to CSTRING.H, the header in which the **string** class is declared—we'll be using that.

The initial contents of INIDATA.CPP are equally mindless: all we have to do is **#include** INIDATA.H:

```
#include "inidata.h"
```

If you like, you can go ahead and start MAIN.CPP as well. In addition to INIDATA.H, we'll want to **#include** IOSTREAM.H, so we can use console I/O to query the contents of **TIniData** objects:

```
#include "inidata.h"
#include <iostream.h>

void main (void)
   {
   }
```

We'll fill in the blanks in the following pages.

Creating TSection

The TSection *class is a specialized* string *intended to hold section names. Here's how it's built.*

You remember the **string** class: it's supplied by Borland as an implementation of the ANSI **String** class, andmysteriously spelled in all lowercase. There are a couple of other quirks in it, too; for example, it doesn't supply a cast to **char** *, or even to **const char** * (although there is a **c_str()** method to accomplish that conversion).

Since our **TSection** class is basically a **string** that has been spun off into its own class simply so C++ will identify it as such, we could get by with implementing it with no more than a constructor. However, I suggest we make it easier to use by including that cast to **const char** *. Both the constructor and the cast overload are simple enough to make them **inline** functions, which makes it possible to implement them in the header file:

```
class TSection : public string
   {
   public:
     TSection (char * aSection = NULL);
     operator const char * (void) const;
     TSection & operator= (TSection aSection);
   };

inline TSection::TSection (char * aSection)
   : string (aSection)
   {
   }

inline TSection::operator const char * (void) const
   {
   return c_str ();
   }
```

The assignment operator, however, needs to be defined in the implementation file. This is because we've given it the argument **TSection aSection**. If we had made **aSection** a *reference* to a **TSection** instead of passing it by value, we could have implemented it **inline**. Had we done so, though, we would have received warnings from the compiler telling us it had to create a temporary object every time we tried to assign a simple string to a **TSection** object.

So, in INIDATA.CPP, we place the implementation of the assignment operator:

```
TSection & TSection::operator= (TSection aSection)
   {
   string::operator=(aSection);
   return *this;
   }
```

This code shows an alternate method of invoking the ancestor version of this operator. Had we preferred, we could have achieved the same goal by casting:

```
((string) *this) = aSection;
```

I like this method because it shows clearly that I am invoking an ancestor method.

Creating the TKey Class

The **TKey** *class is functionally identical to* **TSection***. Most of it, too, can be implemented in the header file. Here's the code.*

Remember, the only reason **TKey** is implemented as a discreet class is so that C++ will recognize it as such. Therefore, the class declaration and **inline** methods look like this:

```
class TKey : public string
   {
   public:
     TKey (char * aKey = NULL);
     operator const char * (void) const;
     TKey & operator= (TKey aKey);
   };

inline TKey::TKey (char * aKey)
   : string (aKey)
   {
   }
```

```
inline TKey::operator const char * (void) const
   {
   return c_str ();
   }
```

Likewise, the INIDATA.CPP file must contain the definition of **TKey**'s assignment operator:

```
TKey & TKey::operator= (TKey aKey)
   {
   string::operator=(aKey);
   return *this;
   }
```

If you are new to Windows programming, don't miss this opportunity to use the Clipboard to save yourself some work! Just copy the **TSection** code, paste it, select the newly pasted lines, and use Edit/ Replace command to replace **TSection** with **TKey**—but don't forget to change it just for the selected text!

And if this seems clunky to you—if you're one of those people who says things like, "This is too much effort. It'll be easier to just retype," remember that *any* new skill seems clunky while you're developing it. You don't get better with chopsticks by using a fork, and you don't become more proficient with Windows editing tools by not using them.

Our First Stab at TIniData

*Now that **TSection** and **TKey** have been defined, we are ready to write the first version of **TIniData**. This version has no additional abilities other than reading values from and writing them to .INI files, but it does provide room for enhancement.*

Unlike **TSection** and **TKey**, **TIniData** cannot be implemented entirely **inline** (or, rather, it *should not* be). So our major INIDATA.H activity is to add the class declaration:

```
class TIniData
   {
   public:
     TIniData (string aPathname = "win.ini", TSection aSection = "");
     TIniData (const TIniData & aIniData);
     TIniData & operator= (const TIniData & aIniData);
     TIniData & operator= (TSection & aSection);
     void SetPathname (string aPathname);
     string GetPathname (void) const;
```

```
   void SetDefault (string aDefault);
   string GetDefault (void) const;
   string GetValue (TKey Key);
   TIniData & operator= (TKey & aKey);
   TIniData & operator= (string & aValue);
   TIniData & operator= (const char * aValue);
   operator TSection (void) const;
   operator TKey (void) const;
   operator string (void) const;
   operator const char * (void) const;
private:
   string Pathname;
   TSection Section;
   TKey Key;
   string Default;
};
```

The **public** entries are usually placed first so that the programmer/user of the class can easily find the elements he or she has to play with. But when studying a class declaration to see how the class works internally, and what the **public** components are *for*, it is often useful to begin with the **private** section, especially the properties. In this case we are storing most of the components of the **GetPrivateProfileString()** function and its relatives.

Pathname, for instance, must be stored if we are to identify the .INI file we intend to manage. **Section** and **Key** not only represent the corresponding components of a .INI file datum, they are the first uses of the **TSection** and **TKey** classes, respectively. Finally, the **Default** property will be used to supply a value if the **Key**, **Section** or **Pathname** doesn't exist when a value is requested.

Now we are ready to look at the methods made **public**. First, of course, is the primary constructor. By supplying default values for both its arguments, the one constructor can double as a default constructor. If you invoke it with no parameters, it constructs a **TIniData** object for the WIN.INI file; but you can also easily create objects for other .INI files. You can even specify a section.

The constructor itself resides in INIDATA.CPP:

```
TIniData::TIniData (string aPathname, TSection aSection)
     : Section (aSection)
   {
   SetPathname (aPathname);
   }
```

Notice that we didn't simply initialize **Pathname** with the **aPathname** parameter, at least not directly. The **SetPathname()** method will fully qualify the supplied name in accordance with Windows' rules (as we'll see when we examine that method).

The next question to ask is, "Do we really *need* a copy constructor?" After all, how often would you want to make a copy of a **TIniData** object—or, for that matter, how often would you even want two of them in a single application? But that isn't the point. Your design time should not be spent exploring ways to *limit* your object's usefulness. Even if you can't think of a reason to copy a **TIniData** object now, does that necessarily mean you never will?

Besides, and more subtly, if you don't create a copy constructor, C++ will—and, as you'll recall, the system-generated copy constructor will perform a shallow copy. We need to create a specific copy constructor. For the same reason, we'll need an assignment operator, which makes the copy constructor easy to implement **inline** in INIDATA.H:

```
inline TIniData::TIniData (const TIniData & aIniData)
   {
   *this = aIniData;
   }
```

Obviously we've begged the question of how the assignment of one **TIniData** object to another is going to take place, but not to worry; the whole **TIniData** assignment operator is defined next in INIDATA.CPP:

```
TIniData & TIniData::operator= (const TIniData & aIniData)
   {
   Pathname = aIniData.Pathname;
   Section = aIniData.Section;
   Key = aIniData.Key;
   Default = aIniData.Default;
   return *this;
   }
```

Setting and retrieving the **Pathname** and **Default** values are operations that probably won't be used very often. After all, the **Pathname** can be specified when a **TIniData** object is constructed, and for most keys the default value is just an empty string. So, rather than implement a **TPathname** or **TDefault** type, which would enable assignments and casts to supply access to these two properties, we can just implement the following methods. The retrieval methods can be implemented **inline**:

```
inline string TIniData::GetPathname (void) const
   {
   return Pathname;
   }
```

```
inline string TIniData::GetDefault (void) const
  {
  return Default;
  }
```

Because Borland C++ won't implement a function requiring intrinsic invocation of a copy constructor **inline** anyway, we may as well place the **SetDefault()** function in the .CPP file:

```
inline void TIniData::SetDefault (string aDefault)
  {
  Default = aDefault;
  }
```

The **SetPathname()** function also goes into the .CPP file; setting the **Pathname** requires a bit more work than retrieving it:

```
void TIniData::SetPathname (string aPathname)
  {
  char Drive[_MAX_DRIVE], Dir[_MAX_DIR], FName[_MAX_FNAME],
Ext[_MAX_EXT];
  char TempName[_MAX_PATH];
  _splitpath (aPathname.c_str(), Drive, Dir, FName, Ext);
  if (! Dir[0])
    {
    GetWindowsDirectory (Dir, sizeof Dir);
    strncpy (Drive, Dir, 2);
    strcpy (Dir, &Dir[2]);
    }
  if (! Ext[0])
    strcpy (Ext, ".INI");
  _makepath (TempName, Drive, Dir, FName, Ext);
  Pathname = TempName;
  }
```

What we do in the method is duplicate Windows' way of hunting for a .INI file. That is, if its name is not already fully qualified, it must reside in the \WINDOWS directory. We'd like a fully qualified pathname for reasons that will become clear in the next couple of sections, so that's what we construct—the standard C library functions **_splitpath()** and **_makepath()**, and the Windows API function **GetWindowsDirectory()** make it easy.

Next come the other assignment operators. Here's where we really use those subsidiary classes like **TSection** and operator overloading to make using the **TIniData** control a snap. We simply provide assignments to **TIniData** objects from **TSection** objects and **TKey** objects. These assignments will apply to the corresponding properties:

```
TIniData & TIniData::operator= (TSection & aSection)
   {
   Section = aSection;
   return *this;
   }


TIniData & TIniData::operator= (TKey & aKey)
   {
   Key = aKey;
   return *this;
   }
```

Since these are more than one-liners, I chose to *not* make them **inline**; they are therefore implemented in INIDATA.CPP.

Microsoft Visual Basic 3.0 has introduced the concept of a "default property." Although we can't implement a default property in quite the same way in C++, we can come close by defining assignments and casts to and from the basic **string** class, with parallel methods for C-style strings (**char far** *). Here are the assignments:

```
TIniData & TIniData::operator= (string & aValue)
   {
   return *this = aValue.c_str();
   }


TIniData & TIniData::operator= (const char * aValue)
   {
   WritePrivateProfileString (Section, Key, aValue, Pathname.c_str());
   return *this;
   }
```

Notice that the **string** assignment just converts the **string** and invokes the **char far** * assignment. This is the function that does the work, and it's the first one we've written for this class that actually ties into the Windows API for management of a .INI file (which the Windows API calls refer to as "profiles").

Casting to **TSection** and **TKey** objects returns, as you might expect, the corresponding property:

```
TIniData::operator TSection (void) const
   {
   return Section;
   }


TIniData::operator TKey (void) const
   {
```

```
return Key;
}
```

With such assignment operators, we'll be able to write code like

```
TIniData IniData ("MYAPP.INI", "Options");
  // Cast of "Options" to TSection made automatically
TSection S = IniData;
  // Cast to TSection made automatically by assignment
S = "Colors";
IniAta = s;
  // Assignment to Section prop made automatically
IniData = TSection ("Sounds");
  // Temporary TSection can be used, too
```

We'll also allow automatic casting to **string** and **char far** * to enable retrieval of the section/key value from the .INI file:

```
TIniData::operator string (void) const
  {
  char Buffer[128];
  GetPrivateProfileString (Section, Key, Default.c_str(),
    Buffer, sizeof Buffer, Pathname.c_str());
  return string (Buffer);
  }

TIniData::operator const char * (void) const
  {
  return ((string) *this).c_str();
  }
```

This time we let **string** do the work while **char far** * gets a free ride. Note the complex casting in the second method; ***this** must be cast to a **string** in order for **c_str()** to be invoked.

But the first method, the cast to **string**, is where the action takes place, such as it is. The Windows API call **GetPrivateProfileString()** is the core. It expects five **char far** * arguments. We provided appropriate casts for **TSection** and **TKey**, so they can be used directly. **Default** and **Pathname** are a little more complex since they are **string** objects and Borland did not implement that class with a cast to **const char** *. They did, however, provide a function called **c_str()** that does the same job; so we invoke it, instead. Finally, we supply a standard C-style **Buffer** into which **GetPrivateProfileString()** can deliver the goods. After competing this task, we can convert **Buffer** into a **string** object, which we then can return.

That, right there, is it—for now. There are definitely more features we'll want to add to **TIniData**, but we have enough now to test: if we can actually read and write .INI file values. Nothing we couldn't have done in C, but we've accomplished it in a much more C++-fashion.

Testing TIniData

*Having gone as far as we have with the **TIniData** class, we'd like to test the thing. We could do this by writing a full-fledged Windows application to do the job. However, since **TIniData** does not make use of ObjectWindows, we can more easily test it in a QuickWin program.*

To test **TIniData** in a QuickWin program, all we have to do is change IniData's target type from static library to QuickWin app, and add a module containing a **main()** function. (Strictly speaking, **main()** could be added to the INIDATA.CPP module; I prefer the discipline of keeping it separate.)

As a less convenient alternative, keep the IniData project as it was, but create a *new* IniTest project that uses INIDATA.LIB.

Either way, the **main()** function simply creates a **TIniData** object and puts it through its paces. Here's an example:

```
#include "inidata.h"
#include <iostream.h>

void main ()
    {
    TIniData Winnie;
    cout << "Pathname is " << Winnie.GetPathname() << endl;
    Winnie = TSection ("Windows");
    Winnie = TKey ("Load");
    cout << "Section is " << (TSection) Winnie << endl;
    cout << "Key is " << (TKey) Winnie << endl;
    cout << "Value is " << Winnie << endl;
    Winnie = "Clock"; // Should change the current Load to Clock
    }
```

Enumerating Sections

One of the few functions oddly missing from Windows' initialization file support is the ability to enumerate section names. Keys within a section can be listed, but users of the Windows API are out of luck if they want to see what sections are already present in a .INI file. If they really want that list, they'll have to open the .INI file using standard file I/O functions and look for the section names themselves.

Of course, we'll have to do the same thing . . . once. But, by building into the *TIniData* class the ability to enumerate section names, we'll never have to worry about writing such code again.

Adding a Sections Bag to TIniData

One of the container classes Borland supplies is the "bag." This is something like an array, except that items "stored" in the bag are not kept in any particular order and therefore cannot be indexed.

If you think about it, sections in a .INI file are, in fact, stored in no particular order; so representing them within a C++ program as a bag makes sense.

If we wanted to, we could create a basic bag directly from the **TIBagAsVector** template class, as described in the chapter on containers. Normal procedure, you'll recall, is to use a **typedef** to provide a more convenient name in place of the awkward template syntax. For example,

```
typedef TIBagAsVector<TSection> TMyBag;
typedef TIBagAsVectorIterator<TSection> T MyIterator;
```

However, I want my sections bag to be a little more specialized. The reason is this: I anticipate that most uses of **TIniData** objects will *not* involve enumerating sections. After all, I've been programming Windows for years now and the only time I actually needed such an ability was the time I wrote a .INI file editor. So I don't want to burden **TIniData** with a blind need to load up all section names every time one of its objects is instantiated.

On the other hand, I'd like the list of section names easily available to the programmer, should he or she want it.

I can achieve both these seemingly contradictory goals by deriving a child class from **TIBagAsVector**. The new class, in addition to inheriting the bag attributes of its ancestor, can add the ability to load section names only if they are requested.

As with **TSection** and **TKey**, the new class can be described in INIDATA.H, at any point after **TSection** has been declared. First, you'll need to **#include** the classlib header file:

```
#include <classlib\bags.h>
```

Note that I have partially qualified the name of the header file, rather than simply adding classlib to the list of directories to be searched. As the number of **#include** headers increases, the more likely it is that we'll run into name conflicts. By adding a portion of the pathname that guarantees uniqueness, and yet works—classlib is always placed by the Borland installation as a subdirectory below BC4\INCLUDE—I help ensure that this module will continue to compile correctly in future years.

Once BAGS.H has been **#include**d, the **TSectionsBag** class can be declared:

```
class TSectionsBag : public TIBagAsVector<TSection>
  {
  public:
    TSectionsBag (string * aPathname);
    unsigned Count (void);
  protected:
    void Refresh (void);
  private:
    string * Pathname;
  };
```

We'll describe the **Flush()**, **Count()**, and **Refresh()** methods shortly, when we define the code for them. For now, we'll just glance at the **Pathname** property and the class's constructor:

```
inline TSectionsBag::TSectionsBag (string * aPathname)
  : TIBagAsVector<TSection> (25), Pathname (aPathname)
  {
  }
```

The ancestral constructor just wants one argument, the number of element positions to be added to the bag whenever the existing number of positions is filled and another one is needed. I picked 25, based on my observation that few .INI files have more sections than that. In the member initialization area, we also initialize the **Pathname** pointer to an address passed to the constructor. Note that there is no default constructor; we'll deal with the ramifications of that shortly.

Next, we need a **typedef** for the specialized iterator for this class:

```
typedef TIBagAsVectorIterator<TSection> TSectionsBagIterator;
```

Strictly speaking, **TSectionsBagIterator** is an iterator, not for **TSectionsBag**, but for *TSectionsBag*'s ancestor class. However, in this case, that's adequate.

Concluding our modifications to the header file, we must add an instance of the new class as a property of the **TIniData** class. Since **TSectionsBag** is a fully implemented object, complete with usage safeguards and so on, we can make it a **public** property. We'll call the new data member **Sections**:

```
class TIniData
   {
   public:
        ⅴ
        ⅴ
     TSectionsBag Sections;
   private:
        ⅴ
        ⅴ
   };
```

I noted that **TSectionsBag** has no default constructor. This is not an oversight; the class doesn't need one. The constructor we did supply requires one argument, a pointer to the .INI file's pathname. It doesn't matter if the pathname is already constructed or not; **TSectionsBag** just needs the pointer. Later, when it needs to reference that pathname, the pathname will have been constructed.

This does mean, however, that we'll have to specify **Sections**' constructor in **TIniData**'s member initialization area. That changes **TIniData**'s copy constructor to:

```
inline TIniData::TIniData (const TIniData & aIniData)
   : Sections (&Pathname)
   {
   *this = aIniData;
   }
```

Turning now to the implementation file, INIDATA.CPP, we also have to modify **TIniData**'s other constructor:

```
TIniData::TIniData (string aPathname, TSection aSection)
     : Section (aSection), Sections (&Pathname)
   {
   SetPathname (aPathname);
   }
```

We'll also have to empty the **Sections** bag whenever its contents (if any) become obsolete—for example, when changing the pathname of the .INI file:

```
void TIniData::SetPathname (string aPathname)
   {
       ⅋
       ⅋
   Sections.Flush (TShouldDelete::Delete);
   }
```

The only change is in the last line, where we invoke **Sections'** inherited **Flush()** method, which will detach and delete any objects the bag might contain.

For the same reason, we'll want to clear the contents of **Sections** if an assignment is made to **Value**. Why **Value** and not **Section**? Because only an assignment to **Value** can cause a new section to be created; simply specifying a non-existent section name is not enough. We could write complex code to see if the section name is already part of the .INI file, but I see no justification in placing such a great CPU-intensive burden in the frequently used **Value** assignment just to support the infrequently used **Sections** collection. So **Value**'s assignment operator is modified just slightly:

```
TIniData & TIniData::operator= (const char * aValue)
   {
   Sections.Flush (TShouldDelete::Delete);
   WritePrivateProfileString (Section, Key, aValue, Pathname.c_str());
   return *this;
   }
```

We also must flush the **Sections** bag if a full **TIniData**-to-**TIniData** assignment takes place; because that could change the **Pathname**:

```
TIniData & TIniData::operator= (const TIniData & aIniData)
   {
   Pathname = aIniData.Pathname;
   Section = aIniData.Section;
   Key = aIniData.Key;
   Default = aIniData.Default;
   Sections.Flush(TShouldDelete::Delete);
   return *this;
   }
```

Now we can look at the three **TSectionsBag** methods declared in the header file: **Flush()**, **Count()** and **Refresh()**.

Be patient. We'll add more code here later.

The **Count()** method replaces the more awkwardly named **GetItemsInCollection()** inherited from the ancestor classes. Other, non-bag collections have a **Count()** method and it's not clear to me why bags were made an exception. But changing its name is not the only reason for the method to exist; invoking it will be the trigger that causes the collection to reach into the .INI file and fill itself with the names of its sections. Here's the code:

```
unsigned TSectionsBag::Count (void)
  {
  if (! TIBagAsVector<TSection>::GetItemsInContainer())
    Refresh ();
  return TIBagAsVector<TSection>::GetItemsInContainer();
  }
```

As you can see—easily, since most of the work was off-loaded into the **Refresh()** method—we simply check to see if the collection is empty. If so, we can assume the .INI file has not yet been read so we invoke **Refresh()** to perform that little task. We then return the count from the base class. Sure, conceivably it could still be zero—but, if so, no harm's been done.

The real work of enumerating sections in a .INI file, then, is encapsulated in the **Refresh()** method. This method will have to do the usual file stuff: open the file, read each line, note if the line begins with the "[" character, and saving the string delimited by the square brackets if it is. Of course, we won't be doing this stuff using standard C file I/O; this is C++ code! So we'll open the .INI as an **ifstream** object:

```
void TSectionsBag::Refresh (void)
  {
  ifstream IniFile (Pathname->c_str());
  while (! IniFile.eof ())
    {
    char Buffer[256];
    IniFile.getline (Buffer, sizeof Buffer);
    if (Buffer[0] == '[')
      {
      char SectionName[64];
      register i = 0, j = 1;
      while (Buffer[j] && (Buffer[j] != ']'))
        SectionName[i++] = Buffer[j++];
      SectionName[i] = 0;
      Add (new TSection (SectionName));
      }
    }
  }
```

Remember, we don't have to explicitly close the file; when the **ifstream** object **IniFile** goes out of scope, the file will be closed automatically.

Testing the Sections Bag

*To test the **Sections** bag it is only necessary to add exercise code for it in the **main()** function.*

In addition (or in place of) the test code you already have in **main()**, here's an example of some code that will enumerate the sections in a given .INI file:

```
void main ()
  {
  TIniData Winnie;
      ∀
      ∀

  TSectionsBagIterator s (Winnie.Sections);
  register n = 1;
  while (s)
    cout << (n++) << ": " << (s++)->c_str() << endl;
  }
```

Enumerating Keys

A handy feature we'd like to add to **TIniData** is the ability to enumerate keys within a section. Although this ability is supplied in the Windows API, it is awkward—some might say "bizarre"—to use. We'll make access to the list of keys as simple as we just made access to the list of sections itself.

How to Access a Key List in the Windows API

Although the Windows API provides no pre-packaged method of enumerating the sections in a .INI file, it does support enumerating the keys within a section. Here's how.

The **GetPrivateProfileString()** function included in the Windows API is usually used to retrieve values from a .INI file, given a section and key name. This is how we implemented the reading of the **Value** property earlier in this chapter. However, it has another function. If the second argument, the one in which the key is usually specified, is passed as a NULL pointer, then the buffer into which the value is usually copied is instead filled with the names of the keys within the specified section.

But it isn't a simple string of key names; that would be too easy. Instead each key in the list is terminated by a single NULL character. So how can you tell where the list itself ends? Just look for the two *adjacent* NULL characters, natch.

To see a sample of how to decode this stream of key names, look ahead to the **TKeys Refresh()** method.

Creating the TKeys Collection

In many ways—especially, in its declaration—the **TKeys** *class resembles the* **TSections** *class. But the superficial similarity ends in the definition of the* **Refresh()** *method.*

Look at the declaration of the **TKeys** class. Look hard; if you spend too little time you may think it's indistinguishable from the **TSections** class:

```
class TKeysBag : public TIBagAsVector<TKey>
  {
  public:
    TKeysBag (string * aPathname, TSection * aSection);
    unsigned Count (void);
  protected:
    void Refresh (void);
  private:
    string * Pathname;
    TSection * Section;
  };

inline TKeysBag::TKeysBag (string * aPathname, TSection * aSection)
  : TIBagAsVector<TKey> (25), Pathname (aPathname), Section
(aSection)
  {
  }

typedef TIBagAsVectorIterator<TKey> TKeysBagIterator;
```

In the interests of brevity I've included the constructor and **typedef** for the iterator. The big difference is really just an extension of what we did with the **TSectionsBag** class: not only is there a pointer to a **Pathname**; there is another pointer to a **Section** name. This follows the hierarchical nature of the .INI file organization: Just as the list of section names will change if the pathname changes, so must the list of key names change if the section changes.

Changes made to **TIniData** also parallel those made when we added the **Sections** bag to it. First, and the simplest, is adding the **Keys** property itself:

```
class TIniData
  {
  public:
        Y
        Y
    TSectionsBag Sections;
    TKeysBag Keys;
  private:
        Y
        Y
  };
```

Then, of course, there's the appropriate modification of the **TIniData** copy constructor:

```
inline TIniData::TIniData (const TIniData & aIniData)
  : Sections (&Pathname), Keys (&Pathname, &Section)
  {
  *this = aIniData;
  }
```

In the implementation file, the **TKeysBag Count()** method is a virtual twin of the **Count()** method of **TSectionsBag**:

```
unsigned TKeysBag::Count (void)
  {
  if (! TIBagAsVector<TKey>::GetItemsInContainer())
    Refresh ();
  return TIBagAsVector<TKey>::GetItemsInContainer();
  }
```

The **Refresh()** method is the one that looks different, because it accomplishes its goal in a totally different manner. Instead of opening a file (at least, explicitly), **Refresh()** must invoke **GetPrivateProfileString()** as described in the previous section, then break the returned string into the separate components:

```
void TKeysBag::Refresh (void)
  {
  char Buffer[512];
  char * Ptr = Buffer;
  GetPrivateProfileString (Section->c_str(),
    NULL,
    "",
    Buffer,
    sizeof Buffer,
    Pathname->c_str());
```

```
while (Ptr[0])
  {
  Add (new TKey (Ptr));
  Ptr = &Ptr[strlen (Ptr)+1];
  }
}
```

The 512-byte size of **Buffer** does limit the amount of key name data that can be returned, but it should be adequate. You can always enlarge it if necessary.

That takes care of the **TKeys** class itself, but of course there's still a little maintenance to be done on the *TIniData* class. There's the standard constructor, for instance, into whose member initialization area a reference to **Keys** must be placed:

```
TIniData::TIniData (string aPathname, TSection aSection)
    : Section (aSection), Sections (&Pathname), Keys (&Pathname,
&Section)
  {
  SetPathname (aPathname);
  }
```

Before, we added a flush of the **Sections** bag to the **TIniData**-to-**TIniData** assignment operator. Now we'll have to do the same for the **Keys** bag:

```
TIniData & TIniData::operator= (const TIniData & aIniData)
  {
  Pathname = aIniData.Pathname;
  Section = aIniData.Section;
  Key = aIniData.Key;
  Default = aIniData.Default;
  Sections.Flush(TShouldDelete::Delete);
  Keys.Flush(TShouldDelete::Delete);
  return *this;
  }
```

Likewise, we must modify **SetPathname( )**:

```
void TIniData::SetPathname (string aPathname)
  {
      ⩒
      ⩒
  Sections.Flush (TShouldDelete::Delete);
  Keys.Flush (TShouldDelete::Delete);
  }
```

But now, we also have to flush the **Keys** bag if the section name alone is reassigned:

```
TIniData & TIniData::operator= (TSection & aSection)
    {
    Section = aSection;
    Keys.Flush (TShouldDelete::Delete);
    return *this;
    }
```

Finally, just as an assignment of a new **Value** could possibly add a new section to an existing .INI file, so might it add a new key. Therefore we must add flushing of the **Keys** bag there, too:

```
TIniData & TIniData::operator= (const char * aValue)
    {
    Sections.Flush (TShouldDelete::Delete);
    Keys.Flush (TShouldDelete::Delete);
    WritePrivateProfileString (Section, Key, aValue, Pathname.c_str());
    return *this;
    }
```

Testing the Keys Bag

*To test the **Keys** bag it is only necessary to add exercise code for it in the **main( )** function.*

In addition to the test code you already have in **main( )**, here's an example of some code that will enumerate the keys in the first section of an .INI file:

```
void main ()
    {
    TIniData Winnie;
        ⋎
        ⋎

    TSectionsBagIterator s (Winnie.Sections);
    register n = 1;
        ⋎
        ⋎

    s.Restart();
    Winnie = *(s.Current());
    int KeyCount (Winnie.Keys.Count());
    cout << endl << "Keys: " << KeyCount << endl;
```

```
TKeysBagIterator k (Winnie.Keys);
n = 1;
while (k)
   cout << (n++) << ": " << (k++)->c_str() << endl;

}
```

Note the way we obtain the first section from the **TSectionsBagIterators**, assigning it to **Winnie** (the **TIniData** object) so that our request of key names becomes meaningful. After all, keys, must reside in a section.

Handling Multiple Values

A quick look at the WIN.INI file will show several examples of keys with multiple values. There are at least two in the [Windows] section alone: *Documents* and *Device*. On my system, *Documents* is equal to "doc txt wri xls xlc bmp wmf" and *Device* is equal to "HP LaserJet III,hppcl5a,LPT1:". (These entries are likely to be somewhat different in your WIN.INI file.)

The Windows API profile calls do not help you parse multi-component values. Of course, accomplishing this is not brain surgery; still, you've got to do it yourself.

But the **TIniData** class is supposed to be *better* than the underlying API functions. So we're going to add automatic parsing of multi-component values, via another collection property: **List**. Once you have specified **List**'s delimiter character, you'll be able to itemize the components in the current section/key's value—without affecting your ability to read values as a whole, as before.

Declaring the TValueList Class

Declaring the **TValueList** *class brings up a chicken-and-egg problem:* **TValueList** *must include a pointer to its* **TIniData** *parent— but* **TIniData** *is going to include a* **TValueList** *property. Which do we declare first?*

The **TSection** class, you'll recall, had as a property a pointer to a pathname. This pointer was passed from the **TIniData** parent, and pointed to the parent's **Pathname** property. This was not a problem, because **Pathname** was a **string** object and the **string** class was predefined.

But **TValueList** will need a pointer to its parent **TIniData** so it can obtain from the parent the value of the current section and key. In order to declare such a pointer, we'll have to include a line like:

```
class TValueList : public TIArrayAsVector<string>
  {
  public:
      ⋎
      ⋎
  private:
    TIniData * Parent;
      ⋎
      ⋎
  };
```

Normally, doing so would require that we previously included a declaration of the **TIniData** class . . . but the **TIniData** class is going to include a line like:

```
class TIniData

  {
  public:
      ⋎
      ⋎
    TValueList List;
      ⋎
      ⋎
  };
```

And that, of course, requires that **TValueList** be previously declared. So what can we do?

Looking at the **TIniData** example, we can see that **TValueList** must be fully declared by the time the compiler reaches this declaration. That's because **List** will be stored **inline**, and the compiler has to know how big it is.

In **TValueList**, on the other hand, we aren't storing an entire **TIniData**, just a *pointer* to one. C++ *knows* how big a pointer is; it doesn't matter what it's a pointer *to*. So we don't have to "fully" declare **TIniData**; just let the compiler know that there will be one declared later; that is, when we say we want a pointer of **TIniData** type, it isn't a typo. We do that with the following statement:

```
class TIniData;
```

With that done, we can declare **TValueList**:

```
class TValueList : public TIArrayAsVector<string>
  {
  public:
    TValueList (TIniData * aParent);
```

```
      TValueList (const TValueList & aValueList);
      TValueList & operator= (char aDelimiter);
      operator char (void) const;
      TValueList & operator= (const TValueList & aValueList);
      int Count (void);
   private:
      TIniData * Parent;
      char Delimiter;
   };
```

You'll note that **TValueList** is based on an array collection rather than a bag, like **TSectionsBag** and **TKeysBag** were. That's because the elements in a compound value might well be positionally significant. That means you'll have to add an **#include** statement to the top of the header file, which now looks like this:

```
#ifndef __INIDATA_H__
#define __INIDATA_H__

#include <cstring.h>
#include <classlib\bags.h>
#include <classlib\arrays.h>
```

I have *not* included an iterator **typedef** because array collections can more easily be iterated by indexing them, just like "normal" C arrays.

Defining the *TValueList* Class

We'll define the **TValueClass** *entirely in the implementation file* ***INIDATA.CPP.** Here's the code.*

The first constructor for **TValueList** is the "normal" one, although it is not a default constructor—it requires a parameter. It looks like this:

```
TValueList::TValueList (TIniData * aParent)
   : TIArrayAsVector<string> (8, 1, 8),
     Parent (aParent),
     Delimiter (0)
   {
   }
```

The parameters being passed to **TIArrayAsVector<string>** set the initial upper bound, lower bound, and delta, respectively. The upper bound can grow as needed, as long as delta is greater than zero. Traditional C programmers will be *aghast* that I set the lower bound to a number other than zero, but I've always hated zero-based arrays. Now, thanks to Borland's class library, I don't have to put up with them any more. I initialized the **Delimiter** to a null byte, so if it isn't changed, the values will be accessible from **List** as an array of one element.

The copy constructor might make you pause for a moment:

```
TValueList::TValueList (const TValueList & aValueList)
    : TIArrayAsVector<string> (aValueList.GetItemsInContainer(), 0, 8),
      Parent (aValueList.Parent),
      Delimiter (aValueList.Delimiter)
{
}
```

It doesn't really look much different than the "normal" constructor, does it? Why aren't we copying the elements of the array?

The reason is, we don't have to. Like **Sections** and **Keys**, **List** won't usually be used at all. If it is accessed, it will fill its own self with the parsed compound values. The only information we copy is that which is required for it to do its job.

To make it easy to set the **Delimiter**, we supply an assignment operator that expects a single character:

```
TValueList & TValueList::operator= (char aDelimiter)
    {
    Delimiter = aDelimiter;
    return *this;
    }
```

Likewise, to *read* the **Delimiter**, we supply a cast to **char**:

```
TValueList::operator char (void) const
    {
    return Delimiter;
    }
```

We also supply an assignment from another **TValueList**, for use in **TIniData**'s assignment. It is similar to the copy constructor, except that it precedes the copying code with an invocation of **Flush()** to clear out any contents it might have already parsed:

```
TValueList & TValueList::operator= (const TValueList & aValueList)
    {
    Flush (TShouldDelete::Delete);
    Parent = aValueList.Parent;
    Delimiter = aValueList.Delimiter;
    return *this;
    }
```

As with **Sections** and **Keys**, we'll trigger the parsing of the input compound value with the invocation of a **Count()** method:

```
int TValueList::Count (void)
   {
   if (! GetItemsInContainer())
      {
      string Value (*Parent);
      char Buffer[128];
      register i, j = 0;
      for (i = 0; i < Value.length(); i++)
         if (Value[i] != Delimiter)
            {
            if (j || (Value[i] != ' '))
               Buffer[j++] = Value[i];
            }
         else
            {
            Buffer[j] = 0;
            Add (new string (Buffer));
            j = 0;
            }
      if (j)
         Add (new string (Buffer));
      }
   return GetItemsInContainer();
   }
```

Adding the List Property to TIniData

We'll next want to add the List property to the TIniData declaration.

Since I showed the addition just a few paragraphs ago, here's the whole **TIniData** declaration as it should now appear:

```
class TIniData
   {
   public:
      TIniData (string aPathname = "win.ini", TSection aSection = "");
      TIniData (const TIniData & aIniData);
      TIniData & operator= (const TIniData & aIniData);
      void SetPathname (string aPathname);
      string GetPathname (void) const;
      void SetDefault (string aDefault);
      string GetDefault (void) const;
      string GetValue (TKey Key);
```

```
      TIniData & operator= (TSection & aSection);
      TIniData & operator= (TKey & aKey);
      TIniData & operator= (string & aValue);
      TIniData & operator= (const char * aValue);
      operator TSection (void) const;
      operator TKey (void) const;
      operator string (void) const;
      operator const char * (void) const;
      TSectionsBag Sections;
      TKeysBag Keys;
      TValueList List;
   private:
      string Pathname;
      TSection Section;
      TKey Key;
      string Default;
   };
```

List is the last of the **public** properties, in case you have trouble finding it. As with **Sections** and **Keys**, we can safely make it **public** because it is a fully functional object, able to fend for itself.

And, also like **Sections** and **Keys**, **List** does not have a default constructor, because **TIniData** must give it a pointer to itself during construction. Here's the **inline** copy constructor:

```
inline TIniData::TIniData (const TIniData & aIniData)
   : Sections (&Pathname),
     Keys (&Pathname, &Section),
     List (this)
   {
   *this = aIniData;
   }
```

Back in the implementation file, the "standard" constructor is also modified to include the **List** construction in the member initialization area:

```
TIniData::TIniData (string aPathname, TSection aSection)
    : Section (aSection), Sections (&Pathname),
      Keys (&Pathname, &Section),
      List (this)
   {
   SetPathname (aPathname);
   }
```

TIniData's assignment operator must also be made to include the copying of the **List** property (although, remember, this only copies the information the target **List** will need to parse a compound value—not the parsed components themselves):

```
TIniData & TIniData::operator= (const TIniData & aIniData)
  {
  Pathname = aIniData.Pathname;
  Section = aIniData.Section;
  Key = aIniData.Key;
  Default = aIniData.Default;
  Sections.Flush(TShouldDelete::Delete);
  Keys.Flush(TShouldDelete::Delete);
  List = aIniData.List;
  return *this;
  }
```

When we added the **Sections** collection, we had to **Flush()** it if the **Pathname** was changed because then the old list of sections would become irrelevant. The same is true of the **List** collection; so now we **Flush()** it, too:

```
void TIniData::SetPathname (string aPathname)
  {
  char Drive[_MAX_DRIVE], Dir[_MAX_DIR], FName[_MAX_FNAME],
Ext[_MAX_EXT];
  char TempName[_MAX_PATH];
  _splitpath (aPathname.c_str(), Drive, Dir, FName, Ext);
  if (! Dir[0])
    {
    GetWindowsDirectory (Dir, sizeof Dir);
    strncpy (Drive, Dir, 2);
    strcpy (Dir, &Dir[2]);
    }
  if (! Ext[0])
    strcpy (Ext, ".INI");
  _makepath (TempName, Drive, Dir, FName, Ext);
  Pathname = TempName;
  Sections.Flush (TShouldDelete::Delete);
  Keys.Flush (TShouldDelete::Delete);
  List.Flush (TShouldDelete::Delete);
  }
```

Likewise, merely changing the **Section** or **Key** invalidates the **List**, as does assigning a new value:

```
TIniData & TIniData::operator= (TSection & aSection)
  {
  Section = aSection;
  Keys.Flush (TShouldDelete::Delete);
```

```
  List.Flush (TShouldDelete::Delete);
  return *this;
  }

TIniData & TIniData::operator= (TKey & aKey)
  {
  Key = aKey;
  List.Flush (TShouldDelete::Delete);
  return *this;
  }

TIniData & TIniData::operator= (const char * aValue)
  {
  Sections.Flush (TShouldDelete::Delete);
  Keys.Flush (TShouldDelete::Delete);
  List.Flush (TShouldDelete::Delete);
  WritePrivateProfileString (Section, Key, aValue, Pathname.c_str());
  return *this;
  }
```

But that's all it takes. You can now use **TIniData**, not only for simple values, but to take the work out of parsing compound values.

Testing the List Property

*Perhaps you'd like to take your **TIniData** object out for a test drive and see how it handles the curves thrown at it by compound values. Here's some suggested test code for* **main()**.

If you've already added MAIN.CPP as suggested in previous sections, then testing the new **List** property will be a piece of cake. Just add the following code (or something similar):

```
void main ()
  {
  TIniData Winnie;
      v
      v
  Winnie = TSection ("Windows");
  Winnie = TKey ("Documents");
  Winnie.List = ' ';
  cout << endl << "Documents=" << ((const char *) Winnie) << endl;
  for (register v = 1; v <= Winnie.List.Count(); v++)
    cout << v << ": " << Winnie.List[v]->c_str() << endl;

  Winnie = TKey ("Device");
  Winnie.List = ',';
```

```
cout << endl << "Device=" << ((const char *) Winnie) << endl;
for (v = 1; v <= Winnie.List.Count(); v++)
    cout << v << ": " << Winnie.List[v]->c_str() << endl;
}
```

In the first block, the **List.Delimiter** is set to a space character by virtue of the overloaded character assignment operator. By setting **Section** to "Windows" and **Key** to "Documents," we obtain a list of the extensions of files Windows considers documents when choosing a representative icon for the file in File Manager.

In the second block, the delimiter is a comma, and we read the current "Device"—that's your current printer. The three components of this value will appear in elements one, two and three of **List**, just the way you'd need them if you planned to use those values (to get a device context, for example).

Now that you have this convenient **TIniData** class, you have no excuse for not supporting user-defined options, lists of last-opened files, and restoring window state and position when restarting your applications.

Using *TIniData* In Your Application

It's all well and good to test the TIniData class from a stand-alone program, but the real test of the class is in a real application. Where is it used? How is it used? Here we'll take the Shapes application as an example and save the user's custom color selection in a .INI file.

After a user has made the effort to create a set of 16 custom colors (as seen in the previous chapter), you can imagine that he or she probably wouldn't want to have to re-create that set each time the application was run. The set of colors presumably has nothing to do with the document *per se*; if it did, it would be saved as part of the document. But some options, such as that set of colors, is *independent* of any document, yet needs to be saved anyway. That's the purpose of .INI files.

You have two choices in locating a *TIniData* object. This first is, you can make one on the stack wherever and whenever you need one—for example, in the *SetupWindow()* method of your main window. In such a case you would need to initialize it each time, but that's not a lot of work. Alternatively, you can make it a property of the application object itself, thus making it accessible from anywhere in the application. Since application options are by definition part of the application as a whole, the second method is the one we'll use.

That means adding a **#include** to SHAPSAPP.H:

```
#include "inidata.h"
```

We'll also have to add a *TIniData* object to the application class declaration:

```
class ShapesApp : public TApplication {
private:

private:
    void SetupSpeedBar (TDecoratedMDIFrame *frame);
    void AddFiles (TFileList* files);

public:
    ShapesApp ();
    virtual ~ShapesApp ();

    ShapesMDIClient  *mdiClient;
    TIniData IniData;
        ⩔
        ⩔
```

Since *TIniData* is a fully-implemented, programmer-safe class, we can make it a public data member without fear.

Of course, we'll have to specify its construction in the implementation file. Here's the change to SHAPESAPP.CPP:

```
ShapesApp::ShapesApp ()
    : TApplication("Shapes"),
      IniData ("Shapes.INI")
  {
  Printer = 0;
  Printing = 0;

  DocManager = new TDocManager(dmMDI | dmMenu);

  // INSERT>> Your constructor code here.
  }
```

The next change is one we wouldn't have to make *if the TXColor* class had been implemented properly. I deliberately left one design flaw in *TXColor* so you'd see the cost of making the same assumption error as in the last chapter.

Here's the problem: I basically copied the code for the *SelectUserColor()* method, which displays the Choose Color common dialog, from the Borland documentation. This code includes two local, but static, data items: the **struct** used by the dialog, and the array of custom colors the **struct** points to. As I explained, they had to be static to preserve their values between calls to the dialog. But *why didn't I make them part of the class?* Well, originally because I didn't think of it. But then, when I did think of it, I realized this was the sort of mistake I make all the time; and so might you, without this object lesson.

The moral of the lesson: *always make static data part of the class* unless there's a definite reason to make it part of the code. You usually be glad you did.

So now we'll just take those variables and make properties of them, by altering the *TXColor* declaration in XCOLOR.H. First, since we'll be referencing the *TChooseColorDialog* class, we'll have to move its **#include** from the implementation file into the header file:

```
#include <owl\chooseco.h>
```

Then we'll add the two properties to the *TXColor* declaration. Notice I've changed the name of the **struct** from *Data*, which was clear enough in the context of the method, to *DlgData*:

```
class TXColor : public TStreamableBase
    {
        Ⅴ
        Ⅴ
    private:
        static TChooseColorDialog::TData DlgData;
        static TColor CustomColors[16];
    DECLARE_STREAMABLE ( , TXColor, 1);
    };
```

Then I move the initialization of the two items out of the function:

```
TChooseColorDialog::TData TXColor::DlgData;

TColor TXColor::CustomColors[16] =
    {
    TXColor::White, TXColor::White,
    TXColor::White, TXColor::White,
    TXColor::White, TXColor::White,
    TXColor::White, TXColor::White,
    TXColor::White, TXColor::White,
    TXColor::White, TXColor::White,
    TXColor::White, TXColor::White,
    TXColor::White, TXColor::White
    };
```

```
void TXColor::SelectUserColor (TWindow * Window)
  {
  if (! DlgData.Flags)
    {
    DlgData.Flags = CC_RGBINIT;
    DlgData.Color = *this;
    DlgData.CustColors = CustomColors;
    }
  if (TChooseColorDialog(Window, DlgData).Execute() == IDOK)
    *this = DlgData.Color;
  }
```

Note how, as a side effect, this makes the code in the *SelectUserColor()* method *appear* simpler and easier to read.

At this point, everything should work as before. (Try it, as an exercise in incremental development. See how warm and confident the success makes you feel!) Now it's time to turn to the question: where do we set and retrieve the custom colors from the .INI file?

The answer to setting the colors is obvious: they must be set when the user returns from the Choose Color dialog, assuming he or she has clicked the OK button. However, setting sixteen colors in the .INI file is going to require at least sixteen lines of code, more than we'd like to clutter this method with. That means: another method!—In fact, two; one for setting and one for retrieving the custom colors. Although the work requires a *TIniData* object, it should be done by *TXColor*. So, the new methods must be passed a *TIniData* object as a parameter, and *that* means *TXColor* must **#include** INIDATA.H:

```
#include "inidata.h"

        ⋎
        ⋎

class TXColor : public TStreamableBase
  {
  public:
        ⋎
        ⋎
    TXColor (string & RGB);
    operator string () const;
    static TXColor GetCustomColor (int i);
    static void SetCustomColor (int i, TXColor aColor);
    static void LoadCustomColors (TIniData & IniData);
    static void SaveCustomColors (TIniData & IniData);
  private:
    static TChooseColorDialog::TData DlgData;
```

```
    static TColor CustomColors[16];
DECLARE_STREAMABLE ( , TXColor, 1);
};
```

Loading *TXColor* values in a .INI file also means the colors must be representable as *strings*, so we've added a constructor that accepts a *string*, and an operator that allows a cast to *string*. Here's the constructor:

```
TXColor::TXColor (string & RGB)
   {
   int R, G, B;
   sscanf (RGB.c_str(), "%d %d %d", &R, &G, &B);
   RValue = R;
   GValue = G;
   BValue = B;
   }
```

I decided the string representation of a color would be each of its red, green and blue values, separated by a space. (This is how most other applications store colors in their .INI files.) The familiar *sscanf* function from the standard C library comes in handy to perform this trick. (Don't forget to add **#include <stdio.h>** to XCOLOR.CPP.)

The cast to *string* is the inverse of the constructor:

```
TXColor::operator string () const
   {
   char Buffer[12];
   wsprintf (Buffer, "%d %d %d", (int) RValue, (int) GValue, (int)
BValue);
   return string (Buffer);
   }
```

The next four methods are marked **static** because they deal only with **static** data members of the class. That provides the extra benefit that the methods can be invoked without an actual instantiated *TXColor* object—something that will come in handy when we're ready to initialize the *CustomColors*.

The code for the two custodial methods is straightforward, supplying that little bit of sanity checking that makes objects more robust than more primitive data types:

```
TXColor TXColor::GetCustomColor (int i)
   {
   if (i >= 0 && i < 16)
     return TXColor (CustomColors[i]);
```

```
  else
    return TXColor::Black;
  }

void TXColor::SetCustomColor (int i, TXColor aColor)
  {
  if (i >= 0 && i < 16)
    CustomColors[i] = aColor;
  }
```

Although we don't need both these methods to implement storing the custom colors in a .INI file, there's no harm in supplying them both—it might make the custom colors array more useful some time in the future.

Our immediate concern is loading and saving these values, given a *TIniData* object to do most of the work. Here's how we load the custom colors *from* a .INI file:

```
void TXColor::LoadCustomColors (TIniData & IniData)
  {
  IniData = TSection ("Custom Colors");
  IniData.SetDefault ("255 255 255");
  char * Key = "Color00";
  register k;
  for (k = 0; k < 16; k++)
    {
    itoa (k+1, &Key[4], 10);
    IniData = TKey (Key);
    string aCustomColor = IniData;
    SetCustomColor (k, TXColor (aCustomColor));
    }
  }
```

The assumption is that the colors will be stored in a section named "Custom Colors," and that each color will be stored via keys "Color1," "Color2," on up to "Color16." We also assume that a missing value has the value of the color white. Since .INI files have no provision for arrays, we have to make our own by constructing each key as needed. When the set the key, the value becomes available and can be read into the *string* object *aCustomColor*. Finally, that string is used to construct a temporary *TXColor* object, which is then used to set the custom color.

As with the constructor/cast operator pair, storing the custom colors *to* a .INI file is the inverse operation:

```
void TXColor::SaveCustomColors (TIniData & IniData)
  {
```

```
IniData = TSection ("Custom Colors");
char * Key = "Color00";
register k;
for (k = 0; k < 16; k++)
   {
   itoa (k+1, &Key[4], 10);
   IniData = TKey (Key);
   IniData = (string) TXColor (CustomColors[k]);
   }
}
```

Again, the key has to be assembled but then it is used to *write* a value to the .INI file—a simple operation, now that *TXColor* objects have the ability to cast themselves to *string*.

Now all that's left is to invoke these functions. The initial loading of custom colors takes place when the application object itself is being constructed, in SHAPSAPP.CPP:

```
ShapesApp::ShapesApp ()
    : TApplication("Shapes"),
       IniData ("Shapes.INI")
   {
   Printer = 0;
   Printing = 0;

   DocManager = new TDocManager(dmMDI | dmMenu);

   TXColor::LoadCustomColors (IniData);
   }
```

The saving of the colors takes place at the only place they might be changed—after the invocation of *SetUserColors()* (and note the change of that method from **void** to *BOOL* to indicate whether the user hit the OK button and, therefore, changes may have taken place):

```
void TShapesView::CmShapesOther ()
   {
   if (Color.SelectUserColor (this))
      Color.SaveCustomColors (((ShapesApp *) GetApplication())-
>IniData);
   }
```

Don't forget to **#include "shapsapp.h"** to allow the *TShapesView* class to recognize the *ShapesApp* class.

Part Overview

PART

4

The World of Custom Controls

One of the hottest areas of Windows programming today is software components. In windows, components are implemented in the form of custom controls (VBXs). A VBX is basically an object with events, properties, and methods. You can use them with your programs to encapsulate low-level functions and create true modular components that can work with different platforms.

In Part 4, we'll explore how controls are built from the ground up in Borland C++. We'll start by creating a useful skeleton control that will serve as a template for writing other controls. Then, I'll show you how to extend the skeleton control so that you can create your very own control for adding file drag-and-drop support to your Visual Basic applications.

Creating a Skeleton VBX

I n *Windows Programming Power with Custom Controls*, Jeff Duntemann and I developed a skeleton custom control that could do double-duty, both as a "traditional" windows custom control and as a VBX (Visual Basic Extension). The fact is, though, that traditional Windows controls are not being sold much by third-party vendors. But VBXs are the hot items.

In this chapter we'll build a skeleton VBX, so that you can learn the correct compiler options and to provide you with a handy tool for developing "real" VBXs later on . . . like, in the next chapter.

Designing and Compiling a Skeleton VBX

What is a VBX? Physically, it is a DLL with certain "hooks"—functions of certain signatures that can be called by an integrated development environment, such as Visual Basic. These hooks allow the control to be included in that environment's toolbox, properties to be listed, and so on.

What is a VBX? Conceptually, it is an object, with properties, events and methods, not necessarily written in C++. (I write mine in C.) VBXs are *usually* user-interface objects, although they are increasingly used as *programmer*-interface objects, invisible to the user.

What is a VBX? Market-wise, it is a way to encapsulate low-level functions in a way that practically guarantees sales to hoards of pan-icky programmers fighting impossible deadlines. The guarantee lies in the fact that the VBX format is supposed to be accepted across a wide range of platforms as diverse as Visual Basic, Borland C++, and PowerBuilder.

Many people, however, took Microsoft and Borland at their respec-tive words and expected Visual C++ and Borland C++ to support the same VBXs they were using in Visual Basic. Unfortunately, they didn't read the fine print: both C++ environments support only *version 1* VBXs, and the current release of Visual Basic—the one most VBXs are written to—is version 3! Still, there is a way to write version-sensitive VBXs, and we'll do that very thing in this chapter.

Learning to Create VBXs

VBXs must adhere to a strict set of rules. Especially, they are built using Microsoft's Control Development Kit (CDK). Here's where to find more information.

The usual method of obtaining Microsoft's Control Development Kit is by purchasing Microsoft Visual Basic 3.0 Professional Edition; the CDK is bundled with VB Pro. However, Microsoft does offer it separately.

When obtained with Visual Basic, the CDK is documented in the manual *Professional Features Book 1*. In addition, many examples come with it. Remember, though, that Microsoft's example code traditionally demonstrates use of an API, not necessarily good programming style.

The CDK also comes with an online help file that is organized in a particularly useful manner. All the functions, structures, and flags—and there are *many* flags—are documented there. In fact, the online help is good enough that I rarely need turn to the actual manual!

At the time of this writing the only other source I know of VBX lore is Jeff's and my own book, mentioned previously: *Windows Programming Power with Custom Controls* by Paul Cilwa and Jeff Duntemann, Coriolis Group Books, ©1994, ISBN # 1-883577-00-4.

Finally, if you don't already have a CompuServe ID, consider getting one. Invaluable assistance can be found in the various Microsoft Windows programming forums.

In this chapter I'll be presenting the skeleton code, but due to space limitations I can't go into the detail you might wish. I will, however, direct you to where you can find out more.

Setting Up the Skeleton Project

Setting up appropriate project options is always crucial to a project's success, but never more so than when using Borland C++ to produce a VBX. Here's how to do it right.

The Skeleton VBX, and most other VBXs, is built from three code modules, MAIN.C, VISUAL.C, and VBXHELP.C; a resource file, MAIN.RC; and a module definition file, MAIN.DEF. If this reminds you of the structure of a plain-C Windows application, don't be surprised. Even though a VBX is a DLL and not a full application, it nevertheless is a window implemented in a module, and that means it must adhere to the same basic principles as a full application.

To start your VBX project, of course, you use the IDE's Project, New project command as you would with any other project, with a project name of "main" (you'll see why shortly). Your Target Type, however, will be Dynamic Library [.dll], and you will not want OWL or the Class Library. The standard library is all right, but you'll probably specify Static rather than have to worry about distributing another DLL with your resulting VBX.

Under Advanced, select your initial node as .C.

When the IDE creates your new project, there will be three nodes: MAIN.C, MAIN.RC, and MAIN.DEF.

Now we start fiddling. Select the node itself, MAIN.DLL and click the right mouse button on it. From the floating menu select Edit node attributes and change the project name to SKELETON.VBX.

Then choose the main menu's Options, Project command to bring up the Project Options dialog box. The settings we make here are crucial.

In the Compiler: Pre-compiled headers section, in the Stop precompiling after header file box, type `MAIN.H`. This designation will make your compiles go much faster.

In the 16-bit Compiler: Memory Model section , select Large model. DLLs should *always* be compiled for large model, unless chasing down erratic bugs is a sort of hobby of yours. In the 16-bit Compiler: Entry/Exit code, select Windows DLL, explicit functions exported. There's no point in exporting all functions; it slows execution down unnecessarily.

We can ignore the 32-bit compiler options; VBXs cannot run in Win32. (They run in Win16 mode under Windows NT.)

Now, you'd think you could ignore the *C++* Options since we're writing the VBX in C, right? Wrong! For some reason, Borland C++ generates code that makes use of Borland's C++ exception handling unless you tell it not to—even if you don't use C++ exception handling in your code! This can cause the environments of other vendors (such as Microsoft) to crash. So go to the C++ Options: Exception handling/RTTI section and check Enable compatible exceptions option. This is good advice for any DLL, by the way, not just VBXs.

The remaining options can be left in their default positions.

Your project is now set up and ready for coding. And, after the skeleton is complete, all you'll have to do to create a "real" VBX from the skeleton is to copy the entire subdirectory, rename the .IDE file appropriately, and select Edit node options to change the project node name.

Writing the Project Header File

By keeping all structure definitions, macros, and function prototypes in one header file, we can take advantage of pre-compiled headers to shorten compile time.

To add MAIN.H to the project, select MAIN.C and click the right mouse button. Choose the Add node command from the floating menu and enter the name MAIN.H. Once it's been added, double-click on MAIN.H. The IDE will create the empty file for you and open a blank window.

Into the window, enter the following code:

```
#include <windows.h>
#include <ver.h>
#include <vbapi.h>
#include <custcntl.h>
#include <string.h>
#include <direct.h>
#include <stdlib.h>

extern HINSTANCE LibInstance;
extern char far * ClassName;

typedef struct
   {
   HFONT Font;
   } MYDATA, far * LPMYDATA;

// VBXHELP.C
HSZ far pascal GetAboutPropertyString (HCTL Control);
HWND far pascal PopupAbout (void);
void far pascal RegisterVbPopups (void);
void far pascal UnregisterVbPopups (void);
LPSTR far pascal HelpFileName (void);
BOOL far pascal vbm_Help
    (
    HWND Window,
    BYTE HelpType,
    BYTE i,
    PPROPINFO Properties[],
    PEVENTINFO Events[]
    );
```

We covered the **MYDATA** structure in the chapter on standard C Windows programming. The **LibInstance** and **ClassName** variables are similar to the **Instance** and **AppName** variables of an application. The remaining items are function prototypes of routines we'll write into VBXHELP.C, as the comment declares.

Writing MAIN.C

In a VBX, the MAIN.C module serves a purpose analogous to the purpose it serves in a standard C application: it provides the focal point for the module, the place where initial code is executed, and home to the window procedure.

Here is the opening to MAIN.C:

```
#include "main.h"

#define GWL_MYDATA 0
#define GWW_EXTRA 4

HINSTANCE LibInstance = 0;
char far * ClassName = "Skeleton";
```

As in an application, the two globals have their values set here and **GWL_MYDATA** and **GWW_EXTRA** serve the same purposes they did in the standard C application.

Many VBX controls are based on standard Windows windows, a technique I often use. It is sometimes convenient to keep the Windows behavior packaged neatly to itself, while placing the special, additional VBX-management code in a place of its own. If you intend to write a standard Windows control and then build the VBX functionality on top of it, you'll need the following framework in MAIN.C:

```
#pragma argsused
static BOOL near pascal OnNcCreate (HWND Window, LPCREATESTRUCT
Create)
    {
    LPMYDATA MyData = (LPMYDATA) calloc (1, sizeof (MYDATA));
    SetWindowLong (Window, GWL_MYDATA, (long) MyData);
    return (MyData != NULL);
    }

static void near pascal OnNcDestroy (HWND Window)
    {
    free ((LPMYDATA) GetWindowLong (Window, GWL_MYDATA));
    }

#pragma argsused
static void near pascal OnCreate (HWND Window, LPCREATESTRUCT Create)
    {
    }

#pragma argsused
static void near pascal OnDestroy (HWND Window)
    {
    }

static HFONT near pascal OnGetFont (HWND Window)
    {
    LPMYDATA MyData = (LPMYDATA) GetWindowLong (Window, GWL_MYDATA);
```

```
  HFONT Result = MyData->Font;
  if (! Result)
    Result = GetStockObject (SYSTEM_FONT);
  return Result;
  }

static void near pascal OnSetFont (HWND Window, HFONT NewFont, BOOL
Repaint)
  {
  LPMYDATA MyData = (LPMYDATA) GetWindowLong (Window, GWL_MYDATA);
  if (NewFont != MyData->Font)
  {
    MyData->Font = NewFont;
    if (Repaint)
      {
      InvalidateRect (Window, NULL, TRUE);
      UpdateWindow (Window);
      }
    }
  }

#pragma argsused
static void near pascal OnDraw (HWND Window, HDC dc, LPMYDATA MyData)
  {
  char Buffer[256];
  WORD Count;
  Count = (WORD)
    SendMessage (Window, WM_GETTEXT, sizeof Buffer, (long)(LPSTR)
Buffer);
  TextOut (dc, 0, 0, Buffer, Count);
  }

static void near pascal OnPaint (HWND Window)
  {
  LPMYDATA MyData = (LPMYDATA) GetWindowLong (Window, GWL_MYDATA);
  PAINTSTRUCT ps;
  HDC dc = BeginPaint (Window, &ps);
  HBRUSH OldBrush;
  HBRUSH NewBrush = (HBRUSH) SendMessage (GetParent (Window),
    WM_CTLCOLOR,
    dc,
    MAKELONG (Window, CTLCOLOR_BTN));
  HFONT OldFont;
  HFONT NewFont = MyData->Font;
  if (NewBrush)
    OldBrush = SelectObject (dc, NewBrush);
  if (NewFont)
    OldFont = SelectObject (dc, NewFont);
  OnDraw (Window, dc, MyData);
```

```
    if (NewBrush)
      SelectObject (dc, OldBrush);
    if (NewFont)
      SelectObject (dc, OldFont);
    EndPaint (Window, &ps);
    }

LRESULT far pascal _export FAR PASCAL WndProc
        (
        HWND Window,
        UINT Msg,
        WPARAM wParam,
        LPARAM lParam
        )
    {
    LRESULT Result = 0;
    switch (Msg)
        {
        case WM_NCCREATE:
          Result = OnNcCreate (Window, (LPCREATESTRUCT) lParam);
          break;
        case WM_NCDESTROY:
          OnNcDestroy (Window);
          break;
        case WM_CREATE:
          OnCreate (Window, (LPCREATESTRUCT) lParam);
          break;
        case WM_DESTROY:
          OnDestroy (Window);
          break;
        case WM_UNDO:
        case WM_CLEAR:
        case WM_COPY:
        case WM_CUT:
        case WM_PASTE:
          break;
        case WM_GETDLGCODE:
          Result = DLGC_STATIC;
          break;
        case WM_GETFONT:
          Result = OnGetFont (Window);
          break;
        case WM_SETFONT:
          OnSetFont (Window, wParam, LOWORD (lParam));
          break;
        case WM_PAINT:
          OnPaint (Window);
          break;
```

```
      case WM_SETTEXT:
        Result = DefWindowProc (Window, Msg, wParam, lParam);
        InvalidateRect (Window, NULL, TRUE);
        break;
      default:
        Result = DefWindowProc (Window, Msg, wParam, lParam);
        }
    return Result;
    }

static WNDCLASS Class =
  {
  CS_HREDRAW | CS_VREDRAW | CS_DBLCLKS | CS_GLOBALCLASS,
  WndProc,
  0,
  GWW_EXTRA,
  0,
  NULL,
  NULL,
  COLOR_WINDOW + 1,
  NULL,
  NULL
  };
```

In a VBX there is no **WinMain()** function, because a DLL is not an application; it's a library, and its functions are called *by* applications. There is an analogous function, however, called **LibMain()** that is invoked when the DLL is first loaded. And, just as it is **WinMain()**'s job to register the application's main window class, it is **LibMain()**'s job to register the window class of the underlying Windows window:

```
#pragma argsused
int far pascal LibMain
    (
    HINSTANCE hInstance,
    WORD DataSeg,
    WORD HeapSize,
    LPSTR CommandLine
    )
  {
  if (HeapSize > 0)
    UnlockData (0);
  LibInstance = hInstance;
  Class.hInstance = hInstance;
  Class.lpszClassName = ClassName;
  return RegisterClass (&Class) ? TRUE : FALSE;
  }
```

If you are not building on a standard window, you can omit the registration code and simply return **TRUE**.

Supplying the Module Definition File

The module definition file supplies information to the linker, enabling it to build the module header. As you will see, .DEF files for VBXs are quite simple.

Here's the module definition file for the Skeleton control:

```
LIBRARY Skeleton
DESCRIPTION "©1994 Paul S. Cilwa All Rights Reserved"
EXETYPE WINDOWS
CODE PRELOAD MOVEABLE DISCARDABLE
DATA PRELOAD MOVEABLE SINGLE
HEAPSIZE  0
```

The biggest difference between this and the .DEF file for an application is that the keyword **LIBRARY** replaces the keyword **NAME**. It serves the same purpose of naming the module, though. Don't forget to change this value each time you derive a new VBX from the skeleton—and you might want to change the **DESCRIPTION**, too.

Some DLLs keep local data of their own. The Windows GDI and USER modules do, for example. If you need to provide this, set **HEAPSIZE** to a value larger than zero. But never imagine you can set a stacksize for a DLL; it always uses the stack of the application calling its functions.

Creating the Skeleton's Resources

A VBX isn't just a custom control—it's a control with a built-in programmer interface! When a VBX is added to an IDE, it shows up in that IDE's toolbox. But when you're writing the VBX, you have to create the bitmap the toolbox displays.

A VBX supplies several different bitmaps to represent itself; the IDE selects the bitmap most suitable to the current video display. As part of the VBX specification, the bitmap identifiers are numbers, commonly based on 8000. See Figure 12.1 for a look at Skeleton's toolbox bitmaps, images of blank buttons as befits an unspecialized control.

VBXs also often supply their very own About boxes so the programmer using them can check on versions, release dates, and so on. The Skeleton

Figure 12.1 The toolbox bitmaps 8000, 8001, 8003, and 8006.

About box is named About; it also uses an icon (created separately) called MAIN. You can see the About box (and the icon) in Figure 12.2.

Lastly, don't forget your VERSIONINFO resource. This is your only defense against the various and many problems DLLs are prone to. Here's a sample:

```
1 VERSIONINFO LOADONCALL MOVEABLE DISCARDABLE
FILEVERSION 1, 0, 0, 0
PRODUCTVERSION 1, 0, 0, 0
FILEOS VOS__WINDOWS16
FILETYPE VFT_DLL
{
 BLOCK "StringFileInfo"
 {
  BLOCK "040904E4"
  {
   VALUE "CompanyName", "Coriolis Group\000"
   VALUE "FileDescription", "Skeleton VBX for Visual Basic\000"
   VALUE "FileVersion", "1.0.0.0\000"
   VALUE "InternalName", "SKELETON\000"
   VALUE "LegalCopyright", "Copyright © Paul S. Cilwa 1994\000"
   VALUE "OriginalFilename", "skeleton.vbx\000"
   VALUE "ProductName", "Borland C++ 4.0 Insider\000"
   VALUE "ProductVersion", "1.0.0.0\000"
   VALUE "Comments", "\000"
  }
 }
}
```

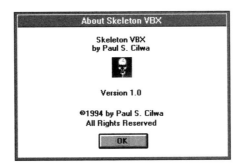

Figure 12.2 The Skeleton VBX's About box.

Supporting Programmer-Help

One of the things that makes VBXs so useful is their built-in, integrated, online help. The programmer can look up properties, events, and methods of a third-party VBX exactly as easily as he or she can look up the VBXs that come with Visual Basic! Here's the module that makes it happen.

This module is written so that it needn't be altered from one project to the next. It is fully described in *Windows Programming Power with Custom Controls,* but you don't have to understand it at all—just let it work for you. (I know that hurts the C programmer's sensibilities, but it's good practice for working with VBXs, *as well as with* C++ objects!)

Add the module VBXHELP.C to the project; it should have the following contents:

```
#include "main.h"

#define _segment(p) ((unsigned int)  (((unsigned long) (void far *)
(p)) >> 16L))

HSZ far pascal GetAboutPropertyString (HCTL Control)
   {
   return VBCreateHsz (_segment (Control), "Click here for About-->");
   }

#pragma argsused
BOOL _export FAR PASCAL AboutDlgProc
    (
    HWND    Dialog,
    WORD    msg,
    WORD    wParam,
    long    lParam
    )
  {
  switch (msg)
    {
    case WM_INITDIALOG:
break;
    case WM_COMMAND:
      switch (wParam)
        {
        case IDOK:
          EndDialog (Dialog, IDOK);
          break;
        default:
          return FALSE;
```

```
            }
          break;
       default:
          return FALSE;
        }
      return TRUE;
   }

LONG _export FAR PASCAL AboutPopupWndProc
      (
      HWND    Window,
      USHORT Message,
      USHORT wParam,
      LONG    lParam
      )
   {
   switch (Message)
      {
      case WM_SHOWWINDOW:
         if (wParam)
   {
            ShowWindow (Window, SW_HIDE);
            PostMessage (Window, WM_USER, 0, 0);
            return 0;
                  }
         break;
      case WM_USER:
         VBDialogBoxParam (LibInstance, "About", AboutDlgProc, NULL);
         return 0;
      }
   return DefWindowProc (Window, Message, wParam, lParam);
   }

static char AboutPopupClass[] = "AboutPopup";

HWND far pascal PopupAbout (void)
   {
   return CreateWindow
      (
      AboutPopupClass,
      NULL,
      WS_POPUP,
      0, 0, 0, 0,
      NULL,
      NULL,
      LibInstance,
      NULL
      );
   }
```

```
static HANDLE IdeTask = FALSE;

static WNDCLASS Class =
   {
   0,
   (WNDPROC) AboutPopupWndProc,
   0,
   0,
   0,
   NULL,
   NULL,
   NULL,
   NULL,
   NULL
   };

void far pascal RegisterVbPopups (void)
   {
   IdeTask = GetCurrentTask();
   Class.hInstance = LibInstance;
   Class.lpszClassName = AboutPopupClass;
   RegisterClass (&Class);
   }

void far pascal UnregisterVbPopups (void)
   {
   if (IdeTask == GetCurrentTask())
      {
      UnregisterClass (AboutPopupClass, LibInstance);
      IdeTask = NULL;
      }
   }

LPSTR far pascal HelpFileName (void)
   {
   static char Pathname[_MAX_PATH] = { 0 };
   if (! Pathname[0])
      {
      char Drive[_MAX_DRIVE];
      char Dir[_MAX_DIR];
      char FName[_MAX_FNAME];
         char Ext[_MAX_EXT];
      GetModuleFileName (LibInstance, Pathname, _MAX_PATH);
      _splitpath (Pathname, Drive, Dir, FName, Ext);
      _makepath (Pathname, Drive, Dir, FName, ".HLP");
      }
    return Pathname;
   }
```

```
BOOL far pascal vbm_Help
    (
    HWND Window,
    BYTE HelpType,
    BYTE i,
    PPROPINFO Properties[],
    PEVENTINFO Events[]
    )
{
BOOL Result = FALSE;
switch (HelpType)
    {
    case VBHELP_PROP:
      if (Properties[i] < PPROPINFO_STD_LAST)
        {
        WinHelp (Window, HelpFileName (), HELP_KEY,
           (DWORD) (LPSTR) Properties[i]->npszName);
        Result = TRUE;
        }
      break;
    case VBHELP_EVT:
      if (Events[i] < PEVENTINFO_STD_LAST)
        {
        WinHelp (Window, HelpFileName (), HELP_KEY,
           (DWORD) (LPSTR) Events[i]->npszName);
        Result = TRUE;
        }
      break;
    case VBHELP_CTL:
      WinHelp (Window, HelpFileName (), HELP_CONTENTS, 0);
      Result = TRUE;
      break;
    }
  return Result;
}
```

By the way, compiling this will bring about one warning, referring to possible segment loss caused by the **_segment()** macro. That is, in fact, the *purpose* of this macro; so you can safely ignore the warning.

Building the VBX Layer

Whether or not your VBX has an underlying window, it will have a VBX layer, and that is housed in the VISUAL.C module. This module provides all the hooks into the Visual programming environment.

After adding the VISUAL.C node to the project, you can start it out this way:

```
#include "main.h"

#define _segment(p) ((unsigned int)  (((unsigned long) (void far *)
(p)) >> 16L))
#define _offsetin(struc, fld) ((USHORT)&(((struc *)0)->fld))
#define VBERR_BADINDEX 381

static long Boolean[2] = { 0, -1 };

typedef struct
   {
   UINT : 16;
   } VBDATA;
typedef VBDATA far * LPVBDATA;
```

VBDATA serves a purpose similar to that of **MYDATA** in the MAIN.C module.

Next in the VISUAL.C module is a structure for each property your VBX will support. The structure is typically filled in at compile-time and kept in the data segment. The Skeleton control only has one property—the About box—but a "real" control would have more, perhaps many more:

```
PROPINFO Property_About =
   {
   "(About)",
   DT_HSZ | PF_fGetMsg | PF_fNoRuntimeW | PF_fGetHszMsg,
   0, 0, 0, NULL, 0
   };
```

After you have defined all the property information structures, you'll need to set up an array. This array will include entries for each of the *standard* properties you feel apply to your VBX, as well as the custom properties you've just defined.

Here's where the first version hurdle is approached. Each version of Visual Basic has added more standard properties. If you want to be compatible with both C++ VBXs (version 1) and Visual Basic (version 3) you need either to restrict yourself to a subset of available standard properties, or to supply *two* property arrays, picking out the appropriate one when the control is registered. That's the approach we'll take.

However, it's not quite that simple because each array of properties implies a *matching* set of values—zero for the first property, one for

the second, and so on. This is normally done with an **enum**. Let's look
at the first array of properties with identifiers:

```
PPROPINFO V3_Properties[] =
   {
   PPROPINFO_STD_NAME,
   PPROPINFO_STD_INDEX,
   PPROPINFO_STD_BACKCOLOR,
   PPROPINFO_STD_FORECOLOR,
   PPROPINFO_STD_LEFT,
   PPROPINFO_STD_TOP,
   PPROPINFO_STD_WIDTH,
   PPROPINFO_STD_HEIGHT,
   PPROPINFO_STD_FONTNAME,
   PPROPINFO_STD_FONTSIZE,
   PPROPINFO_STD_FONTBOLD,
   PPROPINFO_STD_FONTITALIC,
   PPROPINFO_STD_TABINDEX,
   PPROPINFO_STD_TABSTOP,
   PPROPINFO_STD_BORDERSTYLEON,
   PPROPINFO_STD_ENABLED,
   PPROPINFO_STD_PARENT,
   PPROPINFO_STD_TAG,
   PPROPINFO_STD_VISIBLE,
   PPROPINFO_STD_HELPCONTEXTID,
   PPROPINFO_STD_LAST,
   &Property_About,
   NULL
   };

typedef enum
   {
   V3PROP_STD_NAME,
   V3PROP_STD_INDEX,
   V3PROP_STD_BACKCOLOR,
   V3PROP_STD_FORECOLOR,
   V3PROP_STD_LEFT,
   V3PROP_STD_TOP,
   V3PROP_STD_WIDTH,
   V3PROP_STD_HEIGHT,
   V3PROP_STD_FONTNAME,
   V3PROP_STD_FONTSIZE,
   V3PROP_STD_FONTBOLD,
   V3PROP_STD_FONTITALIC,
   V3PROP_STD_TABINDEX,
   V3PROP_STD_TABSTOP,
   V3PROP_STD_BORDERSTYLEON,
   V3PROP_STD_ENABLED,
```

```
V3PROP_STD_PARENT,
V3PROP_STD_TAG,
V3PROP_STD_VISIBLE,
V3PROP_STD_HELPCONTEXTID,
V3PROP_STD_LAST,
V3PROP_About,
V3PROP_End
} V3PROPSIX;
```

As you look up each standard property in the online help, you discover that only **PPROPINFO_STD_HELPCONTEXTID** and **PPROPINFO_STD_LAST** (which is only a placeholder, anyway) were introduced after version 1.0 of Visual Basic. (**PPROPINFO_STD_NAME** is new, but it is a synonym for **PPROPINFO_STD_CTLNAME** which was present in version 1.0.)

So we can create a matching set of array and IDs for version 1.0:

```
PPROPINFO V1_Properties[] =
    {
    PPROPINFO_STD_NAME,
    PPROPINFO_STD_INDEX,
    PPROPINFO_STD_BACKCOLOR,
    PPROPINFO_STD_FORECOLOR,
    PPROPINFO_STD_LEFT,
    PPROPINFO_STD_TOP,
    PPROPINFO_STD_WIDTH,
    PPROPINFO_STD_HEIGHT,
    PPROPINFO_STD_FONTNAME,
    PPROPINFO_STD_FONTSIZE,
    PPROPINFO_STD_FONTBOLD,
    PPROPINFO_STD_FONTITALIC,
    PPROPINFO_STD_TABINDEX,
    PPROPINFO_STD_TABSTOP,
    PPROPINFO_STD_BORDERSTYLEON,
    PPROPINFO_STD_ENABLED,
    PPROPINFO_STD_PARENT,
    PPROPINFO_STD_TAG,
    PPROPINFO_STD_VISIBLE,
    &Property_About,
    NULL
    };

typedef enum
    {
    V1PROP_STD_NAME,
    V1PROP_STD_INDEX,
    V1PROP_STD_BACKCOLOR,
    V1PROP_STD_FORECOLOR,
```

```
V1PROP_STD_LEFT,
V1PROP_STD_TOP,
V1PROP_STD_WIDTH,
V1PROP_STD_HEIGHT,
V1PROP_STD_FONTNAME,
V1PROP_STD_FONTSIZE,
V1PROP_STD_FONTBOLD,
V1PROP_STD_FONTITALIC,
V1PROP_STD_TABINDEX,
V1PROP_STD_TABSTOP,
V1PROP_STD_BORDERSTYLEON,
V1PROP_STD_ENABLED,
V1PROP_STD_PARENT,
V1PROP_STD_TAG,
V1PROP_STD_VISIBLE,
V1PROP_About,
V1PROP_End
} V1PROPSIX;
```

A similar setup is involved with events; however our skeleton VBX has no custom events, only standard ones. Here is the list for version 3.0:

```
PEVENTINFO V3Events[] =
    {
    PEVENTINFO_STD_CLICK,
    PEVENTINFO_STD_DBLCLICK,
    PEVENTINFO_STD_DRAGDROP,
    PEVENTINFO_STD_DRAGOVER,
    PEVENTINFO_STD_GOTFOCUS,
    PEVENTINFO_STD_LOSTFOCUS,
    PEVENTINFO_STD_MOUSEDOWN,
    PEVENTINFO_STD_MOUSEMOVE,
    PEVENTINFO_STD_MOUSEUP,
    PEVENTINFO_STD_LAST,
    NULL
    };

typedef enum
    {
    V3EVENT_STD_CLICK,
    V3EVENT_STD_DBLCLK,
    V3EVENT_STD_DRAGDROP,
    V3EVENT_STD_DRAGOVER,
    V3EVENT_STD_GOTFOCUS,
    V3EVENT_STD_LOSTFOCUS,
    V3EVENT_STD_MOUSEDOWN,
    V3EVENT_STD_MOUSEMOVE,
    V3EVENT_STD_MOUSEUP,
```

```
V3EVENT_STD_LAST,
V3EVENT_End
} V3EVENTSIX;
```

And here is the version 1.0 set:

```
PEVENTINFO V1Events[] =
    {
    PEVENTINFO_STD_CLICK,
    PEVENTINFO_STD_DBLCLICK,
    PEVENTINFO_STD_DRAGDROP,
    PEVENTINFO_STD_DRAGOVER,
    PEVENTINFO_STD_GOTFOCUS,
    PEVENTINFO_STD_LOSTFOCUS,
    PEVENTINFO_STD_MOUSEDOWN,
    PEVENTINFO_STD_MOUSEMOVE,
    PEVENTINFO_STD_MOUSEUP,
    NULL
    };

typedef enum
    {
    V1EVENT_STD_CLICK,
    V1EVENT_STD_DBLCLK,
    V1EVENT_STD_DRAGDROP,
    V1EVENT_STD_DRAGOVER,
    V1EVENT_STD_GOTFOCUS,
    V1EVENT_STD_LOSTFOCUS,
    V1EVENT_STD_MOUSEDOWN,
    V1EVENT_STD_MOUSEMOVE,
    V1EVENT_STD_MOUSEUP,
    V1EVENT_End
    } V1EVENTSIX;
```

The structure of the Visual layer of a VBX is almost identical to that of a window. However, the "thing" we are working with is called a control, not a window, and it is managed from within a *control* procedure, not a window procedure. The control procedure receives many of the same messages a window does, although there are some additional ones. Here are the skeleton handlers for the various messages:

```
#pragma argsused
static void near pascal wm_NcCreate
    (
    HCTL Control,
    LPCREATESTRUCT Create
    )
```

```
      {
      LPVBDATA VbData = (LPVBDATA) VBDerefControl (Control);
      }

static void near pascal wm_NcDestroy
      (
      HCTL Control
      )
      {
      LPVBDATA VbData = (LPVBDATA) VBDerefControl (Control);
      }

typedef struct
      {
      long Count;
      HSZ Item;
      long Index;
      } ADDITEM;
typedef ADDITEM far * LPADDITEM;

typedef struct
      {
      long Count;
      long Index;
      } REMOVEITEM;
typedef REMOVEITEM far * LPREMOVEITEM;

static long near pascal vbm_Method
      (
      HCTL Control,
      HWND Window,
      USHORT Method,
      void far * Args
      )
      {
      LPSTR Text;
      LPADDITEM AddItem = Args;
      LPREMOVEITEM RemoveItem = Args;
      switch (Method)
         {
         default:
            return VBDefControlProc (Control, Window, VBM_METHOD, Method,
(long) Args);
         }
      }

#pragma argsused
static BOOL near pascal vbm_SetProperty
```

```
    (
    HCTL Control,
    HWND Window,
    USHORT Property,
    long Value,
    long far * Error
    )
  {
  LPVBDATA VbData = (LPVBDATA) VBDerefControl (Control);
  switch (Property)
    {
    default:
      return FALSE;
    }
  }

#pragma argsused
static BOOL near pascal vbm_GetProperty
    (
    HCTL Control,
    HWND Window,
    USHORT Property,
    LPVOID Value,
    long far * Error
    )
  {
  LPVBDATA VbData = (LPVBDATA) VBDerefControl (Control);
  switch (Property)
    {
    default:
      return FALSE;
    }
  }

#pragma argsused
static BOOL near pascal vbm_LoadProperty
    (
    HCTL Control,
    HWND Window,
    USHORT Property,
    HFORMFILE FormFile,
    long far * Error
    )
  {
  LPVBDATA VbData = (LPVBDATA) VBDerefControl (Control);
  switch (Property)
    {
    default:
```

```
        return FALSE;
      }
   }

#pragma argsused
static BOOL near pascal vbm_SaveProperty
    (
    HCTL Control,
    HWND Window,
    USHORT Property,
    HFORMFILE FormFile,
    long far * Error
    )
  {
  LPVBDATA VbData = (LPVBDATA) VBDerefControl (Control);
  switch (Property)
    {
    default:
       return FALSE;
    }
  }
```

Here's the control procedure:

```
long far pascal _export CtlProc
    (
    HCTL Control,
    HWND Window,
    USHORT Msg,
    USHORT wParam,
    long lParam
    )
  {
  long Error = 0;
  switch (Msg)
    {
    case WM_NCCREATE:
      wm_NcCreate (Control, (LPCREATESTRUCT) lParam);
      break;
    case VBM_METHOD:
      return vbm_Method (Control, Window, wParam, (void far *) lParam);
    case VBN_COMMAND:
      switch (HIWORD (lParam))
        {
        default:
      break;
        }
      break;
    case VBM_SETPROPERTY:
```

```
      if (vbm_SetProperty (Control, Window, wParam, lParam, &Error))
        return Error;
      break;
    case VBM_GETPROPERTY:
      if (vbm_GetProperty (Control, Window, wParam, (LPVOID) lParam,
          &Error))
        return Error;
      break;
    case VBM_LOADPROPERTY:
      if (vbm_LoadProperty (Control, Window, wParam, (HFORMFILE)
          lParam, &Error))
        return Error;
      break;
    case VBM_SAVEPROPERTY:
      if (vbm_SaveProperty (Control, Window, wParam, (HFORMFILE)
          lParam, &Error))
        return Error;
      break;
    case VBM_GETPROPERTYHSZ:
      switch (wParam)
        {
        case V3PROP_About:
        case V1PROP_About:
          *((HSZ far *) lParam) = GetAboutPropertyString (Control);
          break;
        }
      return 0;
    case VBM_INITPROPPOPUP:
      switch (wParam)
        {
        case IPROPINFO_About:
          return PopupAbout ();
        }
      break;
    case VBM_HELP:
      if (vbm_Help (Window,
          LOBYTE (wParam),
          HIBYTE (wParam),
          Properties, Events))
        return 0;
        break;
    case WM_DESTROY:
      WinHelp (Window, HelpFileName (), HELP_QUIT, 0);
      break;
    case WM_NCDESTROY:
      wm_NcDestroy (Control);
      break;
    }
  return VBDefControlProc (Control, Window, Msg, wParam, lParam);
}
```

Note the response to the **VBM_GETPROPERTYHSZ** message: we check for both **V3PROP_About** and **V1PROP_About**. This is risky code; it works here because there are, in fact, no other properties that would generate this message. In a real control, though, you should probably check the version under which the control is running to decide which set of property identifiers to use. (This is also true of the **vbm_SetProperty()**, **vbm_GetProperty()**, **vbm_LoadProperty()**, and **vbm_SaveProperty()** methods. As I'm sure you have deduced, there is a *lot* of overhead introduced if you intend to support both versions!)

The **MODEL** structure, also pre-initialized and kept in the data segment, is used by a special "hook" function called **VBINITCC()**. This function is called by the Visual environment, partly as a test to make sure the DLL is a legal VBX, and also to actually install the VBX if it is:

```
MODEL Model =
  {
  VB_VERSION,
  MODEL_fFocusOk | MODEL_fArrows,
  (PCTLPROC) CtlProc,
  CS_VREDRAW | CS_HREDRAW,
  WS_BORDER,
  sizeof (VBDATA),
  8000,
  NULL,
  NULL,
  NULL,
  V3_Properties,
  V3_Events,
  V3PROP_STD_NAME,
  V3EVENT_STD_CLICK,
  (BYTE) -1
  };

#pragma argsused
BOOL far pascal _export VBINITCC
    (
    USHORT Version,
    BOOL Runtime
    )
  {
  if (! Runtime)
    RegisterVbPopups ();
  Model.npszDefCtlName =
  Model.npszClassName =
  Model.npszParentClassName = (PSTR) ClassName;
```

```
if (VBGetVersion() < VB300_VERSION)
  {
  Model.npproplist = V1_Properties;
  Model.npeventlist = V1_Events;
  Model.nDefProp = V1PROP_STD_NAME;
  Model.nDefEvent = V1EVENT_STD_CLICK;
  }
return VBRegisterModel (LibInstance, &Model);
}
```

The FileDropper Control

I 'm a whitewater rafting enthusiast. I'm not sophisticated enough to go it on my own, but I've run rivers from Maine to the Grand Canyon with various rafting companies, and all of them keep the special bundled rope we use to throw to "swimmers" in the same place in the raft. You go through some particularly rough rapids, someone falls out, and automatically you reach for the throw rope in the place you know it will be.

Except one time last summer, when I ran with a river guide who kept the throw rope in a different spot. He told us where it was, of course; but when we hit a hole and *he* fell out, I just naturally grabbed for the throw rope in its usual location—and it wasn't there. We were still in class V rapids and that was my last chance to get the throw rope out; I had to take over the guide's position and steer us around a particularly bad "hole" he'd pointed out to us before we started. A hole is like a whirlpool stood on end; if you get caught in a hole—especially if you're swimming—it's very hard to get out. Once we'd reached a safe spot, we dug out the throw rope and, after a couple of tries, managed to get it to the guide while he was at the top of the hole. By the time we fished him into the boat, he wasn't in much of a mood to guide and I wound up with the job for the rest of the run.

So, okay, since we all survived it turned out not to be that bad a thing (for me) that the throw rope was in an unaccustomed position. In fact, it wound up changing a fun rafting trip into a thrilling one, the kind that brings into sharp focus the narrow line between life and death, and makes each moment you live all the more precious.

However, while many of us run white water to learn valuable life lessons, most computer users hope for less from the applications they run; and they *really* prefer all the features to be where they expect to find them. That's why a puzzling lack in Visual Basic is so annoying to Visual Basic developers: Although you can implement file drag-and-drop in any other Windows programming language (App Expert adds the feature automatically), Visual Basic makes no provision for it. This is all the more odd because VB *has* implemented drag-and-drop for controls within a VB application. But you can't drag a file from the File Manager onto a VB application given the tools provided by Visual Basic.

But that's what VBXs are for! And VBXs are why Visual Basic can be a serious development tool: *No one expects to use it as the only development tool!* VB works best as a "glue" to bind various tools, packaged as custom controls, together. Use VB to throw together the user interface, and C or C++ to do the low-level work.

In this chapter we'll develop a custom control that adds file drag-and-drop capability to any Visual Basic application, thus supporting your users' expectation of finding this feature where it belongs. It's not likely anyone will drown if an app doesn't support file drag-and-drop, but—hey!—why take the chance?

Designing the FileDropper Control

Designing any control consists of three steps: first, defining what the control is to accomplish or the behavior it is to encapsulate; second, choosing reasonable properties, events, and methods to make the end-programmer's use of the control simple and straightforward; and third, understanding the algorithm or function calls required to achieve steps one and two.

Defining the FileDropper's Job

The first step in designing a control is to identify the job it is to do and/or the behavior it is to encapsulate. Will it be visible? Will it allow user interaction?

The behavior we want the FileDropper to encapsulate is that of file drag-and-drop. That means, when the user drags a file from the File Manager (or any other replacement, such as the Norton Desktop for Windows' File windows), the FileDropper control will notify the application that files have been dropped. It must also provide a means for the application to find out *which* files, exactly, have been dropped.

Is there any reason to provide a user interface? Not really—no other commercial application that supports file drag-and-drop allows the user to modify that behavior. So, without a user interface needed, our next question is: does the control need a runtime display at all? Obviously, it *could* manifest itself as a file list box; but what would be the point? Most applications do not display a list of the files that have been dropped; they simply open those files. And if you wanted to fill a list box with the filenames, you could always do that. So, final answer: FileDropper will be an invisible-at-runtime control, like the Timer or the CommonDlg control. It exists for the convenience of the programmer, without drawing to itself the attention of the end user.

Defining the FileDropper's Properties, Events, and Methods

The second step in designing a control is choosing reasonable properties, events, and methods to make the end-programmer's use of the control simple and straightforward.

As stated in the previous section, the FileDropper's primary task is to notify its parent application that files have, in fact, been dropped. Such notifications are always implemented as events in Visual Basic. What should we call this event? How about "FilesDropped"? Is that straightforward enough?

But should the event pass the list of dropped files as a parameter? No, for the main reason that you can't easily pass an array as an event parameter. In a more theoretical vein, it isn't commonly done. Events are notifications; what the application does in response to that notification is the application's business. The event, then, should simply do its notifying and get out.

Therefore, we'll need at least a couple of properties: **FileCount** and **FileList**. These names were not chosen by whim. Many custom controls provides lists of one type of item or another; when they do, they also provide a corresponding **Count** property. Lists are always array items, by the way, indexed from zero. The matching **Count** property, therefore, is required to avoid sending an out-of-range index to the list.

But **FileCount** and **FileList** aren't enough, though. A glance at the documentation for the Windows drag-and-drop API reveals that *directories* can be dropped as easily as files! The application could do the job of determining whether a given entry was a file or a directory, but such a job is easier to accomplish in C. Therefore we'll also supply a **DirectoryCount** and **DirectoryList** pair of properties.

The control will also need to know what application window, exactly, expects to have files dropped on it. Is it the form, or just a list box? We'll have to let the form know by passing it the window handle (**Hwnd** property) of the desired form or visible control. We'll call that property **ParentHwnd**.

We should also decide what standard properties to provide. FileDropper will obviously never participate in a DDE conversation, so we can omit all properties that begin with **Link**. And since we've already decided the control will be invisible at runtime, there's no need to worry about any of the **Font** properties. We also won't need the standard **Left**, **Top**, **Height**, and **Width** properties for the same reason;

however, the new **TopNoRun** and **LeftNoRun** properties allow you to specify where the icon that represents the control at design-time will be placed, so we can, and should include them. We'll certainly want the standard **Enabled** property, so the program can turn file dropping on and off. And there's never any harm in including the **Tag** property, which allows the programmer to attach arbitrary text to a control for whatever reasons he or she may have.

Looking through the list of available methods—you can't add custom methods, as you can properties and events—there are none that particularly apply to this control. The only one we *might* be able to use is **Clear** (to release the small amount of memory taken up by the saved lists of dropped files and directories), but it doesn't really add to the value of the control so we won't bother.

A related question is: should we make this a "graphical" control? A graphical control is one that has *no* underlying window. As such, it is insensitive to user interaction (which we don't intend to support anyway) and has much less overhead than a standard control (always a good thing!). With that much information, you would say, "Sure! Make FileDropper a graphical control!" That was my first reaction, too. However, you should know that in this particular case, a subtle algorithmic requirement (explored in the next topic) won't allow it. We'll *need* that underlying window.

Our final implementation consideration is: should we support multiple versions of Visual Basic? As seen in the previous chapter, doing so imposes a considerable amount of overhead on a control, making it both larger and slower than would otherwise be the case. The only benefit is that the control could then be used by Microsoft Visual C++ and Borland C++ applications, as well as Visual Basic apps. But both Microsoft Foundation Classes and ObjectWindows *already support* file dropping; so what would be the point? And so we can heave a sigh of relief and, in the case of FileDropper at least, throw out all that multiple version support.

Understanding the File Dropping Mechanism

The third step in designing a custom control is understanding the algorithm or function calls required to implement it. In the case of FileDropper, that means understanding the mechanism behind file dropping.

File drag-and-drop was introduced with Windows 3.1. It's easy to implement in a simple, C/Windows API application. The app's main window calls the **DragAcceptFiles( )** function to notify Windows it is willing to receive dropped files. If a user drags a file from the File Manager onto an application that has not called **DragAcceptFiles( )** the cursor changes to the universal "no" symbol, and dropping is not allowed.

But once **DragAcceptFiles( )** has been invoked, all that changes. In such a case, when the user drags that file onto the application, the cursor becomes a picture of one or more sheets of paper, depending on whether one or more files is being dragged at once. If the user releases the mouse button, dropping the files, the application receives a **WM_DORPFILES** message. The **wParam** parameter of this message is special handle that is sent to the other file-dropping functions.

One of these functions is **DragQueryFile( )**. Depending on the parameters with which it's called, this function returns either the number of files that have been dropped, or the filename of each by index number. Note that a job that older Windows functions would require the programmer to do—parsing a list of files—is here performed by the function itself, saving us a lot of work.

The **DragQueryPoint( )** function returns the exact point at which the file or files were dropped, relative to the window's client area.

When access of the list of files is complete, the **DragFinish( )** function is invoked to release the dropped files' handle given us by the **WM_DROPFILES** message. Therefore, at the very least, an application that has started file dropping by calling **DragAcceptFiles( )** *must* respond to **WM_DROPFILES** messages by calling **DragFinish( )**; otherwise the application will suffer from a memory leak.

In terms of our custom control, implementing drag-and-drop offers a unique challenge, because the control is not the one we want to implement file dropping on! Most often the target window will be the form itself. How can we implement drag-and-drop on another window— especially, another window whose window procedure we did not write and over which we have no control? The answer to *that* question is *subclassing*.

Similar to the C++ concept, subclassing means replacing an existing windows' window procedure with yours. You can thus intercept any messages of interest, and passing any others on to the original window procedure. What we'll have to do, then, is subclass the target window—the one we've identified with the **ParentHwnd** property—call **DragAcceptFiles( )** in its behalf, intercept any **WM_DROPFILES** messages and handle them, while passing all other messages on to the original window procedure, whatever that may be.

We'll also have to support the **Enabled** property by unsubclassing any window whose **Enabled** property is set to False. A related problem is that we'll have to support a *change* in the **ParentHwnd** property, by unsubclassing the original window and subclassing the new one in turn.

Finally, we need to deal with the possibility that the subclassed window will be destroyed as a result of the application's being closed. In such a case, the parent window, if it is a form, will close *after* any controls on its surface—including the FileDropper. So we have to allow the parent window to unsubclass itself, somehow, if it is destroyed while still subclassed.

Building the FileDropper Control

Now that we have our design reasonably well defined, we can get to work building the control itself.

1. Create a directory for the project (such as FILEDROP).
2. Copy the skeleton control we created in the last chapter into the new directory.
3. Rename SKELETON.* to FILEDROP.*
4. After loading the new project into Borland C++'s IDE, modify the existing code to that shown in the following pages. These modification will involve far more line deletions than additions, because FileDropper is actually a fairly simple control as these things go, in spite of its interesting challenges.

In the code descriptions on the following pages, however, I'm going to build up the control as if it were being written from scratch, rather than specifying which sections to delete. I'll think you'll find the code descriptions a lot simpler to follow this way. As far as making these modifications to the skeleton, well, if I don't mention a function that's present in the skeleton—delete it.

MAIN.DEF

The project's .DEF file is almost unchanged from the skeleton.

Module definition files are usually little trouble because there's usually little you have to do with them other than use them. In fact, if you omit the .DEF file from your project, Borland C++ will use perfectly good default values (perfectly good in most cases, that is)! However, the

FileDropper control will need some heap space of its own. Therefore our module definition file looks like this:

```
LIBRARY FileDropper
DESCRIPTION  "©1994 Paul S. Cilwa All Rights Reserved"
EXETYPE WINDOWS
CODE PRELOAD MOVEABLE DISCARDABLE
SEGMENTS
 _VBXHELP  LOADONCALL
DATA PRELOAD MOVEABLE SINGLE
HEAPSIZE  8192
```

How did I derive a figure of 8K for the heapsize? Simple: I made it up. Windows will increase the heap space if needed, but allocating more memory to this does take a few microseconds. I figured 8K was a reasonable amount and went on to more interesting things.

One of these interesting items was "tweaking" the .DEF file for increased performance. The functions in the VBXHELP.C module are not needed unless the VB programmer asks to see FileDropper's About box or requests its online help. They are *never* needed at runtime. So, using the **SEGMENTS** keyword, I specified that the _VBXHELP code (the name is derived from the filename by prepending an underscore) shouldn't be loaded until requested, unlike the other code modules, which are loaded with the application itself.

MAIN.RC

The resource file for FileDropper must contain the bitmaps for the toolbox button that will represent the control. For the skeleton control we settled for "blank" buttons, but here we'll have to be more creative.

Taking my cue from Visual Basic's drag-and-drop icons—but not copying them!—I came up with the buttons shown in Figure 13.1. These are buttons 8000, 8001, 8003, and 8006; used for VGA normal, VGA pressed, EGA, and CGA, respectively.

The About box is virtually unchanged from the skeleton, except of course for the appropriate names and the MAIN icon, as seen in Figure 13.2.

Figure 13.1 The toolbox buttons for the FileDropper control.

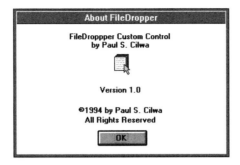

Figure 13.2 The FileDropper's About box.

Finally, as always, never forget the VERSIONINFO resource:

```
1 VERSIONINFO LOADONCALL MOVEABLE DISCARDABLE
FILEVERSION 1, 0, 0, 0
PRODUCTVERSION 1, 0, 0, 0
FILEOS VOS__WINDOWS16
FILETYPE VFT_DLL
{
 BLOCK "StringFileInfo"
 {
  BLOCK "040904E4"
  {
   VALUE "CompanyName", "Coriolis Group\000"
   VALUE "FileDescription", "FileDropper Custom Control for Visual
Basic and Windows\000"
   VALUE "FileVersion", "1.0.0.0\000"
   VALUE "InternalName", "FILEDROP\000"
   VALUE "LegalCopyright", "Copyright © Paul S. Cilwa 1994\000"
   VALUE "OriginalFilename", "filedrop.vbx\000"
   VALUE "ProductName", "Boland C++ 4.0 Insider\000"
   VALUE "ProductVersion", "1.0.0.0\000"
   VALUE "Comments", "\000"
  }
 }
}
```

MAIN.H

***The header file shared by most modules in the FileDropper
project is virtually unchanged from the skeleton.***

Here's FileDropper's MAIN.H header file:

```
#define STRICT
#include <windows.h>
```

```
#include <ver.h>
#include <vbapi.h>
#include <string.h>
#include <direct.h>
#include <stdlib.h>
#include <dos.h>
#include <shellapi.h>

extern HINSTANCE LibInstance;
extern char near ClassName[];

HSZ far pascal GetAboutPropertyString (HCTL Control);
HWND far pascal PopupAbout (void);
void far pascal RegisterVbPopups (void);
void far pascal UnregisterVbPopups (void);
LPSTR far pascal HelpFileName (void);
BOOL far pascal vbm_Help
    (
    HWND Window,
    BYTE HelpType,
    BYTE i,
    PPROPINFO Properties[],
    PEVENTINFO Events[]
    );
```

Notice that two new **#include** files have been added to the list: SHELLAPI.H and DOS.H. The first is the home of the drag-and-drop functions; the second is needed for the functions that determine whether a given name is that of a file or a directory.

MAIN.C

Because the FileDropper control is not based on an underlying standard Windows window, the MAIN.C module is extremely simple. It does have to initialize the DLL, but there is no window procedure to complicate things.

Here is the entirety of MAIN.C:

```
#include "main.h"

HINSTANCE LibInstance = 0;
char near ClassName[] = "FileDropper";

#pragma argsused
int far pascal LibMain
    (
```

```
    HINSTANCE hInstance,
    WORD DataSeg,
    WORD HeapSize,
    LPSTR CmdLine
    )
{
if (HeapSize > 0)
    UnlockData (0);
LibInstance = hInstance;
return TRUE;
}
```

Since there's no underlying Windows window, there's no class registration and no window procedure. Just the **LibMain( )** function, called automatically when the DLL is loaded, and which must return **TRUE** if it succeeds—which it always will; nothing that it does can fail.

VBXHELP.C

The VBXHELP.C file is totally unchanged from the previous chapter.

As mentioned in Chapter 12, the VBXHELP.C file can be used in any custom control project without modification, so there's no point in repeating the code here. The module is invoked on either of two occasions. One, when the programmer asks to see the About box, and two, when the programmer asks for online help for programming the control.

VISUAL.C

All the work is done in the VISUAL.C module, so you'd best take a break now. Once we get into this code, you won't want to quit until you're through!

The first section of VISUAL.C code we'll examine is the subclass procedure, the new window procedure we'll place "in front of" the normal window procedure for the window that the programmer wants to receive dropped files:

```
#include "main.h"

// First: The subclassing code

typedef struct
    {
```

```
    HCTL Control;
    WNDPROC BaseWndProc;
    } LINKBACK, far * LPLINKBACK;

LRESULT far pascal _export SubClassProc
    (
    HWND Window,
    UINT Msg,
    WPARAM wParam,
    LPARAM lParam
    )
{
HANDLE hLinkBack = (HANDLE) GetProp (Window, "Linkback");
LPLINKBACK LinkBack;
LRESULT Result = 0;

if (hLinkBack)
    LinkBack = (LPLINKBACK) LocalLock (hLinkBack);

switch (Msg)
    {
    case WM_DROPFILES:
        Result = VBSendControlMsg
            (
            LinkBack->Control,
            WM_DROPFILES,
            wParam,
            lParam
            );
        break;
    default:
        Result = CallWindowProc
            (
            LinkBack->BaseWndProc,
            Window,
            Msg,
            wParam,
            lParam
            );
        break;
    }

if (hLinkBack && (! Msg == WM_DESTROY))
    LocalUnlock (hLinkBack);

return Result;
}
```

Before the subclass procedure itself is a structure, **LINKBACK**. This structure, which will be set up by the FileDropper control, contains enough information for the subclass procedure to do its job. Specifically, that involves monitoring one message, the **WM_DROPFILES** messages we've heard so much about. If that message arrives, it is simply passed back to the control. All other messages are handled by the original window procedure, guaranteeing that the window's behavior will appear to be entirely normal, whatever kind of window it is—form, or other control.

Next comes the standard Visual layer stuff. The **VBDATA struct** contains room for the list of files and directories. I've somewhat arbitrarily limited this list to 64 items of each:

```
#define _segment(p) ((unsigned int)   (((unsigned long) (void far *)
(p)) >> 16L))
#define _offsetin(struc, fld) ((USHORT)&(((struc *)0)->fld))
#define VBERR_BADINDEX 381

#define MAX_LISTCOUNT 64

typedef struct
    {
    HWND ParentWindow;
    WNDPROC BaseWndProc;
    HANDLE hLinkBack;
    int DirectoryCount;
    HLSTR DirectoryList[MAX_LISTCOUNT];
    int FileCount;
    HLSTR FileList[MAX_LISTCOUNT];
    } VBDATA;
typedef VBDATA far * LPVBDATA;
```

Next comes the property list. The **(About)** property you've seen before; the others are the custom properties we discussed earlier in this chapter. Note that all of them are runtime properties; in addition, the **FileCount**, **FileList**, **DirectoryCount** and **DirectoryList** properties cannot be written to—just read:

```
PROPINFO Property_About =
    {
    "(About)",
    DT_HSZ | PF_fNoRuntimeW | PF_fNoRuntimeR | PF_fGetHszMsg,
    0, 0, 0, NULL, 0
    };
```

```
PROPINFO Property_ParentWindow =
   {
   "ParentHwnd",
   DT_LONG | PF_fSetMsg | PF_fNoShow | PF_fNoRuntimeR,
   0, 0, 0, NULL, 0
   };

PROPINFO Property_FileCount =
   {
   "FileCount",
   DT_LONG | PF_fGetMsg | PF_fNoShow | PF_fNoRuntimeW,
   0, 0, 0, NULL, 0
   };

PROPINFO Property_FileList =
   {
   "FileList",
   DT_HLSTR | PF_fGetMsg | PF_fNoShow | PF_fPropArray |
PF_fNoRuntimeW,
   0, 0, 0, NULL, 0
   };

PROPINFO Property_DirectoryCount =
   {
   "DirectoryCount",
   DT_LONG | PF_fGetMsg | PF_fNoShow | PF_fNoRuntimeW,
   0, 0, 0, NULL, 0
   };

PROPINFO Property_DirectoryList =
   {
   "DirectoryList",
   DT_HLSTR | PF_fGetMsg | PF_fNoShow | PF_fPropArray |
PF_fNoRuntimeW,
   0, 0, 0, NULL, 0
   };
```

Since we are only going to support one (the current) version of VBX
environment, we only need one property array and one **enum** of property IDs:

```
PPROPINFO Properties[] =
   {
   PPROPINFO_STD_CTLNAME,
   PPROPINFO_STD_INDEX,
   PPROPINFO_STD_LEFTNORUN,
   PPROPINFO_STD_TOPNORUN,
   PPROPINFO_STD_ENABLED,
```

```
PPROPINFO_STD_PARENT,
PPROPINFO_STD_TAG,
PPROPINFO_STD_LAST,
&Property_About,
&Property_ParentWindow,
&Property_FileCount,
&Property_FileList,
&Property_DirectoryCount,
&Property_DirectoryList,
NULL
};

typedef enum
    {
    PROP_STD_CTLNAME,
    PROP_STD_INDEX,
    PROP_STD_LEFTNORUN,
    PROP_STD_TOPNORUN,
    PROP_STD_ENABLED,
    PROP_STD_PARENT,
    PROP_STD_TAG,
    PROP_STD_LAST,
    PROP_About,
    PROP_ParentWindow,
    PROP_FileCount,
    PROP_FileList,
    PROP_DirectoryCount,
    PROP_DirectoryList,
    PROP_End
    } PROPSIX;
```

We didn't define any events for the skeleton control in the previous chapter, but here's how to define the one event we've decided to support, the **FilesDropped** event:

```
EVENTINFO Event_FilesDropped = { "FilesDropped", 0, 0, NULL, NULL };

PEVENTINFO Events[] =
    {
    &Event_FilesDropped,
    PEVENTINFO_STD_LAST,
    NULL
    };

typedef enum
    {
    IPEVENTINFO_FilesDropped,
    IPEVENTINFO_STD_LAST,
```

```
IPEVENTINFO_End
} EVENTSIX;
```

The handler for the **WM_NCCREATE** message must allocate space for the **LinkBack** structure, and then provide that structure with initial values. It also supplies initial values to **VbData**:

```
static void near pascal OnNcCreate (HCTL Control)
  {
  LPVBDATA VbData = (LPVBDATA) VBDerefControl (Control);
  LPLINKBACK LinkBack;
  VbData->ParentWindow = 0;
  VbData->BaseWndProc = NULL;
  VbData->hLinkBack = LocalAlloc (LMEM_MOVEABLE, sizeof (LINKBACK));
  LinkBack = LocalLock (VbData->hLinkBack);
  LinkBack->Control = Control;
  LocalUnlock (VbData->hLinkBack);
  VbData->DirectoryCount =
  VbData->FileCount = 0;
  }
```

Since **OnNcCreate()** allocated **LinkBack**, **OnNcDestroy()** must deallocate it:

```
static void near pascal OnNcDestroy (HCTL Control)
  {
  LPVBDATA VbData = (LPVBDATA) VBDerefControl (Control);
  LocalFree (VbData->hLinkBack);
  }
```

Eventually we're going to have to subclass a window, somehow giving it access to that **LinkBack** structure. Here's the function that enables the subclass procedure:

```
static void near pascal EnableSubclassing (LPVBDATA VbData)
  {
  LPLINKBACK LinkBack = LocalLock (VbData->hLinkBack);
  LinkBack->BaseWndProc =
  VbData->BaseWndProc =
    (WNDPROC) GetWindowLong (VbData->ParentWindow, GWL_WNDPROC);
  LocalUnlock (VbData->hLinkBack);
  SetProp (VbData->ParentWindow, "Linkback", VbData->hLinkBack);
  SetWindowLong (VbData->ParentWindow, GWL_WNDPROC,
    (long) SubClassProc);
  DragAcceptFiles (VbData->ParentWindow, TRUE);
  }
```

The **GetWindowLong()** function, provided with the **GWL_WNDPROC** index, returns the address of the requested window's window procedure. The **SetProp()** function is a really cool, but underused way to attach small amounts of data to a window. Since the target window has already been created, but we don't know what class it is, we can't very well add or use existing window bytes. However, you can always attach a "property" (not to be confused with Visual Basic control properties, or C++ properties!) to it. The property is limited to 16 bits, but fortunately that's exactly the size of a handle in Win16. So we provide a property called "LinkBack" and give as its value the handle to **LinkBack**. What could be simpler?

There is one gotcha, though. The property *must* be removed before the target window processes its **WM_DESTROY** message.

Anyway, once the property has been set, we can plug our own subclass procedure into the window, replacing the original, courtesy of the **SetWindowLong()** function. Having done that we are free to call **DragAcceptFiles()**, telling Windows we are ready for it to drop all the files on us it cares to.

As you might expect, disabling the subclass procedure is the inverse of enabling it:

```
static void near pascal DisableSubclassing (LPVBDATA VbData)
  {
  if (VbData->ParentWindow)
    {
    DragAcceptFiles (VbData->ParentWindow, FALSE);
    SetWindowLong (VbData->ParentWindow,
      GWL_WNDPROC, (long) VbData->BaseWndProc);
    RemoveProp (VbData->ParentWindow, "Linkback");
    VbData->BaseWndProc = NULL;
    }
  }
```

After performing the sanity check of verifying there is, indeed, a parent window, we turn off the file dragging (that's the **FALSE** parameter to **DragAcceptFiles()**); restore the original window procedure to the target window, and remove its "LinkBack" property. We do not lose the value of the **VbData->ParentHwnd** because this function's job is just to terminate the subclassing in response to a change in the control's Enabled state. Subclassing may be reinstated later. These operations are driven mainly from the handler for the **WM_ENABLE** message:

```
static void near pascal OnEnable (HCTL Control, BOOL Enabled)
  {
```

```
LPVBDATA VbData = (LPVBDATA) VBDerefControl (Control);
if (! Enabled)
  DisableSubclassing (VbData);
else
  EnableSubclassing (VbData);
}
```

OnEnable() may also be invoked from other places. For example, when the parent window handle is first set:

```
static void near pascal OnSetParentWindow
   (
   HCTL Control,
   HWND Window,
   HWND ParentWindow
   )
{
LPVBDATA VbData = (LPVBDATA) VBDerefControl (Control);
OnEnable (Control, FALSE);
VbData->ParentWindow = ParentWindow;
if (IsWindowEnabled (Window))
  OnEnable (Control, TRUE);
}
```

This function, called when the **ParentHwnd** property is set, first disables any current target window, then changes to the new target window, and (possibly) enables file dropping on the new window, depending on whether the FileDropper itself is currently enabled.

The **vbm_SetProperty()** function has little to do because there's only one property that can be set: the **ParentHwnd** property:

```
#pragma argsused
static BOOL near pascal vbm_SetProperty
   (
   HCTL Control,
   HWND Window,
   USHORT Property,
   long Value,
   long far * Error
   )
{
switch (Property)
   {
   case PROP_ParentWindow:
     OnSetParentWindow (Control, Window, (HWND) Value);
     return TRUE;
   default:
```

```
    return FALSE;
    }
}
```

Getting properties will be more complex; especially fun will be obtaining a single file or directory name from the appropriate array of names. That involves enough code, in fact, to place it in a function by itself—but, at least, the one function is designed to work with *either* list:

```
static void near pascal GetListEntry
    (
    int * Count,
    HLSTR List[],
    LPDATASTRUCT Data,
    long far * Error
    )
{
register i = (int) Data->index[0].data;
if ((i < 0) || (i >= *Count))
    *Error = VBERR_BADINDEX;
else
    {
    register l = VBGetHlstrLen (List[i]);
    Data->data =
        (LONG) VBCreateHlstr (VBDerefHlstr (List[i]), l);
    }
}
```

The **Data struct** is defined by the CDK and is used for array properties such as **FileList**. Even though we intend to store the filenames in the Visual Basic **HLSTR** format (allowing VB to do the memory management for us), we have to duplicate the string we return. That's because, in spite of CDK documentation that doesn't mention it, Visual Basic will assume ownership of the string it is handed here and eventually destroy it. We want to manage our own strings, so we send VB a copy.

The handler for the **VBM_GETPROPERTY** message, then, looks like this:

```
#pragma argsused
static BOOL near pascal vbm_GetProperty
    (
    HCTL Control,
    HWND Window,
    USHORT Property,
    LPVOID Value,
    long far * Error
    )
```

```
{
LPVBDATA VbData = (LPVBDATA) VBDerefControl (Control);
switch (Property)
   {
   case PROP_FileCount:
     *(long far *)Value = VbData->FileCount;
     return TRUE;
   case PROP_FileList:
     GetListEntry (&(VbData->FileCount),
       VbData->FileList,
       (LPDATASTRUCT) Value, Error);
     return TRUE;
   case PROP_DirectoryCount:
     *(long far *)Value = VbData->DirectoryCount;
     return TRUE;
   case PROP_DirectoryList:
     GetListEntry (&(VbData->DirectoryCount),
       VbData->DirecotryList,
       (LPDATASTRUCT) Value, Error);
     return TRUE;
   default:
     return FALSE;
   }
}
```

The next set of functions deals with the array of filenames and directory names. Before we can add a new set of names to the lists, we'll have to clear them of any names left over from the last drop:

```
static void near pascal ClearList (int * Count, HLSTR List[])
   {
   register i;
   for (i = 0; i < *Count; i++)
     VBDestroyHlstr (List[i]);
   *Count = 0;
   }
```

Adding names to the lists is equally simple:

```
static void near pascal AddList
    (int * Count, HLSTR List[], LPSTR Buffer)
   {
   if ((*Count + 1) < MAX_LISTCOUNT)
     {
     List[*Count] = VBCreateHlstr (Buffer, strlen (Buffer));
     (*Count)++;
     }
   }
```

But to which list do we add a name—file or directory? The next task is to tell them apart. Fortunately, there's a C library function that makes that job a trivial one:

```
static BOOL near pascal IsDirectory (LPSTR Buffer)
   {
   unsigned Attribs;
   _dos_getfileattr (Buffer, &Attribs);
   return ((Attribs & _A_SUBDIR) == _A_SUBDIR);
   }
```

We now have all the tools we need to handle that **WM_DROPFILES** message:

```
static void near pascal OnDropFiles (HCTL Control, HDROP Dropped)
   {
   LPVBDATA VbData = (LPVBDATA) VBDerefControl (Control);
   int DragCount = DragQueryFile (Dropped, (UINT) -1, NULL, 0);
   int d;
   char Buffer[128];
   ClearList (&(VbData->DirectoryCount), VbData->DirectoryList);
   ClearList (&(VbData->FileCount), VbData->FileList);
   for (d = 0; d < DragCount; d++)
      {
      DragQueryFile (Dropped, d, Buffer, sizeof Buffer);
      if (IsDirectory (Buffer))
         AddList (&(VbData->DirectoryCount),
            VbData->DirectoryList, Buffer);
      else
         AddList (&(VbData->FileCount),
            VbData->FileList, Buffer);
      }
   DragFinish (Dropped);
   VBFireEvent (Control, IPEVENTINFO_FilesDropped, NULL);
   }
```

After using **DragQueryFile()** to find out how many items have been dropped, we clear the old items from the lists and then add the new items, carefully separating the files from the directories. When we're done with that task we can invoke **DragFinish()** and then fire our custom Visual Basic **FilesDropped** event.

The control procedure, as in the skeleton control, is the message switch for all this activity:

```
long far pascal _export CtlProc
   (
   HCTL Control,
```

```
       HWND Window,
       USHORT Msg,
       USHORT wParam,
       long lParam
       )
{
long Error = 0;
switch (Msg)
   {
   case WM_NCCREATE:
      OnNcCreate (Control);
      break;
   case WM_ENABLE:
      OnEnable (Control, wParam);
      break;
   case WM_DROPFILES:
      OnDropFiles (Control, (HDROP) wParam);
      break;
   case VBM_SETPROPERTY:
      if (vbm_SetProperty (Control, Window, wParam, lParam, &Error))
         return Error;
      break;
   case VBM_GETPROPERTY:
      if (vbm_GetProperty (Control, Window, wParam, (LPVOID) lParam,
            &Error))
         return Error;
      break;
   case VBM_GETPROPERTYHSZ:
      switch (wParam)
         {
         case PROP_About:
            *((HSZ far *) lParam) = GetAboutPropertyString (Control);
            break;
         }
      return 0;
   case VBM_INITPROPPOPUP:
      switch (wParam)
         {
         case PROP_About:
            return (long) (int) PopupAbout ();
         }
      break;
   case VBM_HELP:
      if (vbm_Help (Window,
            LOBYTE (wParam),
            HIBYTE (wParam),
            Properties, Events))
         return 0;
      break;
```

```
    case WM_DESTROY:
      OnEnable (Control, FALSE);
      WinHelp (Window, HelpFileName (), HELP_QUIT, 0);
      break;
    case WM_NCDESTROY:
      OnNcDestroy (Control);
      break;
    }
  return VBDefControlProc (Control, Window, Msg, wParam, lParam);
  }
```

The **MODEL struct** is also similar to that presented in the skeleton:

```
MODEL Model =
  {
  VB_VERSION,
  MODEL_fInvisAtRun,
  (PCTLPROC) CtlProc,
  CS_VREDRAW | CS_HREDRAW,
  WS_BORDER,
  sizeof (VBDATA),
  8000,
  NULL,
  NULL,
  NULL,
  Properties,
  Events,
  PROP_STD_CTLNAME,
  NULL,
  (BYTE) -1
  };
```

Note the **MODEL_fInvisAtRun** flag. This flag tells Visual Basic our control cannot be seen at runtime. More, it says our control doesn't intend to paint itself. You haven't seen a paint routine, have you? And you won't. Visual Basic is considerate enough to use the control's toolbox bitmap as a display for the control at design-time.

Registering the control for a single version of Visual Basic is simpler even than you saw in the skeleton:

```
#pragma argsused
BOOL far pascal _export VBINITCC (USHORT Version, BOOL Runtime)
  {
  if (! Runtime)
    RegisterVbPopups ();
  Model.npszDefCtlName =
  Model.npszClassName = (PSTR) ClassName;
```

```
    return VBRegisterModel (LibInstance, &Model);
    }
```

And terminating the control is the same simple job it always is:

```
VOID FAR PASCAL _export VBTERMCC (void)
    {
    UnregisterVbPopups ();
    }
```

That's it—the whole code for FileDropper. Compile it and then turn to the next sections to watch it work.

Testing the FileDropper Control

Since the FileDropper was written to run under Visual Basic alone, Visual Basic is required to test it. In this section we'll create a test bed for the new control.

Adding the FileDropper to the VB Toolbox

Adding new tools to the Visual Basic toolbox is a basic skill that all Visual Basic programmers develop early on—because VB programming is largely a job of assembly.

To add a new control to the Visual Basic toolbox, after starting Visual Basic, use the File, Add File command. That will bring up a standard File Open dialog box. Simply select the .VBX file that contains the control you want to add and click on the OK button. The new control will be added to the toolbox. Remember, this addition applies only to the current project—you'll have to repeat the operation for any project in which you intend to use a FileDropper control.

Note: You can add the FileDropper to the AUTOLOAD.MAK project in your VB directory; that will make it available to all new projects with no further effort on your part.

Building the FileDropper Test Bed

The FileDropper test application should consist of a couple of list boxes, one of which will contain dropped files; the other, dropped directories.

For my FileDropper tester I placed two list boxes on a form. I also placed a FileDropper in any convenient location—remember, it's invisible at runtime, so the only criteria you have to follow in placing it is that it not get in the way. See Figure 13.3 for a picture of my FileDropper test application.

Just so you'll know, I named the list box that will hold the files, Files; the list box that will hold directory names is called Directories. The FileDropper has its default name, FileDropper1.

Since the FileDropper's **ParentHwnd** property must be set at runtime, we do it in the form's **Load** event:

```
Sub Form_Load ()
FileDropper1.ParentHwnd = hwnd
End Sub
```

The only other required code is the handler for the FileDropper's **FilesDropped** event:

```
Sub FileDropper1_FilesDropped ()
Files.Clear
Directories.Clear
Dim i As Integer
For i = 1 To FileDropper1.FileCount
    Files.AddItem FileDropper1.FileList(i - 1)
Next i
For i = 1 To FileDropper1.DirectoryCount
    Directories.AddItem FileDropper1.DirectoryList(i - 1)
Next i
End Sub
```

Run the application using Visual Basic's Run, Start command; position the File Manager so it shares the screen with the FileDropper test application and try dragging a few files and/or directories and dropping them on top of the tester.

So...how about that?! With relatively little effort, you've created an extremely valuable addition to the Visual Basic armory of weapons

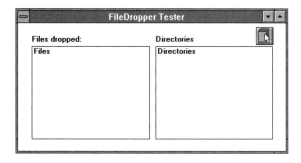

Figure 13.3 The FileDropper test application.

against slow development cycles. Hopefully, this little exercise has convinced you that the world belongs to the programmer who isn't limited to a single tool.

FileDropper Reference

On the disk accompanying this book, in the CHAP13 subdirectory, you'll find the FILEDROP.VBX ready to go. Along with it is FILEDROP.HLP, the accompanying online help file. For your convenience, here is the content of that help file.

FileDropper

FileDropper is a Visual Basic control that adds the ability to drop files onto a VB application from File Manager. It is then up to the application what, exactly, it intends to do with these files.

Properties

(About)
The (About) property is actually a pseudo-property: it doesn't actually store any data. Pressing the "..." button when this property is selected activates the FileDropper About box.

DirectoryCount
This property is available only at run-time, and can only be read. It contains a count of the number of directories last dropped on the window represented by the ParentHwnd property. For example:

```
Sub FileDropper1_FilesDropped ()
Dim i As Integer
For i = 1 To FileDropper1.DirectoryCount
    Directories.AddItem FileDropper1.DirectoryList(i - 1)
Next i
End Sub
```

DirectoryList
This array property is available only at run-time, and can only be read. It contains the names of the directories last dropped on the window represented by the ParentHwnd property. For example:

```
Sub FileDropper1_FilesDropped ()
Dim i As Integer
```

```
For i = 1 To FileDropper1.DirectoryCount
    Directories.AddItem FileDropper1.DirectoryList(i - 1)
Next i
End Sub
```

Enabled
Index
Left
Name
FileCount

This property is available only at run-time, and can only be read. It contains a count of the number of fileslast dropped on the window represented by the ParentHwnd property. For example:

```
Sub FileDropper1_FilesDropped ()
Dim i As Integer
For i = 1 To FileDropper1.FileCount
    Files.AddItem FileDropper1.FileList(i - 1)
Next i
End Sub
```

FileList

This array property is available only at run-time, and can only be read. It contains the names of the files last dropped on the window represented by the ParentHwnd property. For example:

```
Sub FileDropper1_FilesDropped ()
Dim i As Integer
For i = 1 To FileDropper1.FileCount
    Files.AddItem FileDropper1.FileList(i - 1)
Next i
End Sub
```

ParentHwnd

This property must be assigned the Hwnd property of the form or control that is to be the recipient of dropped files. Typically this is the main form. For example:

```
Sub Form_Load ()
FileDropper1.ParentHwnd = Hwnd
End Sub
```

Events

FilesDropped

This event is triggered whenever the user drops one or more files and/or directories onto the form or control represented by the ParentHwnd property. For example:

```
Sub FileDropper1_FilesDropped ()
Files.Clear
Directories.Clear
Dim i As Integer
For i = 1 To FileDropper1.FileCount
    Files.AddItem FileDropper1.FileList(i - 1)
Next i
For i = 1 To FileDropper1.DirectoryCount
    Directories.AddItem FileDropper1.DirectoryList(i - 1)
Next i
End Sub
```

Methods

The FileDropper control supports none of the standard events.

Appendix A: Listings

In Chapters 8 through 11, we built a Shapes application, starting with App Expert, Class Expert, and a lot of our own code. In those chapters, the code was presented piecemeal—we added a bit here, a bit there—in typical C++ coding style. And we didn't bother actually looking at the generated code at all, except where we modified it.

However, many readers prefer a chance to see the code all at once. To accommodate them, this Appendix will present the finished code as it appears at the end of Chapter 11.

APXPREV.H

```
#if !defined(__apxprev_h)          // Sentry, use file only if it's not already included.
#define __apxprev_h

/*  Main Shapes
    The Coriolis Group
    ©1994 Paul S. Cilwa. All Rights Reserved.
    SUBSYSTEM:    shapes.exe Application
    FILE:         APXPrev.H
    AUTHOR:       Paul S. Cilwa
    OVERVIEW
    ========
    Class definition for PreviewWindow (Print Preview).
*/
#include <owl\owlpch.h>
#pragma hdrstop
#include <owl\controlb.h>
#include <owl\printdia.h>
#include <owl\preview.h>
#include "apxprint.h"
#include "shapsapp.rh"

//{{TDecoratedFrame = PreviewWindow}}
class PreviewWindow : public TDecoratedFrame {
public:
    PreviewWindow (TWindow *parentWindow, TPrinter *printer, TWindow* currWindow, const
char far* title, TLayoutWindow* client);
    ~PreviewWindow ();
    int             PageNumber;
    TWindow         *CurrWindow;
    TControlBar     *PreviewSpeedBar;
    TPreviewPage    *Page1;
    TPreviewPage    *Page2;
    TPrinter        *Printer;
    TPrintDC        *PrnDC;
    TSize           *PrintExtent;
    APXPrintOut     *Printout;
```

```
private:
    TLayoutWindow    *Client;
    void SpeedBarState ();
    void CmPrintEnable (TCommandEnabler &tce);
    void CmPrint ();

//{{PreviewWindowVIRTUAL_BEGIN}}
protected:
    virtual void SetupWindow ();
//{{PreviewWindowVIRTUAL_END}}

//{{PreviewWindowRSP_TBL_BEGIN}}
protected:
    void PPR_PreviousEnable (TCommandEnabler &tce);
    void PPR_NextEnable (TCommandEnabler &tce);
    void PPR_Previous ();
    void PPR_Next ();
    void PPR_OneUp ();
    void PPR_TwoUpEnable (TCommandEnabler &tce);
    void PPR_TwoUp ();
    void EvNCLButtonDown (UINT wHitTestCode, TPoint & point);
    void EvClose ();
//{{PreviewWindowRSP_TBL_END}}
DECLARE_RESPONSE_TABLE(PreviewWindow);
};    //{{PreviewWindow}}
#endif        // __apxprev_h sentry.
```

APXPREV.CPP

```
/*  Main Shapes
    The Coriolis Group
    ©1994 Paul S. Cilwa. All Rights Reserved.
    SUBSYSTEM:    shapes.exe Application
    FILE:         APXPrev.CPP
    AUTHOR:       Paul S. Cilwa
    OVERVIEW
    ========
    Source file for implementation of Print Preview.
*/
#include <owl\owlpch.h>
#pragma hdrstop
#include <owl\controlb.h>
#include <owl\buttonga.h>
#include <owl\textgadg.h>
#include "apxprev.h"
#include "shapsapp.h"
#include "shapsapp.rh"

//{{PreviewWindow Implementation}}
DEFINE_RESPONSE_TABLE1(PreviewWindow, TDecoratedFrame)
    EV_COMMAND_ENABLE(APX_PPR_PREVIOUS, PPR_PreviousEnable),
    EV_COMMAND_ENABLE(APX_PPR_NEXT, PPR_NextEnable),
    EV_COMMAND(APX_PPR_PREVIOUS, PPR_Previous),
    EV_COMMAND(APX_PPR_NEXT, PPR_Next),
    EV_COMMAND(APX_PPR_ONEUP, PPR_OneUp),
    EV_COMMAND_ENABLE(APX_PPR_TWOUP, PPR_TwoUpEnable),
    EV_COMMAND(APX_PPR_TWOUP, PPR_TwoUp),
    EV_COMMAND(CM_FILEPRINT, CmPrint),
    EV_COMMAND_ENABLE(CM_FILEPRINT, CmPrintEnable),
```

```
//{{PreviewWindowRSP_TBL_BEGIN}}
    EV_WM_NCLBUTTONDOWN,
    EV_WM_CLOSE,
//{{PreviewWindowRSP_TBL_END}}
END_RESPONSE_TABLE;

PreviewWindow::PreviewWindow (TWindow *parentWindow, TPrinter *printer, TWindow*
                             currWindow, const char far* title, TLayoutWindow* client) :
                TDecoratedFrame(parentWindow, title, client)
{
    CurrWindow = currWindow;
    Printer = printer;
    Client = client;
    Page1 = 0;
    Page2 = 0;

    TPrintDialog::TData& data = Printer->GetSetup();
    PrnDC = new TPrintDC(data.GetDriverName(),
                         data.GetDeviceName(),
                         data.GetOutputName(),
                         data.GetDevMode());
    PrintExtent = new TSize(PrnDC->GetDeviceCaps(HORZRES), PrnDC->GetDeviceCaps(VERTRES));
    Printout = new APXPrintOut(Printer, "Print Preview", currWindow, TRUE);
    SetBkgndColor(GetSysColor(COLOR_APPWORKSPACE));
    //
    // Create default toolbar New and associate toolbar buttons with commands.
    PreviewSpeedBar = new TControlBar(this);
    PreviewSpeedBar->Insert(*new TButtonGadget(APX_PPR_PREVIOUS, APX_PPR_PREVIOUS,
        TButtonGadget::Command, TRUE));
    PreviewSpeedBar->Insert(*new TButtonGadget(APX_PPR_NEXT, APX_PPR_NEXT,
        TButtonGadget::Command, TRUE));
    PreviewSpeedBar->Insert(*new TSeparatorGadget(6));
    PreviewSpeedBar->Insert(*new TButtonGadget(APX_PPR_ONEUP, APX_PPR_ONEUP,
        TButtonGadget::Exclusive, TRUE, TButtonGadget::Down));
    PreviewSpeedBar->Insert(*new TButtonGadget(APX_PPR_TWOUP, APX_PPR_TWOUP,
        TButtonGadget::Exclusive, TRUE));
    PreviewSpeedBar->Insert(*new TSeparatorGadget(12));
    PreviewSpeedBar->Insert(*new TTextGadget(APX_PPR_CURRPAGE, TGadget::Recessed,
        TTextGadget::Left, 10, "Page 1"));
    PreviewSpeedBar->Insert(*new TSeparatorGadget(20));
    PreviewSpeedBar->Insert(*new TButtonGadget(CM_FILEPRINT, CM_FILEPRINT,
        TButtonGadget::Command, TRUE));
    Insert(*PreviewSpeedBar, TDecoratedFrame::Top);

    // We want a window that can be sized, maximized, or minimized.
    Attr.Style &= ~(WS_THICKFRAME | WS_BORDER | WS_MAXIMIZEBOX | WS_MINIMIZEBOX);
    Attr.Style |= (WS_VISIBLE | WS_POPUP | WS_CAPTION | WS_SYSMENU);
    // Don't show the border of the preview window
    Attr.X = -1;
    Attr.Y = -1;
    Attr.W = Parent->GetClientRect().Width() + 2;
    Attr.H = Parent->GetClientRect().Height() + 2;
    parentWindow->MapWindowPoints(HWindow, (TPoint *)&(Attr.X), 1);
}

PreviewWindow::~PreviewWindow ()
{
    delete Page1;
    Page1 = 0;
```

```
    delete Page2;
    Page2 = 0;
    delete PrnDC;
    PrnDC = 0;
    delete PrintExtent;
    PrintExtent = 0;
    delete Printout;
    Printout = 0;
}

void PreviewWindow::SetupWindow ()
{
    TDecoratedFrame::SetupWindow();
    TPrintDialog::TData& data = Printer->GetSetup();
    Page1 = new TPreviewPage(Client, *Printout, *PrnDC, *PrintExtent, 1);
    Page1->SetPageNumber(1);
    data.FromPage = 1;
    data.ToPage = 1;
    data.MinPage = 1;
    data.MaxPage = 1;
    Page2 = 0;
    TLayoutMetrics metrics1;
    metrics1.X.Set(lmLeft, lmRightOf, lmParent, lmLeft, 15);
    metrics1.Y.Set(lmTop, lmBelow, lmParent, lmTop, 15);
    //
    // Determine major axis of preview page.
    // Make minor axis a percentage (aspect ratio) of the page's major axis.
    TRect r = Client->GetClientRect();
    long ratio;
    if (PrintExtent->cx > PrintExtent->cy)
        ratio = ((long)PrintExtent->cy * 100) / PrintExtent->cx;
    else
        ratio = ((long)PrintExtent->cx * 100) / PrintExtent->cy;
    BOOL xMajor = (((r.Width() * ratio) / 100) > r.Height());
    if (xMajor){
        metrics1.Height.Set(lmBottom, lmAbove, lmParent, lmBottom, 15);
        metrics1.Width.PercentOf(Page1, (int)((long)PrintExtent->cx * 95 /
            PrintExtent->cy), lmHeight);
    } else {
        metrics1.Height.PercentOf(Page1, (int)((long)PrintExtent->cy * 95 /
            PrintExtent->cx), lmWidth);
        metrics1.Width.Set(lmRight, lmLeftOf, lmParent, lmRight, 15);
    }
    Page1->Create();
    Client->SetChildLayoutMetrics(*Page1, metrics1);
    Client->Layout();
}

void PreviewWindow::SpeedBarState ()
{
    TPrintDialog::TData &printerData = Printer->GetSetup();
    // Update the page count
    TTextGadget *theTGadget = TYPESAFE_DOWNCAST(PreviewSpeedBar->
        GadgetWithId(APX_PPR_CURRPAGE), TTextGadget);
    if (theTGadget) {
        char    buffer[32];
        if (Page2 && (printerData.FromPage != printerData.ToPage))
            wsprintf(buffer, "Page %d - %d", printerData.FromPage, printerData.ToPage);
        else
            wsprintf(buffer, "Page %d", printerData.FromPage);
```

```
        theTGadget->SetText(buffer);
    }
}

void PreviewWindow::EvClose ()
{
    // Don't call the base class EvClose; we do not want PreviewWindow to be destructed.
    GetApplication()->EndModal(IDCANCEL);
}

void PreviewWindow::PPR_PreviousEnable (TCommandEnabler &tce)
{
    // Only have previous on if we're not at the first page
    TPrintDialog::TData &printerData = Printer->GetSetup();
    tce.Enable(printerData.FromPage != 1);
}

void PreviewWindow::PPR_NextEnable (TCommandEnabler &tce)
{
    // Only have next on if we're not at the last page
    TPrintDialog::TData &printerData = Printer->GetSetup();
    tce.Enable(printerData.ToPage != printerData.MaxPage);
}

void PreviewWindow::PPR_Previous ()
{
    TPrintDialog::TData &printerData = Printer->GetSetup();

    if (printerData.FromPage > printerData.MinPage) {
        printerData.FromPage--;
        printerData.ToPage--;

        Page1->SetPageNumber(printerData.FromPage);
        if (Page2)
            Page2->SetPageNumber(printerData.ToPage);
    }
    SpeedBarState();
}

void PreviewWindow::PPR_Next ()
{
    TPrintDialog::TData &printerData = Printer->GetSetup();
    if (printerData.ToPage < printerData.MaxPage) {
        printerData.FromPage++;
        printerData.ToPage++;
        Page1->SetPageNumber(printerData.FromPage);
        if (Page2)
            Page2->SetPageNumber(printerData.ToPage);
    }
    SpeedBarState();
}

void PreviewWindow::PPR_OneUp ()
{
    if (Page2) {
        Client->RemoveChildLayoutMetrics(*Page2);
        delete Page2;
        Page2 = 0;
        Client->Layout();
        TPrintDialog::TData &printerData = Printer->GetSetup();
```

```
            printerData.ToPage = printerData.FromPage;
            SpeedBarState();
        }
    }

void PreviewWindow::PPR_TwoUpEnable (TCommandEnabler &tce)
{
    // Two up is only available for portrait mode.
    tce.Enable(PrintExtent->cx <= PrintExtent->cy);
}

void PreviewWindow::PPR_TwoUp ()
{
    if (Page2 == 0) {
        Page2 = new TPreviewPage(Client, *Printout, *PrnDC, *PrintExtent, PageNumber + 1);
        Page2->Create();
        TLayoutMetrics metrics2;
        metrics2.X.Set(lmLeft, lmRightOf, Page1, lmRight, 30);
        metrics2.Y.SameAs(Page1, lmTop);
        // Assume portrait
        metrics2.Width.SameAs(Page1, lmWidth);
        metrics2.Height.SameAs(Page1, lmBottom);
        Client->SetChildLayoutMetrics(*Page2, metrics2);
        Client->Layout();
        TPrintDialog::TData &printerData = Printer->GetSetup();
        // Page 2 is the next page.  If the next page is outside of our
        // range then set the first page back one and the 2nd page is
        // the current page.  If the document is only 1 page long then
        // the 2nd page is empty.
        if (printerData.FromPage == printerData.MaxPage) {
            if (printerData.FromPage > 1) {
                printerData.FromPage--;
                printerData.ToPage = printerData.FromPage + 1;
                Page1->SetPageNumber(printerData.FromPage);
                Page2->SetPageNumber(printerData.ToPage);
            } else
                Page2->SetPageNumber(0);
        } else {
            printerData.ToPage = printerData.FromPage + 1;
            Page2->SetPageNumber(printerData.ToPage);
        }
        SpeedBarState();
    }
}

void PreviewWindow::CmPrint ()
{
    ShapesApp *theApp = TYPESAFE_DOWNCAST(GetApplication(), ShapesApp);
    if (theApp)
        theApp->mdiClient->SendMessage(WM_COMMAND, CM_FILEPRINT, 0);
}

void PreviewWindow::CmPrintEnable (TCommandEnabler &tce)
{
   tce.Enable(TRUE);
}

// Don't allow the print preview window to be dragged around.
void PreviewWindow::EvNCLButtonDown (UINT wHitTestCode, TPoint & point)
```

```
{
    // If the LButtonDown isn't in the caption then process it normally
    if (wHitTestCode != HTCAPTION)
        TDecoratedFrame::EvNCLButtonDown(wHitTestCode, point);
}
```

APXPRINT.H

```
#if !defined(__apxprint_h)          // Sentry, use file only if it's not already included.
#define __apxprint_h
/*  Main Shapes
    The Coriolis Group
    ©1994 Paul S. Cilwa. All Rights Reserved.
    SUBSYSTEM:   shapes.exe Application
    FILE:        APXPrint.H
    AUTHOR:      Paul S. Cilwa
    OVERVIEW
    ========
    Class definition for APXPrintOut (TPrintOut).
*/
#include <owl\owlpch.h>
#pragma hdrstop
#include <owl\printer.h>

class APXPrintOut : public TPrintout {
public:
    APXPrintOut (TPrinter *printer, const char far *title, TWindow* window, BOOL scale =
TRUE) : TPrintout(title)
        { Printer = printer; Window = window; Scale = scale; MapMode = MM_ANISOTROPIC; }
    void GetDialogInfo (int& minPage, int& maxPage, int& selFromPage, int& selToPage);
    void BeginPrinting ();
    void BeginPage (TRect &clientR);
    void PrintPage (int page, TRect& rect, unsigned flags);
    void EndPage ();
    void SetBanding (BOOL b)          { Banding = b; }
    BOOL HasPage (int pageNumber);
protected:
    TWindow      *Window;
    BOOL         Scale;
    TPrinter     *Printer;
    int          MapMode;
    int          PrevMode;
    TSize        OldVExt, OldWExt;
    TRect        OrgR;
};
#endif           // __apxprint_h sentry.
```

APXPRINT.CPP

```
/*  Main Shapes
    The Coriolis Group
    ©1994 Paul S. Cilwa. All Rights Reserved.
    SUBSYSTEM:   shapes.exe Application
    FILE:        APXPrint.CPP
    AUTHOR:      Paul S. Cilwa
    OVERVIEW
    ========
    Source file for implementation of Printing.
```

```
*/
#include <owl\owlpch.h>
#pragma hdrstop
#include <owl\listbox.h>
#include <owl\edit.h>
#include <owl\preview.h>
#include "apxprint.h"

// Do not enable page range in the print dialog since only one page is
// available to be printed.
void APXPrintOut::GetDialogInfo (int& minPage, int& maxPage, int& selFromPage, int&
selToPage)
{
    minPage = maxPage = 0;
    selFromPage = selToPage = 0;
}

void APXPrintOut::BeginPrinting ()
{
    TRect clientR;
    BeginPage(clientR);
    TFrameWindow *fWindow = TYPESAFE_DOWNCAST(Window, TFrameWindow);
    HFONT   hFont = (HFONT)fWindow->GetClientWindow()->GetWindowFont();
    TFont   font("Arial", -12);
    if (hFont == 0)
      DC->SelectObject(font);
    else
      DC->SelectObject(TFont(hFont));
    TEXTMETRIC  tm;
    int fHeight=(DC->GetTextMetrics(tm)==TRUE) ? tm.tmHeight+tm.tmExternalLeading : 10;
    DC->RestoreFont();
    // How many lines of this font can we fit on a page.
    int linesPerPage = MulDiv(clientR.Height(), 1, fHeight);
    TPrintDialog::TData &printerData = Printer->GetSetup();
    int maxPg = 1;
    // Get the client class window (this is the content we're going to print).
    TEdit *clientEditWindow = 0;
    TListBox *clientListWindow = 0;
    clientEditWindow = TYPESAFE_DOWNCAST(fWindow->GetClientWindow(), TEdit);
    if (clientEditWindow)
        maxPg = ((clientEditWindow->GetNumLines() / linesPerPage) + 1.0);
    else {
        clientListWindow = TYPESAFE_DOWNCAST(fWindow->GetClientWindow(), TListBox);
        if (clientListWindow)
            maxPg = ((clientListWindow->GetCount() / linesPerPage) + 1.0);
    }
    // Compute the number of pages to print
    printerData.MinPage = 1;
    printerData.MaxPage = maxPg;
    EndPage();
    TPrintout::BeginPrinting();
}

void APXPrintOut::BeginPage (TRect &clientR)
{
    TScreenDC screenDC;
    TSize screenRes(screenDC.GetDeviceCaps(LOGPIXELSX),
                    screenDC.GetDeviceCaps(LOGPIXELSY));
    TSize printRes(DC->GetDeviceCaps(LOGPIXELSX),
                   DC->GetDeviceCaps(LOGPIXELSY));
```

```
    // Temporarily change the window size so any WM_PAINT queries on the total window size
    // (GetClientRect) is the window size for the WM_PAINT of the window and the printer
    // page size when Paint is called from PrintPage. Notice, we don't use
    // AdjustWindowRect because its harder and not accurate.  Instead, we compute the
    // difference (in pixels) between the client window and the frame window.  This
    // difference is then added to the clientRect to compute the new frame window size for
    // SetWindowPos.
    clientR = Window->GetClientRect();
    Window->MapWindowPoints(HWND_DESKTOP, (TPoint*)&clientR, 2);
    // Compute extra X and Y pixels to bring a client window dimensions to equal the frame
    // window.
    OrgR = Window->GetWindowRect();
    int adjX = OrgR.Width() - clientR.Width();
    int adjY = OrgR.Height() - clientR.Height();

    // Conditionally scale the DC to the window so the printout will resemble the window.
    if (Scale) {
        clientR = Window->GetClientRect();
        PrevMode = DC->SetMapMode(MapMode);
        DC->SetViewportExt(PageSize, &OldVExt);
        // Scale window to logical page size (assumes left & top are 0)
        clientR.right = MulDiv(PageSize.cx, screenRes.cx, printRes.cx);
        clientR.bottom = MulDiv(PageSize.cy, screenRes.cy, printRes.cy);
        DC->SetWindowExt(clientR.Size(), &OldWExt);
    }
    // Compute the new size of the window based on the printer DC dimensions.
    // Resize the window; notice position, order, and redraw are not done. The window size
    // changes but the user
    // doesn't see any visible change to the window.
    Window->SetRedraw(FALSE);
    Window->SetWindowPos(0, 0, 0, clientR.Width() + adjX, clientR.Height() + adjY,
                         SWP_NOMOVE | SWP_NOREDRAW | SWP_NOZORDER| SWP_NOACTIVATE);
}

void APXPrintOut::PrintPage (int page, TRect& bandRect, unsigned)
{
    TRect clientR;
    BeginPage(clientR);
    if (Scale)
        DC->DPtoLP(bandRect, 2);
    // Change the printer range to this current page
    TPrintDialog::TData& printerData = Printer->GetSetup();
    int fromPg = printerData.FromPage;
    int toPg = printerData.ToPage;
    printerData.FromPage = page;
    printerData.ToPage = page;
    // Call the window to paint itself to the printer DC
OutputDebugString ("APXPrintOut::PrintPage\n");
    Window->Paint(*DC, FALSE, bandRect);
    printerData.FromPage = fromPg;
    printerData.ToPage = toPg;
    if (Scale)
        DC->LPtoDP(bandRect, 2);
    EndPage();
}

void APXPrintOut::EndPage ()
{
    // Resize to original window size, no one's the wiser.
```

```
    Window->SetWindowPos(0, 0, 0, OrgR.Width(), OrgR.Height(),
                        SWP_NOMOVE | SWP_NOREDRAW | SWP_NOZORDER| SWP_NOACTIVATE);
    Window->SetRedraw(TRUE);
    // Restore changes made to the DC
    if (Scale) {
        DC->SetWindowExt(OldWExt);
        DC->SetViewportExt(OldVExt);
        DC->SetMapMode(PrevMode);
    }
}

BOOL APXPrintOut::HasPage (int pageNumber)
{
    TPrintDialog::TData &printerData = Printer->GetSetup();
    return (pageNumber >= printerData.MinPage) && (pageNumber <= printerData.MaxPage);
}
```

CLIPBRD.H

```
#ifndef __CLIPBRD_H__
#define __CLIPBRD_H__
#include <owl\clipboar.h>
#include <cstring.h>
#include <owl\window.h>

class TXClipboard;
class TClipboardFormat
    {
    public:
        TClipboardFormat (UINT aFormat = CF_TEXT);
        TClipboardFormat (string & aFormatName);
        virtual UINT RenderSize (TWindow & Window) const = 0;
        virtual void RenderToClipboard
            (TWindow & Window, LPVOID & Buffer, LONG BufferLength) const = 0;
        virtual BOOL AcceptFromClipboard
            (TWindow & Window, void far * Buffer, LONG BufferLength) const = 0;
        virtual string GetName (void) const;
        int operator==(const TClipboardFormat & aFormat) const;
        operator UINT (void) const { return Format; }
        virtual void ToClipboard (const TXClipboard & Clipboard) const;
        virtual BOOL FromClipboard (const TXClipboard & Clipboard) const;
    protected:
        UINT Format;
    };

#include <classlib\arrays.h>
typedef TIArrayAsVector<TClipboardFormat> TClipboardFormats;
typedef TIArrayAsVectorIterator<TClipboardFormat> TClipboardFormatsIterator;
class TXClipboard : public TClipboard
    {
    public:
        TXClipboard (TWindow * Window);
        void SetData (void) const;
        void GetData (BOOL GetAll = FALSE) const;
        BOOL IsData (void) const;
        TWindow & GetWindow (void) const { return *Window; }
        TClipboardFormats Formats;
    private:
        TWindow * Window;
    };
```

```cpp
class TClipboardText : public TClipboardFormat
    {
    public:
        virtual UINT RenderSize (TWindow & Window) const;
        virtual void RenderToClipboard
            (TWindow & Window, LPVOID & Buffer, LONG BufferLength) const;
        virtual BOOL AcceptFromClipboard
            (TWindow & Window, void far * Buffer, LONG BufferLength) const;
        virtual BOOL FromClipboard (const TXClipboard & Clipboard) const;
    };

#include <owl\point.h>
#include <owl\gdiobjec.h>
class TClipboardBitmap : public TClipboardFormat
    {
    public:
        TClipboardBitmap (TSize aBounds);
        virtual void RenderToClipboard
            (TWindow & Window, TDC & dc) const;
        virtual BOOL AcceptFromClipboard
            (TWindow & Window, TBitmap & Bitmap) const;
        virtual void ToClipboard (const TXClipboard & Clipboard) const;
        virtual BOOL FromClipboard (const TXClipboard & Clipboard) const;
    protected:
        TSize Bounds;
    private:
        virtual UINT RenderSize (TWindow & Window) const { return 0; }
        virtual void RenderToClipboard
            (TWindow & Window, LPVOID & Buffer, LONG BufferLength) const {}
        virtual BOOL AcceptFromClipboard
            (TWindow & Window, void far * Buffer, LONG BufferLength) const { return FALSE; }
    };

#endif
```

CLIPBRD.CPP

```cpp
#include "clipbrd.h"
#include <string.h>
#include <owl\dc.h>
#include <owl\metafile.h>
//-----------------------------------------------------------
// TClipboardFormat
//-----------------------------------------------------------
TClipboardFormat::TClipboardFormat (UINT aFormat)
    : Format (aFormat)
    {
    }

TClipboardFormat::TClipboardFormat (string & aFormatName)
    {
    Format = RegisterClipboardFormat (aFormatName.c_str());
    }

void TClipboardFormat::ToClipboard (const TXClipboard & Clipboard) const
    {
    LONG OriginalLength = RenderSize (Clipboard.GetWindow());
    if (OriginalLength)
        {
```

```
    HGLOBAL h = GlobalAlloc (GMEM_DDESHARE, OriginalLength);
    LPVOID Original = GlobalLock (h);
    RenderToClipboard (Clipboard.GetWindow(),
        Original, OriginalLength);
    GlobalUnlock (h);
    ((TClipboard &)Clipboard).SetClipboardData (Format, h);
    }
  }

BOOL TClipboardFormat::FromClipboard (const TXClipboard & Clipboard) const
  {
  HGLOBAL h = ((TClipboard &)Clipboard).GetClipboardData (Format);
  LPVOID Buffer = GlobalLock (h);
  BOOL Result = AcceptFromClipboard (Clipboard.GetWindow(),
      Buffer, GlobalSize (h));
  GlobalUnlock (h);
  return Result;
  }

string TClipboardFormat::GetName (void) const
  {
  switch (Format)
      {
      case CF_TEXT:
        return "Text";
      case CF_BITMAP:
        return "Bitmap";
      case CF_METAFILEPICT:
        return "Picture";
      case CF_SYLK:
        return "SYLK";
      case CF_DIF:
        return "DIF";
      case CF_TIFF:
        return "TIFF";
      case CF_OEMTEXT:
        return "OEM Text";
      case CF_DIB:
        return "DIB";
      case CF_PALETTE:
        return "Palette";
      case CF_PENDATA:
        return "Pen Data";
      case CF_RIFF:
        return "RIFF";
      case CF_WAVE:
        return "Wave";
      case CF_OWNERDISPLAY:
        return "Owner Display";
      case CF_DSPTEXT:
        return "Display Text";
      case CF_DSPBITMAP:
        return "Display Bitmap";
      case CF_DSPMETAFILEPICT:
        return "Display Picture";
      default:
        {
        char Buffer[64];
        GetClipboardFormatName (Format, Buffer, sizeof Buffer);
        return string (Buffer);
```

```
          }
       };
   }

int TClipboardFormat::operator==(const TClipboardFormat & aFormat) const
   {
   return (Format == aFormat.Format);
   }
//-----------------------------------------------------------
// TXClipboard
//-----------------------------------------------------------
TXClipboard::TXClipboard (TWindow * aWindow)
   : TClipboard (*aWindow),
     Formats (10, 0, 5),
     Window (aWindow)
   {
   CloseClipboard();
   }

void TXClipboard::SetData (void) const
   {
   ((TClipboard *) this)->OpenClipboard (*Window);
   ::EmptyClipboard();
   TClipboardFormatsIterator f (Formats);
   while (f)
      {
      f.Current()->ToClipboard (*this);
      f++;
      }
   ((TClipboard *) this)->CloseClipboard();
   }

void TXClipboard::GetData (BOOL GetAll) const
   {
   ((TClipboard *) this)->OpenClipboard (*Window);
   TClipboardFormatsIterator f (Formats);
   while (f)
      {
      TClipboardFormat * Format = f.Current();
      if (IsClipboardFormatAvailable (*Format))
         if (Format->FromClipboard (*this) && !GetAll)
            break;
      f++;
      }
   ((TClipboard *) this)->CloseClipboard();
   }

BOOL TXClipboard::IsData (void) const
   {
   TClipboardFormatsIterator f (Formats);
   while (f)
      {
      TClipboardFormat * Format = f.Current();
      if (IsClipboardFormatAvailable (*Format))
         return TRUE;
      f++;
      }
   return FALSE;
   }
```

```
//----------------------------------------------------------
// TClipboardText
//----------------------------------------------------------
UINT TClipboardText::RenderSize (TWindow & Window) const
    {
    return Window.GetWindowTextLength();
    }
void TClipboardText::RenderToClipboard
        (TWindow & Window, LPVOID & Buffer, LONG BufferLength) const
    {
    Window.GetWindowText ((LPSTR) Buffer, (UINT) BufferLength);
    }

BOOL TClipboardText::AcceptFromClipboard
        (TWindow & Window, void far * Buffer, LONG) const
    {
    Window.SetWindowText ((LPSTR) Buffer);
    return TRUE;
    }

BOOL TClipboardText::FromClipboard (const TXClipboard & Clipboard) const
    {
    HGLOBAL h = Clipboard.GetClipboardData (Format);
    LPSTR Buffer = (LPSTR) GlobalLock (h);
    AcceptFromClipboard (Clipboard.GetWindow(),
        Buffer, strlen (Buffer));
    GlobalUnlock (h);
    return TRUE;
    }


//----------------------------------------------------------
// TClipboardBitmap
//----------------------------------------------------------
TClipboardBitmap::TClipboardBitmap (TSize aBounds)
    : TClipboardFormat (CF_BITMAP), Bounds (aBounds)
    {
    }
void TClipboardBitmap::RenderToClipboard
        (TWindow & Window, TDC & dc) const
    {
    TRect Rect (TPoint (0, 0), Bounds);
    Window.Paint (dc, FALSE, Rect);
    }

BOOL TClipboardBitmap::AcceptFromClipboard
        (TWindow &, TBitmap &) const
    {
    return FALSE;
    }

void TClipboardBitmap::ToClipboard (const TXClipboard & Clipboard) const
    {
    TClientDC ClientDC (Clipboard.GetWindow());
    TMemoryDC MemoryDC (ClientDC);
    TBitmap Bitmap (ClientDC, Bounds.cx, Bounds.cy);

    MemoryDC.SelectObject (Bitmap);
    MemoryDC.PatBlt (0, 0,
        Bitmap.Width(), Bitmap.Height(), WHITENESS);
```

```
    RenderToClipboard (Clipboard.GetWindow(), MemoryDC);
    Bitmap.ToClipboard ((TClipboard &) Clipboard);
    }

BOOL TClipboardBitmap::FromClipboard (const TXClipboard & Clipboard) const
    {
    return AcceptFromClipboard (Clipboard.GetWindow(),
        TBitmap (Clipboard));
    }
```

INIDATA.H

```
#ifndef __INIDATA_H__
#define __INIDATA_H__
#include <cstring.h>
#include <classlib\bags.h>
#include <classlib\arrays.h>
class TSection : public string
    {
    public:
        TSection (char * aSection = NULL);
        TSection (const TSection & aSection);
        operator const char * (void) const;
        TSection & operator= (TSection aSection);
    };

inline TSection::TSection (char * aSection)
    : string (aSection)
    {
    }

inline TSection::TSection (const TSection & aSection)
    : string ((string) aSection)
    {
    }

inline TSection::operator const char * (void) const
    {
    return c_str ();
    }

class TKey : public string
    {
    public:
        TKey (char * aKey = NULL);
        TKey (const TKey & aKey);
        operator const char * (void) const;
        TKey & operator= (TKey aKey);
    };

inline TKey::TKey (char * aKey)
    : string (aKey)
    {
    }

inline TKey::TKey (const TKey & aKey)
    : string ((string) aKey)
    {
    }
```

```
inline TKey::operator const char * (void) const
   {
   return c_str ();
   }

class TSectionsBag : public TIBagAsVector<TSection>
   {
   public:
      TSectionsBag (string * aPathname);
      unsigned Count (void);
   protected:
      void Refresh (void);
   private:
      string * Pathname;
   };

inline TSectionsBag::TSectionsBag (string * aPathname)
   : TIBagAsVector<TSection> (25), Pathname (aPathname)
   {
   }


typedef TIBagAsVectorIterator<TSection> TSectionsBagIterator;
class TKeysBag : public TIBagAsVector<TKey>
   {
   public:
      TKeysBag (string * aPathname, TSection * aSection);
      unsigned Count (void);
   protected:
      void Refresh (void);
   private:
      string * Pathname;
      TSection * Section;
   };

inline TKeysBag::TKeysBag (string * aPathname, TSection * aSection)
   : TIBagAsVector<TKey> (25), Pathname (aPathname), Section (aSection)
   {
   }


typedef TIBagAsVectorIterator<TKey> TKeysBagIterator;
class TIniData;
class TValueList : public TIArrayAsVector<string>
   {
   public:
      TValueList (TIniData * aParent);
      TValueList (const TValueList & aValueList);
      TValueList & operator= (char aDelimiter);
      operator char (void) const;
      TValueList & operator= (const TValueList & aValueList);
      int Count (void);
   private:
      TIniData * Parent;
      char Delimiter;
   };

class TIniData
   {
   public:
      TIniData (string aPathname = "win.ini", TSection aSection = "");
      TIniData (const TIniData & aIniData);
```

```
       TIniData & operator= (const TIniData & aIniData);
       void SetPathname (string aPathname);
       string GetPathname (void) const;
       void SetDefault (string aDefault);
       string GetDefault (void) const;
       string GetValue (TKey Key);
       TIniData & operator= (TSection & aSection);
       TIniData & operator= (TKey & aKey);
       TIniData & operator= (string & aValue);
       TIniData & operator= (const char * aValue);
       operator TSection (void) const;
       operator TKey (void) const;
       operator string (void) const;
       operator const char * (void) const;
       TSectionsBag Sections;
       TKeysBag Keys;
       TValueList List;
   private:
       string Pathname;
       TSection Section;
       TKey Key;
       string Default;
   };

inline TIniData::TIniData (const TIniData & aIniData)
   : Sections (&Pathname),
     Keys (&Pathname, &Section),
     List (this)
   {
   *this = aIniData;
   }

inline string TIniData::GetPathname (void) const
   {
   return Pathname;
   }

inline string TIniData::GetDefault (void) const
   {
   return Default;
   }
#endif
```

INIDATA.CPP

```
#include "inidata.h"
#include <stdio.h>
#include <stdlib.h>
#include <fstream.h>
TSection & TSection::operator= (TSection aSection)
   {
   string::operator=(aSection);
   return *this;
   }

TKey & TKey::operator= (TKey aKey)
   {
   string::operator=(aKey);
   return *this;
   }
```

```cpp
unsigned TSectionsBag::Count (void)
   {
   if (! TIBagAsVector<TSection>::GetItemsInContainer())
      Refresh ();
   return TIBagAsVector<TSection>::GetItemsInContainer();
   }

void TSectionsBag::Refresh (void)
   {
   ifstream IniFile (Pathname->c_str());
   while (! IniFile.eof ())
      {
      char Buffer[256];
      IniFile.getline (Buffer, sizeof Buffer);
      if (Buffer[0] == '[')
         {
         char SectionName[64];
         register i = 0, j = 1;
         while (Buffer[j] && (Buffer[j] != ']'))
            SectionName[i++] = Buffer[j++];
         SectionName[i] = 0;
         Add (new TSection (SectionName));
         }
      }
   }

unsigned TKeysBag::Count (void)
   {
   if (! TIBagAsVector<TKey>::GetItemsInContainer())
      Refresh ();
   return TIBagAsVector<TKey>::GetItemsInContainer();
   }

void TKeysBag::Refresh (void)
   {
   char Buffer[512];
   char * Ptr = Buffer;
   GetPrivateProfileString (Section->c_str(),
      NULL,
      "",
      Buffer,
      sizeof Buffer,
      Pathname->c_str());
   while (Ptr[0])
      {
      Add (new TKey (Ptr));
      Ptr = &Ptr[strlen (Ptr)+1];
      }
   }

TValueList::TValueList (TIniData * aParent)
   : TIArrayAsVector<string> (8, 1, 8),
      Parent (aParent),
      Delimiter (0)
   {
   }

TValueList::TValueList (const TValueList & aValueList)
   : TIArrayAsVector<string> (aValueList.GetItemsInContainer(), 0, 8),
      Parent (aValueList.Parent),
```

```
        Delimiter (aValueList.Delimiter)
    {
    }

TValueList & TValueList::operator= (char aDelimiter)
    {
    Delimiter = aDelimiter;
    return *this;
    }

TValueList::operator char (void) const
    {
    return Delimiter;
    }

TValueList & TValueList::operator= (const TValueList & aValueList)
    {
    Flush (TShouldDelete::Delete);
    Parent = aValueList.Parent;
    Delimiter = aValueList.Delimiter;
    return *this;
    }

int TValueList::Count (void)
    {
    if (! GetItemsInContainer())
        {
        string Value (*Parent);
        char Buffer[128];
        register i, j = 0;
        for (i = 0; i < Value.length(); i++)
            if (Value[i] != Delimiter)
                {
                if (j || (Value[i] != ' '))
                    Buffer[j++] = Value[i];
                }
            else
                {
                Buffer[j] = 0;
                Add (new string (Buffer));
                j = 0;
                }
        if (j)
            Add (new string (Buffer));
        }
    return GetItemsInContainer();
    }

TIniData::TIniData (string aPathname, TSection aSection)
        : Section (aSection), Sections (&Pathname),
          Keys (&Pathname, &Section),
          List (this)
    {
    SetPathname (aPathname);
    }

TIniData & TIniData::operator= (const TIniData & aIniData)
    {
    Pathname = aIniData.Pathname;
    Section = aIniData.Section;
```

```
   Key = aIniData.Key;
   Default = aIniData.Default;
   Sections.Flush(TShouldDelete::Delete);
   Keys.Flush(TShouldDelete::Delete);
   List = aIniData.List;
   return *this;
   }

void TIniData::SetDefault (string aDefault)
   {
   Default = aDefault;
   }

void TIniData::SetPathname (string aPathname)
   {
   char Drive[_MAX_DRIVE], Dir[_MAX_DIR], FName[_MAX_FNAME], Ext[_MAX_EXT];
   char TempName[_MAX_PATH];
   _splitpath (aPathname.c_str(), Drive, Dir, FName, Ext);
   if (! Dir[0])
      {
      GetWindowsDirectory (Dir, sizeof Dir);
      strncpy (Drive, Dir, 2);
      strcpy (Dir, &Dir[2]);
      }
   if (! Ext[0])
      strcpy (Ext, ".INI");
   _makepath (TempName, Drive, Dir, FName, Ext);
   Pathname = TempName;
   Sections.Flush (TShouldDelete::Delete);
   Keys.Flush (TShouldDelete::Delete);
   List.Flush (TShouldDelete::Delete);
   }

string TIniData::GetValue (TKey Key)
   {
   return (*this = Key);
   }

TIniData & TIniData::operator= (TSection & aSection)
   {
   Section = aSection;
   Keys.Flush (TShouldDelete::Delete);
   List.Flush (TShouldDelete::Delete);
   return *this;
   }

TIniData & TIniData::operator= (TKey & aKey)
   {
   Key = aKey;
   List.Flush (TShouldDelete::Delete);
   return *this;
   }

TIniData & TIniData::operator= (string & aValue)
   {
   return *this = aValue.c_str();
   }

TIniData & TIniData::operator= (const char * aValue)
   {
```

```
    Sections.Flush (TShouldDelete::Delete);
    Keys.Flush (TShouldDelete::Delete);
    List.Flush (TShouldDelete::Delete);
    WritePrivateProfileString (Section, Key, aValue, Pathname.c_str());
    return *this;
    }

TIniData::operator TSection (void) const
    {
    return Section;
    }

TIniData::operator TKey (void) const
    {
    return Key;
    }

TIniData::operator string (void) const
    {
    char Buffer[128];
    GetPrivateProfileString (Section, Key, Default.c_str(),
        Buffer, sizeof Buffer, Pathname.c_str());
    return string (Buffer);
    }

TIniData::operator const char * (void) const
    {
    return ((string) *this).c_str();
    }
```

SHAPSAPP.H

```
#if !defined(__shapsapp_h)          // Sentry, use file only if it's not already included.
#define __shapsapp_h
/*  Project Shapes
    The Coriolis Group
    ©1994 Paul S. Cilwa. All Rights Reserved.
SUBSYSTEM:    shapes.exe Application
    FILE:         shapsapp.h
    AUTHOR:       Paul S. Cilwa
OVERVIEW
    ========
    Class definition for ShapesApp (TApplication).
*/
#include <owl\owlpch.h>
#pragma hdrstop
#include <owl\statusba.h>
#include <owl\controlb.h>
#include <owl\buttonga.h>
#include <owl\editview.h>
#include <owl\listview.h>
#include <owl\docmanag.h>
#include <owl\filedoc.h>
#include <owl\printer.h>
#include <classlib\bags.h>
#include "inidata.h"
#include "shpsmdic.h"
#include "shapsapp.rh"              // Definition of all resources.
```

```
// TFileDrop class Maintains information about a dropped file, its name, where it was
// dropped, and whether it was in the client area.

class TFileDrop {
public:
    operator == (const TFileDrop& other) const {return this == &other;}
    char*   FileName;
    TPoint  Point;
    BOOL    InClientArea;
    TFileDrop (char*, TPoint&, BOOL, TModule*);
    ~TFileDrop ();
    const char* WhoAmI ();
private:
    //
    // Hidden to prevent accidental copying or assignment.
    //
    TFileDrop (const TFileDrop&);
    TFileDrop & operator = (const TFileDrop&);
};


typedef TIBagAsVector<TFileDrop> TFileList;
typedef TIBagAsVectorIterator<TFileDrop> TFileListIter;


//{{TApplication = ShapesApp}}
class ShapesApp : public TApplication {
private:
private:
    void SetupSpeedBar (TDecoratedMDIFrame *frame);
    void AddFiles (TFileList* files);
public:
    ShapesApp ();
    virtual ~ShapesApp ();
    ShapesMDIClient  *mdiClient;
    TIniData IniData;
    // Public data members used by the print menu commands and Paint routine in MDIChild.
    TPrinter        *Printer;                       // Printer support
    int             Printing;                       // Printing in progress
//{{ShapesAppVIRTUAL_BEGIN}}
public:
    virtual void InitMainWindow();
    virtual void InitInstance();
//{{ShapesAppVIRTUAL_END}}
//{{ShapesAppRSP_TBL_BEGIN}}
protected:
    void EvNewView (TView& view);
    void EvCloseView (TView& view);
    void CmHelpAbout ();
    void EvDropFiles (TDropInfo drop);
    void EvWinIniChange (char far* section);
//{{ShapesAppRSP_TBL_END}}
  DECLARE_RESPONSE_TABLE(ShapesApp);
};    //{{ShapesApp}}
#endif                                  // __shapsapp_h sentry.
```

SHAPSAPP.CPP

```
/*  Project Shapes
    The Coriolis Group
    ©1994 Paul S. Cilwa. All Rights Reserved.
```

```
      SUBSYSTEM:    shapes.exe Application
      FILE:         shapsapp.cpp
      AUTHOR:       Paul S. Cilwa
      OVERVIEW
      ========

      Source file for implementation of ShapesApp (TApplication).
*/
#include <owl\owlpch.h>
#pragma hdrstop
#include "shpsview.h"
#include <dir.h>
#include "shapsapp.h"
#include "shpsmdic.h"
#include "shpsmdi1.h"
#include "shpsabtd.h"                          // Definition of About dialog box.
#include "shpsdoc.h"
#include "xcolor.h"
// Drag / Drop support:
TFileDrop::TFileDrop (char* fileName, TPoint& p, BOOL inClient, TModule*)
{
    char    exePath[MAXPATH];

    exePath[0] = 0;
    FileName = strcpy(new char[strlen(fileName) + 1], fileName);
    Point = p;
    InClientArea = inClient;
}

TFileDrop::~TFileDrop ()
{
    delete FileName;
}

const char *TFileDrop::WhoAmI ()
{
  return FileName;
}


//{{ShapesApp Implementation}}
//{{DOC_VIEW}}
DEFINE_DOC_TEMPLATE_CLASS(TShapesDoc, TShapesView, DocType1);
//{{DOC_VIEW_END}}
//{{DOC_MANAGER}}
DocType1 __dvt1("Shapes files", "*.shp", 0, "shp", dtAutoDelete | dtAutoOpen | dtUpdateDir
| dtPathMustExist | dtFileMustExist);
//{{DOC_MANAGER_END}}


// Build a response table for all messages/commands handled
// by the application.
DEFINE_RESPONSE_TABLE1(ShapesApp, TApplication)
//{{ShapesAppRSP_TBL_BEGIN}}
    EV_OWLVIEW(dnCreate, EvNewView),
    EV_OWLVIEW(dnClose,  EvCloseView),
    EV_COMMAND(CM_HELPABOUT, CmHelpAbout),
    EV_WM_DROPFILES,
    EV_WM_WININICHANGE,
//{{ShapesAppRSP_TBL_END}}
END_RESPONSE_TABLE;
```

```
// ShapesApp
ShapesApp::ShapesApp ()
        : TApplication("Shapes"),
          IniData ("Shapes.INI")
    {
    Printer = 0;
    Printing = 0;
    DocManager = new TDocManager(dmMDI | dmMenu);
    TXColor::LoadCustomColors (IniData);
    }

ShapesApp::~ShapesApp ()
{
    if (Printer)
        delete Printer;
    // INSERT>> Your destructor code here.
}

void ShapesApp::SetupSpeedBar (TDecoratedMDIFrame *frame)
{
// Create default toolbar New and associate toolbar buttons with commands.
    TControlBar* cb = new TControlBar(frame);
    cb->Insert(*new TButtonGadget(CM_MDIFILENEW, CM_MDIFILENEW));
    cb->Insert(*new TButtonGadget(CM_MDIFILEOPEN, CM_MDIFILEOPEN));
    cb->Insert(*new TButtonGadget(CM_FILESAVE, CM_FILESAVE));
    cb->Insert(*new TSeparatorGadget(6));
    cb->Insert(*new TButtonGadget(CM_EDITCUT, CM_EDITCUT));
    cb->Insert(*new TButtonGadget(CM_EDITCOPY, CM_EDITCOPY));
    cb->Insert(*new TButtonGadget(CM_EDITPASTE, CM_EDITPASTE));
    cb->Insert(*new TSeparatorGadget(6));
    cb->Insert(*new TButtonGadget(CM_EDITUNDO, CM_EDITUNDO));
    cb->Insert(*new TSeparatorGadget(6));
    cb->Insert(*new TButtonGadget(CM_FILEPRINT, CM_FILEPRINT));
    cb->Insert(*new TButtonGadget(CM_FILEPRINTPREVIEW, CM_FILEPRINTPREVIEW));
    // Add fly-over help hints
    cb->SetHintMode(TGadgetWindow::EnterHints);
    frame->Insert(*cb, TDecoratedFrame::Top);
}

// ShapesApp
// Application intialization.
void ShapesApp::InitMainWindow ()
{
    mdiClient = new ShapesMDIClient;
    TDecoratedMDIFrame* frame = new TDecoratedMDIFrame(Name, MDI_MENU, *mdiClient, TRUE);
    nCmdShow = (nCmdShow != SW_SHOWMINNOACTIVE) ? SW_SHOWNORMAL : nCmdShow;
// Assign ICON with this application.
    frame->SetIcon(this, IDI_MDIAPPLICATION);
// Menu associated with window and accelerator table associated with table.
    frame->AssignMenu(MDI_MENU);
    // Associate with the accelerator table.
    frame->Attr.AccelTable = MDI_MENU;
SetupSpeedBar(frame);
    TStatusBar *sb = new TStatusBar(frame, TGadget::Recessed,
                                    TStatusBar::CapsLock    |
                                    TStatusBar::NumLock     |
                                    TStatusBar::ScrollLock  |
                                    TStatusBar::Overtype);
    frame->Insert(*sb, TDecoratedFrame::Bottom);
    SetMainWindow(frame);
```

```
    // Borland Windows custom controls.
    EnableBWCC();
}


// ShapesApp
// Response Table handlers:
void ShapesApp::EvNewView (TView& view)
{
  TMDIClient *mdiClient = TYPESAFE_DOWNCAST(GetMainWindow()->GetClientWindow(), TMDIClient);
    if (mdiClient) {
        ShapesMDIChild* child = new ShapesMDIChild(*mdiClient, 0, view.GetWindow());
        // Associate ICON with this child window.
        child->SetIcon(this, IDI_DOC);
        child->Create();
    }
}


void ShapesApp::EvCloseView (TView&)
{}


// ShapesApp
// Menu Help About shapes.exe command
void ShapesApp::CmHelpAbout ()
{
    //
    // Show the Modal dialog box.
    //
    ShapesAboutDlg(MainWindow).Execute();
}


void ShapesApp::InitInstance ()
{
    TApplication::InitInstance();
    // Accept files via drag/drop in the frame window.
    GetMainWindow()->DragAcceptFiles(TRUE);
}


void ShapesApp::EvDropFiles (TDropInfo drop)
{
    // Number of files dropped.
    int totalNumberOfFiles = drop.DragQueryFileCount();
    TFileList* files = new TFileList;
    for (int i = 0; i < totalNumberOfFiles; i++) {
        // Tell DragQueryFile the file interested in (i) and the length of your buffer
        int     fileLength = drop.DragQueryFileNameLen(i) + 1;
        char    *fileName = new char[fileLength];
        drop.DragQueryFile(i, fileName, fileLength);
        // Getting the file dropped. The location is relative to your client coordinates,
        // and will have negative values if dropped in the non-client parts of the window.
        // DragQueryPoint copies that point where the file was dropped and returns whether
        // or not the point is in the client area.  Regardless of whether or not the file
        // is dropped in the client or non-client area of the window, you will still
        // receive the filename.
        TPoint  point;
        BOOL    inClientArea = drop.DragQueryPoint(point);
        files->Add(new TFileDrop(fileName, point, inClientArea, this));
    }
    // Open the files that were dropped.
    AddFiles(files);
```

```
        // Release the memory allocated for this handle with DragFinish.
        drop.DragFinish();
}

void ShapesApp::AddFiles (TFileList* files)
{
        // Open all files dragged in.
        TFileListIter fileIter(*files);
        while (fileIter) {
            TDocTemplate* tpl = GetDocManager()->MatchTemplate(fileIter.Current()->WhoAmI());
            if (tpl)
                tpl->CreateDoc(fileIter.Current()->WhoAmI());
            fileIter++;
        }
}

void ShapesApp::EvWinIniChange (char far* section)
{
        if (lstrcmp(section, "windows") == 0) {
            // If the device changed in the WIN.INI file, the printer
            // might have changed.  If we have a TPrinter (Printer) then
            // check and make sure it's identical to the current device
            // entry in WIN.INI.
            if (Printer) {
                char printDBuffer[255];
                LPSTR printDevice = printDBuffer;
                LPSTR devName = 0;
                LPSTR driverName = 0;
                LPSTR outputName = 0;
                if (::GetProfileString("windows", "device", "", printDevice,
                  sizeof(printDevice))) {
                    // The string which should come back is something like:
                    //       HP LaserJet III,hppcl5a,LPT1:
                    // Where the format is:
                    //       devName,driverName,outputName
                    devName = printDevice;
                    while (*printDevice) {
                        if (*printDevice == ',') {
                            *printDevice++ = 0;
                            if (!driverName)
                                driverName = printDevice;
                            else
                                outputName = printDevice;
                        } else
                            printDevice = AnsiNext(printDevice);
                    }
                    if ((Printer->GetSetup().Error != 0)                         ||
                        (lstrcmp(devName, Printer->GetSetup().GetDeviceName()) != 0)   ||
                        (lstrcmp(driverName, Printer->GetSetup().GetDriverName()) != 0) ||
                        (lstrcmp(outputName, Printer->GetSetup().GetOutputName()) != 0)) {
                        // New printer installed so get the new printer device now.
                        delete Printer;
                        Printer = new TPrinter;
                    }
                } else {
                    // No printer installed (GetProfileString failed).
                    delete Printer;
                    Printer = new TPrinter;
                }
```

```
        }
    }
}

int OwlMain (int , char* [])
{
    ShapesApp      App;
    int            result;
    result = App.Run();
    return result;
}
```

SHAPSAPP.DEF

```
;   Main Shapes
;   The Coriolis Group
;   ©1994 Paul S. Cilwa. All Rights Reserved.
;   SUBSYSTEM:      shapes.exe Module Defintion File
;   FILE:           shapsapp.def
;   AUTHOR:         Paul S. Cilwa
NAME Shapes
DESCRIPTION 'Shapes Application - ©1994 Paul S. Cilwa. All Rights Reserved.'
EXETYPE     WINDOWS
CODE        PRELOAD MOVEABLE DISCARDABLE
DATA        PRELOAD MOVEABLE MULTIPLE
HEAPSIZE    4096
STACKSIZE   8192
```

SHAPSAPP.RH

```
//#if !defined(__shapsapp_rh)        // Sentry, use file only if it's not already
included.
//#define __shapsapp_rh
/*  Main Shapes
    The Coriolis Group
    ©1994 Paul S. Cilwa. All Rights Reserved.
    SUBSYSTEM:      shapes.exe Application
    FILE:           shapsapp.h
    AUTHOR:         Paul S. Cilwa
    OVERVIEW
    ========
    Constant definitions for all resources defined in shapsapp.rc.
*/
// IDHELP BorButton for BWCC dialogs.
#define IDHELP              998         // Id of help button
// Application specific definitions:
#define IDI_MDIAPPLICATION  1001        // Application icon
#define IDI_DOC             1002        // MDI child window icon
#define MDI_MENU            100         // Menu resource ID and Accelerator IDs
#define CM_SHAPESOTHER 24356
#define CM_SHAPESELLIPSE 2
#define CM_SHAPESRECTANGLE  1
#define CM_SHAPESRED   24351
#define CM_SHAPESGREEN 24355
#define CM_SHAPESBLUE  24354
// CM_FILEnnnn commands (include\owl\editfile.rh except for CM_FILEPRINTPREVIEW)
#define CM_MDIFILENEW       24331
#define CM_MDIFILEOPEN      24332
#define CM_FILECLOSE        24339
```

```
#define CM_FILESAVE            24333
#define CM_FILESAVEAS          24334
#define CM_FILEREVERT          24335
#define CM_VIEWCREATE          24341
#define CM_FILEPRINT           24337
#define CM_FILEPRINTERSETUP    24338
#define CM_FILEPRINTPREVIEW    24340


// Window commands (include\owl\window.rh)
#define CM_EXIT                24310


// CM_EDITnnnn commands (include\owl\window.rh)
#define CM_EDITUNDO            24321
#define CM_EDITCUT             24322
#define CM_EDITCOPY            24323
#define CM_EDITPASTE           24324
#define CM_EDITDELETE          24325
#define CM_EDITCLEAR           24326
#define CM_EDITADD             24327
#define CM_EDITEDIT            24328


// Search menu commands (include\owl\editsear.rh)
#define CM_EDITFIND            24351
#define CM_EDITREPLACE         24352
#define CM_EDITFINDNEXT        24353


// Windows menu commands (include\owl\mdi.rh)
#define CM_CASCADECHILDREN     24361
#define CM_TILECHILDREN        24362
#define CM_TILECHILDRENHORIZ   24363
#define CM_ARRANGEICONS        24364
#define CM_CLOSECHILDREN       24365
#define CM_CREATECHILD         24366


// Help menu commands
#define CM_HELPABOUT           2009
// About dialog boxes
#define IDD_ABOUT          22000
#define IDC_VERSION            22001
#define IDC_COPYRIGHT          22002
#define IDC_DEBUG              22003
// OWL defined strings
// Statusbar
#define IDS_MODES              32530
#define IDS_MODESOFF           32531
// EditFile
#define IDS_UNABLEREAD         32551
#define IDS_UNABLEWRITE        32552
#define IDS_FILECHANGED        32553
#define IDS_FILEFILTER         32554
// EditSearch
#define IDS_CANNOTFIND         32540
// General & application exception messages (include\owl\except.rh)
#define IDS_UNKNOWNEXCEPTION   32767
#define IDS_OWLEXCEPTION       32766
#define IDS_OKTORESUME         32765
#define IDS_UNHANDLEDXMSG      32764
#define IDS_UNKNOWNERROR       32763
#define IDS_NOAPP              32762
#define IDS_OUTOFMEMORY        32761
```

```
#define IDS_INVALIDMODULE        32760
#define IDS_INVALIDMAINWINDOW     32759
// Owl 1 compatibility messages
#define IDS_INVALIDWINDOW         32756
#define IDS_INVALIDCHILDWINDOW    32755
#define IDS_INVALIDCLIENTWINDOW   32754
// TXWindow messages
#define IDS_CLASSREGISTERFAIL     32749
#define IDS_CHILDREGISTERFAIL     32748
#define IDS_WINDOWCREATEFAIL      32747
#define IDS_WINDOWEXECUTEFAIL     32746
#define IDS_CHILDCREATEFAIL       32745
#define IDS_MENUFAILURE           32744
#define IDS_VALIDATORSYNTAX       32743
#define IDS_PRINTERERROR          32742
#define IDS_LAYOUTINCOMPLETE      32741
#define IDS_LAYOUTBADRELWIN       32740
// TXGdi messages
#define IDS_GDIFAILURE            32739
#define IDS_GDIALLOCFAIL          32738
#define IDS_GDICREATEFAIL         32737
#define IDS_GDIRESLOADFAIL        32736
#define IDS_GDIFILEREADFAIL       32735
#define IDS_GDIDELETEFAIL         32734
#define IDS_GDIDESTROYFAIL        32733
#define IDS_INVALIDDIBHANDLE      32732
// ListView (include\owl\listview.rh)
#define IDS_LISTNUM               32582
// DocView (include\owl\docview.rh)
#define IDS_DOCMANAGERFILE        32500
#define IDS_DOCLIST               32501
#define IDS_VIEWLIST              32502
#define IDS_UNTITLED              32503
#define IDS_UNABLEOPEN            32504
#define IDS_UNABLECLOSE           32505
#define IDS_READERROR             32506
#define IDS_WRITEERROR            32507
#define IDS_DOCCHANGED            32508
#define IDS_NOTCHANGED            32509
#define IDS_NODOCMANAGER          32510
#define IDS_NOMEMORYFORVIEW       32511
#define IDS_DUPLICATEDOC          32512


// Printing error message string resource IDs (include\owl\printer.rh)
#define IDS_PRNON                 32590
#define IDS_PRNERRORTEMPLATE      32591
#define IDS_PRNOUTOFMEMORY        32592
#define IDS_PRNOUTOFDISK          32593
#define IDS_PRNCANCEL             32594
#define IDS_PRNMGRABORT           32595
#define IDS_PRNGENERROR           32596
#define IDS_PRNERRORCAPTION       32597


// Printer abort dialog & control IDs
#define IDD_ABORTDIALOG           32599
#define ID_TITLE                  101
#define ID_DEVICE                 102
#define ID_PORT                   103
#define ID_PAGE                   104        // Page # text control
```

```
// Print Preview
#define APX_PPR_PREVIOUS        24500
#define APX_PPR_NEXT            24501
#define APX_PPR_ONEUP           24502
#define APX_PPR_TWOUP           24503
#define APX_PPR_CURRPAGE        24504
// TInputDialog DIALOG resource (include\owl\inputdia.rh)
#define IDD_INPUTDIALOG         32514
#define ID_PROMPT               4091
#define ID_INPUT                4090
// TSlider bitmaps (horizontal and vertical) (include\owl\slider.rh)
#define IDB_HSLIDERTHUMB        32000
#define IDB_VSLIDERTHUMB        32001
// Validation messages (include\owl\validate.rh)
#define IDS_VALPXPCONFORM       32520
#define IDS_VALINVALIDCHAR      32521
#define IDS_VALNOTINRANGE       32522
#define IDS_VALNOTINLIST        32523
//#endif          __shapsapp_rh sentry.
```

SHAPSAPP.RC

```
/*  Main Shapes
    The Coriolis Group
    ©1994 Paul S. Cilwa. All Rights Reserved.
SUBSYSTEM:      shapes.exe Application
    FILE:       shapsapp.rc
    AUTHOR:     Paul S. Cilwa
OVERVIEW
    ========
    All resources defined here.
*/
#if !defined(WORKSHOP_INVOKED)
#include <windows.h>
#endif
#include "shapsapp.rh"

MDI_MENU MENU
{
 POPUP "&File"
 {
  MENUITEM "&New", CM_MDIFILENEW
  MENUITEM "&Open...", CM_MDIFILEOPEN
  MENUITEM "&Close", CM_FILECLOSE
  MENUITEM SEPARATOR
  MENUITEM "&Save", CM_FILESAVE, GRAYED
  MENUITEM "Save &As...", CM_FILESAVEAS, GRAYED
  MENUITEM SEPARATOR
  MENUITEM "Print Pre&view...", CM_FILEPRINTPREVIEW, GRAYED
  MENUITEM "&Print...", CM_FILEPRINT, GRAYED
  MENUITEM "P&rint Setup...", CM_FILEPRINTERSETUP, GRAYED
  MENUITEM SEPARATOR
  MENUITEM "E&xit\tAlt+F4", CM_EXIT
 }

 POPUP "&Edit"
 {
  MENUITEM "&Undo\tAlt+BkSp", CM_EDITUNDO, GRAYED
  MENUITEM SEPARATOR
```

```
  MENUITEM "Cu&t\tShift+Del", CM_EDITCUT, GRAYED
  MENUITEM "&Copy\tCtrl+Ins", CM_EDITCOPY, GRAYED
  MENUITEM "&Paste\tShift+Ins", CM_EDITPASTE, GRAYED
  MENUITEM SEPARATOR
  MENUITEM "Clear &All\tCtrl+Del", CM_EDITCLEAR, GRAYED
  MENUITEM "&Delete\tDel", CM_EDITDELETE, GRAYED
  }

 POPUP "&Shapes"
 {
  MENUITEM "&Rectangle", CM_SHAPESRECTANGLE
  MENUITEM "&Ellipse", CM_SHAPESELLIPSE
  MENUITEM SEPARATOR
  MENUITEM "&Red", CM_SHAPESRED
  MENUITEM "&Green", CM_SHAPESGREEN
  MENUITEM "&Blue", CM_SHAPESBLUE
  MENUITEM "&Other...", CM_SHAPESOTHER
 }

 POPUP "&Window"
 {
  MENUITEM "&New Window", CM_VIEWCREATE
  MENUITEM "&Cascade", CM_CASCADECHILDREN
  MENUITEM "&Tile", CM_TILECHILDREN
  MENUITEM "Arrange &Icons", CM_ARRANGEICONS
  MENUITEM "C&lose All", CM_CLOSECHILDREN
 }
POPUP "&Help"
 {
  MENUITEM "&About...", CM_HELPABOUT
 }
}

// Accelerator table for short-cut to menu commands (include\owl\editfile.rc).
MDI_MENU ACCELERATORS
BEGIN
  VK_DELETE, CM_EDITCUT, VIRTKEY, SHIFT
  VK_INSERT, CM_EDITCOPY, VIRTKEY, CONTROL
  VK_INSERT, CM_EDITPASTE, VIRTKEY, SHIFT
  VK_DELETE, CM_EDITCLEAR, VIRTKEY, CONTROL
  VK_BACK,   CM_EDITUNDO, VIRTKEY, ALT
  VK_F3,     CM_EDITFINDNEXT, VIRTKEY
END

// Table of help hints displayed in the status bar.
STRINGTABLE
{
 -1, "File/document operations"
 CM_MDIFILENEW, "Creates a new document"
 CM_MDIFILEOPEN, "Opens an existing document"
 CM_VIEWCREATE, "Create a new view for this document"
 CM_FILEREVERT, "Reverts changes to last document save"
 CM_FILECLOSE, "Close this document"
 CM_FILESAVE, "Saves this document"
 CM_FILESAVEAS, "Saves this document with a new name"
 CM_FILEPRINT, "Print this document"
 CM_FILEPRINTERSETUP, "Setup this document print characteristics"
 CM_FILEPRINTPREVIEW, "Display full pages as read-only"
 CM_EXIT, "Quits ShapesApp and prompts to save the documents"
 CM_EDITUNDO -1, "Edit operations"
```

```
    CM_EDITUNDO, "Reverses the last operation"
    CM_EDITCUT, "Cuts the selection and puts it on the Clipboard"
    CM_EDITCOPY, "Copies the selection and puts it on the Clipboard"
    CM_EDITPASTE, "Inserts the clipboard contents at the insertion point"
    CM_EDITDELETE, "Deletes the selection"
    CM_EDITCLEAR, "Clear the document"
    CM_EDITADD, "Insert a new line"
    CM_EDITEDIT, "Edit the current line"
    CM_EDITFIND -1, "Search/replace operations"
    CM_SHAPESRED, "Draw the next shape in red"
    CM_EDITREPLACE, "Finds the specified text and changes it"
    CM_EDITFINDNEXT, "Finds the next match"
    CM_CASCADECHILDREN -1, "Window arrangement and selection"
    CM_CASCADECHILDREN, "Cascades open windows"
    CM_TILECHILDREN, "Tiles open windows"
    CM_ARRANGEICONS, "Arranges iconic windows along bottom"
    CM_CLOSECHILDREN, "Closes all open windows"
    CM_HELPABOUT -1, "Access About"
    CM_HELPABOUT, "About the Shapes application"
    CM_SHAPESGREEN, "Draw the next shape in green"
    CM_SHAPESBLUE, "Draw the next shape in blue"
    CM_SHAPESRECTANGLE, "Draw a rectangle"
}


// OWL string table
// EditFile (include\owl\editfile.rc and include\owl\editsear.rc)
STRINGTABLE LOADONCALL MOVEABLE DISCARDABLE
BEGIN
    IDS_CANNOTFIND,            "Cannot find ""%s""."
    IDS_UNABLEREAD,            "Unable to read file %s from disk."
    IDS_UNABLEWRITE,           "Unable to write file %s to disk."
    IDS_FILECHANGED,           "The text in the %s file has changed.\n\nDo you want to
                               save the changes?"
    IDS_FILEFILTER,            "Text files (*.TXT)|*.TXT|AllFiles (*.*)|*.*|"
END


// ListView (include\owl\listview.rc)
STRINGTABLE LOADONCALL MOVEABLE DISCARDABLE
BEGIN
  IDS_LISTNUM,  "Line number %d"
END


// Doc/View (include\owl\docview.rc)
STRINGTABLE LOADONCALL MOVEABLE DISCARDABLE
BEGIN
    IDS_DOCMANAGERFILE,        "&File"
    IDS_DOCLIST,               "--Document Type--"
    IDS_VIEWLIST,              "--View Type--"
    IDS_UNTITLED,              "Document"
    IDS_UNABLEOPEN,            "Unable to open document."
    IDS_UNABLECLOSE,           "Unable to close document."
    IDS_READERROR,             "Document read error."
    IDS_WRITEERROR,            "Document write error."
    IDS_DOCCHANGED,            "The document has been changed.\n\nDo you want to save the
                               changes?"
    IDS_NOTCHANGED,            "The document has not been changed."
    IDS_NODOCMANAGER,          "Document Manager not present."
    IDS_NOMEMORYFORVIEW,       "Insufficient memory for view."
    IDS_DUPLICATEDOC,          "Document already loaded."
END
```

```
// Printer (include\owl\printer.rc)
STRINGTABLE LOADONCALL MOVEABLE DISCARDABLE
BEGIN
    IDS_PRNON,                  " on "
    IDS_PRNERRORTEMPLATE,       "'%s' not printed. %s."
    IDS_PRNOUTOFMEMORY,         "Out of memory"
    IDS_PRNOUTOFDISK,           "Out of disk space"
    IDS_PRNCANCEL,              "Printing canceled"
    IDS_PRNMGRABORT,            "Printing aborted in Print Manager"
    IDS_PRNGENERROR,            "Error encountered during print"
    IDS_PRNERRORCAPTION,        "Print Error"
END
// Exception string resources (include\owl\except.rc)
STRINGTABLE LOADONCALL MOVEABLE DISCARDABLE
BEGIN
    IDS_OWLEXCEPTION,           "ObjectWindows Exception"
    IDS_UNHANDLEDXMSG,          "Unhandled Exception"
    IDS_OKTORESUME,             "OK to resume?"
    IDS_UNKNOWNEXCEPTION,       "Unknown exception"
    IDS_UNKNOWNERROR,           "Unknown error"
    IDS_NOAPP,                  "No application object"
    IDS_OUTOFMEMORY,            "Out of memory"
    IDS_INVALIDMODULE,          "Invalid module specified for window"
    IDS_INVALIDMAINWINDOW,      "Invalid MainWindow"
    IDS_INVALIDWINDOW,          "Invalid window %s"
    IDS_INVALIDCHILDWINDOW,     "Invalid child window %s"
    IDS_INVALIDCLIENTWINDOW,    "Invalid client window %s"
    IDS_CLASSREGISTERFAIL,      "Class registration fail for window %s"
    IDS_CHILDREGISTERFAIL,      "Child class registration fail for window %s"
    IDS_WINDOWCREATEFAIL,       "Create fail for window %s"
    IDS_WINDOWEXECUTEFAIL,      "Execute fail for window %s"
    IDS_CHILDCREATEFAIL,        "Child create fail for window %s"
    IDS_MENUFAILURE,            "Menu creation failure"
    IDS_VALIDATORSYNTAX,        "Validator syntax error"
    IDS_PRINTERERROR,           "Printer error"
    IDS_LAYOUTINCOMPLETE,       "Incomplete layout constraints specified in window %s"
    IDS_LAYOUTBADRELWIN,        "Invalid relative window specified in layout constraint in
                                window %s"
    IDS_GDIFAILURE,             "GDI failure"
    IDS_GDIALLOCFAIL,           "GDI allocate failure"
    IDS_GDICREATEFAIL,          "GDI creation failure"
    IDS_GDIRESLOADFAIL,         "GDI resource load failure"
    IDS_GDIFILEREADFAIL,        "GDI file read failure"
    IDS_GDIDELETEFAIL,          "GDI object %X delete failure"
    IDS_GDIDESTROYFAIL,         "GDI object %X destroy failure"
    IDS_INVALIDDIBHANDLE,       "Invalid DIB handle %X"
END

// General Window's status bar messages (include\owl\statusba.rc)
STRINGTABLE
BEGIN
    IDS_MODES                   "EXT|CAPS|NUM|SCRL|OVR|REC"
    IDS_MODESOFF                "   |    |   |    |   |   "
    SC_SIZE,                    "Changes the size of the window"
    SC_MOVE,                    "Moves the window to another position"
    SC_MINIMIZE,                "Reduces the window to an icon"
    SC_MAXIMIZE,                "Enlarges the window to it maximum size"
    SC_RESTORE,                 "Restores the window to its previous size"
    SC_CLOSE,                   "Closes the window"
    SC_TASKLIST,                "Opens task list"
```

```
    SC_NEXTWINDOW,                 "Switches to next window"
END

// Validator messages (include\owl\validate.rc)
STRINGTABLE LOADONCALL MOVEABLE DISCARDABLE
BEGIN
    IDS_VALPXPCONFORM              "Input does not conform to picture:\n""""%s"""""
    IDS_VALINVALIDCHAR             "Invalid character in input"
    IDS_VALNOTINRANGE              "Value is not in the range %ld to %ld."
    IDS_VALNOTINLIST               "Input is not in valid-list"
END

// Bitmaps used by the speedbar.  Each bitmap is associated with a
// particular menu command.
CM_MDIFILENEW BITMAP "new.bmp"
CM_MDIFILEOPEN BITMAP "open.bmp"
CM_FILESAVE BITMAP "save.bmp"
CM_EDITUNDO BITMAP "undo.bmp"
CM_EDITCUT BITMAP "cut.bmp"
CM_EDITCOPY BITMAP "copy.bmp"
CM_EDITPASTE BITMAP "paste.bmp"
CM_FILEPRINTPREVIEW  BITMAP "preview.bmp"
CM_FILEPRINT BITMAP "print.bmp"
// Print Preview speedbar bitmaps
APX_PPR_PREVIOUS BITMAP "previous.bmp"
APX_PPR_NEXT BITMAP "next.bmp"
APX_PPR_ONEUP BITMAP "preview1.bmp"
APX_PPR_TWOUP BITMAP "preview2.bmp"


// Misc. application definitions
// MDI document ICON
IDI_DOC ICON "mdichild.ico"
// Application ICON
IDI_MDIAPPLICATION ICON "appldocv.ico"
// About box.
// BWCC bitmaps for the about box.
#define IDB_BWCC_ABOUT_ICON    1450
#define IDB_BWCC_ABOUT_ICON2   2450 // This definition is for EGA and related video modes.
IDB_BWCC_ABOUT_ICON  BITMAP "borabout.bmp"
IDB_BWCC_ABOUT_ICON2 BITMAP "borabout.bmp"
IDD_ABOUT DIALOG 56, 40, 199, 98
STYLE DS_MODALFRAME | WS_POPUP | WS_CAPTION | WS_SYSMENU
CLASS "bordlg_gray"
CAPTION "About Shapes"
FONT 8, "MS Sans Serif"
BEGIN
    CONTROL "", -1, "BorShade", BSS_GROUP | BSS_CAPTION | BSS_LEFT | WS_CHILD |
        WS_VISIBLE, 48, 6, 144, 51
    CONTROL "Version", IDC_VERSION, "BorStatic", SS_LEFT | WS_CHILD | WS_VISIBLE |
        SS_NOPREFIX | WS_GROUP, 51, 18, 138, 9
    CONTROL "Button", IDB_BWCC_ABOUT_ICON - 1000, "BorBtn", BBS_BITMAP | WS_CHILD |
        WS_VISIBLE | WS_TABSTOP, 6, 9, 39, 42
    CONTROL "Shapes", -1, "BorStatic", SS_LEFT | WS_CHILD | WS_VISIBLE | SS_NOPREFIX |
        WS_GROUP, 51, 9, 138, 9
    CONTROL "", IDC_COPYRIGHT, "BorStatic", SS_LEFT | WS_CHILD | WS_VISIBLE | SS_NOPREFIX
        | WS_GROUP, 51, 27, 138, 27
    CONTROL "", IDC_DEBUG, "BorStatic", SS_RIGHT | WS_CHILD | WS_VISIBLE | SS_NOPREFIX |
        WS_GROUP, 131, 87, 66, 8
    CONTROL "", IDOK, "BorBtn", BS_DEFPUSHBUTTON | WS_CHILD | WS_VISIBLE | WS_TABSTOP, 81,
        66, 37, 25
END
```

```
// Printer abort box
IDD_ABORTDIALOG DIALOG 70, 50, 163, 65
STYLE DS_MODALFRAME | WS_POPUP | WS_VISIBLE | WS_CAPTION | WS_SYSMENU
CLASS "bordlg"
CAPTION "Printing"
BEGIN
    CONTROL "Button", IDCANCEL, "BorBtn", BS_DEFPUSHBUTTON | WS_CHILD | WS_VISIBLE |
WS_TABSTOP, 48, 36, 33, 21
    CTEXT "Now printing Page %d of", ID_PAGE, 0, 8, 130, 8, SS_CENTER | NOT WS_VISIBLE |
WS_GROUP | SS_NOPREFIX
    CTEXT "Now printing", -1, 0, 8, 130, 8, SS_NOPREFIX
    CTEXT "'%s' on the", ID_TITLE, 0, 16, 130, 8, SS_NOPREFIX
    CTEXT "", ID_PORT, 0, 24, 130, 8, SS_CENTER | NOT WS_VISIBLE | WS_GROUP | SS_NOPREFIX
    CTEXT "%s on %s", ID_DEVICE, 0, 24, 130, 8, SS_NOPREFIX
END
// TInputDialog class dialog box
IDD_INPUTDIALOG DIALOG 20, 24, 180, 70
STYLE WS_POPUP | WS_CAPTION | DS_SETFONT
CLASS "bordlg"
FONT 8, "Helv"
BEGIN
    LTEXT "", ID_PROMPT, 10, 8, 160, 10, SS_NOPREFIX
    CONTROL "", ID_INPUT, "EDIT", WS_CHILD | WS_VISIBLE | WS_BORDER | WS_TABSTOP |
ES_AUTOHSCROLL, 10, 20, 160, 12
    CONTROL "Button", IDOK, "BorBtn", BS_DEFPUSHBUTTON | WS_CHILD | WS_VISIBLE |
WS_TABSTOP, 47, 42, 37, 26
    CONTROL "Button", IDCANCEL, "BorBtn", BS_DEFPUSHBUTTON | WS_CHILD | WS_VISIBLE |
WS_TABSTOP, 93, 42, 38, 25
END


// Horizontal slider thumb bitmap for TSlider and VSlider (include\owl\slider.rc)
IDB_HSLIDERTHUMB BITMAP PRELOAD MOVEABLE DISCARDABLE
BEGIN
    '42 4D 66 01 00 00 00 00 00 00 76 00 00 00 28 00'
    '00 00 12 00 00 00 14 00 00 00 01 00 04 00 00 00'
    '00 00 F0 00 00 00 00 00 00 00 00 00 00 00 00 00'
    '00 00 10 00 00 00 00 00 00 00 00 00 C0 00 00 C0'
    '00 00 00 C0 C0 00 C0 00 00 00 C0 00 C0 00 C0 C0'
    '00 00 C0 C0 C0 00 80 80 80 00 00 00 FF 00 00 FF'
    '00 00 00 FF FF 00 FF 00 00 00 FF 00 FF 00 FF FF'
    '00 00 FF FF FF 00 BB BB 0B BB BB BB B0 BB BB 00'
    '00 00 BB B0 80 BB BB BB 08 0B BB 00 00 00 BB 08'
    'F8 0B BB B0 87 70 BB 00 00 00 B0 8F F8 80 BB 08'
    '77 77 0B 00 00 00 08 F8 88 88 00 88 88 87 70 00'
    '00 00 0F F7 77 88 00 88 77 77 70 00 00 00 0F F8'
    '88 88 00 88 88 87 70 00 00 00 0F F7 77 88 00 88'
    '77 77 70 00 00 00 0F F8 88 88 00 88 88 87 70 00'
    '00 00 0F F7 77 88 00 88 77 77 70 00 00 00 0F F8'
    '88 88 00 88 88 87 70 00 00 00 0F F7 77 88 00 88'
    '77 77 70 00 00 00 0F F8 88 88 00 88 88 87 70 00'
    '00 00 0F F7 77 88 00 88 77 77 70 00 00 00 0F F8'
    '88 88 00 88 88 87 70 00 00 00 0F F7 77 88 00 88'
    '77 77 70 00 00 00 0F F8 88 88 00 88 88 87 70 00'
    '00 00 0F F7 77 78 00 88 77 77 70 00 00 00 0F FF'
    'FF FF 00 88 88 88 80 00 00 00 B0 00 00 00 BB 00'
    '00 00 0B 00 00 00'
END


// Vertical slider thumb bitmap for TSlider and HSlider (include\owl\slider.rc)
IDB_VSLIDERTHUMB BITMAP PRELOAD MOVEABLE DISCARDABLE
```

```
BEGIN
    '42 4D 2A 01 00 00 00 00 00 00 76 00 00 00 28 00'
    '00 00 28 00 00 00 09 00 00 00 01 00 04 00 00 00'
    '00 00 B4 00 00 00 00 00 00 00 00 00 00 00 00 00'
    '00 00 10 00 00 00 00 00 00 00 C0 00 00 00 C0'
    '00 00 00 C0 C0 00 C0 00 00 00 C0 00 C0 00 C0 C0'
    '00 00 C0 C0 C0 00 80 80 80 00 00 00 FF 00 00 FF'
    '00 00 00 FF FF 00 FF 00 00 00 FF 00 FF 00 FF FF'
    '00 00 FF FF FF 00 B0 00 00 00 00 00 00 00 00 0B'
    'B0 00 00 00 00 00 00 00 00 0B 0F 88 88 88 88 88'
    '88 88 88 80 08 88 88 88 88 88 88 88 80 0F 77'
    '77 77 77 77 77 77 77 80 08 77 77 77 77 77 77 77'
    '77 80 0F 77 FF FF FF FF FF FF F7 80 08 77 FF FF'
    'FF FF FF FF F7 80 0F 70 00 00 00 00 00 77 80'
    '08 70 00 00 00 00 00 77 80 0F 77 77 77 77 77'
    '77 77 77 80 08 77 77 77 77 77 77 77 80 0F 77'
    '77 77 77 77 77 77 80 08 77 77 77 77 77 77 77'
    '77 80 0F FF FF FF FF FF FF FF F0 08 88 88 88'
    '88 88 88 88 88 80 B0 00 00 00 00 00 00 00 0B'
    'B0 00 00 00 00 00 00 00 00 0B'
END

// Version info
#if !defined(__DEBUG_)
// Non-Debug VERSIONINFO
1 VERSIONINFO LOADONCALL MOVEABLE
FILEVERSION 1, 0, 0, 0
PRODUCTVERSION 1, 0, 0, 0
FILEFLAGSMASK 0
FILEFLAGS VS_FFI_FILEFLAGSMASK
FILEOS VOS__WINDOWS16
FILETYPE VFT_APP
BEGIN
    BLOCK "StringFileInfo"
    BEGIN
        // Language type = U.S. English (0x0409) and Character Set = Windows,
Multilingual(0x04e4)
        BLOCK "040904E4"                // Matches VarFileInfo Translation hex value.
        BEGIN
            VALUE "CompanyName", "The Coriolis Group\000"
            VALUE "FileDescription", "Shapes for Windows\000"
            VALUE "FileVersion", "1.0\000"
            VALUE "InternalName", "Shapes\000"
            VALUE "LegalCopyright", "©1994 Paul S. Cilwa. All Rights Reserved.\000"
            VALUE "LegalTrademarks", "Windows (TM) is a trademark of Microsoft
                                      Corporation\000"
            VALUE "OriginalFilename", "Shapes.EXE\000"
            VALUE "ProductName", "Shapes\000"
            VALUE "ProductVersion", "1.0\000"
        END
    END
    BLOCK "VarFileInfo"
    BEGIN
        VALUE "Translation", 0x0409, 0x04e4   // U.S. English(0x0409) & Windows
                                              Multilingual(0x04e4) 1252
    END
END
#else
```

```
// Debug VERSIONINFO
1 VERSIONINFO LOADONCALL MOVEABLE
FILEVERSION 1, 0, 0, 0
PRODUCTVERSION 1, 0, 0, 0
FILEFLAGSMASK VS_FF_DEBUG | VS_FF_PRERELEASE | VS_FF_PATCHED | VS_FF_PRIVATEBUILD |
    VS_FF_SPECIALBUILD
FILEFLAGS VS_FFI_FILEFLAGSMASK
FILEOS VOS__WINDOWS16
FILETYPE VFT_APP
BEGIN
    BLOCK "StringFileInfo"
    BEGIN
    // Language type = U.S. English (0x0409) and Character Set = Windows, Multilingual(0x04e4)
        BLOCK "040904E4"                    // Matches VarFileInfo Translation hex value.
        BEGIN
            VALUE "CompanyName", "The Coriolis Group\000"
            VALUE "FileDescription", "Shapes for Windows\000"
            VALUE "FileVersion", "1.0\000"
            VALUE "InternalName", "Shapes\000"
            VALUE "LegalCopyright", "©1994 Paul S. Cilwa. All Rights Reserved.\000"
            VALUE "LegalTrademarks", "Windows (TM) is a trademark of Microsoft
                    Corporation\000"
            VALUE "OriginalFilename", "Shapes.EXE\000"
            VALUE "ProductName", "Shapes\000"
            VALUE "ProductVersion", "1.0\000"
            VALUE "SpecialBuild", "Debug Version\000"
            VALUE "PrivateBuild", "Built by Paul S. Cilwa\000"
        END
    END
BLOCK "VarFileInfo"
    BEGIN
        VALUE "Translation", 0x0409, 0x04e4    // U.S. English(0x0409) & Windows
                                                  Multilingual(0x04e4) 1252
    END
END
#endif
```

SHPSABTD.H

```
#if !defined(__shpsabtd_h)      // Sentry, use file only if it's not already included.
#define __shpsabtd_h
/*  Project Shapes
    The Coriolis Group
    ©1994 Paul S. Cilwa. All Rights Reserved.
    SUBSYSTEM:    shapes.exe Application
    FILE:         shpsabtd.h
    AUTHOR:       Paul S. Cilwa
    OVERVIEW
    ========
    Class definition for ShapesAboutDlg (TDialog).
*/
#include <owl\owlpch.h>
#pragma hdrstop
#include "shapsapp.rh"                  // Definition of all resources.
//{{TDialog = ShapesAboutDlg}}
class ShapesAboutDlg : public TDialog {
public:
    ShapesAboutDlg (TWindow *parent, TResId resId = IDD_ABOUT, TModule *module = 0);
    virtual ~ShapesAboutDlg ();
```

```
//{{ShapesAboutDlgVIRTUAL_BEGIN}}
public:
    void SetupWindow ();
//{{ShapesAboutDlgVIRTUAL_END}}
};    //{{ShapesAboutDlg}}
// Reading the VERSIONINFO resource.
class ProjectRCVersion {
public:
    ProjectRCVersion (TModule *module);
    virtual ~ProjectRCVersion ();
    BOOL GetProductName (LPSTR &prodName);
    BOOL GetProductVersion (LPSTR &prodVersion);
    BOOL GetCopyright (LPSTR &copyright);
    BOOL GetDebug (LPSTR &debug);
protected:
    LPBYTE      TransBlock;
    void FAR    *FVData;
private:
    // Don't allow this object to be copied.
    ProjectRCVersion (const ProjectRCVersion &);
    ProjectRCVersion & operator =(const ProjectRCVersion &);
};
#endif                                    // __shpsabtd_h sentry.
```

SHPSABTD.CPP

```
/*  Project Shapes
    The Coriolis Group
    ©1994 Paul S. Cilwa. All Rights Reserved.
SUBSYSTEM:    shapes.exe Application
    FILE:        shpsabtd.cpp
    AUTHOR:      Paul S. Cilwa
OVERVIEW
    ~~~~~~~~~
    Source file for implementation of ShapesAboutDlg (TDialog).
*/
#include <owl\owlpch.h>
#pragma hdrstop
#include <owl\static.h>
#if !defined(__FLAT__)
#include <ver.h>
#endif
#include "shapsapp.h"
#include "shpsabtd.h"

ProjectRCVersion::ProjectRCVersion (TModule *module)
{
    char    appFName[255];
    char    subBlockName[255];
    DWORD   fvHandle;
    UINT    vSize;
    FVData = 0;
    module->GetModuleFileName(appFName, sizeof(appFName));
    DWORD dwSize = GetFileVersionInfoSize(appFName, &fvHandle);
    if (dwSize) {
        FVData  = (void FAR *)new char[(UINT)dwSize];
        if (GetFileVersionInfo(appFName, fvHandle, dwSize, FVData)) {
            // Copy string to buffer so if the -dc compiler switch (Put constant strings
```

```
            // in code segments) is on, VerQueryValue will work under Win16.  This works
            // around a problem in Microsoft's ver.dll which writes to the string pointed
            // to by subBlockName.
            lstrcpy(subBlockName, "\\VarFileInfo\\Translation");
            if (!VerQueryValue(FVData, subBlockName, (void FAR* FAR*)&TransBlock,
              &vSize)) {
                delete FVData;
                FVData = 0;
            } else
            // Swap the words so wsprintf will print the long-charset in the correct format.
                *(DWORD *)TransBlock = MAKELONG(HIWORD(*(DWORD *)TransBlock),
                  LOWORD(*(DWORD *)TransBlock));
        }
    }
}


ProjectRCVersion::~ProjectRCVersion ()
{
    if (FVData)
        delete FVData;
}


BOOL ProjectRCVersion::GetProductName (LPSTR &prodName)
{
    UINT    vSize;
    char    subBlockName[255];
    wsprintf(subBlockName, "\\StringFileInfo\\%08lx\\%s", *(DWORD *)TransBlock,
            (LPSTR)"ProductName");
    return FVData ? VerQueryValue(FVData, subBlockName, (void FAR* FAR*)&prodName, &vSize)
: FALSE;
}


BOOL ProjectRCVersion::GetProductVersion (LPSTR &prodVersion)
{
    UINT    vSize;
    char    subBlockName[255];
    wsprintf(subBlockName, "\\StringFileInfo\\%08lx\\%s", *(DWORD *)TransBlock,
            (LPSTR)"ProductVersion");
    return FVData ? VerQueryValue(FVData, subBlockName, (void FAR* FAR*)&prodVersion,
&vSize) : FALSE;
}


BOOL ProjectRCVersion::GetCopyright (LPSTR &copyright)
{
    UINT    vSize;
    char    subBlockName[255];
    wsprintf(subBlockName, "\\StringFileInfo\\%08lx\\%s", *(DWORD *)TransBlock,
            (LPSTR)"LegalCopyright");
    return FVData ? VerQueryValue(FVData, subBlockName, (void FAR* FAR*)&copyright,
&vSize) : FALSE;
}


BOOL ProjectRCVersion::GetDebug (LPSTR &debug)
{
    UINT    vSize;
    char    subBlockName[255];
    wsprintf(subBlockName, "\\StringFileInfo\\%08lx\\%s", *(DWORD *)TransBlock,
            (LPSTR)"SpecialBuild");
    return FVData ? VerQueryValue(FVData, subBlockName, (void FAR* FAR*)&debug, &vSize) :
```

```
FALSE;
}

//{{ShapesAboutDlg Implementation}}
// ShapesAboutDlg
// Construction/Destruction handling.
ShapesAboutDlg::ShapesAboutDlg (TWindow *parent, TResId resId, TModule *module)
    : TDialog(parent, resId, module)
{
    // INSERT>> Your constructor code here
}

ShapesAboutDlg::~ShapesAboutDlg ()
{
    Destroy();
    // INSERT>> Your destructor code here
}

void ShapesAboutDlg::SetupWindow ()
{
    LPSTR prodName = 0, prodVersion = 0, copyright = 0, debug = 0;
    // Get the static text for the value based on VERSIONINFO
    TStatic *versionCtrl = new TStatic(this, IDC_VERSION, 255);
    TStatic *copyrightCtrl = new TStatic(this, IDC_COPYRIGHT, 255);
    TStatic *debugCtrl = new TStatic(this, IDC_DEBUG, 255);
    TDialog::SetupWindow();
    // Process the VERSIONINFO
    ProjectRCVersion applVersion(GetModule());
    // Get the product name and product version strings
    if (applVersion.GetProductName(prodName) &&
      applVersion.GetProductVersion(prodVersion)) {
        // IDC_VERSION is the product name and version number, the initial value of
        // IDC_VERSION is the word Version (in whatever language) product name VERSION
        // product version.
        char    buffer[255];
        char    versionName[128];
        buffer[0] = '\0';
        versionName[0] = '\0';
        versionCtrl->GetText(versionName, sizeof(versionName));
        wsprintf(buffer, "%s %s %s", prodName, versionName, prodVersion);
        versionCtrl->SetText(buffer);
    }
    //Get the legal copyright string
    if (applVersion.GetCopyright(copyright))
        copyrightCtrl->SetText(copyright);
    // Only get the SpecialBuild text if the VERSIONINFO resource is there
    if (applVersion.GetDebug(debug))
        debugCtrl->SetText(debug);
}
```

SHPSDOC.H

```
#ifndef __SHPSDOC_H__
#define __SHPSDOC_H__
#include <owl\filedoc.h>
#include "shape.h"

class TShapesDoc : public TFileDocument
    {
```

```
     public:
        TShapesDoc (TDocument * Parent = 0);
        virtual ~TShapesDoc ();
        void Add (TShape * aShape);
        void Draw (TDC & dc);
        virtual BOOL IsOpen (void);
        virtual BOOL Open (int Mode, LPCSTR Path = 0);
        virtual BOOL Commit (BOOL Force);
        virtual BOOL Revert (BOOL Clear);
        virtual BOOL Close (void);
     protected:
        TShapeArray Data;
        BOOL Opened;
     };

typedef enum
     {
     vnAppend = vnCustomBase,
     vnModify,
     vnClear
     } TShapesEvents;
NOTIFY_SIG (vnAppend, TShape *)
NOTIFY_SIG (vnModify, void)
NOTIFY_SIG (vnClear, void)
#define EV_VN_APPEND VN_DEFINE(vnAppend, VnAppend, long)
#define EV_VN_MODIFY VN_DEFINE(vnModify, VnModify, void)
#define EV_VN_CLEAR VN_DEFINE(vnClear, VnClear, void)
#endif
```

SHPSDOC.CPP

```
#include <owl\owlpch.h>
#pragma hdrstop
#include "shpsdoc.h"
#include "waitcur.h"
TShapesDoc::TShapesDoc (TDocument * Parent)
     : TFileDocument (Parent), Data (100, 0, 50), Opened (FALSE)
     { }

TShapesDoc::~TShapesDoc ()
     { }

void TShapesDoc::Add (TShape * aShape)
     {
     Data.Add (aShape);
     SetDirty (TRUE);
     }

void TShapesDoc::Draw (TDC & dc)
     {
     TShapeArrayIterator S (Data);
     while (S)
        {
        S.Current()->Draw (dc);
        S++;
        }
     }
```

```
BOOL TShapesDoc::IsOpen (void)
   { return Opened; }

BOOL TShapesDoc::Open (int, LPCSTR)
   {
   TWaitCursor Wait;
   ifpstream In (GetDocPath());
   Data.Flush();
   WORD ShapeCount;
   In >> ShapeCount;
   while (ShapeCount--)
      {
      TShape * Shape;
      In >> Shape;
      Add (Shape);
      }
   SetDirty (FALSE);
   Opened = TRUE;
   return TRUE;
   }

BOOL TShapesDoc::Commit (BOOL Force)
   {
   if (! TFileDocument::Commit (Force))
      return FALSE;
   TWaitCursor Wait;
   ofpstream Out (GetDocPath());
   WORD ShapeCount = Data.GetItemsInContainer();
   Out << ShapeCount;
   for (register WORD s = 0; s < ShapeCount; s++)
      Out << Data[s];
   SetDirty (FALSE);
   return TRUE;
   }

BOOL TShapesDoc::Revert (BOOL Clear)
   {
   if (! TFileDocument::Revert (Clear))
      return FALSE;
   if (! Clear)
      Open (NULL);
   return TRUE;
   }

BOOL TShapesDoc::Close (void)
   {
   if (! TFileDocument::Close ())
      return FALSE;
   Opened = FALSE;
   return TRUE;
   }
```

SHPSMDI1.H

```
#if !defined(__shpsmdi1_h)        // Sentry, use file only if it's not already included.
#define __shpsmdi1_h
/*  Project Shapes
    The Coriolis Group
    ©1994 Paul S. Cilwa. All Rights Reserved.
```

```
    SUBSYSTEM:     shapes.exe Application
    FILE:          shpsmdi1.h
    AUTHOR:        Paul S. Cilwa
    OVERVIEW
    ========
    Class definition for ShapesMDIChild (TMDIChild).
*/
#include <owl\owlpch.h>
#pragma hdrstop
#include <owl\editfile.h>
#include <owl\listbox.h>
#include "shapsapp.rh"              // Definition of all resources.
//{{TMDIChild = ShapesMDIChild}}
class ShapesMDIChild : public TMDIChild {
public:
    ShapesMDIChild (TMDIClient &parent, const char far *title, TWindow *clientWnd, BOOL
                    shrinkToClient = FALSE, TModule* module = 0);
    virtual ~ShapesMDIChild ();
//{{ShapesMDIChildVIRTUAL_BEGIN}}
public:
    virtual void Paint (TDC& dc, BOOL erase, TRect& rect);
//{{ShapesMDIChildVIRTUAL_END}}
//{{ShapesMDIChildRSP_TBL_BEGIN}}
protected:
    void EvGetMinMaxInfo (MINMAXINFO far& minmaxinfo);
//{{ShapesMDIChildRSP_TBL_END}}
DECLARE_RESPONSE_TABLE(ShapesMDIChild);
};      //{{ShapesMDIChild}}

#endif                                      // __shpsmdi1_h sentry.
```

SHPSMDI1.CPP

```
/*  Project Shapes
    The Coriolis Group
    ©1994 Paul S. Cilwa. All Rights Reserved.
    SUBSYSTEM:     shapes.exe Application
    FILE:          shpsmdi1.cpp
    AUTHOR:        Paul S. Cilwa
    OVERVIEW
    ========
    Source file for implementation of ShapesMDIChild (TMDIChild).
*/
#include <owl\owlpch.h>
#pragma hdrstop
include "shapsapp.h"
#include "shpsmdi1.h"
#include <stdio.h>

//{{ShapesMDIChild Implementation}}
// Build a response table for all messages/commands handled
// by ShapesMDIChild derived from TMDIChild.
DEFINE_RESPONSE_TABLE1(ShapesMDIChild, TMDIChild)
//{{ShapesMDIChildRSP_TBL_BEGIN}}
    EV_WM_GETMINMAXINFO,
//{{ShapesMDIChildRSP_TBL_END}}
END_RESPONSE_TABLE;
```

```
// ShapesMDIChild
// Construction/Destruction handling
ShapesMDIChild::ShapesMDIChild (TMDIClient &parent, const char far *title, TWindow
  *clientWnd, BOOL shrinkToClient, TModule *module)
    : TMDIChild (parent, title, clientWnd, shrinkToClient, module)
{
    // INSERT>> Your constructor code here.

}

ShapesMDIChild::~ShapesMDIChild ()
{
    Destroy();

    // INSERT>> Your destructor code here.

}

// Paint routine for Window, Printer, and PrintPreview for an TEdit client
void ShapesMDIChild::Paint (TDC & dc, BOOL Erase, TRect & Rect)
   {
   ShapesApp * App = TYPESAFE_DOWNCAST(GetApplication(), ShapesApp);
   if (App)
     if (App->Printing && App->Printer && ! Rect.IsEmpty())
        {
        TWindowView * Client =
           TYPESAFE_DOWNCAST(GetClientWindow(), TWindowView);
        Client->Paint (dc, Erase, Rect);
        }
   }

void ShapesMDIChild::EvGetMinMaxInfo (MINMAXINFO far& minmaxinfo)
{
    ShapesApp *theApp = TYPESAFE_DOWNCAST(GetApplication(), ShapesApp);
    if (theApp) {
        if (theApp->Printing) {
            minmaxinfo.ptMaxSize = TPoint(32000, 32000);
            minmaxinfo.ptMaxTrackSize = TPoint(32000, 32000);
            return;
        }
    }
    TMDIChild::EvGetMinMaxInfo(minmaxinfo);
}
```

SHPSMDIC.H

```
#if !defined(__shpsmdic_h)        // Sentry, use file only if it's not already included.
#define __shpsmdic_h
/* Project Shapes
   The Coriolis Group
   ©1994 Paul S. Cilwa. All Rights Reserved.
   SUBSYSTEM:    shapes.exe Application
   FILE:         shpsmdic.h
   AUTHOR:       Paul S. Cilwa
   OVERVIEW
   ========
   Class definition for ShapesMDIClient (TMDIClient).
*/
```

```
#include <owl\owlpch.h>
#pragma hdrstop
#include <owl\opensave.h>
#include "shapsapp.rh"              // Definition of all resources.

//{{TMDIClient = ShapesMDIClient}}
class ShapesMDIClient : public TMDIClient {
public:
    int                    ChildCount;              // Number of child window created.
    ShapesMDIClient ();
    virtual ~ShapesMDIClient ();
    void OpenFile (const char *fileName = 0);
private:
    void LoadTextFile ();
//{{ShapesMDIClientVIRTUAL_BEGIN}}
protected:
    virtual void SetupWindow ();
//{{ShapesMDIClientVIRTUAL_END}}
//{{ShapesMDIClientRSP_TBL_BEGIN}}
protected:
    void CmFilePrint ();
    void CmFilePrintSetup ();
    void CmFilePrintPreview ();
    void CmPrintEnable (TCommandEnabler &tce);
    void EvDropFiles (TDropInfo);
//{{ShapesMDIClientRSP_TBL_END}}
DECLARE_RESPONSE_TABLE(ShapesMDIClient);
};    //{{ShapesMDIClient}}
#endif                              // __shpsmdic_h sentry.
```

SHPSMDIC.CPP

```
/*  Project Shapes
    The Coriolis Group
    ©1994 Paul S. Cilwa. All Rights Reserved.
    SUBSYSTEM:    shapes.exe Application
    FILE:         shpsmdic.cpp
    AUTHOR:       Paul S. Cilwa
    OVERVIEW
    ========
    Source file for implementation of ShapesMDIClient (TMDIClient).
*/
#include <owl\owlpch.h>
#pragma hdrstop
#include <dir.h>
#include "shapsapp.h"
#include "shpsmdic.h"        ‛
#include "shpsmdi1.h"
#include "apxprint.h"
#include "apxprev.h"

//{{ShapesMDIClient Implementation}}
// Build a response table for all messages/commands handled
// by ShapesMDIClient derived from TMDIClient.
DEFINE_RESPONSE_TABLE1(ShapesMDIClient, TMDIClient)
//{{ShapesMDIClientRSP_TBL_BEGIN}}
    EV_COMMAND(CM_FILEPRINT, CmFilePrint),
    EV_COMMAND(CM_FILEPRINTERSETUP, CmFilePrintSetup),
    EV_COMMAND(CM_FILEPRINTPREVIEW, CmFilePrintPreview),
```

```
    EV_COMMAND_ENABLE(CM_FILEPRINT, CmPrintEnable),
    EV_COMMAND_ENABLE(CM_FILEPRINTERSETUP, CmPrintEnable),
    EV_COMMAND_ENABLE(CM_FILEPRINTPREVIEW, CmPrintEnable),
    EV_WM_DROPFILES,
//{{ShapesMDIClientRSP_TBL_END}}
END_RESPONSE_TABLE;

// ShapesMDIClient
// Construction/Destruction handling
 ShapesMDIClient::ShapesMDIClient ()
 : TMDIClient ()
{
    ChildCount = 0;
    // INSERT>> Your constructor code here.
}

 ShapesMDIClient::~ShapesMDIClient ()
{
    Destroy();
    // INSERT>> Your destructor code here.
}

// ShapesMDIClient
// MDIClient site initialization
void ShapesMDIClient::SetupWindow ()
{
    // Default SetUpWindow processing.
    TMDIClient::SetupWindow ();
    // Accept files via drag/drop in the client window.
    DragAcceptFiles(TRUE);
}

// ShapesMDIClient
// Menu File Print command
void ShapesMDIClient::CmFilePrint ()
{
    // Create Printer object if not already created.
    ShapesApp *theApp = TYPESAFE_DOWNCAST(GetApplication(), ShapesApp);
    if (theApp) {
        if (!theApp->Printer)
            theApp->Printer = new TPrinter;
        // Create Printout window and set characteristics.
        APXPrintOut printout(theApp->Printer, Title, GetActiveMDIChild(), TRUE);
        theApp->Printing++;
        // Bring up the Print dialog and print the document.
        theApp->Printer->Print(GetActiveMDIChild()->GetClientWindow(), printout, TRUE);

        theApp->Printing--;
    }
}

// ShapesMDIClient
// Menu File Print Setup command
void ShapesMDIClient::CmFilePrintSetup ()
{
    ShapesApp *theApp = TYPESAFE_DOWNCAST(GetApplication(), ShapesApp);
    if (theApp) {
        if (!theApp->Printer)
            theApp->Printer = new TPrinter;
        // Bring up the Print Setup dialog
```

```
            theApp->Printer->Setup(this);
    }
}

// ShapesMDIClient
// Menu File Print Preview command
void ShapesMDIClient::CmFilePrintPreview ()
{
    ShapesApp *theApp = TYPESAFE_DOWNCAST(GetApplication(), ShapesApp);
    if (theApp) {
        if (!theApp->Printer)
            theApp->Printer = new TPrinter;
        theApp->Printing++;
        PreviewWindow *prevW = new PreviewWindow(Parent, theApp->Printer,
            GetActiveMDIChild(), "Print Preview", new TLayoutWindow(0));
        prevW->Create();
        GetApplication()->BeginModal(GetApplication()->GetMainWindow());
        // We must destroy the preview window explicitly.  Otherwise, the window will not
        // be destroyed until it's parent the MainWindow is destroyed.
        prevW->Destroy();
        delete prevW;
     theApp->Printing--;
    }
}

// ShapesMDIClient
// Menu enabler used by Print, Print Setup, and Print Preview
void ShapesMDIClient::CmPrintEnable (TCommandEnabler &tce)
{
    if (GetActiveMDIChild()) {
        ShapesApp *theApp = TYPESAFE_DOWNCAST(GetApplication(), ShapesApp);
        if (theApp) {
            // If we have a Printer already created, just test if all is okay.
            // Otherwise, create a Printer object and make sure the printer
            // really exists and then delete the Printer object.
            if (!theApp->Printer) {
                theApp->Printer = new TPrinter;
                tce.Enable(theApp->Printer->GetSetup().Error == 0);
            } else
                tce.Enable(theApp->Printer->GetSetup().Error == 0);
        }
    } else
        tce.Enable(FALSE);
}

void ShapesMDIClient::EvDropFiles (TDropInfo)
{
    Parent->ForwardMessage();
}
```

SHPSVIEW.H

```
#if !defined(__shpsview_h)     // Sentry, use file only if it's not already included.
#define __shpsview_h
/*  Project shapes
    The Coriolis Group
    ©1994 Paul S. Cilwa. All Rights Reserved.
    SUBSYSTEM:    shapes.apx Application
    FILE:         shpsview.h
```

```
    AUTHOR:        Paul S. Cilwa
    OVERVIEW
Class definition for TShapesView (TWindowView).
*/
#include <owl\owlpch.h>
#pragma hdrstop
#include <owl\docview.h>
#include "shapsapp.rh"            // Definition of all resources.
#include "shpsdoc.h"
#include "clipbrd.h"
#include "xcolor.h"
//{{TWindowView = TShapesView}}
class TShapesView : public TWindowView {
public:
    TShapesView (TDocument& doc, TWindow* parent = 0);
    virtual ~TShapesView ();
protected:
  TXColor Color;
  enum { SHAPE_RECTANGLE, SHAPE_ELLIPSE } Geometry;
  TXClipboard Clipboard;
//{{TShapesViewRSP_TBL_BEGIN}}
protected:
    void EvLButtonDown (UINT modKeys, TPoint& point);
    void CmShapesRectangle ();
    void CmShapesEllipse ();
    void CmShapesRed ();
    void CmShapesGreen ();
    void CmShapesBlue ();
    void CmShapesOther ();
    void CmShapesRectangleEnable (TCommandEnabler &tce);
    void CmShapesEllipseEnable (TCommandEnabler &tce);
    void CmShapesRedEnable (TCommandEnabler &tce);
    void CmShapesGreenEnable (TCommandEnabler &tce);
    void CmShapesBlueEnable (TCommandEnabler &tce);
    void CmShapesOtherEnable (TCommandEnabler &tce);
    virtual void Paint(TDC& dc, BOOL erase, TRect& rect);
    TShapesDoc & GetDocument (void);
    BOOL VnAppend (TShape * Shape);
    BOOL VnModify (void);
    BOOL VnClear (void);
    void CmEditCopy ();
    void CmEditPaste ();
    void CmEditPasteEnable (TCommandEnabler &tce);
    //{{TShapesViewRSP_TBL_END}}
DECLARE_RESPONSE_TABLE(TShapesView);
};    //{{TShapesView}}

inline TShapesDoc & TShapesView::GetDocument (void)
   {
   return (TShapesDoc &) TWindowView::GetDocument();
   }
#endif                                   // __shpsview_h sentry.
```

SHPSVIEW.CPP

```
/*  Project shapes
    The Coriolis Group
    ©1994 Paul S. Cilwa. All Rights Reserved.
SUBSYSTEM:    shapes.apx Application
```

```
    FILE:       shpsview.cpp
    AUTHOR:     Paul S. Cilwa
OVERVIEW
    ========
    Source file for implementation of TShapesView (TWindowView).
*/
#include <owl\owlpch.h>
#pragma hdrstop
#include "shpsview.h"
#include "shape.h"
#include "shapsapp.h"
// Build a response table for all messages/commands handled
// by the application.
DEFINE_RESPONSE_TABLE1(TShapesView, TWindowView)
//{{TShapesViewRSP_TBL_BEGIN}}
    EV_WM_LBUTTONDOWN,
    EV_COMMAND(CM_SHAPESRECTANGLE, CmShapesRectangle),
    EV_COMMAND(CM_SHAPESELLIPSE, CmShapesEllipse),
    EV_COMMAND(CM_SHAPESRED, CmShapesRed),
    EV_COMMAND(CM_SHAPESGREEN, CmShapesGreen),
    EV_COMMAND(CM_SHAPESBLUE, CmShapesBlue),
    EV_COMMAND(CM_SHAPESOTHER, CmShapesOther),
    EV_COMMAND_ENABLE(CM_SHAPESRECTANGLE, CmShapesRectangleEnable),
    EV_COMMAND_ENABLE(CM_SHAPESELLIPSE, CmShapesEllipseEnable),
    EV_COMMAND_ENABLE(CM_SHAPESRED, CmShapesRedEnable),
    EV_COMMAND_ENABLE(CM_SHAPESGREEN, CmShapesGreenEnable),
    EV_COMMAND_ENABLE(CM_SHAPESBLUE, CmShapesBlueEnable),
    EV_COMMAND_ENABLE(CM_SHAPESOTHER, CmShapesOtherEnable),
    EV_VN_APPEND,
    EV_VN_MODIFY,
    EV_VN_CLEAR,
    EV_COMMAND(CM_EDITCOPY, CmEditCopy),
    EV_COMMAND(CM_EDITPASTE, CmEditPaste),
    EV_COMMAND_ENABLE(CM_EDITPASTE, CmEditPasteEnable),
//{{TShapesViewRSP_TBL_END}}
END_RESPONSE_TABLE;

//{{TShapesView Implementation}}
TShapesView::TShapesView (TDocument& doc, TWindow* parent)
    : TWindowView(doc, parent),
      Color (TColor::LtRed),
      Geometry (SHAPE_RECTANGLE),
      Clipboard (this)
    {
    Clipboard.Formats.Add (new TClipboardText);
    Clipboard.Formats.Add (new TClipboardBitmap (TSize (1000, 1000)));
    }

TShapesView::~TShapesView ()
{
    Destroy();
    // INSERT>> Your destructor code here.
}

void TShapesView::EvLButtonDown (UINT modKeys, TPoint& point)
    {
    TWindowView::EvLButtonDown(modKeys, point);
    TRect Rect (point, TSize (50, 50));
    TShape * Shape;
```

```
    if (Geometry == SHAPE_RECTANGLE)
       Shape = new TShapeRectangle (Color, Rect);
    else
       Shape = new TShapeEllipse (Color, Rect);
    GetDocument().Add (Shape);
    GetDocument().NotifyViews (vnAppend, (long) Shape);
    }

void TShapesView::CmShapesRectangle ()
   { Geometry = SHAPE_RECTANGLE; }

void TShapesView::CmShapesEllipse ()
   { Geometry = SHAPE_ELLIPSE; }

void TShapesView::CmShapesRed ()
   { Color = TColor::LtRed; }

void TShapesView::CmShapesGreen ()
   { Color = TColor::LtGreen; }

void TShapesView::CmShapesBlue ()
   { Color = TColor::LtBlue; }

void TShapesView::CmShapesOther ()
   {
   if (Color.SelectUserColor (this))
      Color.SaveCustomColors (((ShapesApp *) GetApplication())->IniData);
   }

void TShapesView::CmShapesRectangleEnable (TCommandEnabler &tce)
   { tce.SetCheck (Geometry == SHAPE_RECTANGLE); }

void TShapesView::CmShapesEllipseEnable (TCommandEnabler &tce)
   { tce.SetCheck (Geometry == SHAPE_ELLIPSE); }

void TShapesView::CmShapesRedEnable (TCommandEnabler &tce)
   { tce.SetCheck (Color == TColor::LtRed); }

void TShapesView::CmShapesGreenEnable (TCommandEnabler &tce)
   { tce.SetCheck (Color == TColor::LtGreen); }

void TShapesView::CmShapesBlueEnable (TCommandEnabler &tce)
   { tce.SetCheck (Color == TColor::LtBlue); }

void TShapesView::CmShapesOtherEnable (TCommandEnabler &tce)
   {
   tce.SetCheck (Color != TColor::LtRed &&
   Color != TColor::LtGreen &&
      Color != TColor::LtBlue);
   }

void TShapesView::Paint(TDC& dc, BOOL, TRect &)
   {
   char Buffer[128];
   GetWindowText (Buffer, sizeof Buffer);
   dc.TextOut (0, 0, Buffer);
   GetDocument().Draw (dc);
   }
```

```
BOOL TShapesView::VnAppend (TShape * Shape)
   {
   TClientDC dc (*this);
   Shape->Draw (dc);
   return TRUE;
   }

BOOL TShapesView::VnModify (void)
   {
   Invalidate();
   return TRUE;
   }

BOOL TShapesView::VnClear (void)
   {
   Invalidate();
   return TRUE;
   }

void TShapesView::CmEditCopy ()
   { Clipboard.SetData(); }

void TShapesView::CmEditPaste ()
   {
   Clipboard.GetData();
   Invalidate();
   }

void TShapesView::CmEditPasteEnable (TCommandEnabler &tce)
   { tce.Enable (Clipboard.IsData()); }
```

WAITCUR.H

```
#ifndef __WAITCUR_H__
#define __WAITCUR_H__
#include <owl\gdiobjec.h>
class TWaitCursor :  protected TCursor
   {
   public:
      TWaitCursor (BOOL StartWait = TRUE);
      ~TWaitCursor ();
      void Wait ();
      void Done ();
   private:
      HCURSOR OldCursor;
   };
#endif
```

WAITCUR.CPP

```
#include <owl\owlpch.h>
#pragma hdrstop
#include "waitcur.h"
TWaitCursor::TWaitCursor (BOOL StartWait)
   : TCursor (0, IDC_WAIT), OldCursor (0)
   {
   if (StartWait)
      Wait();
   }
```

```
TWaitCursor::~TWaitCursor ()
   {
   Done();
   }

void TWaitCursor::Wait ()
   {
   OldCursor = SetCursor (*this);
   }

void TWaitCursor::Done ()
   {
   if (OldCursor)
      SetCursor (OldCursor);
   OldCursor = 0;
   }
```

XCOLOR.H

```
#ifndef __XCOLOR_H__
#define __XCOLOR_H__
#include <classlib\objstrm.h>
#include <owl\color.h>
#include <owl\chooseco.h>
#include <cstring.h>
#include "inidata.h"

class TColorComponent : public TStreamableBase
   {
   public:
      TColorComponent (BYTE aValue) : Value (aValue) {}
      TColorComponent (TColorComponent & aComponent) : Value (aComponent.Value) {}
      TColorComponent operator+ (BYTE aValue) const;
      TColorComponent operator+ (TColorComponent aComponent) const;
      TColorComponent operator- (BYTE aValue) const;
      TColorComponent operator- (TColorComponent aComponent) const;
      TColorComponent operator* (BYTE aValue) const;
      TColorComponent operator/ (BYTE aValue)const;
      operator BYTE () const { return Value; }
   protected:
      BYTE Value;
   DECLARE_STREAMABLE (, TColorComponent, 1);
   };

class TRed : public TColorComponent
   {
   public:
      TRed (TRed & R) : TColorComponent (R.Value) {}
      TRed (BYTE aValue = 0) : TColorComponent (aValue) {}
      TRed & operator= (BYTE aValue);
      TRed & operator= (TRed & R);
      TRed & operator+= (BYTE aValue);
      TRed & operator+= (TRed & R);
      TRed & operator-= (BYTE aValue);
      TRed & operator-= (TRed & R);
      TRed & operator*= (BYTE aValue);
      TRed & operator/= (BYTE aValue);
   DECLARE_STREAMABLE ( , TRed, 1);
   };
```

```
class TGreen : public TColorComponent
   {
   public:
      TGreen (TGreen & G) : TColorComponent (G.Value) {}
      TGreen (BYTE aValue = 0) : TColorComponent (aValue) {}
      TGreen & operator= (BYTE aValue);
      TGreen & operator= (TGreen & G);
      TGreen & operator+= (BYTE aValue);
      TGreen & operator+= (TGreen & G);
      TGreen & operator-= (BYTE aValue);
      TGreen & operator-= (TGreen & G);
      TGreen & operator*= (BYTE aValue);
      TGreen & operator/= (BYTE aValue);
   DECLARE_STREAMABLE ( , TGreen, 1);
   };

class TBlue : public TColorComponent
   {
   public:
      TBlue (TBlue & B) : TColorComponent (B.Value) {}
      TBlue (BYTE aValue = 0) : TColorComponent (aValue) {}
      TBlue & operator= (BYTE aValue);
      TBlue & operator= (TBlue & B);
      TBlue & operator+= (BYTE aValue);
      TBlue & operator+= (TBlue & B);
      TBlue & operator-= (BYTE aValue);
      TBlue & operator-= (TBlue & B);
      TBlue & operator*= (BYTE aValue);
      TBlue & operator/= (BYTE aValue);
   DECLARE_STREAMABLE ( , TBlue, 1);
   };

class TXColor : public TStreamableBase
   {
   public:
      TXColor ();
      TXColor (TXColor & aColor);
      TXColor (TRed R, TGreen G, TBlue B);
      TXColor (COLORREF aValue);
      TXColor (int anIndex);
      TXColor(const PALETTEENTRY far & pe);
      TXColor(const RGBQUAD far & q);
      TXColor(const RGBTRIPLE far & t);
      operator COLORREF () const;
      operator TColor () const;
      short operator== (const TXColor & aColor) const;
      TXColor & operator= (COLORREF aValue);
      TXColor & operator= (int anIndex);
      TXColor & operator= (TRed R);
      TXColor & operator= (TGreen G);
      TXColor & operator= (TBlue B);
      TXColor & operator+= (TXColor aColor);
      TXColor & operator+= (COLORREF aColor);
      TXColor & operator+= (TRed R);
      TXColor & operator+= (TGreen G);
      TXColor & operator+= (TBlue B);
      TXColor operator+ (TXColor aColor) const;
      TXColor operator+ (COLORREF aColor) const;
      TXColor operator+ (TRed R) const;
      TXColor operator+ (TGreen G) const;
      TXColor operator+ (TBlue B) const;
```

```
        TXColor & operator-= (TXColor aColor);
        TXColor & operator-= (COLORREF aColor);
        TXColor & operator-= (TRed R);
        TXColor & operator-= (TGreen G);
        TXColor & operator-= (TBlue B);
        TXColor operator- (TXColor aColor) const;
        TXColor operator- (COLORREF aColor) const;
        TXColor operator- (TRed R) const;
        TXColor operator- (TGreen G) const;
        TXColor operator- (TBlue B) const;
        TXColor operator* (BYTE aValue) const;
        TXColor & operator*= (BYTE aValue);
        TXColor & operator/= (BYTE aValue);
        TXColor operator/ (BYTE aValue) const;
        TXColor & operator>>= (int Shift);
        TXColor & operator<<= (int Shift);
        TXColor operator>> (int Shift) const;
        TXColor operator<< (int Shift) const;
        void SetSysColor (int anIndex);
        TRed RValue;
        TGreen GValue;
        TBlue BValue;
        static const COLORREF Red;
        static const COLORREF Green;
        static const COLORREF Blue;
        static const COLORREF White;
        static const COLORREF Black;
        TXColor (string & RGB);
        operator string () const;
        BOOL SelectUserColor (TWindow * Window);
        static TXColor GetCustomColor (int i);
        static void SetCustomColor (int i, TXColor aColor);
        static void LoadCustomColors (TIniData & IniData);
        static void SaveCustomColors (TIniData & IniData);
    private:
        static TChooseColorDialog::TData DlgData;
        static TColor CustomColors[16];
    DECLARE_STREAMABLE ( , TXColor, 1);
    };
#endif
```

XCOLOR.CPP

```
#include <owl\owlpch.h>
#pragma hdrstop
#include "xcolor.h"
#include <stdio.h>

static BYTE near Normalize (int Test)
    {
    if (Test > 255)
        return 255;
    else if (Test < 0)
        return 0;
    else
        return (BYTE) Test;
    }


TColorComponent TColorComponent::operator+ (BYTE aValue) const
    {
```

```
   TColorComponent Temp (*this);
   Temp.Value = Normalize ((int) Temp.Value + (int) aValue);
   return Temp;
   }

TColorComponent TColorComponent::operator+ (TColorComponent aComponent) const
   {
   TColorComponent Temp (*this);
   Temp.Value = Normalize ((int) Temp.Value + (int) aComponent.Value);
   return Temp;
   }

TColorComponent TColorComponent::operator- (BYTE aValue) const
   {
   TColorComponent Temp (*this);
   Temp.Value = Normalize ((int) Temp.Value - (int) aValue);
   return Temp;
   }

TColorComponent TColorComponent::operator- (TColorComponent aComponent) const
   {
   TColorComponent Temp (*this);
   Temp.Value = Normalize ((int) Temp.Value - (int) aComponent.Value);
   return Temp;
   }

TColorComponent TColorComponent::operator* (BYTE aValue) const
   {
   TColorComponent Temp (*this);
   Temp.Value = Normalize ((int) Temp.Value * (int) aValue);
   return Temp;
   }

TColorComponent TColorComponent::operator/ (BYTE aValue) const
   {
   TColorComponent Temp (*this);
   Temp.Value = Normalize ((int) Temp.Value / (int) aValue);
   return Temp;
   }

IMPLEMENT_STREAMABLE (TColorComponent);
void * TColorComponent::Streamer::Read (ipstream & in, uint32) const
   {
   TColorComponent * Me = GetObject();
   in >> Me->Value;
   return Me;
   }

void TColorComponent::Streamer::Write (opstream & out) const
   {
   out << GetObject()->Value;
   }

TRed & TRed::operator= (BYTE aValue)
   {
   Value = aValue;
   return *this;
   }

TRed & TRed::operator= (TRed & R)
   {
```

```
      return *this = R.Value;
      }

  TRed & TRed::operator+= (BYTE aValue)
      {
      Value = Normalize ((int) Value + (int) aValue);
      return *this;
      }

  TRed & TRed::operator+= (TRed & R)
      {
      return *this += R.Value;
      }

  TRed & TRed::operator-= (BYTE aValue)
      {
      Value = Normalize ((int) Value - (int) aValue);
      return *this;
      }

  TRed & TRed::operator-= (TRed & R)
      {
      return *this -= R.Value;
      }

  TRed & TRed::operator*= (BYTE aValue)
      {
      Value = Normalize ((int) Value * (int) aValue);
      return *this;
      }

  TRed & TRed::operator/= (BYTE aValue)
      {
      Value = Normalize ((int) Value / (int) aValue);
      return *this;
      }

IMPLEMENT_STREAMABLE1 (TRed, TColorComponent);
void * TRed::Streamer::Read (ipstream & in, uint32) const
      {
      ReadBaseObject (STATIC_CAST(TColorComponent *, GetObject()), in);
      return GetObject();
      }

void TRed::Streamer::Write (opstream & out) const
      {
      WriteBaseObject (STATIC_CAST(TColorComponent *, GetObject()), out);
      }

TGreen & TGreen::operator= (BYTE aValue)
      {
      Value = aValue;
      return *this;
      }

TGreen & TGreen::operator= (TGreen & G)
      {
      return *this = G.Value;
      }
```

```
TGreen & TGreen::operator+= (BYTE aValue)
   {
   Value = Normalize ((int) Value + (int) aValue);
   return *this;
   }

TGreen & TGreen::operator+= (TGreen & G)
   {
   return *this += G.Value;
   }

TGreen & TGreen::operator-= (BYTE aValue)
   {
   Value = Normalize ((int) Value - (int) aValue);
   return *this;
   }

TGreen & TGreen::operator-= (TGreen & G)
   {
   return *this -= G.Value;
   }

TGreen & TGreen::operator*= (BYTE aValue)
   {
   Value = Normalize ((int) Value * (int) aValue);
   return *this;
   }

TGreen & TGreen::operator/= (BYTE aValue)
   {
   Value = Normalize ((int) Value / (int) aValue);
   return *this;
   }

IMPLEMENT_STREAMABLE1 (TGreen, TColorComponent);
void * TGreen::Streamer::Read (ipstream & in, uint32) const
   {
   ReadBaseObject (STATIC_CAST(TColorComponent *, GetObject()), in);
   return GetObject();
   }

void TGreen::Streamer::Write (opstream & out) const
   {
   WriteBaseObject (STATIC_CAST(TColorComponent *, GetObject()), out);
   }

TBlue & TBlue::operator= (BYTE aValue)
   {
   Value = aValue;
   return *this;
   }

TBlue & TBlue::operator= (TBlue & B)
   {
   return *this = B.Value;
   }

TBlue & TBlue::operator+= (BYTE aValue)
   {
   Value = Normalize ((int) Value + (int) aValue);
```

```
    return *this;
    }

TBlue & TBlue::operator+= (TBlue & B)
    {
    return *this += B.Value;
    }

TBlue & TBlue::operator-= (BYTE aValue)
    {
    Value = Normalize ((int) Value - (int) aValue);
    return *this;
    }

TBlue & TBlue::operator-= (TBlue & B)
    {
    return *this -= B.Value;
    }

TBlue & TBlue::operator*= (BYTE aValue)
    {
    Value = Normalize ((int) Value * (int) aValue);
    return *this;
    }

TBlue & TBlue::operator/= (BYTE aValue)
    {
    Value = Normalize ((int) Value / (int) aValue);
    return *this;
    }

IMPLEMENT_STREAMABLE1 (TBlue, TColorComponent);
void * TBlue::Streamer::Read (ipstream & in, uint32) const
    {
    ReadBaseObject (STATIC_CAST(TColorComponent *, GetObject()), in);
    return GetObject();
    }

void TBlue::Streamer::Write (opstream & out) const
    {
    WriteBaseObject (STATIC_CAST(TColorComponent *, GetObject()), out);
    }

TXColor::TXColor ()
    : RValue (0), GValue (0), BValue (0)
    {
    }

TXColor::TXColor (TXColor & aColor)
    {
    RValue = aColor.RValue;
    GValue = aColor.GValue;
    BValue = aColor.BValue;
    }

TXColor::TXColor (TRed R, TGreen G, TBlue B)
    : RValue (R), GValue (G), BValue (B)
    {
    }
```

```
TXColor::TXColor (COLORREF Value)
   {
   *this = Value;
   }

TXColor::TXColor (int anIndex)
   {
   *this = anIndex;
   }

TXColor::TXColor(const PALETTEENTRY far & pe)
   {
   *this = TColor (pe);
   }

TXColor::TXColor(const RGBQUAD far & q)
   {
   *this = TColor (q);
   }

TXColor::TXColor(const RGBTRIPLE far & t)
   {
   *this = TColor (t);
   }

TXColor::operator COLORREF () const
   {
   return RGB (RValue, GValue, BValue);
   }

TXColor::operator TColor () const
   {
   return TColor ((COLORREF) *this);
   }

short TXColor::operator== (const TXColor & aColor) const
   {
   return ((RValue == aColor.RValue) &&
      (GValue == aColor.GValue) &&
      (BValue == aColor.BValue));
   }

TXColor & TXColor::operator= (COLORREF Value)
   {
   RValue = GetRValue (Value);
   GValue = GetGValue (Value);
   BValue = GetBValue (Value);
   return *this;
   }

TXColor & TXColor::operator= (int anIndex)
   {
   return *this = GetSysColor (anIndex);
   }

TXColor & TXColor::operator= (TRed R)
   {
   RValue = R;
   return *this;
   }
```

```
TXColor & TXColor::operator= (TGreen G)
    {
    GValue = G;
    return *this;
    }

TXColor & TXColor::operator= (TBlue B)
    {
    BValue = B;
    return *this;
    }

TXColor & TXColor::operator+= (TXColor aColor)
    {
    RValue += aColor.RValue;
    GValue += aColor.GValue;
    BValue += aColor.BValue;
    return *this;
    }

TXColor & TXColor::operator+= (COLORREF aColor)
    {
    TXColor C (aColor);
    return *this += C;
    }

TXColor & TXColor::operator+= (TRed R)
    {
    RValue += R;
    return *this;
    }

TXColor & TXColor::operator+= (TGreen G)
    {
    GValue += G;
    return *this;
    }

TXColor & TXColor::operator+= (TBlue B)
    {
    BValue += B;
    return *this;
    }

TXColor TXColor::operator+ (TXColor aColor) const
    {
    return TXColor (*this) += aColor;
    }

TXColor TXColor::operator+ (COLORREF aColor) const
    {
    return TXColor (*this) += aColor;
    }

TXColor TXColor::operator+ (TRed R) const
    {
    return TXColor (*this) += R;
    }

TXColor TXColor::operator+ (TGreen G) const
    {
```

```
    return TXColor (*this) += G;
    }

TXColor TXColor::operator+ (TBlue B) const
    {
    return TXColor (*this) += B;
    }

TXColor & TXColor::operator-= (TXColor aColor)
    {
    RValue -= aColor.RValue;
    GValue -= aColor.GValue;
    BValue -= aColor.BValue;
    return *this;
    }

TXColor & TXColor::operator-= (COLORREF aColor)
    {
    TXColor C (aColor);
    return *this -= C;
    }

TXColor & TXColor::operator-= (TRed R)
    {
    RValue -= R;
    return *this;
    }

TXColor & TXColor::operator-= (TGreen G)
    {
    GValue -= G;
    return *this;
    }

TXColor & TXColor::operator-= (TBlue B)
    {
    BValue -= B;
    return *this;
    }

TXColor TXColor::operator- (TXColor aColor) const
    {
    return TXColor (*this) -= aColor;
    }

TXColor TXColor::operator- (COLORREF aColor) const
    {
    return TXColor (*this) -= aColor;
    }

TXColor TXColor::operator- (TRed R) const
    {
    return TXColor (*this) -= R;
    }

TXColor TXColor::operator- (TGreen G) const
    {
    return TXColor (*this) -= G;
    }
```

```
TXColor TXColor::operator- (TBlue B) const
    {
    return TXColor (*this) -= B;
    }

TXColor & TXColor::operator*= (BYTE aValue)
    {
    RValue *= aValue;
    GValue *= aValue;
    BValue *= aValue;
    return *this;
    }

TXColor TXColor::operator* (BYTE aValue) const
    {
    return TXColor (*this) * aValue;
    }

TXColor & TXColor::operator/= (BYTE aValue)
    {
    RValue /= aValue;
    GValue /= aValue;
    BValue /= aValue;
    return *this;
    }

TXColor TXColor::operator/ (BYTE aValue) const
    {
    return TXColor (*this) / aValue;
    }

TXColor & TXColor::operator>>= (int Shift)
    {
    Shift %= 3;
    while (Shift > 0)
        {
        TColorComponent Temp (BValue);
        BValue = GValue;
        GValue = RValue;
        RValue = Temp;
        --Shift;
        }
    return *this;
    }

TXColor & TXColor::operator<<= (int Shift)
    {
    Shift %= 3;
    while (Shift > 0)
        {
        TColorComponent Temp (RValue);
        RValue = GValue;
        GValue = BValue;
        BValue = Temp;
        --Shift;
        }
    return *this;
    }

TXColor TXColor::operator>> (int Shift) const
    {
```

```
   return TXColor (*this) >>= Shift;
   }

TXColor TXColor::operator<< (int Shift) const
   {
   return TXColor (*this) <<= Shift;
   }

void TXColor::SetSysColor (int anIndex)
   {
   COLORREF Color (*this);
   SetSysColors (1, &anIndex, &Color);
   }

TChooseColorDialog::TData TXColor::DlgData;
TColor TXColor::CustomColors[16] =
   {
   TXColor::White, TXColor::White,
   TXColor::White, TXColor::White,
   TXColor::White, TXColor::White,
   TXColor::White, TXColor::White,
   TXColor::White, TXColor::White,
   TXColor::White, TXColor::White,
   TXColor::White, TXColor::White,
   TXColor::White, TXColor::White
   };

TXColor::TXColor (string & RGB)
   {
   int R, G, B;
   sscanf (RGB.c_str(), "%d %d %d", &R, &G, &B);
   RValue = R;
   GValue = G;
   BValue = B;
   }

TXColor::operator string () const
   {
   char Buffer[12];
   wsprintf (Buffer, "%d %d %d", (int) RValue, (int) GValue, (int) BValue);
   return string (Buffer);
   }

BOOL TXColor::SelectUserColor (TWindow * Window)
   {
   if (! DlgData.Flags)
      {
      DlgData.Flags = CC_RGBINIT;
      DlgData.Color = *this;
      DlgData.CustColors = CustomColors;
      }
   if (TChooseColorDialog(Window, DlgData).Execute() == IDOK)
      {
      *this = DlgData.Color;
      return TRUE;
      }
   else
      return FALSE;
   }
```

```
TXColor TXColor::GetCustomColor (int i)
    {
    if (i >= 0 && i < 16)
        return TXColor (CustomColors[i]);
    else
        return TXColor::Black;
    }

void TXColor::SetCustomColor (int i, TXColor aColor)
    {
    if (i >= 0 && i < 16)
        CustomColors[i] = aColor;
    }

void TXColor::LoadCustomColors (TIniData & IniData)
    {
    IniData = TSection ("Custom Colors");
    IniData.SetDefault ("255 255 255");
    char * Key = "Color00";
    register k;
    for (k = 0; k < 16; k++)
        {
        itoa (k+1, &Key[4], 10);
        IniData = TKey (Key);
        string aCustomColor = IniData;
        SetCustomColor (k, TXColor (aCustomColor));
        }
    }

void TXColor::SaveCustomColors (TIniData & IniData)
    {
    IniData = TSection ("Custom Colors");
    char * Key = "Color00";
    register k;
    for (k = 0; k < 16; k++)
        {
        itoa (k+1, &Key[4], 10);
        IniData = TKey (Key);
        IniData = (string) TXColor (CustomColors[k]);
        }
    }

IMPLEMENT_STREAMABLE (TXColor);
void * TXColor::Streamer::Read (ipstream & in, uint32) const
    {
    TXColor * Me = GetObject();
    in >> Me->RValue >> Me->GValue >> Me->BValue;
    return Me;
    }

void TXColor::Streamer::Write (opstream & out) const
    {
    TXColor * Me = GetObject();
    out << Me->RValue << Me->GValue << Me->BValue;
    }
const COLORREF TXColor::Red = RGB (255, 0, 0);
const COLORREF TXColor::Green = RGB (0, 255, 0);
const COLORREF TXColor::Blue = RGB (0, 0, 255);
const COLORREF TXColor::White = RGB (255, 255, 255);
const COLORREF TXColor::Black = RGB (0, 0, 0);
```

Index

The book you are holding was designed and produced
by the Coriolis Group, with the aid of the latest desktop publishing
software, including Aldus PageMaker, Adobe Illustrator, Aldus Freehand,
Adobe PhotoShop, Microsoft Word, and of course, Microsoft Windows 3.1.
The cover concepts were designed by Marek Antoniak.
The interior design is by Keith Weiskamp and Frank Grazioli.
The body text is 10.5/12.5 ITC Garamond Light.
Technical illustrations were provided by Rob Mauhar and Brad Grannis.
The text was edited by Jenni Aloi-Wolfson.

Borland C++ Insider
Disk Offer!

The Borland C++ Insider Disk contains all of the units and programs described in this book. The diskette is arranged by chapter so you can easily find the code you want. In addition, we've included some utilities which you may find useful. **A great deal at $20.**

To order, just fill out the coupon below, telling us how many diskettes you want. Check the appropriate box for diskette type: 5 1/4" 360K, or 3 1/2" 720K. Add 6% sales tax if the order is to be shipped within Arizona.

Include payment in the form of check or money order in U.S. funds, or else VISA/MasterCard authorization. CODs and open account purchase orders are not accepted.

Mail the coupon to:

The Coriolis Group
Insider Disks Offers
7339 E. Acoma Dr., #7
Scottsdale, AZ 85260

Shipping and handling is $2 for orders shipped to the U.S. and Canada, and $6 for airmail shipping to the rest of the world. Please make all checks and money orders payable to The Coriolis Group.

- -

Qty	Complete disk for:	Each	Total
___	*Borland C++ Insider*	$20	_____
	Arizona orders please add 6% sales tax:		_____
	Shipping and handling:		_____
	Total due, in U.S. funds:		_____

Disks size: 5 1/4" 3 1/2"
  ☐   ☐

Get it fast—Call:

Phone (602) 483-0192
Fax: (602) 483-0193

Name _____

Company _____

Address _____

City/State/ZIP _____

Phone _____

VISA/MC # _____ Expires: _____

Signature for charge orders: _____

(John Wiley & Sons, Inc., is not responsible for orders placed with the Coriolis Group.)